ACADEMIE DU VIN
WINE COURSE

ACADEMIE DU VIN
WINE COURSE

The complete course in wine appreciation, tasting and study of the Académie du Vin

STEVEN SPURRIER
& MICHEL DOVAZ
Introduction by Hugh Johnson

MITCHELL BEAZLEY
in association with
Direct Wines (Windsor) Limited

First published in Great Britain in 1983
by Century Publishing Co. Ltd
in association with Christie's Wine Publications
Revised edition 1990
Reprinted 1994

A CIP catalogue record for this book is available from the British Library.

ISBN 1 85732 368 8

Typeset by Litho Link Ltd, Welshpool, Powys, Wales

Printed and bound in Hong Kong

Special Contributors

Muriel de Potex
Special Studies

Ian Jamieson
Germany

Fenella Pearson
Italy

Geoffrey Roberts
California, Australia & New Zealand

Note: Measurement Conversion

Measurements of volume and area in the sections on European wines have been expressed in hectolitres (hl) and hectares (ha):

1 hectolitre = 26.4 U.S. gallons
1 hectare = 2.471 acres

CONTENTS

The Académie du Vin 8
Introduction by Hugh Johnson 10

1. FOUNDATION COURSE

Tasting 16
The Vine 28
Vinification 38
Vintage 56
Wine Buying & Transport 62
Wine Storage 64
Chemical Composition 66

2. INTERMEDIATE COURSE

Grape Varieties 70
Wine Producing Regions 86
France/Bordeaux 86
France/Burgundy 90
France/Champagne 94
France/Rhône 98
France/Alsace 100
France/Loire 102
France/Jura/Savoy/Provence 104
France/Languedoc and the South-west 106
Germany 108
Italy 112
Spain and Portugal 118
Austria/Switzerland/Luxembourg 122
California 124
Rest of United States 134
Australia and New Zealand 136
South America 138
South Africa 139

3. ADVANCED COURSE

Very Dry Whites 142
Dry Whites 144
Sweet & Aromatic Whites 146
Light Reds 148
Medium Reds 150
Full-bodied Reds 152
Sparkling Wines 154
Rosés 156
Riesling 157
Sauvignon Blanc 159
Chardonnay 160
Chenin Blanc 162
Sémillon 163
Cabernet Sauvignon 164
Pinot Noir 166
Merlot 168
Syrah 169
Horizontal Tasting/Red Burgundy 1978 170
Horizontal Tasting/Red Bordeaux 1983 172
Vertical Tasting/Red Burgundy 174
Vertical Tasting/Red Bordeaux 176
Fortified and Dessert Wines 178
Colour of Wine 180

4. SPECIAL STUDIES

Wine & Food 188
Serving Wine 196
Fortified Wines 200
Distilled Wines 204
Oak 208
Wine & Health 209
Tasting Cards 210
Tasting Terms 212
Vintage Chart 216
Glossary 218
Index 219
Bibliography & Acknowledgements 223

The Académie du Vin

The aim of L'Académie du Vin, the wine school I founded in Paris 20 years ago, was to teach people about wine. Whenever I was asked what L'Académie du Vin actually was, I replied that it was the wine version of Le Cordon Bleu: they taught cooking, we taught drinking. In fact, we taught much more than the simple "how to ..." by going back to basics: why taste, what to look for, where to find it, how to recognise it, how to remember it. The way we did it was through all sorts of wine courses, the gist of which are reproduced in this book.

There are hundreds of good books about the history and geography of wine, many of the best written by The Wine Club President himself, but few compare wines rather than regions. Wine Courses are held 'glass in hand' as the moment of truth comes not when you read about a wine, nor even when you buy it, but when you drink it. Wine growers produce wine for a variety of reasons: some because their land won't produce anything else and others through a passion to create something individual and wonderful. But wine drinkers should only open the bottles for one reason - pleasure; and pleasure is increased the more you know. This book is a step by step approach to knowing more about wine.

The book is divided into four sections: the Foundation Course, covering all aspects of tasting, easy-to-follow vine cultivation, vinification, and the purchase, transport and storage of wine; the Intermediate Course explains the major (and minor) grape varieties, where they are planted around the world and what sort of wine they produce; the Advanced Course puts this knowledge into practice through a series of tastings, comparing and contrasting over 200 wines; finally the Special Studies section discusses serving wine, wine and food, wine and health, tasting terms and vintages.

This, therefore, is the Complete Handbook for you to dip into at your leisure. It will be brought to life by the tasting cards and feature articles sent to you every three months covering in more detail tasting, storing, maturing and serving wine, as well as an in depth look at wine and food, wine in restaurants and other essential wine topics. These will be specially written to gradually build up your understanding of the World of Wine. So knowledge and pleasure go together 'glass in hand'.

Steven Spurrier

BARSAC
1978

Introduction

The more you know, the more you enjoy. From The Wine Club's foundation 20 years ago, this has been our underlying philosophy. The Club was founded at a time when The Sunday Times had just uncovered practices in the British Wine trade which it would be kind to call cynical. (Bottling so-called 'Bordeaux', 'Rhône' and 'Beaujolais' from the same vat was then a time-honoured procedure among some merchants).

The new Wine Club, in partnership with Tony Laithwaite's Bordeaux Direct (established four years earlier), promised a fresh start, direct supplies and full explanations. Both have come a long way from their humble origins under a Windsor railway arch, but this openness, this conviction that a well-informed wine-drinker is going to enjoy his wine more, is still fundamental to what we do.

You can see it in action at our annual Vintage Festival. Some long-serving members will remember our 'Bottle University' of the early '80s. Now, with our new wine course, we are redoubling our pedagogic efforts, offering liquid lessons in a structured way steered by one of the most experienced teachers in the wine world.

Steven Spurrier founded L'Académie du Vin in 1972. He can justly claim to be a true pioneer in wine-teaching in the most practical and direct way - over bottle and glass. It was phenomenal the way Paris (yes, Paris) flocked to his lectures. He restructured them as a book that became the basis for L'Académie du Vin courses in countries around the world - and now for The Wine Club and Bordeaux Direct. Liquid illustrations are delivered to your home complete with book, tasting cards and the first of your lively and informative feature articles written by some of the top British wine writers.

The last thing in the world we want you to become is a wine bore. But this is exactly why we are inviting you to taste and learn. The one thing wine bores have in common is that they don't know what they are talking about.

Hugh Johnson
Club President

Grand Vin de Bourgogne
Pouilly-Fuissé

THE ACADEMIE DU VIN COURSES

1
FOUNDATION COURSE

2
INTERMEDIATE COURSE

3
ADVANCED COURSE

4
SPECIAL STUDIES

1
FOUNDATION COURSE

As an introduction to the main subject areas of the Foundation Course (tasting, vine cultivation, vinification, and the purchase, transport and storage of wine), it may be helpful to say something about identifying wine.

Even before protective legislation had been introduced, it was generally recognized that different wines needed to be clearly defined in the interests of authenticity. This was basically in order to protect the producer, who would otherwise be vulnerable to inferior imitations which might eventually damage both the prestige of his wine and his business.

It was soon evident that the best way to assure and protect the authenticity of various wines was to adopt a system based on the place of origin. French wine producers, in any event, were in the habit of forming regional federations, since they had to deal with similar problems of cultivation on similar types of soil, using identical grape varieties. As a consequence, their wines were bound to have much in common.

Nowadays, the area which forms the basis of wine identification may be very large or tiny. It is obvious that a wine from a small, well-defined region is more likely to maintain a consistently high quality. By the same token, wines from a vast area will not be given individual identification. These are simply brand wines, the familiar *vins de table*. To label such wines as the produce, say, of the European Economic Community or the United States, would provide a vague, unhelpful indication of origin; and even to describe a wine as coming from France, California, Italy or Spain, is fairly meaningless. These would still be wines of very imprecise identification, way down the scale.

Tasting/Aims

There are two distinct types of wine-tasting, which can broadly be termed 'technical' and 'hedonistic'. They differ both in method and purpose.

Technical tasting is for the professionals and its principal aim is to assess the wine from a commercial viewpoint. It has to determine, firstly, whether the wine has any faults, and secondly whether it conforms to the characteristics of its *appellation* and satisfies certain requirements of quality. Technical tasting must endeavour to be as objective as possible. The taster, in fact, is required to answer a series of questions set out on a tasting card. The pleasurable experience afforded by a given wine is not a prime consideration in this context. As a rule, wines are tasted at a uniform temperature of 15°C; ideally this may often be too cold or too warm, but it does provide an additional criterion by which the wines can be compared, and it is, in fact, a suitable temperature for critical tasting.

Hedonistic tasting is quite a different matter, for the emphasis here is on the actual pleasure afforded by drinking the wine. The taster must experience the wine as fully and subtly as possible in the best possible conditions. Thus it is a question of intelligent drinking – leading, it is to be hoped, to intelligent buying. To know that it is a good investment is to enhance the pleasure of drinking the wine.

Our experience at the Académie du Vin has shown us, however, that the two types of tasting do overlap. Neither should be pursued to the exclusion of the other. The most rewarding experience for the drinker comes from combining the strict technique and the pleasurable art of tasting.

Acquiring the technical expertise for tasting is really a matter of mastering a series of operations which, after a time, virtually become automatic. Once this happens, the taster can quickly go on to appreciate bouquet, aromatic strength, length of taste in the mouth, and so on. A more 'cultural' experience of wine takes much longer to acquire and does need a lengthy apprenticeship. It requires, for instance, a knowledge of *appellations* and their characteristics, and an ability to recognize the influence of the vintage. At an even more subtle level, it may be possible to distinguish the individual qualities of a particular wine maker and the vital importance of grape variety, soil, climate and vinification techniques.

Opposite *Perfect conditions for a professional tasting at the Académie du Vin in Paris.*

Below *Hedonistic tasting: members of the wine cooperative of Vaux-en-Beaujolais (the original of Gabriel Chevalier's 'Clochemerle') sample the previous year's vintage, while waiting for the start of the* vendange.

Tasting/Conditions

The only adjunct to the taster's own skill and experience is the wine glass – though not, as we shall see, just any glass. The other important conditions relate to the taster himself and the setting for the actual tasting. Firstly, the taster must be in good physical shape; a cold or influenza makes tasting impossible. The palate must be fresh, and have had no recent contact with spicy dishes, chocolate, mint, strong drink or cigarettes. The best time for tasting is about 10 or 11 a.m.

The setting is also very important. Ideally, the room should be quiet, well lit and well aired, to banish any lingering smells; needless to say, no odour of perfume, tobacco or cooking should be allowed to seep in. The room should have light walls and a table with a white cloth. The temperature should be 20–22°C and humidity 60–70%. These conditions are about standard for any dining room in which fine wines are to be drunk.

Such preparations, however, are pointless, if the glasses themselves are unsuitable. Various types of glass have been studied by specialist bodies; the form of glass generally recognized to be the best has now been internationally adopted and conforms to standards laid down by the International Standards Organization (ISO).

The standard glass is clear and relatively thin. It has the exceptional quality of being suitable for tasting all kinds of drinks: champagne, sparkling wines, all reds and whites, ports and other fortified wines, and *eaux-de-vie* made from wine, fruit and grain. The tulip form of this perfect and universally applicable glass both retains the bouquet within the glass and also enables the processes of oxidation and oxygenation to take place through contact with the surrounding air. The foot and stem make it possible for tasters to hold it without warming the liquid; it is also an easy form to handle during the various actions which precede the tasting proper.

The ISO Wine Glass

Total height 155mm ± 5
Bowl height 100mm ± 2
Base and stem height 55mm ± 3
Diameter of top 46mm ± 2
Diameter of bowl at its widest 65mm ± 2
Thickness of stem 9mm ± 1
Diameter of base 65mm ± 5
Total capacity 215ml ± 10
Tasting quantity 50ml

Tasting/The Eye 1

The glass must first be placed on a white surface and filled up to one-third of its volume. The eye is then the first organ used in the tasting of wine. Even though it is nowadays rare to find wines possessing faults which can be seen by the eye alone, all tastings must begin visually by the inspection of the disc, the robe and, finally, the 'legs'.

The disc

The disc is the upper surface of the wine in the glass. It should be examined from above and then from the side. The surface of the disc should be bright and free from all dust or other solid matter. If the disc is matt, this is almost certainly a sign that all is not well with the wine, which is probably suffering from a microbic ailment. Lateral examination of the disc may reveal flocculation and deposits. The presence of any floating matter in the wine, so-called 'fliers', is clearly unacceptable, for it is a sure sign that the wine has been vinified badly and will therefore not age. The best that can be said about such a wine is that it is 'dubious'.

The collection of deposits at the bottom of the glass is not serious. These are generally made up of insoluble crystals, or precipitates of potassium bitartrates (cream of tartar), a sign that the wine has been subjected to a cold shock after bottling and the wine maker has not precipitated the bitartrates.

The results of these first visual examinations are described in very simple terms. Good wines are **limpid, bright** or **brilliant**: the others are **troubled, dubious, opaque, hazy, milky, flocculent, dim, murky,** etc.

The robe

The robe is the colour of the wine; it is assessed for its hue and the intensity of the hue. These two factors change together as the wine ages and are often pointers to its condition and quality. The robe also helps to assess the vintage of a wine, whether white, rosé or red and, in the case of the latter, to recommend how long it should be kept. The hue of white wines may range from light yellow to bronze, and once again colour can be used to evaluate age.

Colour is such an important factor in the wines of Bordeaux, that one well-known *négociant* made it his major criterion when buying. He painted the courtyard wall opposite his office white, and whenever he had to judge a wine he filled the glass and flung its contents at the wall. He always bought the wine which stained the wall (which needed regular repainting) most deeply. This procedure was not as eccentric as might at first appear. In comparing the vintages of 1960 and 1961 or 1969 and 1970, it would certainly have led him to choose the better ones (1961 and 1970). Indeed, colour is so important that certain grape varieties are planted solely for the purpose of colouring the wine. Such varieties, called *teinturiers*, produce special grapes containing a dark juice. The best known of these is the Alicante Bouschet, and more than 60,000 hectares of this variety are planted in France. An older procedure is to add the juice of elderberries. Such practices do not apply to fine wines.

Left *The robe and disc seen to best advantage in a standard ISO tasting glass.*

Appearance and Colour

White wines are often described in the following terms: *colourless, yellow, yellow* linked to the words *pale, straw, lemon, green, golden, dark* and *gold*; furthermore there is *white gold*, with additional nuances expressed by *pale gold, green gold, red gold* and *bronze gold*; and older wines may be termed *topaz, burnt topaz, maderized, amber, brown, caramel, mahogany* or *black*.

Rosé wines are often termed *grey, light red, 'partridge eye', rose* or *violet*; and older rosés may be described as *rosé yellow, rosé orange, russet, salmon pink* or even as *having the colour of onion skin*.

Red wines are often described as *light, violaceous, dark, garnet, ruby, vermilion, purple* or *black*; and older reds are termed *bisque, orange, tile-red* or *maroon*.

Tasting/The Eye 2

Opposite *The taster inclines his glass, then allows the wine to run back down the sides, leaving the 'legs' to trickle down more slowly.*

The vocabulary used to describe the visual appearance of wines is essentially one of analogy. Flowers, fruits, woods, precious stones – all these are regularly used to evoke the colour of wine; but, although in theory the range of this vocabulary and system of analogies is limitless, a restricted number of terms have become almost standard by reason of frequent use.

Such terms are mainly intended to evoke the nuance and shade of a wine, which can of course be of a greater or lesser intensity. The robe of the wine can therefore be further qualified by such words as **deep, consistent, ample, dense, rich, heavy** or, in contrast, **light, weak, poor.** The description of a wine's hue is almost always accompanied by an opinion on the ageing of the wine, and the vocabulary may thus be extended by such terms as **fresh, sound, clear, true,** or **faded, over-aged, past its best, worn out, oxidized, maderized.**

Although the hue of a wine can nowadays be measured scientifically with a spectrometer, the taster's eye still remains the surest method of relating colour to quality by the comparative method. Professional tasters are offered four wine samples of varying degrees of colour intensity, positioned in front of a light source. They will arrive at their opinion of a particular wine by comparing it with the other samples offered for inspection.

The 'legs'

The 'legs' are the subject of the third type of visual examination.

The taster inclines his glass or makes a circular movement with it, so that the wine rises and then runs back down the sides of the glass. As this happens, the wine will form 'legs' or 'tears' which trickle down more slowly. This is the result of two processes. The first is due to the differences in surface tension between water and alcohol, which creates a capillary effect; the second is related to the viscosity of the wine, the 'legs' or 'tears' being formed by glycerols and residual sugar together with the alcohol. There has been much inconclusive discussion about the relationship between the quality of a wine's taste and the degree to which it forms 'legs'. Suffice it to say that the presence of the 'legs' is no guarantee of the balance or harmony of a wine. Too much alcohol or an excess of glycerol will also help the formation of very fine 'legs'. A poor wine which is weak both in extract and alcohol will be too fluid to develop 'legs'; in contrast, a Grand Cru Burgundy, because it is legally obliged to attain a high level of alcohol to qualify for its *appellation*, will always form very marked 'legs'.

Below *The effect of 'legs' or 'tears' on the side of a glass.*

The vocabulary relating to the **fluidity** or **viscosity** of a wine is more limited: **watery, liquid, fluid,** as opposed to **heavy, syrupy, unctuous, high on glycerol, forming 'legs', forming 'tears', weeping.** The terms **oily, viscous** and **thick** are used to describe sick wines, especially those attacked by 'ropiness', a rare bacteriological ailment.

Sparkling wines

Wines which contain less than 100 mg/l of carbonic gas are referred to as 'still wines'; wines which contain more are known by a number of terms ranging from **effervescent** to **sparkling.** The various intermediate degrees between still and sparkling wines are described as **lively, pearly, 'moustillant'** and **semi-sparkling**, since carbon dioxide can be traced from a level of 1.5–2 gr/l.

Wines which do contain carbon dioxide need special attention, as the presence of the gas may be either a fault or a virtue, according to whether or not it is supposed to be present in the type of wine to be considered. In the context of visual inspection, it effectively entails examination of the bubbles, their diameter, frequency and rapidity with which they recur. These bubbles can create a fine cream on the surface of the wine (Champagne Crémant) or a very thick 'head', likewise made up of small bubbles, all equal in diameter, but only lasting for a few seconds. The transformation of groups of small bubbles into larger bubbles only occurs in beer. Once the 'head' on the wine has disappeared, the cream forms a ring, called the *cordon*, around the side of the glass, which remains there as long as the bubbles are renewed.

The major champagnes are all better drunk mature than young and none should ever be drunk too cold. In the context of our visual examination, however, the taster will be looking for an attractive pale colour and a constant flow of bubbles. Old champagnes will display certain changes in their visual characteristics: the customary palish colour will deepen to something close to gold, while the actual 'bubbly' quality will be less vigorous and lively.

Tasting/The Nose 1

Once the visual stage of the tasting is over, it is the turn of the olfactory senses. There is obviously no need for the two stages to follow each other in separate sequence; after some practice, during a purely hedonistic tasting or in the course of a meal, eye and nose can go to work simultaneously and with the same glass of wine. For present purposes, however, let us imagine that the glass used for the visual examination has been put to one side and that a new glass has been poured for the next stage. In this way we can discuss the significance of the 'first nose' and then compare the condition of the wine in the two glasses.

The first nose

The newly filled glass is left to stand on the table. The taster expels the air from his lungs and then, nose in glass, inhales deeply.

The 'first nose', even though it is often only a pale reflection of the ensuing 'second nose', enables the taster to become aware of the presence of a number of highly volatile and fugitive chemical elements which quickly disappear into the surrounding air or are transformed by oxidation or combination. In many cases, the first nose is strongly influenced, or even dominated, by parasitic odours caused by the wine having been kept in a bottle and by the presence of gas which the wine maker tries to eliminate before bottling; such odours may arise from sulphur dioxide (SO_2), from the fermentation process, the lees, mercaptan, hydrogen sulphide and other chemicals.

The second nose

The second phase of the olfactory examination of the wine begins with a familiar action. The taster takes the glass by its foot and swivels it to make the wine revolve inside. This is done in order to oxygenate the liquid and accelerate the process of oxidation. The oxygenation or aeration of the wine helps to get rid of the gases in solution and the oxidation opens up the various aromatic elements of the wine.

The third nose

Oxidation is a continuous process in that the complex chemical composition of wine is constantly changing through the loss of volatile elements, coupled with the oxidation of volatile products and the interaction of the remaining constituent elements. For this reason, we can now turn back to the first glass, which was served for the visual examination, to see how these various processes have

Opposite *The 'first nose': the taster inhales deeply, nose in glass.*

Tasting: the olfactory senses

The olfactory appreciation of a glass of wine takes place by way of the nostrils and also from behind the soft palate.

1. Front sinus
2. Olfactory bulb
3. Nasal cavities
4. Vapour rising directly through the nostrils
5. Roof of mouth
6. Upper lip
7. Soft palate
8. Vapour rising behind the soft palate

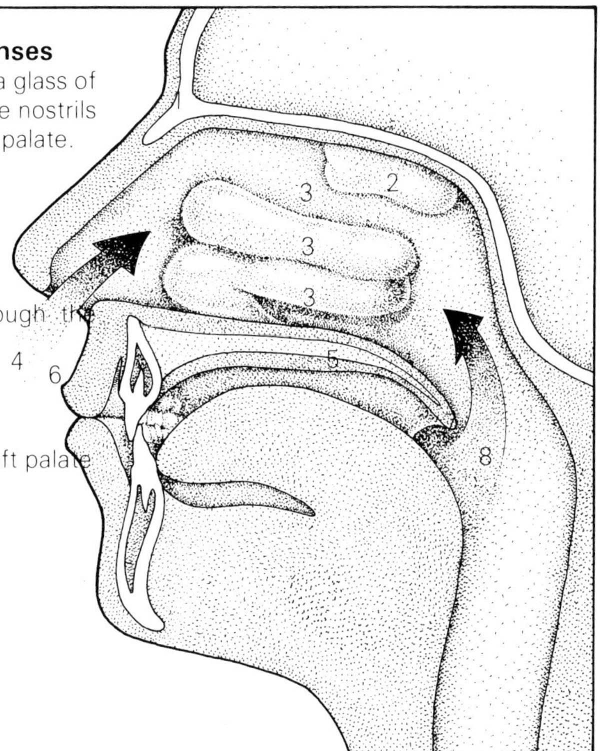

Tasting/The Nose 2

begun to affect the wine. Professional tasters may complete this part of the examination by testing the condition of the wine in the glass, which involves leaving it for twelve hours. Another method entails emptying the glass and then following the olfactory development of the remaining aromatic constituents, since they are then free from the influence of the alcohol. This procedure is especially useful in tasting wines with very high alcohol content, such as fortified wines, and *eaux-de-vie.*

The sense of smell plays an essential part in wine tasting in order to establish the nature and intensity of the wine's aromatic elements.

The intensity is expressed in terms of strength or weakness, and there are many words to describe the stages between two extremes. The most frequently used terms, in sequence of increasing approval, are **null, weak, small, poor, short, hollow, closed, medium, normal, strong, rich, developed, intense, ample** and **generous.**

Primary aromas refer to the fruity qualities of the grape and it is by these that the grape variety is most easily identified. Such aromas are especially noticeable in very young wines or wines made from very aromatic varieties for drinking young (e.g. Alsatian and German wines).

Secondary aromas (sometimes called fermentative) are those that refer more specifically to the wine itself; they are caused by the transformation of the must into wine, which brings into existence a number of elements not present in the must before fermentation, such as succinic acid. These aromas depend on the type of must (vines, soils), on yeasts and on the method of fermentation.

Tertiary aromas only begin to appear during the maturing period in cask or vat (oxidation) and/or after a period of ageing in the bottle. Such aromas are sometimes termed post-fermentative.

It would probably be true to say that the taster will find most of the olfactory sensations he is likely to derive from a given glass of wine when he first passes his nose over it and inhales relatively lightly. Indeed, there is little point in lingering too long over the first nose of a wine, since too long an exposure to the initial bouquet will rapidly reduce its interest. It is better to pass on to the other stages of the olfactory examination which will then yield a much more rounded appreciation of the varied odours given off by the wine.

Opposite *Swivelling the glass accelerates the process of oxidation and opens up the various aromatic elements of the wine.*

Odours and Aromas

There is likewise an accepted vocabulary for the various aromatic categories. Wine can never be defined in terms of one aromatic element, even if it is the dominant one; there are always several. For the sake of convenience, these elements have been classified into nine principal categories.

Animal odours: *game, gamey, venison, meaty, musk, musky, 'catty';*
Balsamic odours: all *resins, juniper, turpentine, vanilla, pine, benjamin;*
Empyreumatic odours: everything *dry, smoked, toasted bread, almond, hay, straw, coffee, wood*; also *leather* and *tar*;
Chemical odours: *spirituous, acetone* (nail varnish), *acetic, phenol, carbolic, mercaptan, sulphur* (and its derivatives), *lactic, iodized, oxidized, yeast, ferment*;
Spicy odours: all spices, but most frequently *clove, laurel, pepper, cinnamon, nutmeg, ginger, rosemary, truffle, liquorice, mint*;
Floral odours: all flowers but most frequently *violet, hawthorn, rose, citronella, jasmine, iris, geranium, acacia, lime*;
Fruit odours: all fruits but most frequently *blackcurrant, raspberry, cherry, grenadine, gooseberry, plum, almond, quince, apricot, banana, nuts, fig*;
Vegetable and mineral odours: *herbaceous, hay, tea, dead leaves, truffle, mushroom, damp straw, damp moss, damp undergrowth, chalk, fern, ivy, green leaves.*

These terms do not differ greatly from those used for making qualitative judgments; and the more subjective the tasting becomes, the more this is reflected in the terminology. Thus, the nose may be described as **ordinary, vulgar, uninteresting, simplistic, lacking complexity** and **banal** or **refined, fine, sophisticated, stylish, complex, distinguished** and **exemplary.**

The aromas are sometimes further subdivided into three categories.

Tasting/The Mouth

It is not generally realized that the 'taste' of a wine depends more on the nose than the mouth. In other words, it is more of an olfactory than a merely gustatory experience. Expert wine tasters therefore rely heavily on the first purely nasal appreciation of wine in the knowledge that almost all its aromas travel to the mouth through the back passages of the nose. The effect is double-acting, since the olfactory glands, in addition to being stimulated directly when the nose is passed over the wine, are again alerted once the wine is actually inside the mouth, the vaporized aromas exciting one or more of the 50 million or so nasal nerve cells.

An understanding of this process helps to explain the logic of the tasting ritual and the reasons why the wine must always be distributed around the mouth. The taster takes a small quantity of wine into his mouth and, instead of swallowing, allows it to roll around his tongue while slowly inhaling. The wine's aromatic vapours are released more strongly through being warmed gently in the mouth and by its evaporation in the air.

Some tasters prefer to 'chew' the wine, turning it round and round in the mouth, enabling the olfactory glands to confirm the sensations initially registered during the nasal phase. These sensations will not be identical, however, since the wine will have been warmed slightly inside the mouth, releasing a quantity of less volatile molecules that generate a complementary set of aromas; these are described in the same terms as those used for the purely nasal perception.

Taste in the mouth proper

The human tongue distinguishes four basic types of flavour: sweet on the tip of the tongue, salty just behind the tip and on either side of it, acidic on the sides, and bitter at the back. These four primary flavours are modified by sensations perceived by the tongue and the whole oral cavity: sensations of heat and temperature, touch, feel and consistency (fluidness, viscosity, etc.) and of chemistry, such as astringency and gas.

Aftertaste

It might be assumed that the taster, having looked at the wine, tasted it and analysed his oral sensations, would swallow it and pass on to the next sample. Not so, however, for there is one final factor that in itself can enable him to distinguish a great wine from an ordinary vintage. This is the wine's 'length' or persistence inside the mouth – on the face of it quite simple, yet in reality a rather complex phenomenon. After the wine is swallowed, its aromatic power tends to fill the mouth and then fade away gradually; the duration of this sensation determines the wine's persistence or ability to linger, and is measured in seconds. The longer or more persistent the aftertaste, the greater the wine will be; conversely, a short wine is never really acceptable.

Unfortunately there is one minor problem, namely that sensations are always mixed, since a wine's aromatic components are supported by its structure; and, in determining the wine's persistence in the mouth, sensation of structure plays no part. The structure of the wine is affected by acidity and by certain tannins yielded by the alcohol. To give just one simple example of how 'structure' and 'length' can be confused: vinegar leaves a persistent memory in the mouth but is not long in flavour, for it is only the acetic acid that is left behind. The length of more successful wines is, however, relatively easy to measure since their structure, body and aromas will be more evenly and equally balanced and so should provide an aftertaste that lingers and fades in perfect harmony.

Tasting: harmony and rhythm

The harmony that tasters expect of great wines presupposes an uninterrupted succession of positive impressions; in other words, the eye must herald the 'nose' that will be confirmed by the mouth. A red wine with a white wine flavour would never do, while a champagne that had a Bordeaux nose and a Blanquette de Limoux taste would be devoid of all interest.

The first in the sequence of sensations is the wine's 'attack', which should be clean, natural and precise. Many southern wines or wines made in very hot years have little or no attack. Secondly, the mouth should be wholly suffused with the wine's flavours and aromas. Finally, there is the aftertaste, the impressions of which must continue and prolong the original taste sensation without a break.

Comparative tastings presented in the Advanced Course (page 140) will enable the reader to become acquainted with the techniques described here and with the terminology of tasting.

Tasting/Balance

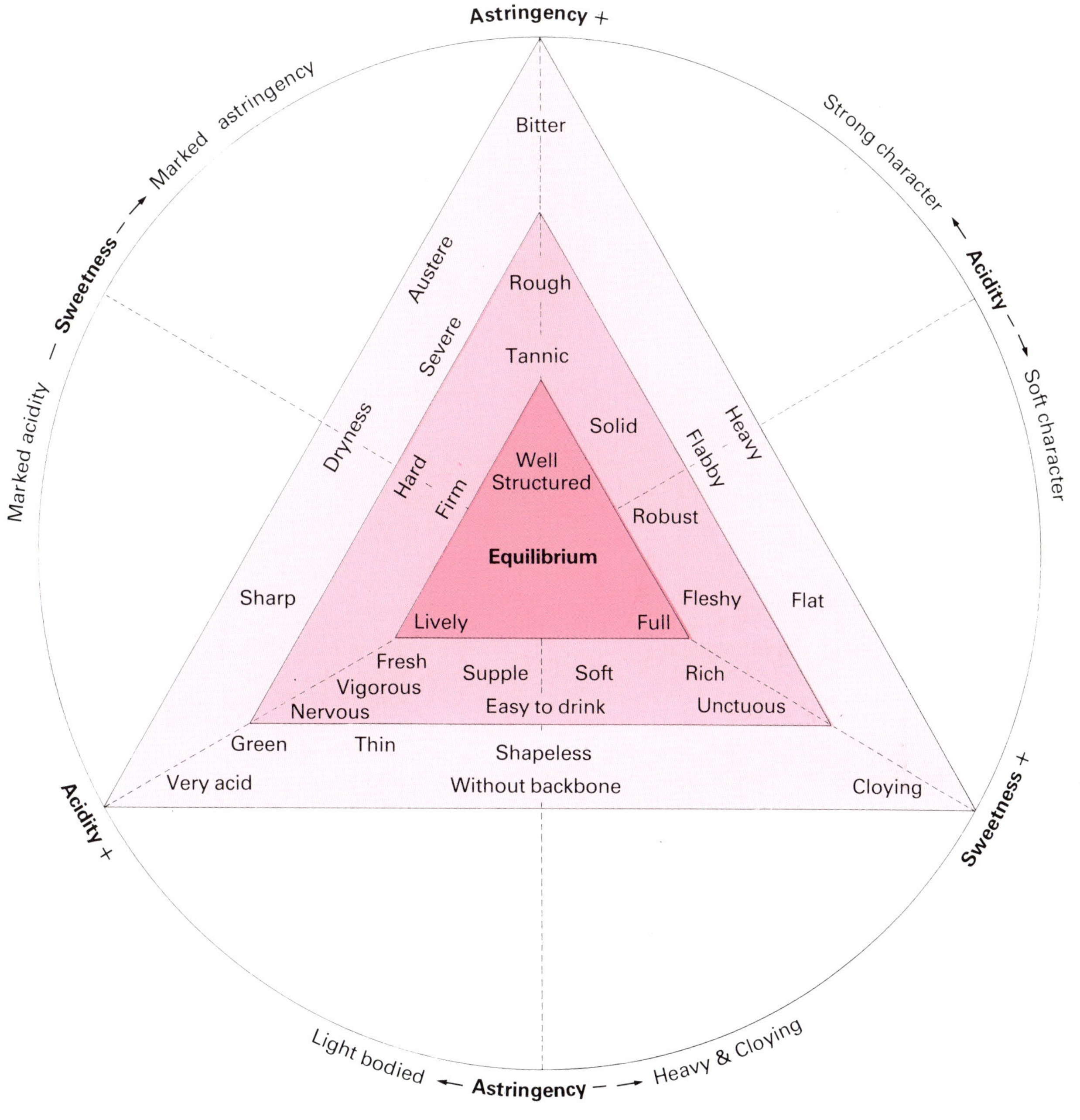

Tasting: balance

Tasting wine is like appreciating good music. Just as we can derive additional pleasure from reading the score, identifying the instruments, recognizing changes of key and so forth, we can enhance our enjoyment of a wine by seeking out the essential elements, determining which are complementary and which incompatible. A wine of quality imparts a sense of balance, created by a harmonious merging of constituent factors.

The diagram above, taken from *Le goût du vin* by Emile Peynaud (Bordas, second edition, 1983) explains the components and mechanics of this balancing process in red wines.

The Vine/Life Cycle

Right *The life cycle of the vine – from new leaves to ripe grapes.*

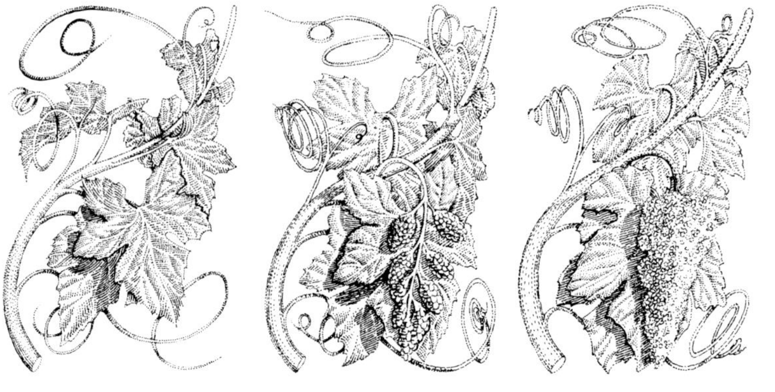

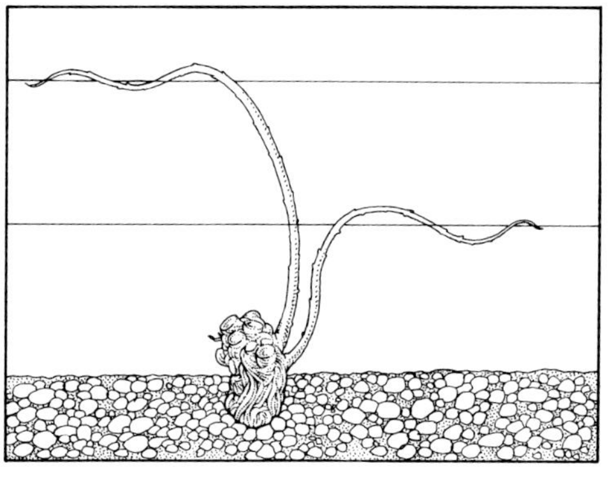

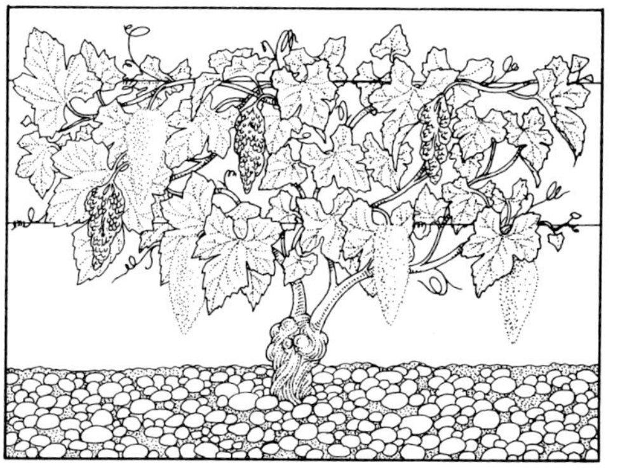

The vine is a humble plant, simply a domesticated creeper that happens to thrive well in a number of different soils, even poor ones, provided the climate is temperate and its roots do not rot with excessive dampness. The vine's most interesting feature – at any rate from our viewpoint – is that it bears fruit, the grape, that can be turned into wine. Here we are immediately confronted by a paradox, for experience shows that the best wines come from vines that in a sense, are made to 'suffer'. It is a fact that rich, well irrigated soils which get a lot of sunshine do not produce really great wines. At the opposite extreme, soils that are excessively wet and deprived of sunlight are equally unsuitable for growing vines. Scientific research has shown that the finest wines come from vines planted around the northern boundaries of areas given over to particular grape varieties. Of course, not every geographical region will be suitable for all the different varieties of grape, if only because their life cycles tend to vary. These matters are dealt with in greater detail in the Intermediate Course.

The life cycle of the vine is such that the grower must give it his constant, unflagging attention. Like all plants, the vine lies dormant in winter, and revives in the spring when the soil starts to warm up. This is true at any rate of temperate climates; in the tropics the various phases of a plant's life cycle may occur simultaneously, so that the vine will bear blossom, green grapes and ripe grapes all at the same time, in which case only rigorous pruning can establish a logical sequence. In Europe, winter cold and frost suspend the vine's growth but normally – since it is a hardy plant – do not kill it. Only if very cold conditions persist, as in 1956 when there were protracted frosts of – 20°C, will it be finished off.

In spring, when the temperature starts to rise to around 11°C, the sap rises and can be seen running from pruned shoots, when the vine is said to be 'weeping'. This is the moment when the buds develop and burst, breaking the soft down that protected them from the cold. The buds split open at different times, depending on the variety of grape. Early-budding varieties may still be threatened by late frosts, and therefore extra protection must be provided either by heating the surrounding air or by watering the vines,

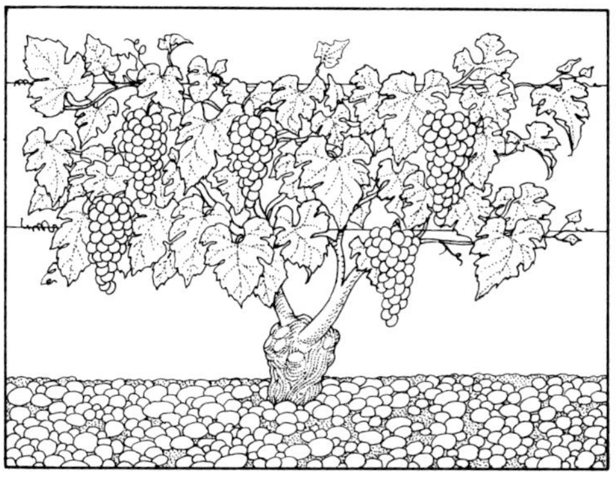

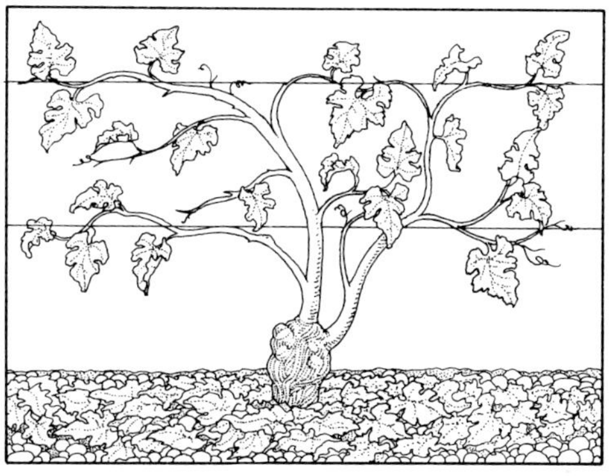

Below *The vine needs careful protection from adverse weather conditions: anti-frost stoves in California's Napa Valley.*

since the resulting layer of ice insulates the buds (Chablis, Champagne).

Another risky moment for the vine comes in June when the plant flowers. Fertilization is essential if the blossom is to give way to grape berries, but in poor atmospheric conditions this will not happen and the plant will yield little fruit. Sometimes small grapes without pips will form, indicating a partial crop failure, known as *millerandange*. The annual harvest yield is often decided at this particular stage.

One hundred days elapse between flowering and harvesting, and during this period sunshine is of prime importance. Temperatures of around 30°C are ideal, especially if accompanied by a little rainfall from 15 to 20 August. Too much rain, of course, is detrimental to the vine and will never produce a great wine even though all other requirements may have been met (Bordeaux 1974 is an example). After harvesting, the leaves redden and fall and the vineyard returns to its winter slumbers.

The vine has a need for constant attention if it is to fulfil its role in the delicate chain from individual vineyard to wine glass.

The Vine/Cultivation

Below *The vines of Châteauneuf-du-Pape growing in characteristically pebbly soil.*
Below right *Vines need repeated spraying to combat the ravages of bacteria, fungi and insects; hand-spraying in a vineyard of Jurançon in south-west France.*

Vines are usually uprooted between the ages of 40 and 50 years, but the grower is faced with a dilemma. Although the vine's grape yield diminishes with age, the quality of the wine improves, and so a choice has to be made between quantity and quality. The older the vineyard, the less plentiful and more expensive the wine, as is the case with all Bordeaux first growths. In practice, however, things are not quite so simple, and the vines are replaced piecemeal in order to keep the quality consistent.

In France a vine has to be at least four years old before its grapes can be made into *appellation contrôlée* wines. The great châteaux wait as much as eight years before permitting grapes to go into their *grands vins*, so wary are they of unsuitably light wines from young plants. Replanting will depend on the variety of grape grown and the cultivation density, which may range from 5000 to 10,000 vines per hectare. It will also depend on the type of stock that is to be planted, since all post-phylloxera vines comprise a root (*porte-greffe*) to which the visible part of the vine is grafted. The branches therefrom produce the grapes.

Cultivation and treatment

Although, as mentioned, the vine thrives in poor soils, it stands to reason that enormous amounts of fertilizer, both natural and man-made, have to be applied to the vineyard. To begin with, each hectare is treated with 25 to 30 tonnes of natural manure together with about half a tonne of phosphates and, at time of planting, one tonne of potassium. The soil is treated in similar fashion approximately every four years. The vineyard requires constant attention: earthing-up in autumn to protect the base of the vine, de-earthing in spring to free the base, turning over the soil between the rows of the vine, tamping down the earth in May and finally topsoil dressing and hoeing in summer.

Some growers prefer natural cultivation, allowing grass to grow amongst the vines, though most make use of grass- and weed-killers. All, however, are engaged in a constant battle against vine diseases, which may either

be due to soil deficiencies, to bacteria or to fungi (mildew, oidium, blackrot, botrytis) and combated by means of fungicides, while others are animal in origin (weevils, mealy bugs, cochylis bugs, caterpillars, phylloxera and spiders). All diseases require a specific treatment and some – botrytis, for instance – need repeated spraying.

Pruning

The quality of the wine depends on the quality of the grape. As Jean-Paul Gardère, director of Château Latour, says: 'Give me good grapes and good vats and I will make you a great wine.' The fight against vine diseases does much to protect the grape's health, and pruning is equally valuable. Lack of pruning causes the shoots to grow too long and the yield to drop, since the older branches will cease to bear bunches of berries; incorrect pruning, on the other hand, may produce huge yields but the grapes may turn out to be weak and insipid.

Winter pruning Not all grape varieties are pruned in the same manner. There is, for example, the 'goblet' cut, used in the south of France, in the Rhône Valley, in Beaujolais, Burgundy and the Champagne region. According to this method, the stock or stem supports three to five branches each bearing one or two spurs dressed to form loops.

The Chablis cut is a variation of the 'goblet' system (four arms radiating directly from the main stem) and is the method used in the Champagne region for white-grape vines.

Then there are the Royat cordon cut (Pinot Champenois) and the single or double Guyot (Bordeaux) in which one arm of the stem (or both in double Guyot) follows the training of the plants and includes 6 to 8 loops (2×3 or 2×4 in the double Guyot). Whatever the method employed, the purpose of pruning is to expose the vine to as much sun as possible, to simplify cultivation and in some cases to facilitate mechanized harvesting.

Spring and summer dressing This includes disbudding – removing unwanted buds – topping to remove the uppermost branches, clipping to take off the ends of the twigs and, finally, thinning out of leaves.

Below *Pruning vines in Champagne.*

The Vine/Soil & Climate

Experts agree that the quality of wine depends on four factors and four factors alone: geology, climate, vine stock and vinification (method of wine-making) under which heading we must include growing and maturing. It could be argued that conditions of tasting are also important, but as far as the Académie du Vin is concerned these are the main areas of interest and research.

Subsoil and topsoil

Geology is for our purposes virtually synonymous with soil. It is not always easy to decide where the subsoil ends and the topsoil begins. The vine will often put down its roots to great depths in search of sustenance; for instance, cellars cut into the rock 10 to 15 metres beneath the Saint-Emilion vineyards at Château Ausone and Château Pavie reveal the roots of very old vines. As mentioned, the vine does poorly in very wet soil, but like any other plant it does need water and will probe deep down to find it. Thus the best soil for the vine is one with good natural drainage and free from obstacles likely to impede the roots. Such conditions are met by deep gravel and, to a lesser extent, by asteriated limestone of the type found in the Médoc and Saint-Emilion regions. In gravelly soil, where water cannot collect, the vine roots are free to grow and develop; in limestone soils, they burrow deep into the fissures between the solid blocks of rock.

Sandy and siliceous soils frequently produce wines that are fine but over-light, whereas limestone and clayey soils yield

Right *The vines of Châteauneuf-du-Pape frequently grow on scree slopes; the pebbles improve the aeration and drainage of the soil and also store daytime warmth for release during the night.*

vintages which are more robust than sophisticated. The actual presence of pebbles improves the soil's aeration and drainage as well as acting as a 'storage heater', releasing at night the warmth accumulated during the hours of sunshine. This is the case at Châteauneuf-du-Pape where the vines grow on a virtual scree slope. The actual colour of the soil also plays a part, since pale soils such as marls, chalks and tuff are better for white varieties, while the darker soils are more suited to red wines.

Climate

The four principal interactive elements of climate are sunshine, rainfall, temperature and wind. Areas that enjoy an abundance of sunshine will produce grapes that are rich in sugar but low in acidity. Regions with too much sun tend to yield wines that lack breeding. Too little sunshine, on the other hand, leads to wines that are over-acidic but low in alcohol and hence thin and feeble.

The vine requires from 16 to 24 inches of rain a year, though not at random: rain is welcome in winter and early spring but potentially harmful in summer and early autumn.

Wine-growing becomes a problem when mean annual temperatures fall below 10°C, and the quality of each year is usually decided in the months of August and September, when temperatures above 30°C enhance the prospects of the new vintage.

North winds are favourable in hot regions as they cleanse and purify the vineyard, but excessively strong winds cause damage.

Left *Close inspection of the dusty soil in a Napa Valley vineyard in California.*

The Vine/Grafting

All the diseases mentioned previously will have a detrimental effect on the wine's quality, but there is one more that very nearly exterminated the vine for good in the 19th century. This disease was caused by the phylloxera bug (*Dactylosphera vitifolii*), an aphid brought across the Atlantic from America in the early 1860s, possibly on vine scions or table grapes. In 1863 phylloxera appeared in the extensive vineyards of the *département* of Gard, in Languedoc, and then moved northwards to Orange, in Vaucluse, and the Drôme; by 1868 vineyards in Bordeaux and Portugal had been attacked. American vines were fortunately immune to phylloxera, but within half a century it had destroyed all of Europe's vineyards, since the only treatment found against it – carbon disulphide – proved difficult to apply, being highly flammable and giving off a foul odour, besides having toxic effects on humans.

The *vignerons* hit on the idea of replacing their defunct European vines with phylloxera-proof American ones, but the latter on their own proved incapable of producing wines of sufficient quality and distinction for European tastes. However, when European *vinifera* shoots were grafted on to them the grapes – and hence the wines – took on the characteristics of the new shoots. Nowadays, quality vines the world over are grafted in this way. Only plants grown in sand can be left ungrafted because phylloxera cannot survive in this element.

Ever since this major replanting exercise – from 1¼ to 1½ million hectares were reconstituted in this way – experts have discussed and argued the various merits of grafting and its effects on the quality of the wine. Comparisons are difficult because pre-phylloxera vines are by now very old. The last quality vineyard to preserve ungrafted plants was Romanée-Conti, until the end of World War II; and at the moment the well known champagne firm Bollinger is cultivating two small plots of ungrafted Pinot Noir (so-called 'old French vines'), by way of experiment.

Any valid opinion must take into account the fact that the ungrafted vine has the great advantage of longevity – it survives for almost a century. As already mentioned, a wine's quality improves with the age of the vine, the bouquet becoming more refined and the structure more complex.

So what, apart from their resistance to phylloxera, are the benefits and drawbacks of grafted vines? Whereas ungrafted varieties grow in just about any type of soil apart from ground that is too wet, clayey or salty (chloride), the American vines that constitute the basis of present-day vineyards do poorly in limestone, which etiolates them (turns the leaves yellow); furthermore, grafted vines have a shorter life. On the other hand, they are many and varied; in France a grower has the choice of some 30 different vine stocks (including hybrids) which enables him to find exactly the right kind for the shoots, depending on the particular type of soil and the type of grape he wants to cultivate. Factors such as strength, sugar, yield and resistance to disease, all vary according to selection of the stock for a particular environment.

Wine growers everywhere periodically come up with new stocks which they hope will be better suited to their particular soil, especially limestone, and yield even more fruit. The most recent is called Fercal, and great things are expected of it in Saint-Emilion and Champagne. In France alone, over 4000 hectares are devoted to the production of vine stocks for replenishing purposes.

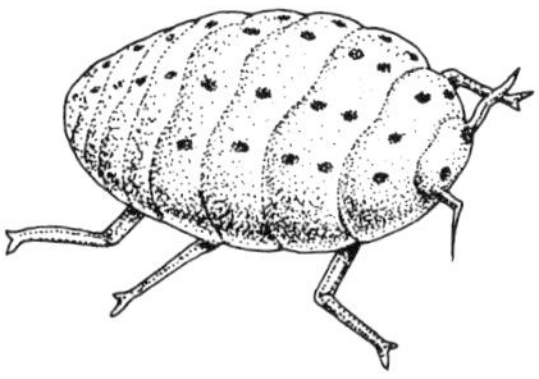

Above *The phylloxera bug (*Dactylosphera vitifolii*).*

Right *Vine twigs for grafting, showing the W-form 'join'.*

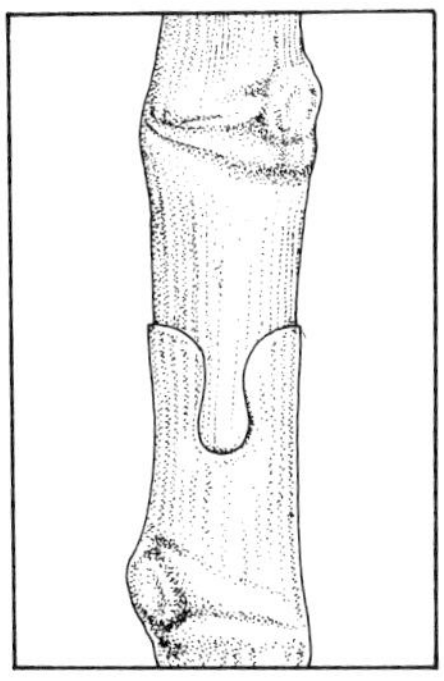

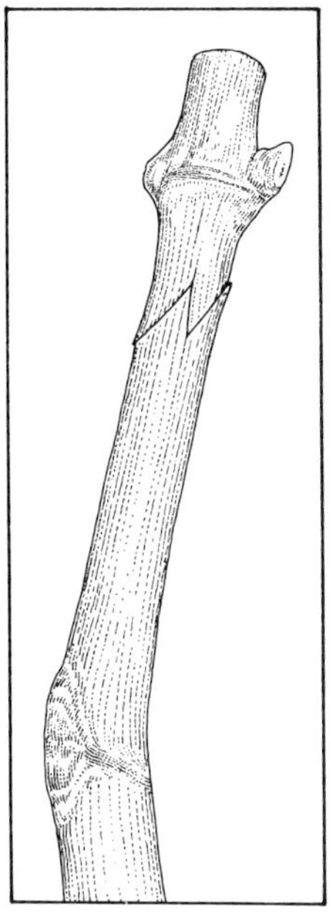

Top *The modern U-form vine graft, which can be done with a stamping machine.*
Above *The more traditional W-form.*
Right *Cutting and joining American root stock (dark twigs) to the desired French variety (pale twigs).*

The Vine/Mechanized Cultivation

Mechanization made its first appearance in vineyards just after World War II. The recently invented straddler tractor has transformed the lives of the growers, making possible a wide range of different treatments and processes. These vehicles have an adjustable track and the more sophisticated types are equipped with hydraulic levellers for safe working on hillside vineyards where rows of vines do not evenly follow the slope.

Winches are used on steeply inclined hills with rows that follow the line of the slope; and these have proved highly effective in reclaiming vineyards abandoned because of the difficulty and cost of manual labour (e.g. Sancerre and Switzerland). Trials are currently being conducted to test new tractors for the more precipitous, inaccessible slopes. These machines have articulated legs and feet in place of the normal wheels and are able to cope with any gradient while remaining in a horizontal position. This type of tractor is particularly suited to terraced vineyards thus far wholly reliant on manual labour.

The straddler tractors can be fitted with a range of attachments for various functions,

Below *Manuring a vineyard in Savoy, using a tractor specially designed for this purpose.*

such as earthing up and de-earthing, including sensor-controlled ploughs that till between the rows of vines without damaging the precious plants. The machines are also used for treating the vines, notably for spraying them with the innumerable fungicides and insecticides so essential for modern vineyard practice.

No machine has so far been invented for automatic pruning; nevertheless, pneumatic and hydraulic secateurs minimize physical effort and increase individual productivity. There is, however, a machine that collects and breaks up the pruned twigs and branches, incinerating them or burying them in the soil as additional fertilization.

Topping has also been mechanized, and rotary toppers and dressers mounted on the tractors help give the vineyard the ordered neatness and regularity of a formal garden. Dressing, of course, must be done with extreme care, for photosynthesis of the leaves determines the grape's sugar content.

Finally, and particularly if the grape harvest itself is automated, the straddler tractor can be converted into a pneumatic stripper which separates the bunches and eliminates unwanted leaves.

Mechanical harvesting

These machines are being used to an increasing extent. The bunches of grapes, provided they are correctly dressed, should develop and grow at specific heights above the ground, and so it is a simple matter for harvesters to drop the berries and grapes onto a moving conveyor where residual leaves are removed by powerful air blowers; under normal conditions the machines operate as well as, if not better than, teams of pickers.

Machines also have the additional obvious advantage of needing no sleep and so can work round the clock if there is a threat of bad weather. Last but by no means least, machinery enables the *vigneron* to start and finish the harvest when the grapes are fully ripened. Note, however, that mechanical harvesting is prohibited in Champagne.

Below *A mechanical harvester at work in a vineyard at Cahors.*

Vinification/Introduction

Vinification is the collective term for all the operations and processes which turn grapes into wine. Authoritative books on wine written before World War II make no mention of vinification, but since then the art of wine-making has made great strides and a new kind of expert has emerged, the oenologist. The oenologist's mastery of vinification techniques is just as important as the grape variety, the soil and the climate. Not only is he a technician who must be versed in physics and chemistry, but he is also something of an artist, and a great wine represents his masterpiece. A good oenologist can stamp a wine with distinction; a bad oenologist can produce a bad wine even from excellent grapes.

Gifted oenologists tend to divide into two types, some being pure technicians, others more aesthetic. The technicians produce correspondingly technical wines, that is to say wines which, though faultless, are devoid of charm; the more artistic oenologists can also be further subdivided into those who impose their personality on the wine, 'signing' it, often to the detriment of the distinctive local or native tang, and those who, more self-effacingly, allow the characteristic qualities of the grape to speak for themselves.

Vignerons have repeatedly confirmed that the method of vinification is at least 50% responsible for the final quality of a wine. Naturally, therefore, the Académie du Vin attaches great importance to the various problems involved.

The same red grapes are capable of producing either a wine that is light, fresh and fruity rather than full-bodied, which should be drunk young or even very young, or a wine that is rich, dark and generous, heavy on extract, of great aromatic complexity and not to be drunk in the first ten years of its life. The grapes could even be used to make a light rosé for summer drinking or a fine and vinous white wine.

The same applies to white grapes. The wine maker can use them to create a fruity wine with an alluring primary bouquet, a somewhat facile dry white wine to accompany hors d'oeuvres, a truly great white wine with highly evolved secondary aromas from which the grape flavour has quite disappeared, or finally a sparkling or slightly sparkling dry white wine.

The type and quality of the finished product are thus dependent on the vinifier; and at the Académie du Vin it is our business to determine, simply by tasting, the method chosen by the wine maker and to compare wines, which, although they come from the same village or commune, possess different properties because they have been made on different estates. A knowledge of the principles of vinification is essential for this rather more sophisticated approach to wine.

Right *The quality of a wine depends greatly on the ability and taste of the vinifier: tasting wine from the cask in Beaujolais.*

Opposite Pesage *at Margaux, Bordelais.*

Vinification/The Cuverie

Adjoining the actual fermenting room – where the must is transformed into wine – is an area that usually features a *fouloir-érafloir* (or *égrappoir*) which simultaneously removes the stalks from the grapes and crushes them. After fermentation, the wine is aged and matured in storage vats and casks. The wine is then fined, filtered and bottled; and finally the bottles are labelled and packed into cases.

Each of these operations has led to the invention of special equipment. The crusher, as its name suggests, is used to squeeze the grape, thereby bursting its skin and releasing the juice. Crushing was once done by 'treading' the wine in huge tubs, but nowadays the berries are passed between two rollers which are close enough to burst the grape but not to crack the pips. This is important, for the pips contain substances that give the wine an unpleasant taste.

The *érafloir* or *egrappoir* is a machine that separates the stalks and stems from the berries, although certain estates, e.g. Château Palmer, still carry out this work traditionally by hand.

The fermenting vats themselves may be made of wood, cement, plastic, enamelled metal or stainless steel, and can be open (Burgundy) or closed (Bordeaux). Vat capacities range from just a few to several thousand hectolitres; some white wines ferment in 2-hectolitre barrels! The temperature of the grape must has to be monitored and controlled, and fermenting temperatures are regulated by means of water cooling systems, heat pumps or heat exchanger coils. The pumps circulate the wine around the vats, conveying it from the base to the surface of the liquid, a process known as *remontage* and highly important for the quality of red wines. Pumps are also used to transfer the wine from one vat to another, and this is called *écoulage*. The 'cake' *(marc)* or residue collected inside the vat is transferred to a press, but since

Above right *Old-style press still in use for producing fine Sauternes at Château d'Yquem.* ***Right*** *A modern drum press at Château Beychevelle in the Médoc.*

there is no *écoulage* for white wines these are routed directly to the press.

Most modern presses are pneumatic or electrically operated horizontal machines with pressure control. As mentioned, it is essential never to crack the grape pips because they contain a bitter oil fatal to the quality of the wine. Inside the press, two screw-driven plates compress the 'cake' of skin, pips and sometimes stalks. A new model of press known as a balloon press has a rubber bag that presses the grape against a cylindrical grid when inflated. Pressing is done several times and between each pressing the 'cake' is broken up by removal of the plates and a system of chains or, in the balloon press, by deflating the balloon and rotating the cylinder. Once all the juice has been expressed, the press is emptied and the dried 'cake' is turned into fertilizer or supplied to a distillery for conversion into *marc* brandy.

The wine is then put into an insulated vat which may be artificially heated to encourage malolactic fermentation or cooled to promote the precipitation of bitartrate. Finally it will be stored in huge vats pending bottling or pumped to the maturing cellars where it will rest in wooden barrels or casks.

The following sections take a fairly detailed look at the various vinification methods and their respective effects on the taste of the finished wine.

Above *Stainless steel tanks in a modern Californian winery can be used for both fermentation and storage.*

Left *Oak casks in the maturing cellar of a French* négociant; *the age and method of manufacture of a cask can have an influence on the eventual taste of the wine.*

Vinification/Red Wine

Red wine is obtained by fermenting red grapes, although some white berries may be added to the process – something that is tolerated in Burgundy, common practice in the Rhône Valley and until recently a tiresome obligation in Chianti. For the wine to be red, the pigments that give the grape skin its characteristic colour must dissolve in the colourless grape juice and this occurs under the influence of heat or alcohol, or both.

Sorting and pressing

When the grapes arrive at the fermenting room, they may be more or less sorted: in Champagne the sorting is thorough, in the Rhône Valley it is compulsory (at Châteauneuf, for instance, 5% are discarded), and this has an initial effect on quality. The harvest may also have been pressed and/or de-stalked, and manual de-stalking, as practised at Château Palmer, may necessitate additional sorting. Although all harvests are pressed (except in the special cases described on pages 54–55), de-stalking is a more complex issue, for the retention of stalks may actually be beneficial in certain grape varieties, harmful in others. The stalks of Pinot or Merlot, for example, make a positive contribution to the quality of the fermented wine, while those of the Cabernet or Carignan varieties give rise to disagreeable features. Generally speaking, the removal and elimination of the vine stalks will enhance the distinction and breeding of the wine, but in certain cases good stalks may strengthen its tannin and make it longer-lived.

Fermentation

Pressed grapes – whether or not partially or wholly de-stalked – are placed in the fermenting vats and at this point the vinifier has three parameters to consider: fermentation, temperature and *remontage.*

Fermentation ceases at temperatures below 15°C, while above 35°C the yeasts are killed off by the heat. Lower temperatures encourage primary aromas that are the attributes of wine which must be drunk young; hot fermentation tends to extract the polyphenols and tannins so essential for making great vintage wines. Similar criteria govern the actual fermenting time – short fermentation (24 to 36 hours only) produces light, so-called 'overnight' wines. Lengthy fermentation, as much as one month, produces more ambitious wines.

In deciding the fermenting period, the *vigneron* must take into account the potential of the vintage, the grape variety and his own personal taste. He may even increase the wine's degree of alcohol by adding sugar during the fermenting process. This practice, known as chaptalization, is the subject of much controversy but is nevertheless regulated to a maximum of 2° extra alcohol. In mediocre years the fermenting time may have to be increased, but if the grape is unhealthy it will have to be cut short.

The influence of the grape variety is very important. The fermenting period for Bordeaux varieties is, for example, two times longer than for the Pinot. It sometimes happens that the *vigneron*, when tasting the wine, feels the need for a little extra fermenting; yet to prolong it may be dangerous since risks of bacteriological disease (volatile acidity, etc.) are always present.

Remontage

The wine-maker also has to decide how many times to carry out *remontage.* During fermentation, the solids tend to float to the top of the vat, forming a thick crust called the 'cap' which floats on or just below the surface of the wine. This cap, buoyed up by the rising carbon dioxide gas, has to be kept immersed, or at least constantly pressed under (a process called *pigeage*); alternatively, it may be sprayed with wine pumped from beneath and back again over the cap, which is thereby kept wet. These essential operations increase extraction.

Vin de goutte and vin de presse

Next comes the process of running off the fermented wine from the vat (*écoulage*). This wine is the *vin de goutte*, of fine, sometimes great, quality. The solids taken from the fermenting vats are then pressed two or three times to yield the *vin de presse* (first pressing, second pressing and so on) which constitutes some 20% of the total volume. This is a very dark, extremely tannic wine which is slightly lower in alcohol and rather more acid. It is less refined and very unpleasant to taste on its own; some or all of it will eventually be added to the *vin de goutte*, depending upon the latter's constitution and the vinifier's preferences. In any event, both *goutte* and *presse* will first undergo malolactic fermentation, in which malic acid is converted to lactic acid under the action of lactic ferments.

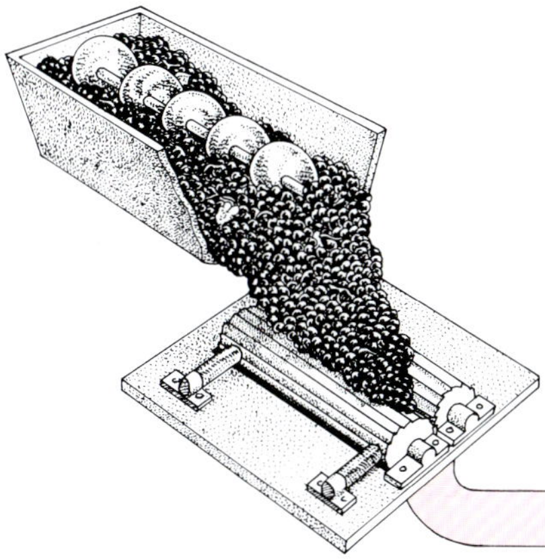

The black grapes are first crushed before removal to the fermenting vat; red wine takes its colour from the pigments present in the skins.

The solids taken off from the fermenting vat, about 20% of the total volume, are pressed two or three times to yield the vin de presse.

The fermented wine is run off from the fermenting vat straight to the storage vat or barrel; this is the vin de goutte.

A certain amount of the vin de presse *may be added to the* vin de goutte, *depending on the type of wine preferred by the vinifier.*

Wine run off for storage in oak barrels takes on different characteristics from the wood; other wine may be aged in the bottle.

Vinification/Rosé Wine

In Europe, one region apart, rosé wines cannot be made by blending red wines with white. The exception is in Champagne where *vignerons* may legally tint their white wine by adding red wine from the same area of *appellation*. Otherwise there are three types of rosé, each the product of a special vinification technique: they are the pressed rosés, the 'bled' rosés (*saignée*) and rosés made from pink grapes.

The pressed rosé is made from red grapes but using the white grape method, bearing in mind the fact that good-quality red grapes are filled with colourless juice. These grapes are crushed, strained and pressed, and in very hot weather some of the pigments that give the skin its characteristic colour are dissolved, encouraged by alcoholic fermentation. Subsequent pressings will be increasingly coloured, and the first pressing is normally used to give the wine its pink hue. These relatively pale rosés are frequently sold as *vin gris* (grey wines), and are similar in taste to white wines (*vin gris de Toul, vin gris d'Orléans*). The Cabernets of Anjou and Saumur are vinified in this way to make the famous Rosé d'Anjou.

Unlike the must of white grapes, the two kinds of must, *goutte* and *presse*, are mixed in the vat without their solids having been removed, and allowed to ferment under the same conditions as white wine musts, i.e. at low temperatures and heavily protected from oxidation. Like white wines, they may or may not undergo malolactic fermentation, as the individual wine maker eventually chooses.

The rosés *de saignée* are in fact red wine grapes that are partially macerated or fermented for a short period. Unlike the pressed rosés, therefore, they result from the vinification of red grapes by the red wine method whereby maceration is restricted from a few hours to two or three days according to the final colour desired; after this time the vat is 'bled' or tapped to remove a quarter or a third of its contents, and the rest made into standard red wine. The tapped amount continues to ferment but is no longer in contact with the grape skins and so cannot be additionally coloured. These rosé wines are superior in quality to pressed rosés, and all undergo malolactic fermentation.

The third type of rosé is also the least common and found almost solely in the Jura region. It is produced by the red vinification of a very special grape, the Poulsard, special because of its pink skin and pink juice. This means that the grapes can macerate at length, the extraction of colouring and aromatic agents being extremely important. It is vinified in exactly the same way as a red wine, and is even referred to, if somewhat superficially, as a very light red. Another characteristic of the Poulsard rosé that gives it a resemblance to reds is its longevity, for its quality improves with age. Pressed rosés, on the other hand, should be drunk quickly, if possible within 12 months, while the rosés *de saignée* can wait a little longer but will hardly improve with age.

Opposite *Grapes from the vineyards of Tavel, Côtes-du-Rhône. One of the rare* appellations *to allow the mixing of red and white varieties.*

Vinification/White Wine

White wine is made by the direct pressing of white grapes or black grapes with colourless juice, although the great white wines – apart from champagne – are always made with white grapes.

Crushing and pressing

Once the grapes are harvested, they are immediately crushed and strained, mechanically or naturally, then pressed. Mechanical strainers can extract 75% of the must, which will be of a high quality. Subsequent pressings will be of lesser quality and the final 10–15% will be low in acidity, containing much tannin and iron; they are, in any event, coloured and so will not be used to make the wine.

At all stages of vinification the must has to be protected against oxidation, and this is done by sulphuring, i.e. treating the must with sulphur dioxide (8–10 gr/hl) which is both an antioxidant (a reducing agent) and antioxidasic. Oxidases (oxidation enzymes) are harmful to white wines and are capable of destroying them altogether (oxidasic breakdown); they attack the phenol components, giving bitterness, harshness and colour. Since they attach themselves to the solid matter of the berries, these solids have to be removed by a process known as *débourbage* and the juice allowed to ferment by itself. *Débourbage* may be natural – by means of sedimentation with the must cooled to prevent fermentation (– 10°C) – or forced by filtration (bentonite), flocculation or centrifuging. These traditional techniques all help to improve the quality of white wines.

Below *Sorting Chardonnay grapes at Cramant for the production of Blanc de Blancs champagne.*

Fermentation

The clear grape must now begins to ferment and selected yeasts are added to the wine inside the vat or tank. Depending on the type of wine desired and the size of the estate, these fermenting vats may either take the form of wooden barrels, to contain about 2 hectolitres, or be huge cement or stainless steel tanks of up to 1000 hectolitres.

The wine maker must, of course, pay particular attention to the fermenting temperature, since experience shows that anything over 19–20°C can jeopardize the potential aromas. White wine is best fermented in relatively small quantities: the process of fermentation gives off much heat and in large vats there is always a tendency to overheat, whereas in small ones the surface area of the walls is relatively greater, causing less trouble. The problem of vat size can be overcome by the use of internal or external refrigeration to regulate the temperature.

Low-temperature fermentation may take up to one month and the wine is considered to be dry when laboratory analysis shows it to contain only 2 grams of sugar per litre.

Malolactic fermentation

This is the moment when the wine maker is faced with a crucial decision: whether or not to allow malolactic fermentation to take place. Malolactic fermentation is triggered by heating the vats; otherwise the wine is sulphited (10 gr/hl) to destroy the lactic bacteria. The decision depends on the overall acidity of the young wine (and hence on the grape variety and year) as well as on the type of wine the vinifier wants to achieve. Malolactic fermentation is practised in Burgundy, where a degree of suppleness is sought, and in Switzerland, despite the Chasselas grape's lack of acidity. In Germany, the Bordelais and most of the Champagne region, however, it is avoided. It is worth noting that the conversion of malic acid into lactic acid reduces the wine's acidity, since 10 grams of malic acid produce 6.7 grams of lactic acid plus 3.3 grams of carbon dioxide which escapes as gas. Generally speaking, a standard dry white wine with 11–11.5° of alcohol is judged successful when its acidity reaches 4–5 grams per litre.

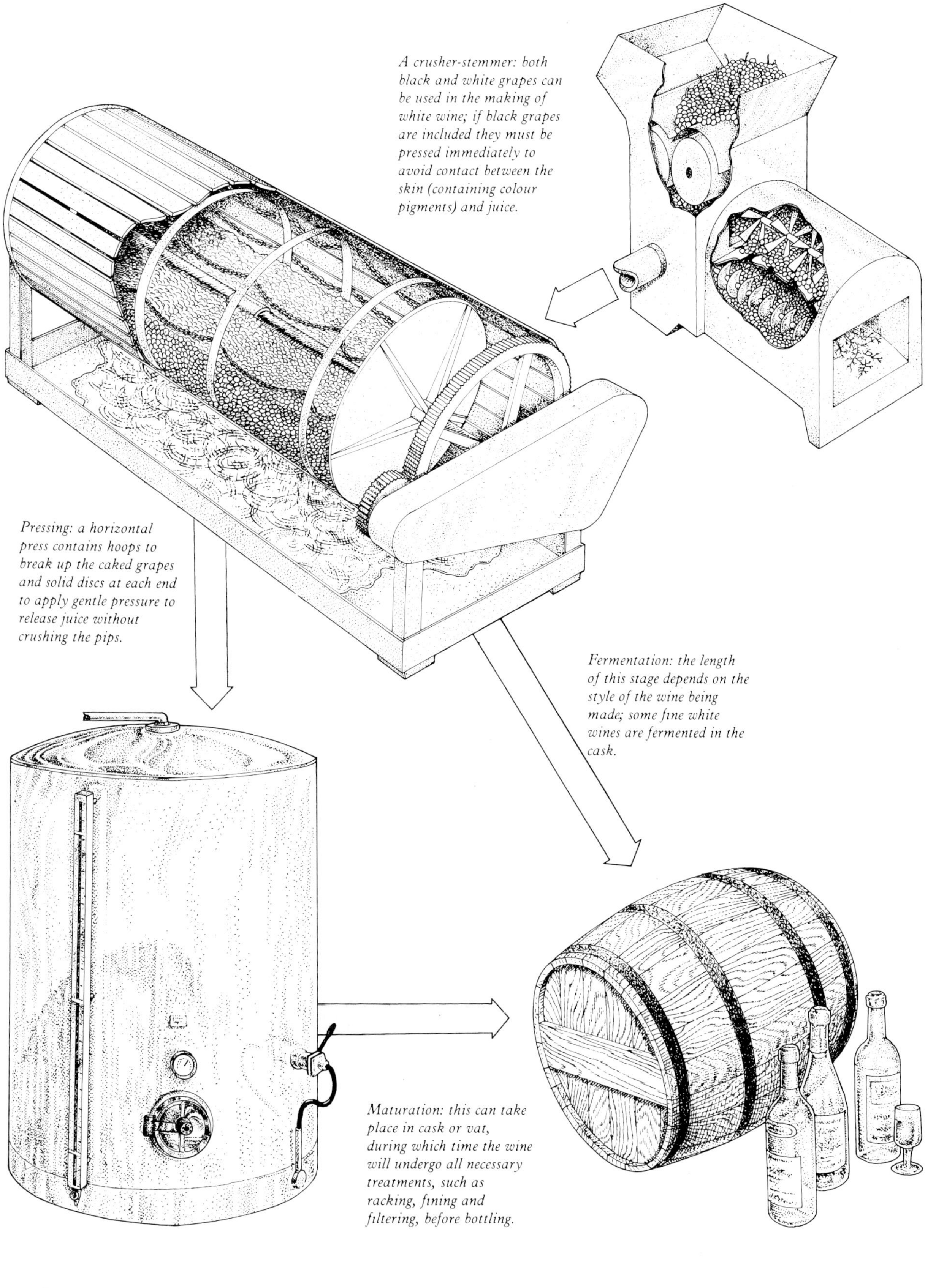

A crusher-stemmer: both black and white grapes can be used in the making of white wine; if black grapes are included they must be pressed immediately to avoid contact between the skin (containing colour pigments) and juice.

Pressing: a horizontal press contains hoops to break up the caked grapes and solid discs at each end to apply gentle pressure to release juice without crushing the pips.

Fermentation: the length of this stage depends on the style of the wine being made; some fine white wines are fermented in the cask.

Maturation: this can take place in cask or vat, during which time the wine will undergo all necessary treatments, such as racking, fining and filtering, before bottling.

Vinification/Elevage

We have so far described the ways in which grapes are transformed into wine. But the tasks of the *vigneron* do not cease until the wine is actually bottled, and this may be early or after a period of one or two years. We have therefore to consider two types of wine, those that 'see wood' *(faire du bois)* and the rest. 'Seeing wood' means being left to mature, for a fairly long time, in wooden casks (usually 225 litres) or tuns, instead of being placed in neutral tanks – neutral because, being made of metal, enamel or plastic, they have no effect whatsoever on the wine, regardless of how long it is stored.

The wooden cask, on the other hand, has a considerable effect on the wine, depending on the type of wood, its age, its cut and the period of storage. Two main factors are influential: first, the wood releases tannins which pass into the wine (200 mg per litre in the first year with new casks), second, the wine oxidizes because the wood is slightly permeable, unlike metal. Researchers have measured the annual amount of oxygen that passes through the wood as between 2 and 5 cc per litre, more than offset by the 15 to 20 cc per litre that enter the wine through its upper surface. In addition, the wine is racked *(soutirage)* four times a year to separate it from its deposit and lees and to aerate it. Each time this is done, 3 or 4 cc of oxygen per litre are dissolved in the wine. It is this process, together with a slight loss of alcoholic potency, that helps to transform primary aromas into secondary aromas and to develop the wine's colour: the violet-red of the anthocyanes which disappear by precipitation is gradually replaced by the brownish-yellow-red of the tannins.

The wine maker controls the maturing process according to his taste for wines that are more or less woody, selecting new or used casks depending on the year, varying the number of *soutirages* and leaving the wine inside the casks for as long as he wishes.

Actual bottling is prefaced by a number of processes designed to clarify or fine the wine. White wines will be drastically cooled over a period of eight to ten days down to below 0°C in order to precipitate the cream of tartar. This lends the wine softness, causing it to lose its acerbic properties, and also prevents the formation of *gravelle* or crystalline deposit.

All wines, red, white and rosé, are fined. This is done by adding a coagulant (fish-glue, ox-blood, casein, gelatine, white of egg, bentonite, etc.) to remove impurities by flocculation and sedimentation. After fining, and

Right *Heating dampened barrel staves, which have been hooped at one end so that the other end can be shaped by pulling on a looped hawser.*
Far right *New oak barrels at Château Lascombes, Margaux.*

sometimes instead of it, wine may be filtered through meshes of varying grade (cloth, cellulose, mineral substances). The more modern estates employ sterilized filtration followed by bottling under sterile conditions.

Certain *maîtres de chai* claim nowadays that they prefer to reverse the order of these operations, filtering prior to maturing in cask (Château Cos Labory, for instance), but it is too soon to make any definite pronouncement on the advantages of this method. It is worth noting that wines matured in small quantities (in cask) over long periods, say three years, will self-clarify through sedimentation, although it is rare for a wine never to be fined or filtered.

Left *The practice of 'thieving': using a* velenche *(pipette) to inspect and taste wine as it ages in barrels at Château Grand-Puch, Entre-Deux-Mers, Bordeaux.*

Vinification/Special Methods 1

Right *Turning the grapes over in a press used specifically for making champagne; many of the grapes are still whole after the first pressing.*

Wines are basically still or sparkling: the former contain a few milligrams (75 per litre) of carbon dioxide in solution, undetectable to the palate and the eye, while in the latter the presence of CO_2 creates pressures inside the bottle that can reach 6 atmospheres. This is only found in whites and rosés, since gas and red wine go badly together (although this rule is successfully defied by certain Italian Barberas).

Slightly sparkling wines

Some white wine labels, bearing the words *mis sur lie* or *mis en bouteilles sur lie*, recommend that the bottle should be drunk while young, and a slight prickling sensation on the tongue will indicate that the wine contains a little carbon dioxide gas. This is not a defect of vinification but is done deliberately to give the impression of crispness, making up for a lack of acidity (Swiss white wines). Wines that are *mis sur lie* are bottled the moment they leave the fermenting vat while it is still 'on its lees' and before it has been de-gassed by repeated *soutirages*. The process offers certain advantages: re-casking a wine increases its oxidation and is harmful to white wines, but the lees act as a reducing agent and are antioxidant (Muscadet, Vin de Savoie, etc.). Sparkling rosés are made for the same reason.

Sparkling wines

Very different techniques are used to make sparkling wines, which occupy a special position by reason of their history, their taste and their usage. Some wines are carbonated artificially, but these are usually rough, coarse varieties without interest or *appellation*. More distinctive are wines that have been made to sparkle by the *méthode rurale*, by closed vat vinification or by the *méthode champenoise*. In all cases the carbon dioxide given off by the fermentation of the grape sugar or added sugar has to be dissolved.

The *méthode rurale* is undoubtedly the most ancient method, and is used for making what is perhaps the world's oldest sparkling wine, Gaillac – a title it contests with the Blanquette de Limoux. This was the method used by Dom Pérignon, and it was not until the first half of the 18th century that the *vignerons* of the Champagne region perfected a new technique of putting the bubbles into wine.

The *méthode rurale* is simplicity itself: the wine is bottled before fermentation is complete. Once fermentation is over, the bottle will contain carbon dioxide and fermentation residues – the deposit known as *lie*. This deposit may be removed by expelling a minute quantity of wine after the process of *dégorgement*, whereby the bottle is stacked on its neck or by decanting at low temperature in a vat under pressure, then filtering and re-bottling at the same pressure.

The *méthode champenoise* also works on the principle of carbon dioxide being dissolved after fermentation; but this fermentation is not natural, being induced by the addition of sugared liquor and yeasts in a mixture known as the *liqueur de tirage*. The wine ferments in very small quantities (by the bottle, in fact) and very slowly at low temperatures (10°C) to guarantee best results. The bottles are clarified by *dégorgement*.

The *closed vat* sparkling wines are made by adding sugared liquor and yeasts to a vat capable of withstanding high pressures. This brings about a second fermentation, followed by filtration and bottling under pressure. Such wines may prove satisfactory provided their second fermentation is slowed down by the cold. Asti Spumante is a sparkling wine produced in closed vats from which nitrogenous matter has been removed by filtration and centrifuging, then sterilized (filtration or pasteurization) to prevent further fermentation of the residual sugar it contains.

Left *Giving the bottles their daily twist and shake* (remuage) *in the cellars of a champagne house; since the bottles are stored sloping downwards towards the neck,* remuage *causes sediment to be dislodged from the glass on to the cork.*

Below *Sediment in a champagne bottle after second fermentation.*

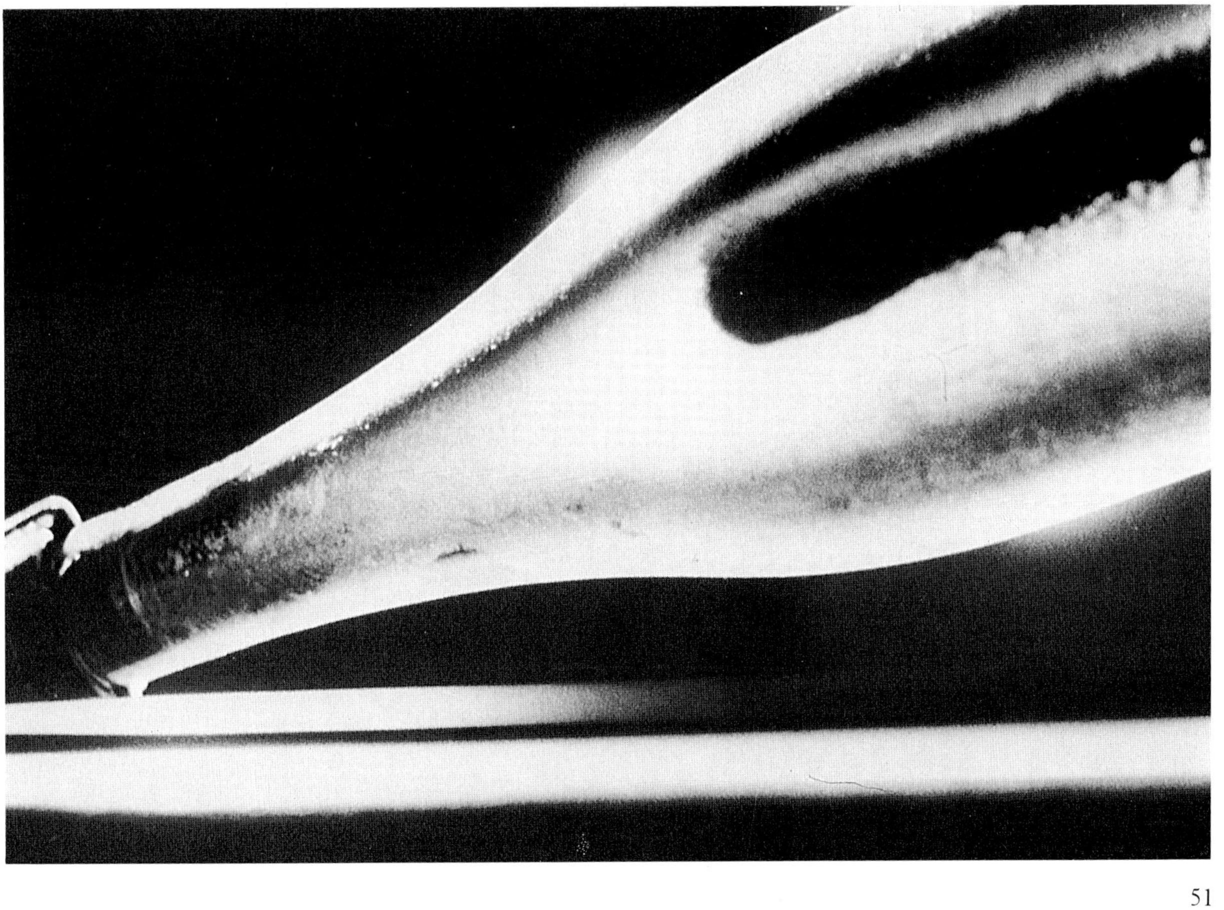

Vinification/Special Methods 2

White wines are said to be dry when they contain under 4 grams of residual sugar per litre. Above this level, the wine may be medium (20 gr sugar/litre) or sweet (40 gr/l); and thereafter it is a fortified wine.

The presence of residual sugar, i.e. sugar that has not turned into alcohol, poses problems for the vinifier, since the yeasts that transform the sugar into alcohol cannot withstand high alcoholic concentration. They multiply in sugared liquids at moderate temperatures (approx. 10–35°C) with an alcohol content up to 15–16°, but beyond this they are killed off by the alcohol itself.

Since it is a fact that 17 grams of sugar produce one degree of alcohol, musts that are rich in sugar should in theory be capable of producing wines with a strength of 20° or more. But because the yeasts die at over 15° alcohol, the *vigneron* is left with 5° of potential alcohol in the form of unconverted sugar, and the wine is said to have 15° of actual

Right Vendange *on the Premières Côtes de Bordeaux for sweet white wines.*

Left *Rotted Sémillon grapes going into the press to make the finest Sauternes at Château d'Yquem.*
Far Left *Tasting a Barsac by pipette.*

alcohol and 5° of potential alcohol – or 85 grams of residual sugar.

For many years fortified wines were only made from exceptional vintages that were unusually rich in sugar. Over the last two centuries – longer in Hungary (Tokay) – growers have allowed the grapes to desiccate (*vin de paille*, Jura) or have picked overripe berries attacked by *pourriture noble* or noble rot (Sauternes) in order to enrich the sugar content of their harvests. Even so, the sugar content is seldom high enough, and except in a rare year or on the occasional estate (Yquem) the wine maker has to interrupt the fermentation process artificially in order to strike an acceptable balance between sugar and alcohol. In general this balance is found at 14° of actual and 4° of potential alcohol; the process of halting fermentation is known as 'muting'.

There are several ways of killing or removing the yeasts, the simplest being to raise the alcohol level by adding more alcohol. This artificial fortification (*mutage*) is prohibited in the production of wine but permitted for making *vins doux naturels* (VDN wines include port, sherry, Banyuls, etc.). The second, commoner way uses sulphur dioxide (SO_2) to kill the yeasts. In order to work well, this method requires a massive quantity of SO_2 which contravenes current legislation and in any event ruins the taste. Only the best wine makers manage to use it properly, and generally in conjunction with other procedures such as:

- eliminating the nitrogen on which the yeasts depend, accompanied by filtration and centrifuging;
- sterile filtration to eliminate the yeasts;
- refrigeration or cooling, which halts fermentation but only renders the yeasts dormant.

Other techniques include thermolization (partial pasteurization at 45°), flash pasteurization at 70°, and normal pasteurization at 70° and over, all somewhat drastic processes that are never inflicted upon the great wines.

Muting a wine is a tricky business; the fermentation of fortified wines is also hazardous, because the large amount of sugar present leads to botryticine, an antibiotic produced by botrytis. Since *débourbage* is practically impossible, there is always the risk of oxidation and volatile acidity. Fortified wines enjoy very rich and highly complex aromas but are the most difficult to vinify.

Vinification/Special Methods 3

Whole-grape vinification

We have so far discussed what are usually referred to as 'traditional' wine-making techniques, the methods used everywhere to make the great vintage wines. Yet a substantial portion of wine is vinified in other ways, one of which is whole-grape vinification.

It is possible that all wines were once made in this manner, to be superseded later by the 'traditional' method. This would imply, for example, that the *vignerons* of Beaujolais, rather than inventing a new and special technique, were continuing an ancient practice.

The great advantage of whole-grape vinification is its ability to extract powerful aromas, but its major drawback is its failure to endow the wine with the structure so vital for good maturing and ageing. The method derives its name from the fact that whole grapes (even whole bunches) are carefully placed inside a closed fermenting vat, being neither de-stalked nor crushed. The vat is saturated with carbon dioxide (hence 'carbonic maceration') supplied from another vat or gas bottle. Fermentation cannot take place in an atmosphere that lacks oxygen, but intracellular fermentation does occur inside each separate berry: two degrees of alcohol form inside each grape, while half the malic acid disappears and the juice takes on colour. It is to this enzyme fermentation that these first-pressing wines (*vins de primeur*) owe their unmistakable aromas. After one week oxygen is supplied to the vat and the yeasts do their work. Malolactic fermentation takes place, *vin de goutte* and *vin de presse* blend together.

This type of vinification has spread to the Rhône Valley and has even extended its range to certain *appellation* wines around Crozes-Hermitage and Châteauneuf. It is possible to blend carbonic wines with those macerated in the traditional manner (Château Beaurenard) so as to combine the aromatic exuberance of the former with the structure and roundness of the latter. Broadly speaking, *vins de primeur* are vivid and very fruity mild wines for quick consumption, since they do not improve with age.

Vin jaune

There is another type of oxidized wine – *vin jaune* – which truly defies all the laws of oenology. It is actually a white wine left for six years in an open 225-litre cask, without *ouillage*, i.e. topping up of wine lost by evaporation. As a general rule, wine left in this

Opposite above *Taking semi-fermented must from a traditional square press.*
Opposite below *The cake of* marc *left after pressing.*
Above *Vats for whole-grape vinification in Beaujolais.*

way turns sour to become, at best, vinegar, but with *vin jaune* a crust forms on the surface to protect it against oxygen. This *fleur du vin* consists of yeasts (*Saccharomyces oviformis*) that cause part of the alcohol in the wine to oxidize into ethyl aldehyde, contributing to the famous 'yellow flavour', a taste reminiscent of walnuts.

The *vin jaune* method is rare, costly and not always successful. It is practised mainly in the Jura, the most famous exponent being the Château-Chalon which produces a strong, dry yellow wine that may be drunk as soon as it is bottled. It is somewhat similar to sherry, and it is interesting to note that the latter, which is a fortified wine, also depends on the magical effects of the *fleur du vin.*

Heating the maceration process

All maceration is hot because fermentation heats up the grape must. This 'natural' heat is sometimes artificially boosted to 50–80°C; the grapes may or may not be crushed. At these temperatures the extraction of colour is reinforced (almost double the number of anthocyanes are developed); this high-temperature maceration is followed, after cooling, by the fermentation of the now deeper coloured must. The wine is then matured in the traditional manner.

This method has three distinct advantages: it destroys the oxidases, makes it easier to vinify rotten grapes and stimulates the extraction of the anthocyanes, which disappear after two years. The aromatic implications of this method have been much debated. At Château de Beaucastel (Châteauneuf-du-Pape) it has been employed for some 50 years, and the principle itself has been known for at least two centuries.

Vintage/Introduction

The year in which a wine is made is of tremendous importance, and if a year is not declared it must be with good reason. The quality – and price – of a wine may vary enormously from year to year; and in bad years even great *appellation* wines will not be marketed because they are considered unworthy of their domaine or château.

Not every wine-growing region is equally reliant on the concept of year or vintage or on the success – or failure – of a harvest. Certain regions benefit from a very even climate, but whether such a climate creates average conditions and hence unvaryingly average wines, or ideal conditions conducive to perennially perfect vintages, is a debatable point.

We at the Académie du Vin feel that the difference in vintage years only stresses the diversity of the wines themselves, underlining certain aspects and characteristics of the wine as a consequence of capricious weather conditions. The vintage adds an extra dimension to a wine, instantly appreciated by the connoisseur.

There is no way of guessing at the quality of a wine unless it is seen and tasted – 'experienced' – and a particular vintage cannot be selected or recommended without some personal knowledge or recollection of it. Quality ratings by region and by year can help to refresh hazy memories; and, generally speaking, such ratings are agreed by experts, even if sometimes disputed by wine merchants who have to sell the 'little' years as well as the great ones. In any event, the development of the wine memory is of paramount importance in this context and great emphasis is placed on this in these courses.

An understanding of the interplay between climatic conditions and quality is essential when choosing a wine, for regions, grape varieties and types of wine all react differently to changing weather conditions.

It is obvious, for example, that a region close to the sea will be much influenced by the ocean's thermal fluctuations. Temperature, however, is only one climatic factor, and the sea offers no protection against rain, nor does it guarantee sun. A thorough understanding of these three factors, *temperature, rainfall* and *sunshine*, affords a sound basis on which to approach and evaluate a year, although they are insufficient on their own. It is vital to have accurate information on hourly distribution and incidence, to know that the sun shone towards the end of the summer, that it did not rain before or during the harvest, and that temperatures were sufficiently high.

Distribution is the essential question. Annual statistics of temperature, rainfall and sunshine are virtually useless, since they do not reveal whether it rained a little every day or if there were just two weeks of pouring rain during the whole year. Nor will they indicate whether it was too mild in winter or too cool in summer. To ascertain this, figures would have to be provided only for the growing period from March to October, taking account of the vine's very specialized requirements. In fact, studies for collating all this information, including hourly variables and time factors, are currently under way. It may not be long before it is possible to predict the likely effects of climate on each vintage and to use this as a standard for rating wine.

***Above** The year of a wine is part of its unique individuality: one of the prime factors in determining quality and price.*

Left *White wine ageing in the cellar of a* négociant *(Calvet) in Beaune.*

Vintage/Principal Influences

Weather conditions affect the grape in two ways. Firstly, they can accelerate or impede the growth and ripening of the grape; secondly, they may create conditions favourable or detrimental to the proliferation of parasites. Both contingencies affect quantity and quality.

It is often assumed that quantity and quality are incompatible, although this is not always the case. Certainly, when yield per hectare tends to be excessive, quantity is harmful to quality, and the distinctive characteristics of the wine become 'diluted'. This always happens if there is rain just before the harvest when the vine plant is still actively growing: the berries fill with water pumped up from the roots and the result is almost certainly a wine lacking in colour, substance and density, irrespective of previous weather conditions. Such rainfall may have even more drastic consequences if it has been preceded by a succession of very dry months, if the grapes are small and if, as sometimes occurs, the skin of the grape lacks suppleness. Because the berry cannot swell, it cracks and the harvest is lost.

Rain does not always have the same effect. Cold rain will increase the hectare yield, whereas warm, mild rains will create ideal conditions for the development of grey rot – fatal to wine, especially red wine, which has to macerate to extract colour. Spring rain can threaten the very existence of the wine, washing away the pollen from the flowers so that there are no grapes.

Premature growth of the vine is another cause of anxiety, for spring frosts can destroy pollen and buds. However, if the vine survives this ordeal, its chances of success are much higher. Since the grapes are usually harvested 100 days after the plant flowers, the sooner the flowers fade and die, the earlier the grapes can be picked. It often rains at the autumn equinox – around 21 September – and if the grapes are harvested before then, it augurs well for the wine.

Until 1978, all the great vintages were the result of early harvests; recently, however, the vine has become a much tougher plant, capable of withstanding the attacks of parasites following in the wake of bad weather. This increased resistance on the part of the vine is the consequence of successful treatments which are discussed later.

Too much heat and sunshine are not necessarily good for the vine; although this gives a red wine more colour, it reduces acidity (red and white) and impairs finesse. Furthermore, vintages exposed to excessive heat frequently fail to develop or last well.

Right *Young vine shoots are especially vulnerable to frost in spring. One means of protecting them against the frost involves the use of rapid burners to heat the atmosphere around the shoots.*
Opposite *Syrah grapes growing in the strong sunshine of the Côtes-du-Rhône.*

Vintage/Choice

Right *The vine is a pampered and cosseted plant: hand-spraying in Burgundy against parasites.*

Whereas the year is an important consideration for southern vineyards, it is absolutely vital for those farther north, where the climate is more extreme. Another significant factor is the grape variety, since not all grapes are equally capable of resisting climatic catastrophes. Each region, in fact, has discovered varieties best suited to its own particular climate. The Cabernet Sauvignon, for example, needs intense heat, and is thus not found north of the Loire; and both the thin-skinned Grenache and the Merlot, being prone to rot, are vulnerable to rain.

In choosing a wine it is a help to know something of the vine's idiosyncrasies as well as the age of the vineyard. Young vines react strongly to climatic conditions, so much so that in 1976, during the very long, dry summer, the youngest vines all but died. The older vines, capable of pumping up much-needed water through their longer roots, and generally adapting to changing weather conditions, had no difficulty in surviving.

Geology also provides a guide, especially in the case of difficult years. A soil's permeability and capacity for drainage will affect its absorption of heavy rainfall, and the advantage of deep gravel (10 to 15 metres) is obvious. The presence of impermeable layers of soil, as, for instance, at Château Haut Bailly (Graves), prevents good drainage and hinders root growth, so that the wine is highly sensitive to the year.

Apart from the direct consequences of climatic conditions, there are the indirect effects of parasites, although much progress has been made in recent years, notably systemic preventive sprays for saving harvests and vintages. Proper treatment enables the vine to come through the dangerous periods unscathed, and so allows the grapes to ripen fully. The excellent late vintages in Bordeaux in 1978 and 1979 bear witness to this success.

Such treatments have greatly improved the strength of white and red grapes but are difficult to apply to vineyards producing fortified wines since these are harvested late. Autumn is the important season, and although some years may be average for a red wine because of a mediocre summer, they may be highly rated for a fortified wine thanks to autumnal morning mists and sunny afternoons. This happened in 1967, though more often it is the other way round.

Below *Nylon filaments are sometimes draped over vines to protect them from the ravages of birds.*

Wine Buying & Transport

Wine can be bought through many channels, directly from the producer, from a wholesaler, in a supermarket, by mail order, or in a wine shop. Yet it is likely that the same bottle of the same wine will vary in quality or flavour in each of these establishments. Wine is a living thing that improves or deteriorates according to how and where it is stored, and the wine lover must remember this when purchasing.

The ideal but least convenient way for many is to buy straight from the producer, for this is where the wine is born and raised, and the maker has a reputation to safeguard. You can also taste beforehand. A word of advice on this. Do not be tempted by accompanying appetizers since these will mask possible defects in the wine.

Wholesalers are usually well equipped to

Above left *Buying from the producer: a grower's sign at Chinon on the Loire.*
Below left *Direct sales by the producer: Maurice Gousset, l'Aiglerie, Anjou.*

Right *The wines of the Bergerac and Bordeaux regions displayed in a wine shop in Périgueux.*

store wine correctly but sometimes refuse to sell retail. Grocers will not necessarily have a good cellar for storage and the wines may be kept too warm. Nor are they likely to have the time or expertise to select the best suppliers.

Supermarket wines are generally over-exposed to both heat and light. White wines in particular are liable to deteriorate by photosynthesis, which is why champagne bottles are always protected by an opaque sheet of paper. The specialist wine merchant or cellar will offer the best guarantee of good wine, with a greater selection of the better vintages and estates.

Travelling

Transporting wine after purchase demands as much care as any other aspect of handling. If you buy your wine straight from the producer, whether in bottles or in quantity (barrels, 'bonbonnes' or cubitainer), load it carefully into your car and make sure that it will not be exposed to too much heat either from the sun or the heater. Try to avoid sudden changes in temperature. Wine will be damaged if transferred from a cellar at 11°C to a car at 25°C, and vice-versa. Buying from a shop poses the same problems, though not so serious because the distances will probably be shorter.

If the wine is for early consumption the bottles should be transported and stored upright; always allow the bottles to stand for a day or two following a journey, even a week or more when the wine is worth it. A good bottle taken to friends for drinking the same day can often turn out to be a considerable disappointment.

Wine Storage

If circumstances permit, bulk buying for home bottling is a worthwhile investment. Wine that is transported in plastic containers should be bottled as soon as possible; if purchased in a barrel it is best left for up to two weeks, preferably in the place where bottling will eventually be done, and set up with an air space to aid ventilation.

Bottling should be done when the weather is dry and fine and atmospheric pressure high – rain and thunderstorms are fatal. The process should never be interrupted for any reason; leaving a half-empty barrel will destroy all the remaining wine. Before starting, therefore, make sure there is an adequate reserve of clean bottles and suitable corks. The bottles must be filled by siphoning the wine and allowing it to run down the sides to avoid frothing which will lead to oxidation. Corks must be long (38 to 52 mm) if the wine is to mature, and previously softened by soaking for ten minutes in very hot, but not boiling, water or, even better, in steam. Corks must be rinsed in cold water before being inserted far enough into the neck to leave little or no air between cork and wine. Once the cork is dry, the bottle may be capped or waxed, then labelled – a very important detail in the practical life of wine.

The cellar

The cellar, preferably with a solid door and strong locks, must afford the wine the best chances of development and improvement, and all bottles should be sensibly arranged so that they are accessible for supervision and consumption. Ready-made wine racks can be bought anywhere and are ideal.

A good cellar should protect the wine from outside odours, vibration and light. Never use a room that smells, for example, of domestic heating oil or one exposed to regular vibrations (as from a nearby underground railway). The cellar should be quiet, with a relative humidity of around 90% and a constant temperature as near as possible to 10–11°C. Minor variations in temperature are permissible provided it never exceeds 16°C, since sudden changes will ruin the wine, and a cellar that is always warm will accelerate ageing and deprive the wine of its very best quality.

The cellar register

A cellar register is essential if the wines are to be enjoyed at their best. Besides recording the contents of the cellar, the register should also contain notes, made after each tasting, on how the wine is developing and maturing.

Right *Bottling by hand in the cellars of Marc Brédif, producers at Vouvray, Loire.*

Left *A mechanical bottling line in the champagne house of Pommery & Greno.*

Below *A range of traditional bottle shapes for different wines; left to right: Tokay, Verdicchio, Chianti, Alsace/Rhine, Claret, Burgundy and Champagne.*

The Chemical Composition of Wine

Components and effects

SUBSTANCE	WEIGHT	WINE	REMARKS
SWEET			
Sugar	1–4 g	Dry white Red Medium white Sweet white Fortified	Sugar has not fermented
Ethanol (alcohol)	70–120 g	All wines	Preserving agent. Gives body
Glycerol	5–10 g up to 18 g	Quality wines Fortified	Gives density, though some deny this effect
BITTERNESS (and ASTRINGENCY)			
Tannins (leucoanthocyanes) (phenolic)	1–4 g 0.1–0.3 g	Red wine White wine	Colour structure, falls off with age Supports but hardens white wines
Anthocyanes (phenolic)	0.1–0.5 g	Red wine	Colour of young wines Disappears in 2 years Monoglucide in European wines Diglucide in American wines
Malic acid	0.1–5 g	White wines (not all)	Apple-greenness, acerbic, not found in the grape
Succinic acid	0.5–5 g	All wines	Product of fermentation
ACIDITY			
Succinic acid	0.5–1 g	All wines	
Lactic acid	2–8 g	All wines	Breakdown of malic acid Product of fermentation
Tartaric acid		All wines	Precipitates in cold (deposit)
Citric acid	traces	All wines	Disappears during vinification
Acetic acid (volatile acidity)	0.6 g 0.9 g	All wines Fortified	Too much indicates disease and careless vinification
SALTY			
Succinic acid	0.5–1 g	All wines	Product of fermentation
Mineral and organic acids	2–3 g	All wines	Enhance sense of freshness
Trace elements	traces	All wines	Enhance sense of freshness

Components without flavours or aromas

SUBSTANCE	QUANTITY	
Water	850–900 g	Pure water, biggest component by volume
Nitrogenous substances	1–3 g	Feed the yeasts; becoming rarer in modern wines
Vitamins	Traces	Helpful to yeasts
Gums	0–3 g	Becoming rarer in modern wines
Carbon dioxide Sulphur dioxide	2–3 mg	Irritate the mucous membranes CO_2 is unacceptable in tannic red wines, but is capable of improving certain whites and rosés SO_2 is always a mistake as soon as it becomes noticeable

Aromas

The aromatic components of wine run to several hundreds, including acids, alcohol, aldehydes and cetones.

AROMAS	SUBSTANCES
FLORAL	
Geranium	Hexane dienol
Rose	Geraniol Phenyl alcohol Phenyl acetate
Iris	Irone
FRUITY	
	Acetates of isoamyl, methyl, ethyl, butyl, isobutyl, isobutyl amyl, hexyl
Banana	Butyrates of isoamyl, butyl amyl Various alcohols: methanol, ethanol, propanol, butanol, pentanol, hexanol
Cherry	Benzaldehyde cyanhydride
Strawberry Raspberry Blackcurrant	Various acids, alcohol, aldehydes and cetone
Bitter almond Almond	Benzoic aldehyde, acetoin, (cetone)
Hazelnut Apple	Diacetyl (cetone) 50 components!
Peach	Undecalatone (alcohol)
SPICES AND OTHERS	
Cinnamon	Cinnamic aldehyde
Liquorice	Glycyrrhyzine
Honey	Phenylethyl acid
Rancid butter	Excessive diactyl (cetone)
Sour wine	Ethyl acetate (ester)

2
Intermediate Course

Wine is a complex business, its harmony and balance being matters of extreme delicacy. Each component exerts an influence upon another, which is why any blinkered study of a single constituent must be doomed to failure. Nevertheless, the Académie du Vin has decided to devote a special course to the varieties of wine grape, in the belief that this subject is fundamental to the better understanding of all other branches of the business and art of wine-making. For the grape, in its diversity, its sensitivity to different soils and climates, and the potentialities it offers to the wine producer, is an extraordinary fruit.

Our investigation of the principal grape varieties will be followed by a tour of France and indeed of the whole world, for each region and each country possesses its own stocks which it nurtures, improves and crosses with other stocks to create hybrids with the aim of modifying, both directly and artificially, the biological genotypes. Having described these varieties and the ways in which they are affected by soil, climate and vinification, we shall be ready to go on to the Advanced Course in appreciation, which deals with the wine itself, in all its marvellous diversity.

In accordance with the established principles of the Académie du Vin, we shall try to identify some causal relationships between the conditions in which wine is nurtured and developed, and the wine itself.

Quite apart from the intrinsic interest of this study, we are convinced that the wine lover who knows how a wine comes into being is better equipped to appreciate it, to remember it and to choose it wisely. Wine, after all, is more than a casual, pleasant diversion. If, as we must surely believe, the art of living is a cultural phenomenon, it follows that the knowledge and use of wine are cultural activities, part and parcel of a civilized and satisfactory existence.

Grape Varieties/Introduction

The study, description and classification of grape varieties is called *ampelography*. Though ancient, this science is nevertheless imprecise, and differences of opinion often occur. For example, in the texts of ratifications published by the French Institut National des Appellations d'Origine Contrôlée (INAO) in the *Journal Officiel* (French law gazette), Chardonnay is always referred to as Pinot-Chardonnay. Now it is well known that there is no connection at all between the Pinot and the Chardonnay, that they do not belong to the same family, that the white grape close to the Pinot is the Pinot Blanc, and finally that it has to be called Pinot Blanc Vrai in order to indicate its true affiliation. The term Pinot-Chardonnay can thus breed confusion.

Correct nomenclature is important because varieties are designated and regulated for each *appellation*. The wine grower buys his grapes from nurserymen, and when he plants Cabernet, he has no more desire to pick Sémillon grapes than a tree grower wishes to see an oak when he has planted a cherry tree! Ampelography aims to define the varieties of grape and to classify them family by family. The task, however, is not made easier by the fact that the science must deal only with pure varieties; and they cannot be judged pure before they are defined. Many systems of definition have been suggested. Some are based on the particular date of budding, flowering, ripening, maturing or defoliation, while others are related to the type of vine shoots, roots, flowers or even leaves. This last

Below *Merlot grapes growing in Saint-Estèphe.*

system, extremely meticulous, is based on the angles of the veins in the leaves, and it originated a branch of the science known as *ampelometry*. The latest classification, based on phenotypes, takes account of all the visible hereditary features of the vine.

A serious study of grape varieties must embrace both the vine plant and its stocks. Whereas the variety of vine determines the variety of grape, the quality depends on the stocks that bear the vine. For example, the stock known as SO4 (Berlandieri-Riparia No. 4, selected at Oppenheim) increases the hectare output and reduces the grape's sugar content.

The grape's quality is also modified by selection. Mixed selections have long been the rule, but more recently cloned selections have come into fashion, raising the prospect of vineyards being nothing more than an infinite reproduction of a single vine stock, which would greatly impoverish the wine. Selectors who tend to promote quantity at the expense of quality are therefore to be treated with circumspection. In addition to the selectors, nurserymen and research centres can also influence grape varieties.

Since the vine is a sexed plant it can be cross-bred. First cross-fertilizations give hybrids, sometimes directly productive, of two different species, while second cross-fertilizations, using varieties of the same species, yield hybrids with remarkable characteristics. Thus the most popular variety in Germany is the Müller-Thurgau, a cross between Riesling and Sylvaner.

Left *Gamay grapes in the Beaujolais.*

Grape Varieties/Influence

The influence of the grape variety on the finished wine cannot be over-stressed. It gives it colour, of course, but much more than that, as is testified, for example, by the wines of Germany and Alsace, which are derived from the same soil, the same vineyard and the same vinification processes, yet bear the names of individual grapes. There is no confusing a Riesling with a Gewürztraminer. The effects of soil and climate must not be underestimated, but it is the historical connection over many centuries between specific grapes and specific regions that has created the ideal growing environments.

Three distinct techniques of wine-making have emerged over the years. The first, and the simplest, produces wine from a single grape variety. The wines of Germany, Alsace, Burgundy and the Loire illustrate this process.

The second is more sophisticated – several varieties of grape are simultaneously introduced into the *cuves* (wine vats) and ferment together. This is the process employed in the Rhône Valley and a number of Italian regions, and it is suitable for producing both red and white wines; furthermore, both white and black grapes can go into the vat to make red wines. Châteauneuf-du-Pape, for instance, comes from the in-vat fermentation of between one and 13 varieties of *Vitis vinifera.* It is obvious that only white grape varieties are vatted together in the case of white wines.

The third method of processing different varieties of grape into a single wine is known as blending. Two, three or four grape varieties are vatted separately, and each produces its own wine. During February-March, after the harvests, these wines are blended in proportions specified by the cellar-master after tasting. The wines of Bordeaux and south-western France, both white and red, are produced according to this principle.

The pros and cons of blending grapes and wines are topics of endless discussion. The

Below *An impressive array of grape varieties awaiting pressing at a wine producer's in the Pays d'Aude.*

partisans of grape blending assert that mixed fermentation causes interactions among the particular components of each variety, and the complexity of chemical reactions during fermentation may indeed give some credit to this theory.

Nevertheless, the method has its drawbacks. Not all the varieties of grape will achieve full maturity at one and the same time, but if each is vinified separately they can be harvested at exactly the right moment. On the other hand, it is impossible to alter the contents of the vat, whereas blending, by definition, facilitates precise, proportional adjustments. Once adopted, methods are not necessarily permanent. In Champagne, for instance, grapes used to be blended in the lifetime of Dom Pérignon, but today it is the wines that are blended. Mixed methods are also practicable. In the Rhône Valley some wines are produced by blending the grapes in the vat and then blending its contents.

Left and below *Tasting for blending at the champagne house of Moët & Chandon; the* chef de cave, *Dominique Foulon, is working on the* cuvée *before second fermentation takes place.*

Grape Varieties/International Reds 1

The Cabernets

This is a large and well-bred family which includes the Cabernet Sauvignon, the Cabernet Franc and the closely related Petit Verdot and Carmenère.

Cabernet Sauvignon

The origins of this patriarch of the Cabernet family are obscure, but it is assumed to be derived from a wild vine of the Bordeaux region. This is a late ripening variety, with buds that also open late, best suited to warm climates. The Sauvignon is an expanding variety, grown in Europe, the Americas, Africa, Australia, New Zealand and elsewhere.

In France it is grown in the Loire, the Midi, the south-west and also Bordeaux. Its tiny spherical black berries with their colourless juice produce wines that are very tannic, astringent and highly coloured, of moderate alcoholic strength and with complex aromas, including cedar, but more often of a fruity blackcurrant type. This harsh wine is long-lived and continues to improve with age. It plays a major role in the blending of Médocs (50–80%) and a minor one in the Graves and Saint-Emilion. It helps to produce reds and rosés in Anjou and Saumur wines.

Cabernet Franc

This is the Bouchy of the Pyrenees and the Breton of the Loire. It is a late ripening variety, budding just before the Cabernet Sauvignon and rather eclipsed by the latter's showy splendour. Its wines are less tannic, have a greater 'nose' (violet, raspberry, blackcurrant, gooseberry, liquorice) and are more refined. It is always blended in the Bordeaux region but is nevertheless the basis of the Chinon, Bourgueil and Saumur Champigny of the Loire. Its finest wine is Château Cheval Blanc (Saint-Emilion), accounting for two-thirds of the constituents.

Below *Cabernet Franc.*

Merlot Noir

Yet another expanding variety of wine grape, occupying more surface area in the Bordelais region than the two Cabernets together. It extends to southern France and is much prized in Italy, the Americas, South Africa and many other countries.

The Merlot Noir is an early-budding, second-vintage variety which often falls victim to spring frosts. The thin skin of its berries is susceptible to rotting; the rather

Far left *Cabernet Sauvignon.*

small black berries have colourless juice and are very numerous. Yields can be substantial (100 hl/ha). The wines of Merlot are stronger than those of Cabernet but of low acidity – often too low – supple and velvety with animal and truffle fragrances, and should be drunk fairly rapidly.

In France, Merlot wine is rarely pure (as it is in Italy and on other continents). Merlot Blanc has been grown for about 75 years and yields a weak wine of poor quality.

Pinot Noir

This very old traditional grape of Burgundy, perhaps originating there, used to be called Morillon or Auvernat.

The Pinot Noir is an early ripening grape which can be planted anywhere from south to north, although nocturnal warmth impairs the finesse of its wines. It buds very early and is thus susceptible to spring frosts, which may cause total or partial crop failure. Its finest wines are produced on limestone soil, and in more northerly regions. The blue-black berries are small, spherical, compact and thick-skinned, although their very compactness encourages mould. The juice is colourless. The Pinot wines are usually more acid than those of the Cabernet, but less tannic, rich ruby in colour with aromas of the red soft fruits. The Pinot grape is always vinified on its own, except for the Bourgogne Passetoutgrains (⅓ Pinot and ⅔ Gamay).

The Pinot thrives best in Burgundy. In Champagne the grape is vinified into a white wine, and in Alsace it makes light-coloured wines, and is particularly successful as a rosé. In Germany and farther east it is used to make a variety of light coloured wines. Pinot Noir wines from California tend to be fatter and richer.

Mourvèdre

This important variety, of Spanish origin, was widespread in the south of France in the days before phylloxera. It was not replanted because no suitable stock could be found. This problem, however, has been solved since World War II, and Mourvèdre is now increasingly found improving Côtes de Provence, Châteauneuf-du-Pape and other wines of the Midi.

It is a contradictory plant since it needs a lot of warmth but is susceptible to drought, and because it likes hillsides yet needs rich soils. This is a late-budding, very late-harvest grape with medium-sized bunches bearing very small, black and compact berries with thick skins and an unbearably tart taste if eaten. Yields are low to medium. Mourvèdre wine is usually average in alcohol, highly coloured, well constructed and very tannic, with a spicy bouquet that has a hint of violets. The grape has the unique characteristic of being anti-oxidant (very useful when blended with Grenache). The Mourvèdre has risen in stature in recent years to vie with the Syrah in the southern Rhône.

Above *Pinot Noir.*

Grape Varieties/International Reds 2

Zinfandel

This grape is most probably of Austro-Hungarian origin, or possibly Italian, but it has found its adopted soil in the United States where it was imported in 1851 by Baron Agoston Haraszthy, who first planted it at San Diego.

Zinfandel buds late and is very late ripening with a life cycle that is even later than that of the Cabernet Sauvignon. Its long bunches of blue-violet, compact and medium-sized grapes give very varied hectare yields. It does not thrive in flat, open country or strong heat, preferring chalky-limestone, slightly sandy soil of dry hillsides.

Well situated vines that are over 25 years of age produce highly coloured wines with spicy, black pepper and raspberry aromas. They are long-lived and the best of them come from the high hillsides of the Napa Valley in California.

Cot or Malbec

This variety is said to originate in the Bordeaux area, although each region gives it a different name: Malbec in its supposed place of birth, Auxerrois around Cahors, Cot in the Loire Valley, Pressac towards Saint-Emilion. Despite so many names, it is a vanishing variety, although it continues to form the basis of the Cahors vineyard. One reason for its gradual decline is its high failure rate, a tendency accentuated by its life cycle, since it buds very early and is thus susceptible to winter frosts. This early ripening variety bears medium-sized bunches of grapes that are round, small to medium in size, fleshy, black with a colourless juice. Yields can be high.

The wine of the Malbec is highly coloured and markedly tannic. It is well constituted but the aroma is somewhat feeble, which is why preference is often given to the Cabernets and Merlot. It is grown in the south-west and on the banks of the Loire where it goes into the making of rosés and uncomplicated reds.

Gamay Noir

Reputed to originate in the Côte d'Or, having taken its name from a village where, ironically, only Pinot grows today, this grape is so closely associated with Beaujolais that it is sometimes called Gamay-Beaujolais. It is, in fact, the most fashionable variety of red grape, precocious, early ripening and suitable for planting practically anywhere; indeed, it has already invaded the foothills of the Lyonnais, Jura and Savoie, lined the higher banks of the Loire and Rhône, and even extended south-west as far as Gaillac. Its progress is only resisted – at least for the time being – by Alsace in the east, the Bordelais region and the Midi in the south. The warmer climates do not seem to suit its attractive bunches of medium-sized, oval berries (the juice is colourless) with their high yields (100 hl and more). This early-budding variety thrives best in granite soils, and although it may succumb to spring frosts, it is fairly resilient, with second buds appearing to bear grapes.

Above *Gamay Noir.*

To give of their very best, the grapes have to be vinified whole (semi-carbonic maceration). Good Gamay wines are light, fresh, and with a pleasant bouquet, provided they have not been subjected to over-zealous 'chaptalization' (sugaring of the wine during fermentation). They should be drunk while still young. Gamay grapes planted in clayey limestone soils (Côte d'Or, for instance) produce uninteresting wines.

There used to be a number of *teinturier* Gamays, so called because the juice of their berries was coloured. These wines lacked finesse and they were used to give colour to others.

Syrah

This is a high-quality grape provided its yield never exceeds 40 hl/ha. Recent developments in this variety reflect the errors of ill-advised cloned selections. Its low yield, rarely exceeding 30 hl/ha, has been forced up to 100 hl/ha, resulting in wines of little or no quality.

It is a late ripening variety that has been grown in the Rhône Valley for over 1000 years. Nowadays, it has spread abroad to California, South Africa and Australia, and other regions. The grapes are small, oval, purple-violet and bloomy, in medium-sized bunches.

The quality of the Syrah grape in the northern Rhône is such that for a long time it improved the great wines of Bordeaux, including Château Latour, which was called 'hermitaging'. Needless to say, the system of *appellations* has put paid to this practice.

The wine from the Syrah grape is strong in colour and alcohol (11–13°), tannic, and endowed with the bouquet of violets highlighted by cherry and blackcurrants. Syrah shows at its best in the wines from Hermitage.

Left *Syrah.*

Grape Varieties/Local Reds

Grenache Noir

As its name might suggest, the Grenache, a round, medium-sized grape with colourless juice, is Spanish in origin and is one of the principal varieties in the wines of Rioja. It is a very late-ripening grape requiring much warmth, and therefore valued on the west coast of the Mediterranean. It is also extensively used in Australia and California to make a number of rosés.

It is not, however, without faults: it buds early, thus exposing it to spring frosts, it often suffers from irregular flowering and, like many varieties, it is prone to rot. Moreover, the wine it produces lacks acidity and oxidizes extremely quickly. How then to account for its popularity and success? The answer is that when it is planted *en coteau*, grafted onto a not too vigorous rootstock, and when one is satisfied with half its yield from the plain (130 hl/ha), it forms the base wines that are high in alcohol, fleshy, with a rich, round flavour. It is blended in the vat with other grapes (Cinsault, Mourvèdre, Syrah, Carignan, etc.), constituting as much as 70% of the make-up of Châteauneuf-du-Pape and the Côtes-du-Rhône.

There is a Grenache Blanc in the Roussillon but this variety produces no great wines since it is too strong in alcohol, oxidizes too rapidly and lacks acidity.

The Grenache Gris, i.e. pink, produces the fortified *vins doux naturels* (VDN) in the Roussillon.

Carignan

This variety takes its name from the Aragon town of Cariñena in Spain, where it probably originated. It occupies nearly 220,000 hectares of French soil, making it the most widely grown grape, but quantity is not necessarily conducive to quality. The grape only ripens with plenty of sunlight, and for this reason is chiefly found along the Mediterranean coastline. A late-budding, late-ripening variety, it does best near the Pyrénées Orientales provided it is grown on hillsides and the vines are fairly old, thus giving a low yield. On the plain it is capable of producing over 150 hectolitres per hectare.

Its usually large, compact bunches consist of medium-sized, spherical berries that are black-skinned with a colourless juice; the skin is thick and highly astringent.

The wine of Carignan averages 9 degrees on the plain and 13 on the hillside; it is dark coloured, very harsh in its youth and frequently bitter even when mature. Its participation is always limited in AOC wines (40% or less) falling to nil in the better wines. It is very seldom made as a single variety wine. In Languedoc tests have shown that Carignan would require at least 20% Cinsault to refine it and 20% Grenache to lend it body and softness.

Cinsault

This is both a table grape and a wine grape, good for eating because of its large, thin-skinned berries. It hails from southern France, the Midi, but is being more widely cultivated as growers come to appreciate its versatility, for it can go into *primeur* wines and even rosés (Tavel). Cinsault lends finesse and softness to the great *appellation* wines (Châteauneuf-du-Pape, Gigondas, etc.) but is also capable of high yields (100 hl/ha). This late-ripening variety should never be grafted onto over-vigorous stocks nor be planted in the plain, where yields tend to be too high.

Its bunches are large, the berries black, elliptical and compact (with colourless juice), bloomy and fleshy.

The Cinsault wines are usually full-coloured, very soft, low in tannin, with a medium alcoholic strength, maturing very quickly. Its floral aromas are elegant and sophisticated. In red wines it makes an excellent complement to the great varietals, but should not be used on its own.

The fact that it is sometimes called Hermitage in South Africa causes confusion, all the more since the world-famous original *appellation* comes only from a single variety, the Syrah.

Petit Verdot

A very late variety of Médoc which does not always ripen. It produces wines that are highly coloured, tannic and with a respectable alcohol content.

Carmenère

An excellent Médoc variety which has disappeared. It is currently being re-selected in the experimental plantation of the Château Dillon (Médoc).

Pinot Meunier

A variant of the Pinot, dating from the 16th century. It buds and ripens after the Pinot Noir, etiolates (turns white) in limestone soils and is resistant to frosts. Its bunches are large with round, compact, blue-black grapes that give good yields. Its wines are less acid, less vigorous and less sophisticated than those of the incomparable Pinot Noir. These versatile wines mature quickly and have found their true place in Champagne.

Tannat

A robust grape of ancient origin, from the Béarn region, it buds late and ripens correspondingly very late. The compact bunches with their tightly packed, small round berries, give good yields.

Tannat wine is highly coloured and very tannic, a characteristic to which it probably owes its name. It is a long-lasting wine which softens only with time.

Tannat used to be blended with Bordeaux wines to give them body and colour. Nowadays, it is blended where harvested with other quality grapes of a gentler nature, such as Bouchy, alias the Cabernet Franc. This is the way in which Madiran is made.

One also finds the Tannat in other wines: Tursan, Béarn, Irouléguy and Côtes de Saint Mont.

Poulsard

This is a very ancient grape from the Jura, being some 2000 years old and known by its present name since the 14th century. It appears to thrive only in the clayey schists and blue marl of the Jura.

It is an early-budding, but latish-ripening variety with large, loose and oval grapes with thin skins of a pinkish-violet colour. Its juice is slightly rosé. Poulsard is a table and wine grape that produces naturally rosé wines.

Trousseau

Another variety from the Jura, recorded by Olivier de Serres. It buds late and ripens during the autumn. The bunches bear very black, thick-skinned ovoid grapes of medium size. It produces wines that are highly coloured, firm, tannic and strong in alcohol, best when old.

Negrette

A grape from the south-west which buds late but ripens relatively early. It is widespread in the Middle Garonne basin where it produces fruity, soft and highly coloured wines for drinking within two years. Its finest example bears the AOC label of the Côte du Fronton-Villaudric. This is the wine drunk in Toulouse.

Jurançon Noir

This south-western variety is often called Folle Noire. It buds late and ripens in mid-October. Bunches are large, and the grapes round, medium-sized and bluish, giving respectable yields.

Its wines are light in colour, pleasant but of little character. It forms a make-up grape for certain lesser *appellations* of the south-west (Lavilledieu, etc.).

Mondeuse

This is a typical medium quality, late-budding grape from the Savoie producing large bunches of small, blue-black, oval berries. Yield per hectare is high. The wines of the Mondeuse are rich ruby in colour. They are clean, honest and uncomplicated, firm and rather harsh in youth, although they soften with age. Good Mondeuse wines can be found under the Vin de Savoie Chautagne label.

It is, however, a vanishing variety, being gradually superseded by Pinot Noir and Gamay.

Grolleau

In the Loire Valley, its birthplace, this grape bears several different names: Gros Lot de Cinq Mars or Pineau de Saumur, but its nickname seems to describe it exactly: Aramon du Val de Loire, an allusion to the southern variety of Aramon, a table-wine grape that produces a 'gros rouge qui tache' (literally 'a coarse red wine that stains' – a polite name for 'plonk'). The Grolleau wine hardly stains at all because it is weak in colour and frequently vinified into rosé (Anjou and Touraine). Its bunches are large with medium-sized, bluish, round and compact berries full of colourless juice that gives substantial yields (120 hl/ha).

Pineau d'Aunis

This is an authentic black variety of the Loire sometimes called Chenin Noir. It is a late-ripening grape that produces good-quality yet light coloured wines that are delicate with a raspberry fragrance (Coteaux du Loir).

Grape Varieties/International Whites 1

Chardonnay

This is the grape of the world's greatest dry white wines, probably Burgundian in origin, or perhaps from the Mâconnais, if we believe the story that it was selected close to the village alleged to be responsible for its name.

It is, in fact, known by different names, Beaunois in Chablis (an allusion to the town of Beaune), Melon Blanc in Arbois (Jura) and, quite stupidly and misleadingly, Pinot-Chardonnay.

This relatively early-ripening grape buds and ripens a little after Pinot. It is not surprising, therefore, that it is found in the same areas, especially since it has the same preference for poor, rocky, clay-limestone soil.

These strains of Chardonnay are carefully selected, for the grape is highly vulnerable to *court noue*, a viral disease that has greatly impaired the quality of Montrachet and other wines since the war.

Its small spherical yellow berries colour slightly at maturity; yields can be high in fertile soil (100 hl/ha). The Chardonnay wines excel by their delicacy, their balance of acid with alcohol, their aromatic richness and their capacity for improvement with age.

The pink Chardonnay is an anomaly, while the musky Chardonnay with its odd flavour offers little interest.

Riesling

Riesling is to Germany what Chardonnay is to France. Originating along the banks of the Rhine, it spread to Alsace and Luxembourg before extending into Italy, Yugoslavia and Hungary, and then abroad to the United States, South Africa and Australia. It is a late-ripening grape (15 October) and a late budder, thus escaping the rigours of early frost; all the same, it needs a clement autumn, and is best suited to the continental climate.

Its bunches are small, compact and plentiful; the small round berries are golden yellow, tinged with green. Yields are high (100 hl/ha). The grape is susceptible to *Botrytis cinerea* (*pourriture noble*) which develops favourably thanks to the dawn mists of the Rhine, in which case the yield may fall by as much as 90%.

Riesling can therefore produce both dry and sweet wines, and is the most delicate of all the German-Alsatian aromatic varieties. Apart from its delicacy, Riesling wine is clean, honest, precise, distinguished and elegant, with excellent acidity-alcohol balance. It is free from the fault that other aromatic varieties display of being over-exuberant.

If harvested late and vinified into a sweet wine, it becomes more dense and complex.

Its wines are among the best in the world; whether sweet or dry; the acidic strength of the grape allows them to age and improve over long periods.

Gewürztraminer

This grape is a native of Germany and more specifically of the Palatinate (Pfalz). Its popularity has since spread to neighbouring Alsace, Austria, etc. and its range has extended abroad to the United States, South Africa and elsewhere.

The life cycle of the Gewürztraminer precedes that of the Riesling, alongside which it is often grown. This is an early-ripening and early-budding variety and is therefore best suited to continental climates.

Below *Riesling.*

Its small bunches of equally small, oval and loosely spaced berries are easily recognized by their pinkish hue. Hectare output is moderate. Although thick-skinned, it is a prime target for *pourriture noble*, when yields can drop drastically. The still, soft, golden Gewürztraminer wine is immediately recognizable. Its musky, spicy, rose-scented aromas are well sustained by average acidity, giving an impression of richness on the palate which may be supported by residual sugar in a late-picked wine.

Chenin Blanc

This is, in every sense, a universal grape, firstly because it is found in Europe, the United States, South Africa, Australia and other areas, and secondly because it forms the basis of dry, semi-sweet, sweet or sparkling wines. In France, except for a few plants which have migrated towards Aveyron (Entraygues and Fel), it is found only in the Loire Valley, apparently its birthplace, where it is known as Pineau de la Loire.

It is a late-ripening grape with a regrettably early budding that can pose problems with spring frosts.

The medium-sized bunches of golden, oval grapes, over one centimetre in diameter, can produce yields of up to 100 hectolitres, although such yields are not achieved in the better vineyards on the *tuffeau*, i.e. chalk.

Without sufficient sunshine Chenin wines will suffer from unbearable acidity, but in sunny years they can offer aromas reminiscent of lemon-apricot, acacia honey and quince, while the sparkling wines that improve with age – more than champagne – take on the aromas of lime and honey.

Sémillon

The Sémillon grape, occupying nearly one-quarter of all Bordeaux vineyards, is thus the principal variety of this region, even though on the decline. Many Bordeaux growers have uprooted Sémillon and replaced it with Sauvignon. This is because of the fashion for dry white wine (for which Sauvignon is better suited) and the declining popularity of sweeter wines based on the Sémillon.

It is a middle-budding variety which ripens fairly late. Its round berries, a centimetre or so in diameter, range from greenish-yellow to yellowish-pink. Sémillon lacks a little fruit on the palate and the aroma, especially of young dry white wines, is reminiscent of green apples. Once bottled, it must wait five years to attain rich and complex tertiary aromas.

It is largely affected by *pourriture noble* and used for the greater Sauternes, almost always supported by a little Sauvignon (10-20%).

The Sémillon is planted with particular success in Australia, where it is often blended with Chardonnay or Sauvignon.

Left *Gewürztraminer.*

Grape Varieties/International Whites 2

Ugni Blanc – Trebbiano

Originating in Tuscany, this is the most commonly grown white variety in Italy and in France (100,000 hectares).

It needs much sun to ripen since it is a very late-ripening vine and a late budder. In France, it produces drinkable wine only in the south and in Corsica, although growers from the Cognac and Armagnac regions plant numerous specimens to make so-called *vin de chauffe*, i.e. wine intended for distillation.

The wine is thus nothing special, acidic and sharpish, with 7–8° of alcohol. Ugni Blanc, which is known locally as Saint-Emilion, achieves yields of 150 hl/ha. Its bunches are very large and the round, golden grapes darken when fully ripe.

In the south of France and Italy – especially in Tuscany, where the grape is called Trebbiano – the wines, a very pale yellow, are stronger in alcohol and more acidic, something that is often lacking in warm regions where white wines are often too soft. Ugni Blanc is unfortunately rather poor in aroma. It is blended to make that well-known red wine, Chianti. This is a pity, as it does nothing for it!

Pinot Blanc

Pinot Blanc is itself a mutation of the Pinot Noir. Although Burgundy is its birthplace, it is hardly found there today. In Alsace it is known as Clevner (Klevner); in Italy it is made into a dry sparkling wine, while in California it is sold under its proper name. Pinot Blanc is a productive variety of grape that forms the basis for well-rounded, well-balanced wines which are nevertheless far less sophisticated than those from the Chardonnay.

Pinot Gris

Yet another derivative of the Pinot Noir, the Pinot Gris is found in small quantities in Burgundy, where it is called Pinot Beurot; in Alsace it is known as Tokay and in Germany as Ruländer. This pink-graped variety gives well-constructed and full-bodied wines of moderate acidity and a respectable alcohol content.

Right *Pinot Gris.*

Sylvaner

The Sylvaner grape is grown all over central Europe, having originated in Austria. In Germany it is second in importance, or first if Rheinhessen is considered separately. In California it is sometimes called Riesling, confusingly so, for the banal Sylvaner does not bear comparison with that noble wine.

This is a variety that buds neither early nor late, with grapes that ripen late in autumn. Bunches are medium-sized, as are its grapes, which are round, compact and light yellow. Like many other grape varieties, Sylvaner is prone to excessive yield (over 100 hl/ha), and then the faintly scented, pale, thin Sylvaner wine lacks charm.

The grape loosely resembles the Chasselas, and may be eaten as a table grape.

The best Sylvaner vinification takes place in Germany. German Sylvaner is a great wine which unfortunately underlines the insignificance of many Alsatian Sylvaners.

Muscat

Muscat varieties, genuine or false, black or white, are found all over the world, though originating in Greece. The grapes can be distilled, turned into dry wines like those of Alsace, sparkling wines such as Clairette de Die, Asti Spumante, or even 'natural sweet wines' like Rivesaltes, Beaumes de Venise, Lunel, Frontignan, etc. The Muscat from Hamburg is a large, black table grape. Drinking varieties include the Muscats of Frontignan (these small grapes are the best), Alexandrie and Ottonel. Bunches ripen fairly late, but the buds open early. Its small to medium-sized round grapes are amber, tinged with red. Once grown in Alsace, its late maturity is causing it to be superseded by the earlier-ripening Muscat Ottonel. The Muscat d'Alsace is, in fact, the only Muscat-based still, dry wine produced in France. It is very delicate, very aromatic and must be drunk young.

The Muscat d'Alexandrie produces wine comparable to those made from the Frontignan grape but are rather less refined. This is a variety that ripens very late indeed, best suited to very warm, very dry regions (Aude-Pyrénées Orientales). Its medium-sized bunches bear huge, elliptical, yellow and thin-skinned grapes that are fleshy and musky. This is an all-purpose grape used for making aromatic sparkling wines in Italy.

Left *Chardonnay.*

Sauvignon

This variety enjoys universal popularity. It is known by different names, including Blanc Fumé (Fumé Blanc in California), which is found under the *appellation* of Pouilly Blanc Fumé. It is a relatively early-flowering grape that ripens quickly.

Its numerous small bunches of musky, golden yellow, little oval-shaped berries give respectable yields of up to 100 hl/ha. In a relatively cool climate, limestone soils enhance the floral bouquets of the wine, while gravelly or siliceous soils tend to moderate it.

Until quite recently, in the Bordeaux region, the Sauvignon merely played a supporting rôle in the great sweet wines based on the Sémillon. But it is gradually replacing the Sémillon, even though the latter is still the most widely planted white grape in Bordeaux and is emerging as a varietal for dry whites.

In other parts of the south-west it is displacing the local grapes, and already reigns supreme on the banks of the Loire around Sancerre, Pouilly-sur-Loire, Quincy, Reuilly, etc.

Its often accentuated aromas are reminiscent of spices, straw, blackcurrant leaves and gooseberries. On the palate it is aggressively fruity, with excellent acidity.

Grape Varieties/Local Whites

Colombard

The life cycle of this grape is similar to that of the Folle Blanche, which it resembles in many different respects. Like Folle Blanche, its wine can be drunk as it is or may be distilled into Cognac or Armagnac. Colombard brandies are slightly inferior in quality to those made from the Folle Blanche grape, more or less on a par with brandies made from the distillation of Ugni Blanc wine (Saint-Emilion) but better than those made from the Baco 22A.

The Colombard may be blended together with grapes of the great classical varieties to make Bordeaux wines such as Entre-Deux-Mers; by itself it produces Côtes de Blaye.

This is a quite late-ripening grape variety. Its medium-sized bunches bear light golden, oval-shaped grapes, a centimetre in diameter, with substantial yields exceeding 100 hl/ha.

The Colombard grape has its own particular character. Quite a full yellow in colour, it has a pleasant bouquet, a good alcohol-acid balance, but should be drunk young to be at its best.

Muscadelle

Muscadelle is one of the three varieties used for the great Bordeaux white wines, albeit the least popular and least widely grown. Yet despite a slight decline, Bordeaux growers stick by it and it gives them good wine in return. The plant itself is frail and is invariably the first to be affected by disease in a vineyard, sounding the alarm for growers to treat the other varieties. Though frequently sick, it is very consistent, yielding relatively few grapes, but giving them every year, whatever happens.

It is a late budder that ripens correspondingly late. Its large bunches bear round, medium-sized, pinkish-yellow berries that take on colour as they mature, and with a musky flavour which is transferred to the wine. Output per hectare is modest.

Chasselas

Chasselas is grown far more as a table grape than as a wine grape, but nevertheless forms the basis of *appellation contrôlée* wines such as Crépy, Ripaille, Marignan (AOC Savoie) in the Haute-Savoie, Pouilly-sur-Loire, Gutedel – the Alsace name for Chasselas – and more especially the white wines of French-speaking Switzerland, where it is known as Fendant or Dorin.

It is an undistinguished early-ripening variety able to withstand the very varied climates of Languedoc, Alsace and the sub-alpine plains. Bunches are medium sized, and the grapes hardly exceed one centimetre in diameter, being greenish-yellow, very juicy and thin-skinned. Hectare yields can attain 100 hectolitres.

Aligoté

This grape, probably a native of Burgundy, and cultivated since ancient times, cannot compete in that region with the incomparable Chardonnay. It has been given an *appellation* that prevents any confusion with the latter, since it is the only Burgundy wine to bear the name of the variety – Bourgogne Aligoté.

Folle Blanche

This variety goes by several names. In the Nantes region it is called Gros Plant, and has also given its name to a VDQS wine (*vin délimité de qualité supérieure*), the Gros Plant du Pays Nantais, which is a sort of sub-Muscadet.

In southern France it is called Picpoul, where it is the basis of another VDQS wine, the Picpoul de Pinet. It is best known in Cognac and Armagnac, whose finest brandies come from the distillation of the lean, light and acidic wines of Folle Blanche.

The plant itself is very vulnerable to cryptogamic attack and is being gradually superseded by its descendant, created by a cross with the Noah grape – the Baco 22A.

Mauzac or Blanquette

The Mauzac is a very ancient variety from south-western France. In the Aude, known as Blanquette, it has given its name to the Blanquette de Limoux *appellation*, generally known as a sparkling wine made according to the *méthode champenoise*, although probably better still is the Vin de Blanquette, which is made to sparkle by the *méthode rurale*. It is also used to make the still and sparkling white wines of Gaillac.

This middle-budding variety ripens late. Its largish bunches are laden with spherical, thick-skinned grapes containing large pips, making them unsuitable for eating. In flat, open country, yields are high (100 hl/ha) but the quality suffers, while on hillsides output falls off and quality improves. Mauzac can be harvested over-ripe or mouldy with noble rot, when they produce rich, sweet wines.

Clairette

Clairette has given its name to a number of *appellations* and hails from southern France, where it has been grown for centuries. The high sugar content of its grapes, and hence the alcoholic strength of the Clairette wines and their ability to maderize, once made the grape an ideal raw material for aperitif wines. Nowadays, however, the Clairette grape, if well tended, is reserved for AOC wines, provided yields do not exceed 50 hl/ha. In fertile alluvial soils the yield doubles at least, and Clairette produces only table wines.

Clairette wine is excellent, provided it is not over 12.5°; the aromas are flowery, it oxidizes quickly and is low on acidity. Poorly made, it is heavy and strong. Clairette may be either vinified alone or blended. In the former case, the grape produces the Clairette de Bellegarde, the Clairette du Languedoc and the sparkling Clairette de Die made by the *méthode champenoise*. When blended, it is used to make Côtes-du-Rhône and Châteauneuf-du-Pape (white) as well as the sparkling Clairette de Die Tradition (with Muscat).

Melon or Muscadet

The Melon de Bourgogne is indeed a native of Burgundy and has only been called Muscadet since it was first planted around Nantes, in the Loire Atlantique and in Anjou during the 16th century. It is said to have replaced the local varieties in these regions that were killed off by very cold winters.

The Melon de Bourgogne is undoubtedly hardy and resistant to frost, as was proved in the winter of 1956 when the vineyards were ravaged and decimated by cold.

No longer grown in Burgundy, where because of its susceptibility to rot (*pourriture grise*) it earned the nickname *pourrisseux*, it seems better suited to the crystalline schists of the Nantes region. It is an early-ripening, early-budding variety; its medium-sized bunches bear small, round berries with thick golden skins. Yields are respectable though not excessive. The wine made from Melon de Bourgogne, i.e. Muscadet, is pale gold with a green lustre. Its delicate, accentuated floral aromas, though not very full or complex, are nevertheless clean and light. In the mouth, a musky flavour accounts for its name.

Other White Varieties of Grape

Viognier

Otherwise known as golden Viognier, from the northern Rhône Valley. An extraordinary, late-ripening grape with a low yield but with very rich and complex aromatic powers (Condrieu, Château Grillet).

Roussanne

An excellent, low-yield grape from the northern part of the Rhône Valley, it ripens late. Its wine is very refined and improves with age (Hermitage, Saint-Joseph). Unfortunately the greed of some growers is causing them to replace it by Marsanne. It is called Bergeron in Savoie.

Marsanne

A productive, very late-ripening variety, with large bunches and round grapes. Gives same wine as above (Roussanne) though less refined and not so intense.

Traminer–Savagnin

Otherwise known as Naturé. The only variety from the celebrated Château-Chalon (Jura). Low in yield, late-ripening. Compact bunches of small berries. An unforgettable wine.

Jacquère

A typical Savoyard variety that is late for the region. Productive plants produce round, compact and thick-skinned berries. Makes for moderately good local wines, the most representative being the AOC wine of Savoie, Apremont.

Bourboulenc

A white grape used to blend Châteauneuf-du-Pape. Grapes are reasonably compact, of good aromatic strength, delightfully fresh and persistent.

Maccabeu (Maccebeo)

A late budder, ripening very late, for dry regions only. Wine is golden, full-bodied, strong and fruity but lacking in finesse. Well suited to fortified wines. Grown in Roussillon.

Ondenc

A grape from the south-west of France with early budding and early ripening. Yields are low but the wine is well balanced, strong in alcohol and in most instances blended with others.

Baroque

A good variety from south-west France (Tursan) that is growing in popularity. Late-maturing; the wine is balanced and strong in alcohol.

Wine Producing Regions/France/Bordeaux 1

The Bordeaux *appellation* area comprises 100,000 hectares of vines, and is the world's largest producer of fine wines.

There are three types of soil: the Graves soil, limestone soil and sandy soil, although these may overlap and mingle. The region roughly coincides with the *département* of Gironde, and can be further subdivided into three sections: the left bank of the Garonne and Gironde; the right bank of the Dordogne and Gironde; the centre between the Garonne and the Dordogne.

In each of these areas there are at least a dozen sub-regional or local *appellations*. The latter, the commune *appellations*, are the cradle of the *crus*, the Châteaux, the Clos and the smaller properties so typical of the Bordeaux vineyards. The great wines are made from three red varieties (Cabernet Sauvignon, Cabernet Franc and Merlot) and three white varieties (Sémillon, Sauvignon and Muscadelle). Almost all fine Bordeaux wines are made from a blend of more than one grape variety. The few exceptions, such as Château Pétrus, prove this rule.

In order to simplify the commercial side of their activities, the Bordelais invented a system of classification by quality – in fact, by price – for their growths (*crus*). The first official classification came in 1855, covering five different classes of Médoc and Sauternes-Barsac (plus one Graves) only. In 1973 it was revised to allow Château Mouton-Rothschild to move up from Second to Premier Cru. Allowing for all the various divisions and groupings, 87 châteaux are currently classified.

In 1953 and 1959, 14 Graves châteaux (white and red) were classified without any specific placing, while the Saint-Emilions were classed in three categories in 1955 and 1958. This particular classification at present covers 84 châteaux.

The wines of Pomerol and the other regions are unclassified, although Château Pétrus (Pomerol) is included in the innermost circle of greats which also encompasses Margaux, Latour, Mouton-Rothschild, Lafite Rothschild (Pauillac); Haut-Brion (Graves); Yquem (Sauternes); Cheval Blanc and Ausone (Saint-Emilion).

Left bank of the Gironde

Médoc This is divided into Haut and Bas Médoc. Haut Médoc is in turn subdivided into six communal *appellations*:

Margaux (R)' This *appellation* extends beyond the Margaux commune into the neighbouring parishes of Soussans, Arsac, Cantenac and Labarde. Here, in gravelly soil, we find the finest Médoc wines with *sève*, grace, softness and distinction. One Premier Cru, five second, ten third, three fourth, and two fifth *crus* are classified.

Right *Château Margaux, home of one of the Premiers Crus of the Bordelais.*

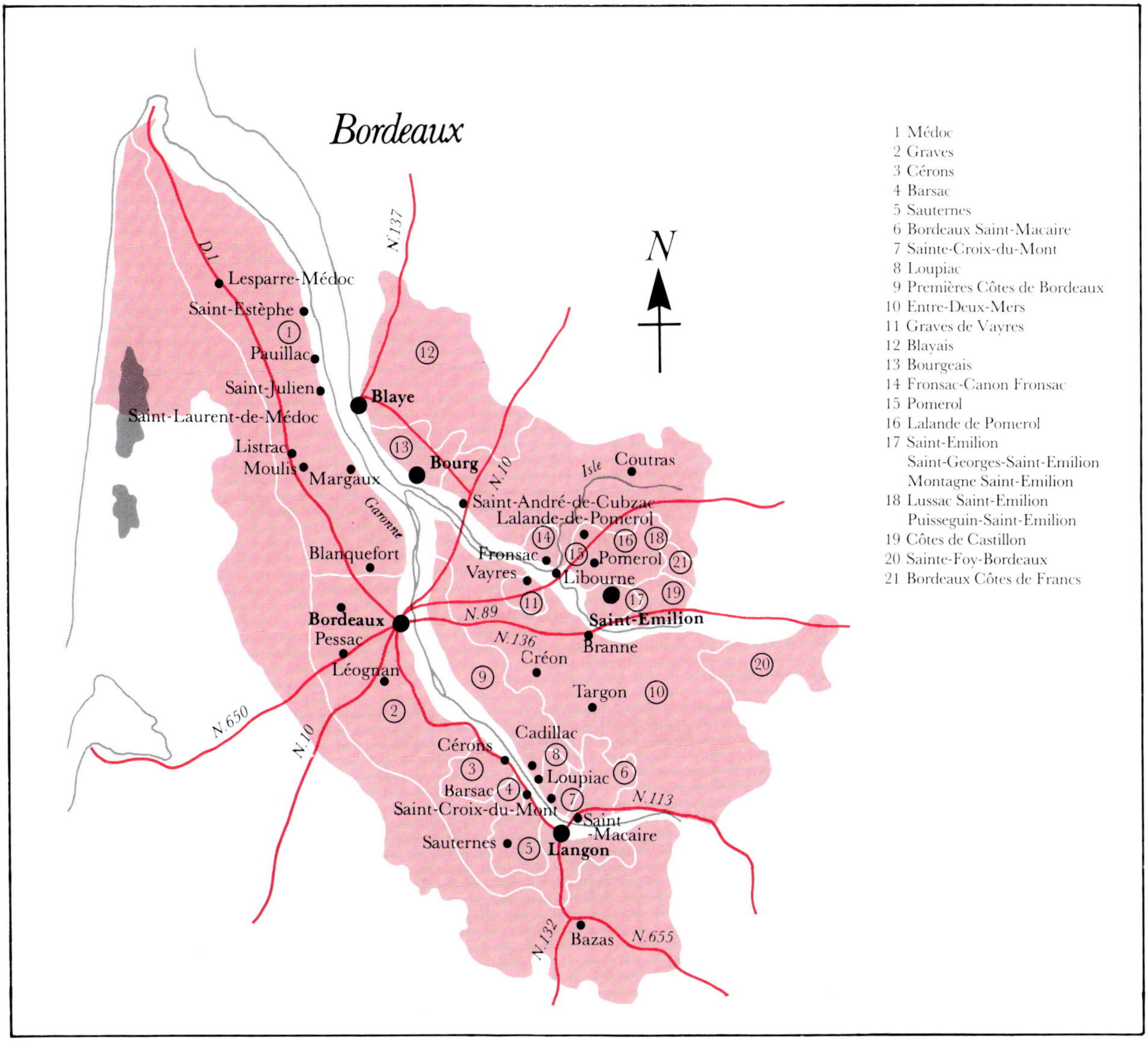

Saint-Julien (R) These are great wines of balance, elegance and mellowness. There are five classified second, two third, and four fourth *crus*.

Pauillac (R) An AOC that spills over the communes of Saint-Estèphe, Cissac and Saint-Julien. These great wines are tannic, full-bodied with plenty of *sève*, taking time to mature. There are three Premier Crus, two second, one third and twelve fifth *crus*.

Saint-Estèphe (R) Well-structured, powerful wines but less refined than Pauillac. Two second, one third, one fourth and one fifth *cru* are classified.

Moulis (R) Well-made, supple wines but with neither the finesse nor the ambition of the *crus* mentioned above.

Listrac (R) Close to Moulis in style but perhaps a shade more rustic.

Haut-Médoc (R) This is the *appellation* on the labels of five classified *crus* from communes not mentioned above.

Médoc This AOC encompasses all the *appellations* so far mentioned plus those wines produced in the northern part of Médoc whose rough and less gravelly terrain tends to impair their finesse.

The *crus exceptionnels, crus bourgeois exceptionnels* or *supérieurs*, and the *crus bourgeois* number 117 in all, some equivalent to a kind of 'sixth *cru*'. The (rare) white wines produced in the Médoc region are only entitled to the *appellation* Bordeaux or Bordeaux Supérieur.

Wine Producing Regions/France/Bordeaux 2

Left bank of the Garonne

Graves (R & W) A distinction is made between the northern Graves which now has its own *appellation* Pessac-Léognan, and the softer, more supple wines of the southern Graves. The red Graves can claim to be as great as the Médocs. They improve over 10 to 15 years.

Sauternes, Barsac (sweet white) These regions are bordered by the Graves to the south, some 50 kilometres from Bordeaux. In theory, the grapes are only harvested one by one when they have been affected by *pourriture noble*.

The fact that this noble rot develops irregularly means that harvesting must sometimes be done piecemeal, each picking being a *trie* (or *tri*). The harvest is sometimes split up into as many as ten *tries*, each being separately pressed, vinified, then reassembled or blended before bottling.

The sweet wines are very aromatic (honey, quince, acacia, etc.), and have a particular and complex balance, the sugar and alcohol being offset by the acid and the bitterness.

Right bank of the Dordogne

Saint-Emilion (R) An AOC comprising the commune of Saint-Emilion and eight others adjacent to it. A distinction has to be made between the Saint-Emilions from the slopes close to the town itself, with their limestone soil, and those of the more sandy *graves* terrain which include two great Saint-Emilions, Château Cheval Blanc and Château Figeac. Of the 11 Premier Grand Crus Classés, these are the only ones grown on the *graves* soil, the nine others coming from the *côtes* grown on limestone. They are as fine as the best classified *crus* of Médoc, but more round and with more vinosity. While lamb is the perfect partner of Pauillac, beef goes beautifully with Saint-Emilion. Some of the neighbouring communes are allowed to add the distinction of 'Saint-Emilion' (Saint Georges-Saint-Emilion, Lussac-Saint-Emilion, etc.) after their name, although their wines are less substantial than the real thing.

Pomerol (R) Separated from Saint-Emilion only by a few yards, Pomerol brings out the

Below *Château d'Yquem, producer of the finest Sauternes.*

best in the Merlot grape. The richness and generosity of these wines has earned them the nickname of 'the Burgundies of Bordeaux'. The communes of Néac and Lalande de Pomerol produce wines that are less rich and less rounded.

Fronsac, Canon-Fronsac (R) A firm, well-built wine offering an excellent introduction to the classified Bordeaux *crus*.

Côtes de Bourg, Côtes de Blaye (R & W) A vast region producing wines that are generally well made and for the most part inexpensive.

Bordeaux Côtes de Castillon (R) Honest wines typical of the communes surrounding Saint-Emilion, offering a good value for money.

Bordeaux Côtes de Francs (R & W) Better than Bordeaux AOC in character, with some of the fruit of Saint-Emilion. The white wines are usually dry.

Between Garonne and Dordogne

This is a huge triangle with ten or so *appellations* of red, dry white and sweet white wines.

Entre-Deux-Mers (W) A crisp dry white wine with finesse but not much body. Very agreeable.

The red wines are only entitled to be called Bordeaux or Bordeaux Supérieur.

Premières Côtes de Bordeaux (R & W) An honest, uncomplicated wine. The white may be dry or sweet.

Cadillac, Loupiac, Sainte Croix du Mont (sweet W) Sauternes style with less richness and not so rounded. The Sainte Croix du Mont are often very sophisticated, with a rich smoothness.

Côtes de Bordeaux Saint Macaire (W) Dry or sweet. Similar to the Premières Côtes de Bordeaux.

Saint Foy de Bordeaux, Graves de Vayres (R & W) Again, similar to the Premières Côtes. The Graves de Vayres are quality wines that are certainly worth looking out for.

Neighbouring regions

These regions, with the town of Bergerac at their centre, are extensions, both geographically and in terms of grape variety, of the Bordelais.

Monbazillac (sweet W) A sweet wine, historically perhaps older than Sauternes, with the same varieties of grape and the same vinification. Honey, violet, plum and crystallized apricot. Sweetness compensated by good acidic backbone.

***Above** Château de Monbazillac, where a sweet white wine similar to Sauternes is produced.*

Haut Montravel, Côtes de Montravel, Rosette (sweet W) Lighter than the Monbazillac, same style.

Montravel (dry W)**, Côtes de Bergerac, Bergerac Côtes de Saussignac** (R & W)

***Above** Château La Jaubertie produces wines under the Bergerac* appellation.

The reds are reminiscent of the light Bordeaux, while the whites are nearly always on the dry side.

Côtes de Duras (R & W sweet or dry) Red wines in the Bergerac style. The dry whites are legally obliged to state 'sec' on their labels.

Pécharmant (R) This is the best of all the reds in the region. It can be considered a sort of Bergerac Premier Cru.

Wine Producing Regions/France/Burgundy 1

The wine-growing part of Burgundy starts 120 kilometres south of Paris and extends almost as far as Lyons. This is a distance of 350 kilometres but that in itself is misleading on three counts. In the first place, the northern vineyards of Burgundy stop at Chablis and only continue after Dijon, a break of 100 kilometres; secondly, because Burgundy proper does not extend beyond the southern boundary of the *département* of Côte d'Or, above Chagny, another 50 kilometres, and finally, because the vineyard is narrow, with widths ranging from a few hundred metres to several kilometres.

Six separate zones may be distinguished: Chablis, the Côtes de Nuits and de Beaune, followed by the Côte Chalonnaise, the Mâconnais and Beaujolais. All these vineyards are based on a handful of grape varieties. The more serious wines are all single varieties: i.e. the white of Chardonnay, the reds of Pinot Noir and the Beaujolais of Gamay. The less ambitious Bourgogne Aligoté wines are made from the white Aligoté variety.

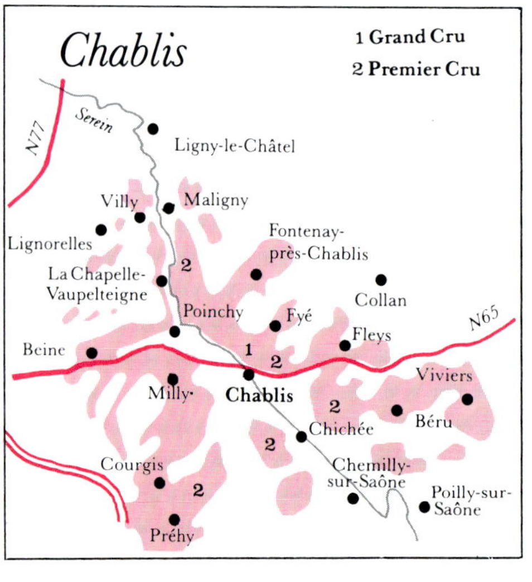

Chablis (W) A truly world-famous white wine *appellation*. One should separate four *appellations* according to their soil and exposition.

Petit Chablis (W) These are not quite authentic since the *appellation* covers an area of soil that is not Kimmeridgian (i.e. limestone marl), an essential prerequisite for true Chablis.

Petit Chablis is nevertheless a pleasant and drinkable wine when still young.

Chablis, Chablis Premier Cru, Chablis Grand Cru These are the real Chablis, in order of increasing quality. There are seven Grand Crus and eleven Premiers Crus. They achieve a really high quality, being dry, rounded and full, without any sweetness; their colour is green or yellow golden.

They improve over 8–10 years, are excellent with shellfish, poultry and white meats.

Côte de Nuits Along the Côte de Nuits and the Côte de Beaune, there is an ascending hierarchy of quality starting with the *appellations communales*, the *appellations communales premier cru* and culminating with the Grands Crus, without naming the commune. Here are the more prestigious *appellations*:

Fixin (R & W) Mostly red, well-constructed, keeps well.

Gevrey-Chambertin (R) The best are the Chambertins, being full, well-structured, with great flavour and immense length, best drunk between the ages of 10 and 20 years.

Morey Saint-Denis (R & W) Has a raspberry and violet bouquet, with a full flavour. The five Grands Crus include the famous Clos de Tart and the Bonnes Mares which we come across again at Chambolle-Musigny.

Chambolle-Musigny (R) The most sophisticated and delicate of the Côte de Nuits. The exceptional wine here is le Musigny, of which a tiny amount is white.

Vougeot (R & W) Clos de Vougeot is the Grand Cru of this commune. The style is ruby-coloured with an aroma of truffles.

Echézeaux and Grands Echézeaux (R) Two Grands Crus from the commune of Flagey-Echézeaux. An aristocratic wine with a bouquet of violet and a hint of raspberries on the palate.

Vosne-Romanée (R) Both commune and wines are legendary, with five outstanding Grands Crus: la Romanée-Conti, a silky, suave and superbly elegant wine; la Romanée, the smallest AOC in France (only 8345 square metres), which is sometimes equal in quality to Romanée-Conti, but rather less silky; Richebourg, powerful and authoritative; La Tâche, the synthesis of all that is best in the *appellation*; and Romanée Saint-Vivant, elegant but less reliable.

Nuits Saint-Georges (R & W) There are some marvellous Premiers Crus: Vaucrains, Saint-Georges and Boudots are powerful, with a hint of strawberries, while Les Pruliers and Les Porrets are rounded and firm, but with great finesse. The wines of this commune tend to be full-bodied and age well.

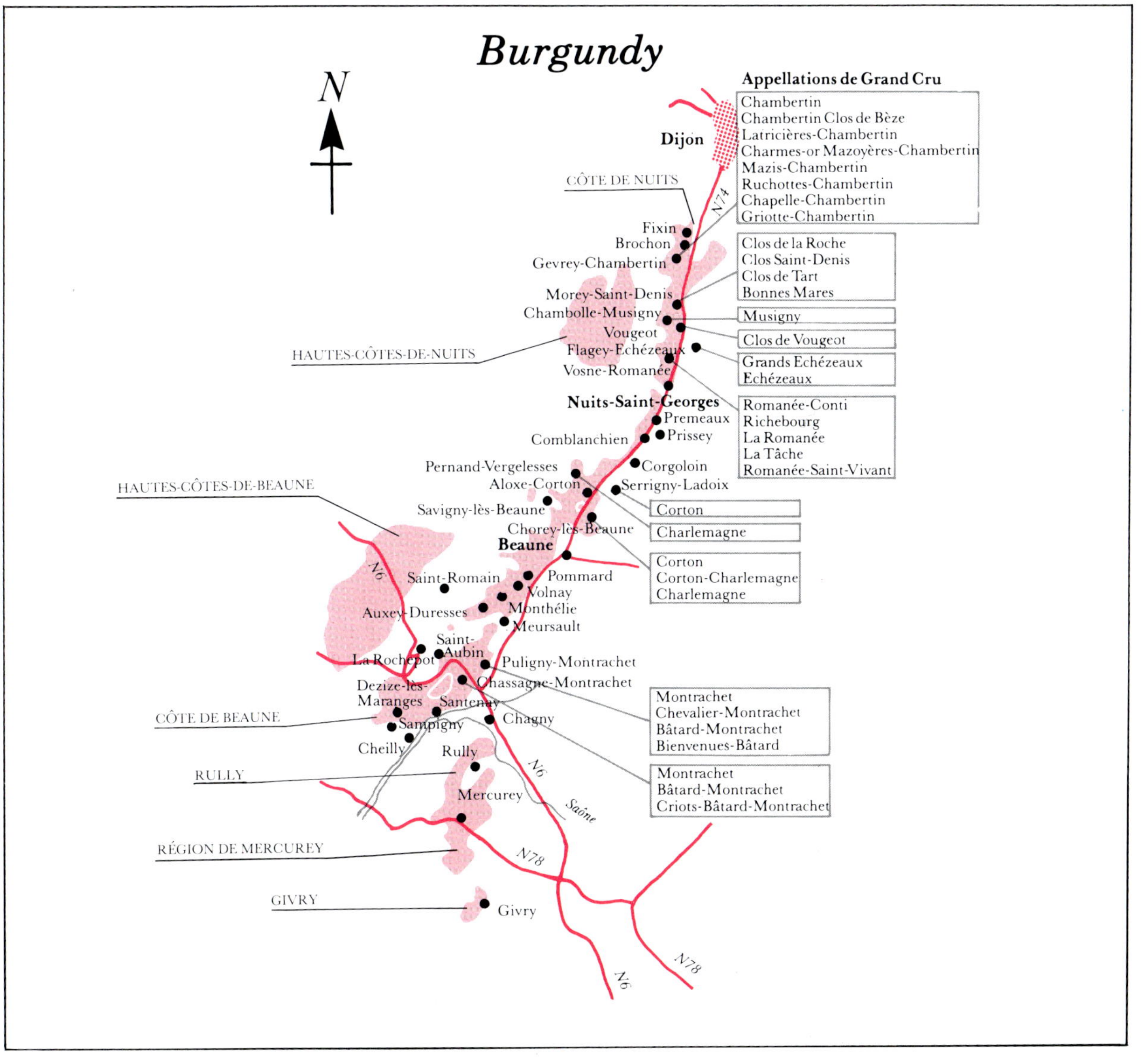

Hospices de Beaune Founded in 1443 by Nicolas Rolin, Chancellor to the Duke of Burgundy, and his wife Guigone de Salins. Today the Hospices (hospital) of Beaune owns 125 acres of the finest vineyards (all in the Côtes de Beaune with the exception of a parcel of Mazis-Chambertin). The wines are auctioned every year on the third Sunday in November, the proceeds going to the Hospices, making it the largest charity in the world. After many years of variable quality, wines bearing the Hospices label now justify their high price. The Hospices de Nuits, a much smaller affair, holds its auction in the spring following the vintage.

Left *First spraying at the Clos de Vougeot, Côte de Nuits, Burgundy.*

Wine Producing Regions/France/Burgundy 2

Côte de Beaune

Corton and Corton-Charlemagne (R & W) The red Grand Cru is clean, firm and full, with aromas of peach, blackcurrant and raspberry. The white Grand Cru is full-bodied, generous and rounded, with plenty of *sève*; a spicy cinnamon, floral bouquet and backed up by good acidity.

Pernand-Vergelesses, Savigny-lès-Beaune, Ladoix-Serrigny (R & W) In the style of the Corton but less full-bodied.

Chorey-lès-Beaune (R & W) More modest than those above.

Beaune (R & W) Fine, delicate wines which mature fairly quickly, with a floral nose of hawthorn and rose.

Pommard (R) A full, generous, virile wine. The Rugiens are the most potent while the Epenots are the most refined.

Volnay (R) The most refined and elegant of the Côte de Beaune. The Caillerets is the best vineyard.

Monthélie, Auxey-Duresses, Saint-Romain, Saint-Aubin (R & W) A firm, precise, straightforward red wine which is typically Pinot. The white is sophisticated, delicate and clean.

Meursault (R & W) A generous white *grand vin*, dry without being parched, hint of hazelnut on the palate.

Puligny-Montrachet (R & W) A great wine with a complex flowery aroma.

The Montrachets (W) These are the world's greatest dry white wines; they are potent, full-bodied and generous, with floral and fruity aromas and flavours reminiscent of almond, hazelnut and honey. They have a long, lingering aftertaste and keep well (15 years).

Chassagne-Montrachet (R & W) The white is fruity, full of vigour and keeps well, while the red is well-built and full-bodied.

Santenay (R & W) The red Santenay is well-

Mâconnais and Beaujolais

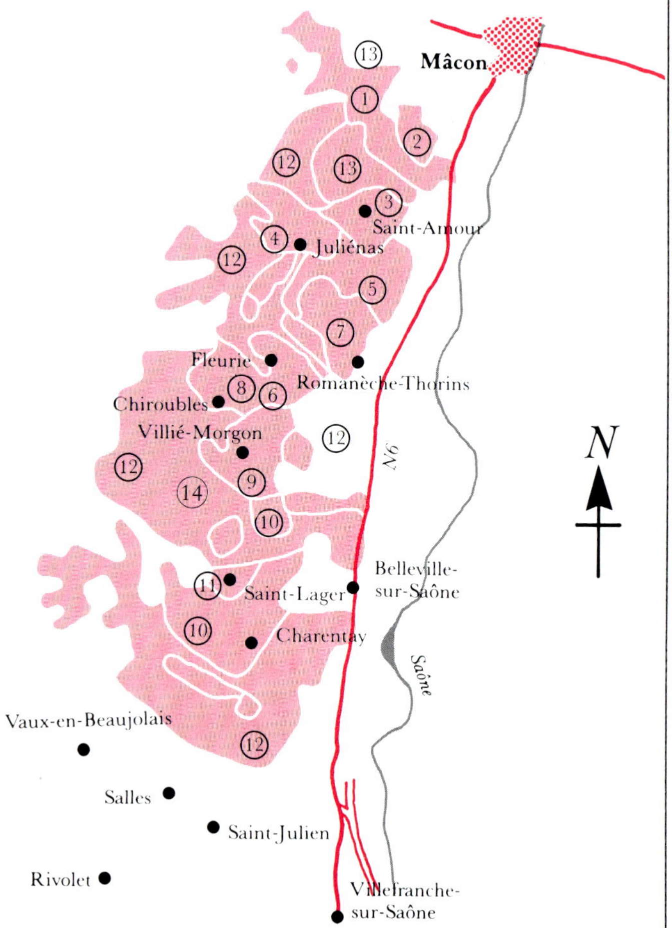

1 Pouilly-Fuissé	8 Chiroubles
2 Pouilly-Loché Pouilly-Vinzelles	9 Morgon
3 Saint-Amour	10 Brouilly
4 Juliénas	11 Côte de Brouilly
5 Chénas	12 Beaujolais
6 Fleurie	13 Saint-Véran
7 Moulin-à-Vent	14 Régnié

constructed although rather less virile than the Pommard. White Santenay is a rarity.

Côte de Nuits-Villages, Côte de Beaune-Villages, Hautes Côtes de Nuits, Hautes Côtes de Beaune (R & W) These are wines of somewhat less sophistication, without aromatic intricacy and lighter in structure.

Côte Chalonnaise

The Côte Chalonnaise has no Grands Crus although it does possess a few Premiers Crus that are outstanding, though little known.

Rully (R & W) Although less floral, the white wines of Rully can compare with the Savigny-lès-Beaune and Pernand-Vergelesses.

The red Rully wines are reminiscent of Volnay but without the latter's finesse and complexity.

Mercurey (R & W) Mercurey is highly successful. It resembles the wines of Beaune, but is a little rougher and has less finesse. The whites are floral, quite rich, yet occasionally a little dull.

Givry (R & W) Close in style to Mercurey, Givry is less generous and open. The very rare white Givry is similar to Rully, but lighter.

Montagny (W) A light, fresh white wine for summer or afternoon drinking.

Mâconnais

The 50 kilometres that separate the Côte Chalonnaise from the Beaujolais region are filled with vineyards planted with Chardonnay, Pinot Blanc, Pinot Noir and Gamay, this last *cépage* forming the transition to Beaujolais itself.

Wines made from the Chardonnay, Pinot Blanc and Pinot Noir grapes are allowed to bear the Burgundy label – the whites are generally better than the reds. They can all have the following labels, in order of improving quality: Mâcon, Mâcon Supérieur and Mâcon followed by the name of the locality; the white can also be Mâcon-Villages. Both the white and red Mâcons preserve their quality and refinement well, but should not be over-aged owing to their relative lack of substance and fullness.

Pouilly-Fuissé, Pouilly-Loché, Pouilly-Vinzelle, Saint-Véran (W) are four different wines all made from the Chardonnay. Pouilly-Fuissé is undoubtedly the best, with its pale golden colour tinged with emerald, its violet and acacia-honey nose and flavour of honey and almonds.

Beaujolais

True Beaujolais wine is a product of the Gamay grape granitic soil and, let it be admitted, some aggressive marketing. Only the northern part of the *appellation* region is actually granitic, so that southern Beaujolais wines are really 'illegitimate'. The range includes Beaujolais Primeur, sold from mid November onward, Beaujolais, Beaujolais Supérieur, Beaujolais-Villages (red, rosé and white) as well as the Beaujolais *crus* (red only). Only the *villages* and the *crus* grow in ideal soil.

Moulin-à-Vent is the finest and most full-bodied and can keep up to five years, while the **Fleurie** is its elegant cousin. **Saint-Amour** is fruity, light and pleasant. **Chénas** is robust yet smooth, **Juliénas** fruity and more showy, while **Chiroubles** is soft and ideally light. **Morgon** has a violet nose and is best enjoyed when a year or more old. **Brouilly** is luscious and rich in alcohol; **Côte de Brouilly** is full-bodied, well-rounded and strongly flavoured.

Opposite left *Courtyard of the Hôtel-Dieu, Hospices de Beaune.*

Below *The hill of Solutré towers over the vineyards of Pouilly-Fuissé in the Mâconnais.*

Wine Producing Regions/France/Champagne 1

Contrary to what one hears all the time, Dom Pérignon (1639– 1715) did not invent champagne; neither did he make it nor even drink it. What he did make were outstanding country-style sparkling wines. True champagne is produced by a second in-bottle fermentation, a method first employed after the death of the famous monk from the abbey of Hautvillers.

Dom Pérignon is also said to have invented the art of blending, the second principal characteristic of champagne. The truth is that he blended grapes, never wines, and only Pinot grapes, whereas nowadays 80% of champagnes are the result of blending Chardonnay with Pinot Noir and Pinot Meunier.

Right *Statue of Dom Pérignon outside the headquarters of Moët & Chandon, Epernay.*

According to the modern pressing procedure, the black grapes are put in a specially designed press that is broad yet shallow, and the colourless juice is rapidly squeezed out of the whole grapes without allowing them time to discolour. The wine produced from fermenting this clear must is a Blanc de Noirs as opposed to a Blanc de Blancs, resulting from the pressing of white Chardonnay grapes.

Generally speaking, champagne is a two-thirds/one-third or three-quarters/one-quarter blend of Blancs de Noirs and Blancs de Blancs respectively, and it is the way the wine is elaborated and blended that gives each champagne its personality. Champagne is usually a *vin de marque* or brand, made by *négociants* who buy the grapes from the grower and press and blend them into champagne. They are called *négociants manipulants* (NM), as opposed to *recoltants manipulants*, who both grow and process the grapes. Other champagnes are made by cooperatives (CM) whose members supply the grapes for vinifying, blending and processing (i.e. turning into champagne). These abbreviations are important because they must be shown on champagne labels to identify its origin. The letters MA mean that the champagne has been bought from a merchant, grower or cooperative to be marketed under a *marque auxiliaire* (secondary brand) or *marque d'acheteur* (buyer's own brand).

To be entitled to an *appellation*, champagne must come from a specific area, chiefly from the *départements* of Marne or Aube, east of Paris, and be made from the Chardonnay, Pinot Noir and Pinot Meunier grapes. Because vineyards produce grapes of varying quality, communes have been classed and quoted in percentage terms (80%–100%).

Nine communes in the Montagne de Reims and four in the Côte des Blancs are quoted 100% and so are entitled to be called Grand Cru. Premier Cru identifies communes quoted between 90% and 99%.

The grapes themselves are pressed several times; and each stage in the process is traditional and strictly controlled. Every 4000 kg (four tonnes) of grapes yields 2050 litres of top-quality grape-must called the *cuvée*[1], 410 litres of *première taille* and 205 litres of *deuxième taille* (subsequent pressings). The finer champagnes are made only from the *cuvée* and the *deuxième taille* is never used by serious *manipulants*.

The champagne *appellation* cannot be used for more than one hectolitre (100 litres) for every 150 kilograms of grapes.

The *cuvée* is colourless and refined, with good acidity, the first *taille* lacks finesse and a little acidity, while the second *taille* is inferior still, being harsh and rather coloured.

The final blend is born from these wines, from grapes of different varieties and various origins and even by the addition of reserve wines, i.e. wines held over from previous years. In the latter case the champagne cannot be 'vintaged' but can be sold 12 months after bottling, unlike vintage champagnes which stay in the cellars for at least three years.

[1] The word *cuvée* has two meanings:
a) first pressing, *vin de cuvée*
b) the blending of wines.

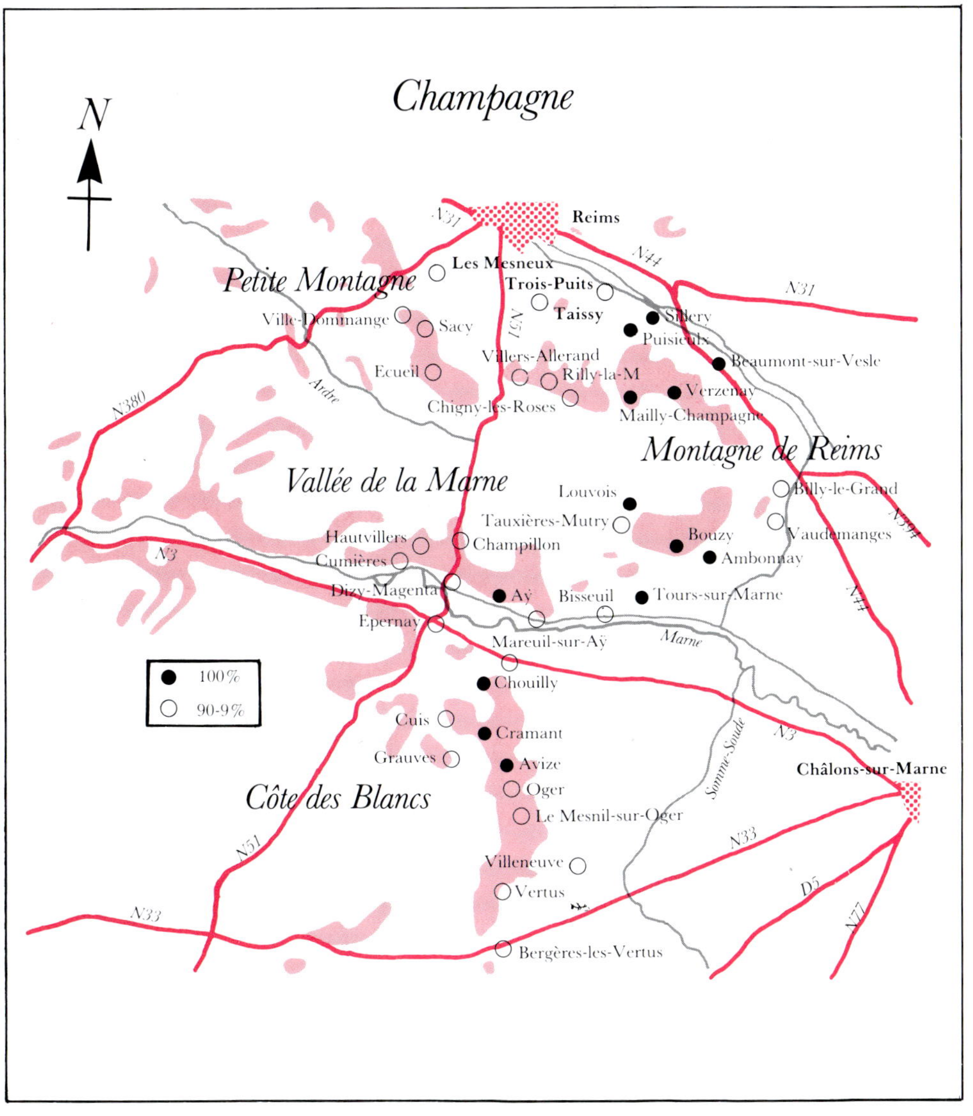

There are many different styles of champagne and many champagne lovers have a preference for a particular house or *marque*. Most of the 'grandes marques' produce a full range of wines, both sparkling and still: Coteaux Champenois; Brut non-vintage; Blanc de Blancs (vintage or non-vintage); Brut vintage; Rosé; Luxury Cuvées.

While the luxury blends capture the headlines, the original and still the most famous being Moet et Chandon's Dom Pérignon, most houses maintain that their reputation rests on the quality of their non-vintage Brut. With the increasing popularity of champagne, even the houses with the best reputation are releasing their Brut shortly after disgorgement, and importers, wholesalers and retailers move their lines as quickly as possible. There is no doubt that a non-vintage improves immeasurably with a year's cellarage. Vintage champagnes are generally released at five years old. A further two years allows them to blossom, and with few exceptions, they reach their peak at 7-10 years.

Although it is very resistant to rough handling, champagne is one of the wines most affected by heat and especially sunlight, and must be kept in cellars as cool as those from where it came.

Wine Producing Regions/France/Champagne 2

Coteaux Champenois (R, W and rosé)

This is the second *appellation contrôlée* of the Champagne region and only came into being in 1974, the AOC Coteaux Champenois replacing the old Vin Nature de Champagne which in turn replaced Champagne Nature from 1953 onwards.

Since the word 'Champagne' is exclusive to the celebrated wines of the area, the new Coteaux Champenois *appellation* was created because the qualifying word *nature* somehow implied that the other wines were 'artificial'. These wines may be red, white or rosé and their very existence is erratic since the Coteaux Champenois are only made when there are 'too many' grapes, in other words more grapes than can be vinified into champagne, which was not the case in 1978, 1980 or 1981.

The white Coteaux Champenois are historically interesting inasmuch as they resemble the Champagne wines that existed before the age of Dom Pérignon. The pale rosé wines of the 16th and 17th centuries were probably much like today's white Coteaux Champenois.

These are dry, fresh and moderately fruity wines, light and relatively simple in character; like champagne itself, they may be made from a single variety of grape or blended. The Blancs de Blancs – the Chardonnay wines – are the best and finest, though less typical because the grape's character does not come out so much in Champagne soil, something that the *vignerons* positively appreciate. A more pronounced influence would mark the *cuvée* too much during blending.

It is therefore pointless to compare wines made from Champagne Chardonnay on the one hand and Burgundy Chardonnay on the other.

The best red Coteaux Champenois come from the Pinot Noir grown in the commune of Bouzy (100% Grand Cru). This is a wine vinified *à la bourguignonne*: it is clean and well-structured without ever attaining the complexity, roundness or richness of its Burgundian counterpart. Coteaux Champenois rosé wines are rare.

Above Remuage *of champagne bottles in the Heidsieck cellars.*

Rosé des Riceys

This is the only *appellation d'origine*, apart from Tavel, reserved exclusively for a rosé. Riceys, a little commune in the *département* of Aube, has been making rosé for over 1000 years and once used Gamay as an ingredient. Some are bottled straight from the vat and resemble the rosé wines of Sancerre, while others are kept for a year in *pièces champenoises*, wood barrels containing 205 litres. The taste of the Riceys is unmistakable and only appears during fermentation after a variable lapse of time, requiring great expertise on the part of the *vignerons*. It is a very rare wine, a mere 60 hectolitres being produced each year, and is every bit as expensive as champagne.

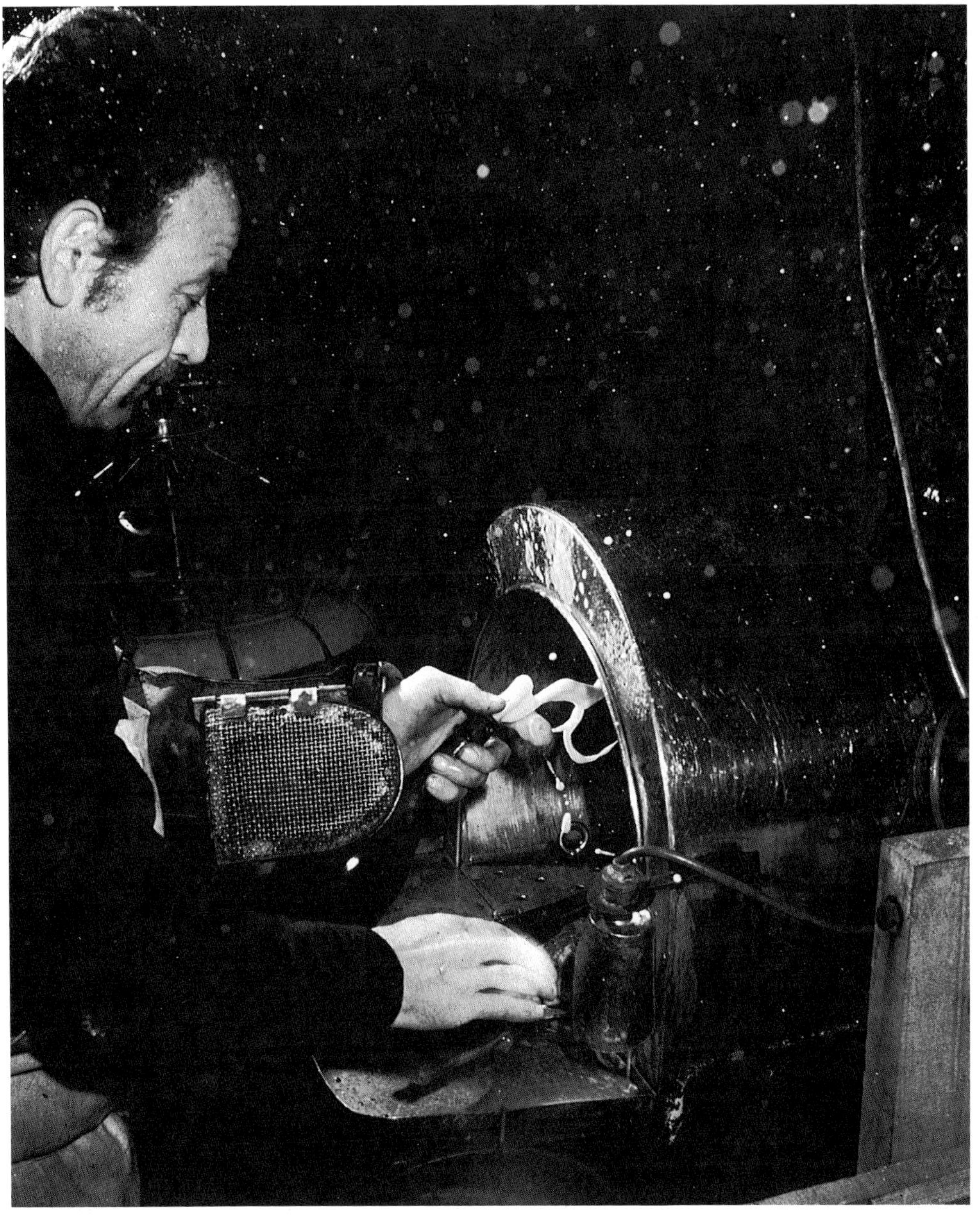

Left *Removing the sediment from a bottle of champagne* (dégorgement)*; a wrist guard is worn for protection against bursting bottles.*

Vinification

Once the *cuvée* has been blended (February-March) the wine is bottled with the addition of *liqueur de tirage* (24gr sugar dissolved in wine and yeast). This is the second fermentation in the bottle, called *prise de mousse* (March to May); the bottles are laid horizontally on *lattes* for about one year at 10°C, then stored on their *pointes* (neck down) with the fermentation deposit (stored at 10°C from a few months to several years) to enable the sediment to rest on the cork. The process by which this sediment is removed is called *dégorgement*. The expert *dégorgeur* takes each bottle and removes the cork with one hand to let the sediment fly out. After a fraction of a second he prevents further loss of liquid by placing his thumb over the neck of the bottle, then deftly inserts a fresh cork. The lost liquid is made up by the so-called *liqueur d'expédition* or *liqueur de dosage* which consists of pure cane sugar adjusted to suit the champagne's intended market (dry, medium or sweet) The illustration above shows how cork and sediment are removed with the aid of 'lobster' pincers.

Wine Producing Regions/France/Rhône

The Rhône vineyards occupy the hillsides on the left and right banks of the Rhône a little below Lyons, extending to and beyond Avignon. They can be split into two types of wine corresponding to distinct plant families and geological categories. The two zones, with nothing in common except the river and a hot to very hot climate, more or less correspond to the northern and southern Rhône respectively.

Northern Côtes-du-Rhône

These remarkably steep, terraced vineyards have always been worked by hand, being virtually inaccessible to machines. The heat is stifling, magnified as it is by the reflection from the Rhône itself and the narrowness of the river valley.

The white and red wines of this region are some of the best in the world, although they no longer enjoy their former immense reputation. The vineyards date back to Roman times when the wines produced around the town of Vienne graced the tables of the imperial capital. The glory of the Rhône wines has, for about a century, now been somewhat overshadowed by the Bordeaux and Burgundies. Hardly surprising, since the great Rhône wines are rare and the vineyards cannot be expanded, making their wines the prerogative of the lucky few who have discovered them.

Côte Rôtie (R) As its name suggests, this region is literally 'roasted' by heat and sun. These rich ruby wines with their violet aromas derive their vigour and luxuriance from the admirable Syrah grape, assisted by the no less respectable white variety, Viognier. They are tannic, well-built wines that require years of maturing, and go perfectly with game. There are differences in style between the top-quality wines from the Côte Brune and Côte Blonde.

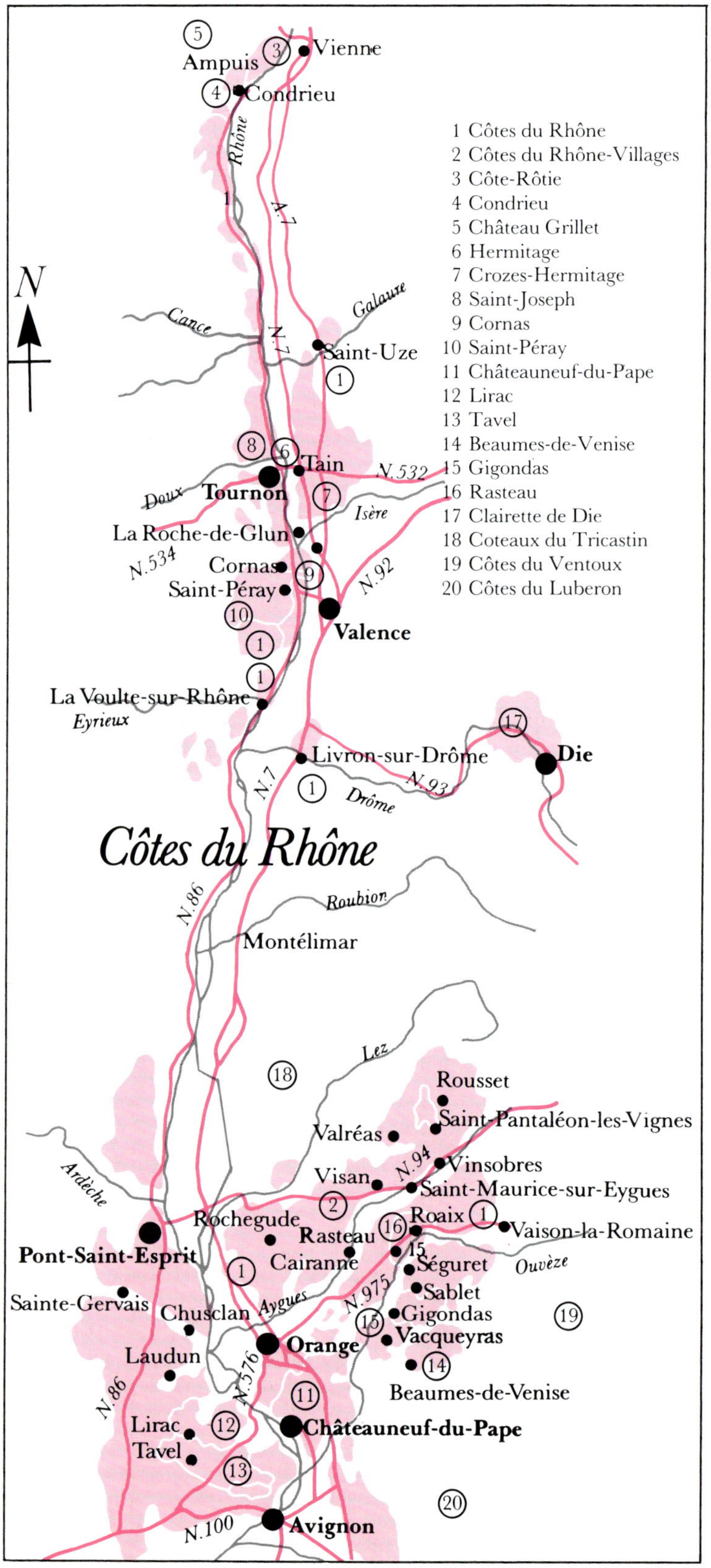

Condrieu – Château Grillet (W) Two white wines which are very similar both in soil and taste, produced by the Viognier vine planted in the thin mica soil of the region. These golden wines are distinguished by their exuberant floral and fruity aromas, and go excellently with fish and shellfish. Must be drunk very young, and do not travel.
Hermitage (R & W) A red wine made only from the Syrah grape, and one of the greatest in the world. This dark ruby wine is rich in tannin, well-balanced and with aromas of violet and hawthorn; it keeps well, and is best enjoyed with red meat or game.

The greatest white Hermitage wines are made from the Roussanne grape, while the rest are blended with Marsanne. This very distinguished wine is complex, with clean aromas of wild flowers, and great finesse. It perfectly complements the better fish dishes.
Crozes-Hermitage (R & W) Similar to Hermitage but not quite so distinguished. Should be drunk before it is five years old.
Saint-Joseph (R & W) Not unlike the Crozes-Hermitage and occasionally better.
Cornas An imposing red wine made from Syrah with an extrovert, virile character; it resembles Hermitage but is less complex.
Saint-Péray (still white and sparkling) Made from the same grape variety as Hermitage, with a pale yellow hue and bouquet of violets and hazelnut. More often produced as a sparkling wine by the *méthode champenoise*.

Southern Côtes-du-Rhône

This vast area of the Côte-du-Rhône *appellation* is also the home of a great wine which is gradually regaining the quality that once made it so celebrated: Châteauneuf-du-Pape. Taken all together, the wines of this region including the more modest, are constantly improving.
Châteauneuf-du-Pape (R & W) These warm, rich, full-bodied and spicy wines are produced in extensive vineyards, often on a bed of round pebbles, and planted with Grenache, Cinsault, Mourvèdre, Syrah or other varieties (13 permitted in all, including some whites) set out in broad rows. These are winter-evening wines designed to accompany red meats and cheeses; their very potency often detracts from their finesse, and they can be drunk between 4 and 15 years old. Some domaines are making wine by *macération carbonique*; these have some finesse but are not typical Châteauneufs.

Above *Château des Fines Rochers, Châteauneuf-du-Pape.*

Gigondas (R, rosé) The best of these are comparable to the Châteauneuf-du-Pape in quality and style.
Tavel (rosé) Ten different varieties, including some white, go into the making of this wine, long claimed to be the best French rosé. This is a wine for summer evenings, complementing poultry and white meats.
Lirac (R, W, rosé) The rosés fall somewhere between the Tavels and the Côtes-du-Rhône rosés, while the reds are as good as the best Côtes-du-Rhône-Villages. The white tend to be short on finesse and vigour.
Côtes-du-Rhône-Villages (R, W, rosés) Seventeen communes, all renowned for their quality, are entitled to use this *appellation* in conjunction with their own name. The absence of such a name indicates that the wine originates from more than one commune. The reds are the best known, with their deep ruby colour and nose of blackcurrant and raspberry. They are well-rounded, full and spicy to the taste, with more body than finesse.
Côtes-du-Rhône (R, W, rosé) Everyday wines; many are made by *macération carbonique* and sold *en primeur*.

Opposite left *Vines on the banks of the Rhône, Côte Rôtie.*

Wine Producing Regions/France/Alsace

The vineyards of Alsace lie on the left bank of the Rhine in the French *départements* of the Bas-Rhin and the Haut-Rhin, stretching from Mulhouse to Strasbourg. It is an extremely picturesque region of valleys dotted with ancient hamlets that have preserved their character quite successfully by resisting modern development. The soil is varied but mostly limestone, and the climate is pre-continental with low rainfall and plenty of sunshine.

Alsace has frequently been at the heart of wars between France and Germany and has been occupied several times, even annexed to Germany from 1870 to 1918. These disputes have had lasting side-effects, not the least of which is that the system of *appellation d'origine contrôlée* in use since 1962 – the year in which the Alsatian vineyards were elevated to AOC status – much resembles customs still practised in Germany itself. As in Germany, the variety of grape takes precedence over the *cru*; as in the German Palatinate or Rheingau, the cooperatives turn out a large proportion of the total production; and finally, like many German wines, the wines of Alsace come in a 'flute' bottle so typical of hocks and Mosels.

The shape of the bottle has been laid down and regulated since 1972 by the Comité Interprofessionel des Vins d'Alsace. Yet there is no rule that dictates the shape of bottle for any particular *appellation*, except for Château-Chalon; and a Bordeaux may theoretically grace a Burgundy bottle (or vice versa). In reality, of course, this never happens, although specially designed bottles are not hard to find. Château Haut-Brion, for instance, is a Bordeaux wine but is never sold in a classic Bordeaux bottle.

The Comité Interprofessionel has another apparently beneficial rule, that no Alsace wine (AOC) may leave the region before being bottled. It is unlikely that this type of regulation offers the same sort of guarantee as 'château bottling'. At most, if the wine does not satisfy the consumer or fails to live up to its label, it can be traced back to Alsatian soil.

The appellations and the wines

The wine can be sold as a *vin d'Alsace* pure and simple, or as a *vin d'Alsace* made from a specific and identified grape; a commune may also be mentioned, and an Alsace Grand Cru category has existed since 1975, and the number of vineyards with Grand Cru status now stands at 45. The yield per hectare for

Below *Young vines at the village of Turkheim, Alsace.*
Opposite left *Vineyards on slopes facing the Rhine, Alsace.*

these Grands Crus is low (70 hl/ha) but a higher degree of alcohol is required. Only the very best grapes have a right to the *appellation* (Gewürztraminer, Riesling, Pinot Gris, Muscat).

Riesling (W) This is the best, most refined of Alsace wines, aristocratic and full of character. It goes excellently with chicken, fish and even sauerkraut.

Gewürztraminer (W) The most aromatic. Not easy to enjoy with meats, and goes better with foie gras and spicy dishes.

Pinot Gris (Tokay) (W) A round, mouth-filling wine best suited to white meats.

Muscat (W) An extraordinary wine that successfully expresses the aromas and finesse of the variety. It is the perfect aperitif wine and should be drunk without fail while still young and fresh.

Sylvaner (W) Pleasant and dry, but has little finesse. It can be drunk with hors d'oeuvres but does little for them.

Clevner (Pinot Blanc) (W) Minor version of a Tokay, with a good price/quality level.

Edelzwicker (W) Mixed varieties of noble grapes. Nothing special, but agreeable.

Pinot Noir (R) A very light red, or rosé, wine. Clean, fruity, not very complex.

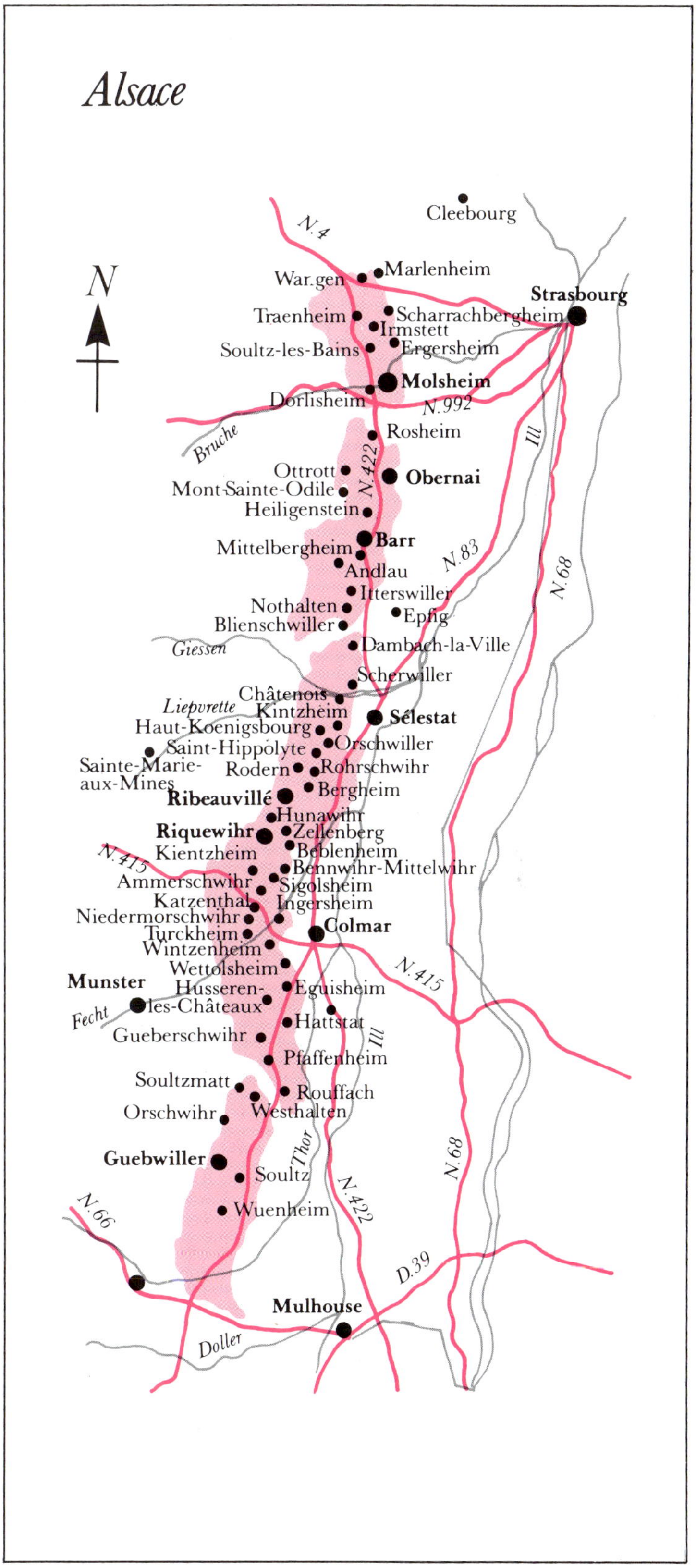

Wine Producing Regions/France/Loire

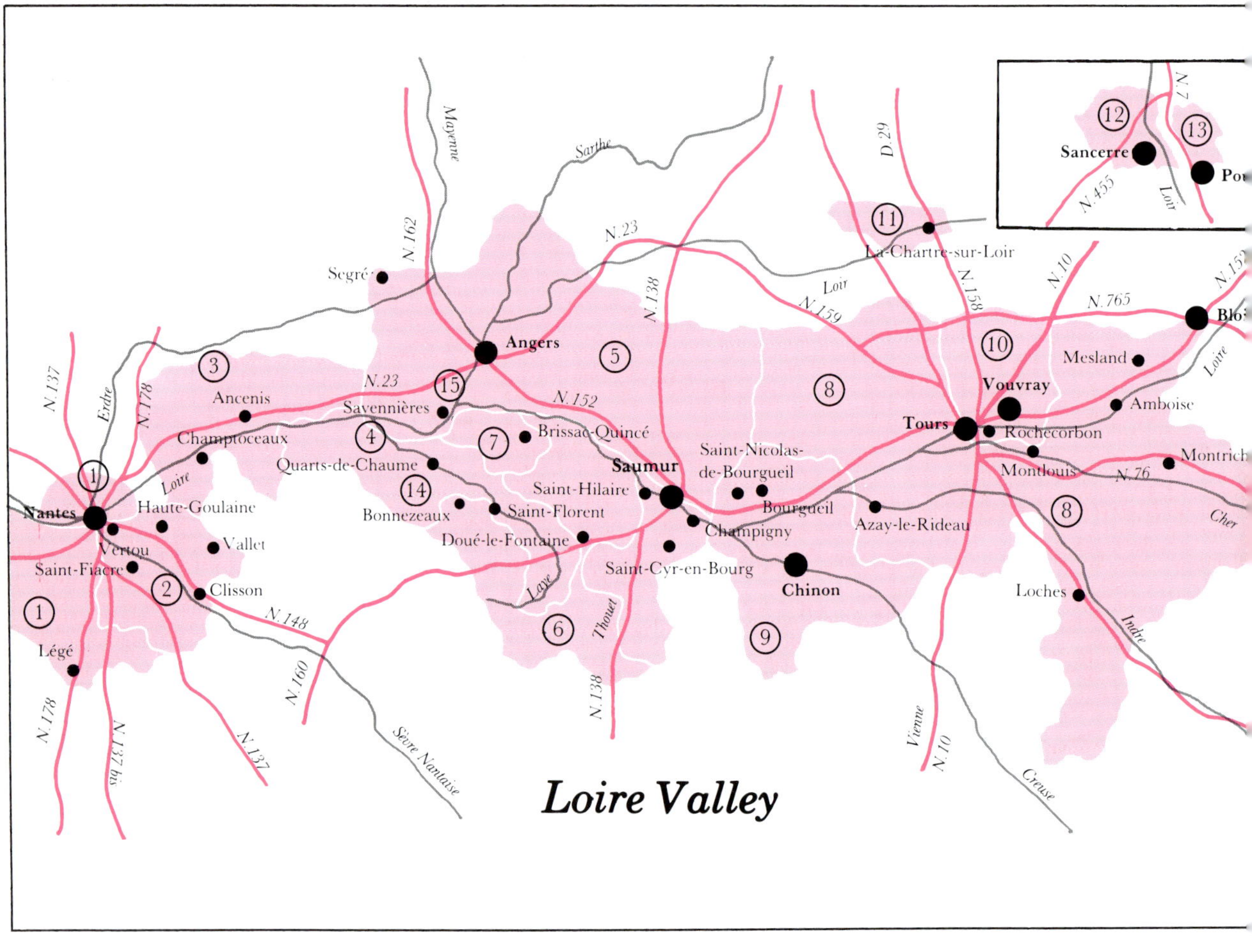

The Loire is a very old wine region. Saint Martin founded a religious order and an abbey in AD 372. It was he who, so the legend goes, first made wine here. The vineyards flank the River Loire and its tributaries for over almost 1000 kilometres. For simplicity, the middle and lower Loire is here divided into five sections, corresponding to five styles of wine and to specific grape varieties.

Sauvignon

Pouilly Blanc Fumé (W) A dry white wine with strong floral aromas. This is a summer wine that owes its freshness and finesse to the clayey-limestone soil where it is grown. Not to be confused with the lesser *appellation* of **Pouilly-sur-Loire**, an everyday carafe wine made from Chasselas grapes.

Sancerre (R, W and rosé) Sancerre illustrates the almost over-emphatic characteristics of Sauvignon wines that are derived from clayey-limestones, marls and chalk soils. Much like Pouilly Blanc Fumé. The red is made from Pinot Noir grapes and is half-way between a light Burgundy and an Alsace Pinot Noir.

Quincy (W), Reuilly, Ménétou Salon (R, W and rosé) In the style of Sancerre but with less pronounced qualities.

Wines of the Orléans Region

Strictly for the record, France's largest vineyard, until the 17th-18th centuries, produced a Gris d'Orléans, a pale rosé wine made from the Pinot Meunier grape.

Wines of Touraine

From Blois to Vouvray we find a number of AOC Touraine wines, red, white, rosé and sparkling, all based on Burgundy grapes and varieties native to the Loire.

Great Wines of the Loire

Vouvray and Montlouis (W) Until 1937 these two AOC white wines, mellow-sweet or sparkling, belonged to the same *appellation*.

1 Muscadet des Coteaux de la Loire
2 Muscadet de Sèvre-et-Maine
3 Coteaux d'Ancenis
4 Coteaux du Layon
5 Anjou Saumur
6 Saumur
7 Coteaux de l'Aubance
8 Touraine
9 Bourgueil-Chinon
10 Vouvray-Montlouis
11 Coteaux du Loir
12 Sancerre
13 Pouilly-sur-Loire
14 Bonnezeaux
15 Savennières

They are very typical of the Chenin grape from which they are made, and the dry wines can be over-acidic in poor years. They have a long lifespan, up to half a century.

Bourgueil and Saint-Nicholas de Bourgueil (R, rosé) A sturdy red wine made from the Cabernet Franc grape; when the soil is limestone rock, the wine is tannic and firm, while the more sandy, or even pebbly soil (*graves*) yields a gentler red wine.

Chinon (R, W and rosé) Grown on the left bank, opposite the last two. The same soil with the same grape variety yields a very similar though often softer wine with a bouquet of violets.

Jasnières (W), **Coteaux du Loir** (R, W and rosé) The Jasnières is a Chenin wine close to the Vouvray, with a nose and aroma of peach and apricot. Coteaux du Loir wines are soft and friendly, and there are even a few red wines with a raspberry aroma. These are made from the Pineau d'Aunis.

Saumur (sparkling, R & W) The white Saumur is made from Chenin, the red from the Cabernet Franc varieties. They are clean, firm and straightforward.

Saumur Champigny (R) The true *cru* of Saumur, with a dark ruby colour. It has a nose of violet and raspberry and is subtle in the palate. The great old vintages are outstanding.

Rosé d'Anjou is a medium light rosé; Anjou Gamay is characterized by the Gamay grape, Cabernet d'Anjou; Rosé de Loire is a mediocre rosé; Coteaux du Layon, Coteaux de l'Aubance, Bonnezeaux and Quart de Chaumes are mellow, even luscious white wines from the Chenin grape. The last two *appellations*, equivalent to the Grands Crus of Layon, are complex, rich and even sublime in a good year.

Anjou Coteaux de la Loire (W), **Savennières** (W), **Savennières Coulée de Serrant** (W), **Savennières Roche aux Moines** (W) There is very little to distinguish these wines from each other, although the last two are the Grand Crus of Savennières, the best commune in the area.

The Chenin grape finds its best expression in the Coulée de Serrant, a truly great and generous dry wine.

Muscadet

Three wines make use of the Muscadet or Melon de Bourgogne grape: first upstream is the rather solid Muscadet des Coteaux de la Loire, then Muscadet de Sèvre-et-Maine, which is the finest and best balanced, and finally Muscadet, a *vin de carafe* without much complexity, crisp, fresh, to be drunk young. Slightly more acid is the VDQS le Gros Plant.

Le Jardin de La France

Apart from the internationally known names like Muscadet, Pouilly-Fumé and Sancerre, Loire wines have been little exported. The vast range of wines produced makes the region less easy to assimilate than, say, Bordeaux or Burgundy. For many years the Loire has produced regional wines par excellence, and the improvements in viticulture and wine making that have been so apparent in Bordeaux, have finally come to this region, where dedication to quality and above all maintaining the individuality of their *appellation* has been the hallmark. The Loire Valley is probably the most interesting wine region for the next decade.

Wine Producing Regions/France/Jura, Savoy & Provence

Jura

This rocky and mountainous region produces one of the world's really great white wines, the Château-Chalon, so long lived that outstanding pre-revolutionary bottles still exist. The vineyards of the Jura cover the same area – 1200 hectares – as those of the neighbouring Savoy region, and are special in that they produce all types of wine (except for sweet white) including 'straw' or dessert wine, as well as reds, rosés, whites, *vins jaunes* and sparkling wines.

The Côtes de Jura regional *appellation* comprises all the various types of wine produced in the area. White wines are made from the Chardonnay, and especially the Savagnin grape, the reds from Trousseaus, Poulsard and Pinot Noir, alone or blended, while the best rosés come from the Poulsard variety on its own.

Vin de paille is made by a special process, and is so named because the grapes were once dried on straw, although nowadays they are dried on mats or hung up. After drying for some two months, the grapes are pressed and the resulting must, very rich in sugar, ferments slowly. *Vin de paille* is not unlike white port, but is richer and more complex.

The best still Jura wines are labelled Arbois and Arbois Pupillin, while the best sparkling wines are from the Etoile *appellation*.

Red Jura wines made from Trousseau grapes are richly coloured, robust and long-lived, going well with grilled red meats.

The white Arbois wines are full, dry and well-rounded in good years. As for the *vins jaunes*, their extraordinariness surpasses comment!

Savoy

Savoy possesses no great wines but has some excellent ones which are true examples of their grape variety.

The region of Savoy makes the best Chasselas wine, Crépy. The vineyards rise above Lake Geneva and lie facing those that produce the Swiss Fendant (also from Chasselas). This is a golden-yellow wine of medium acidity and with a hazelnut aroma. It should be drunk young, ideally with fresh perch or dace from the lake.

The Roussette de Savoie is named after its grape, which should not be confused with Roussanne. Altesse is another name for this delicately structured, well-balanced wine with its pale golden hue. It is best enjoyed

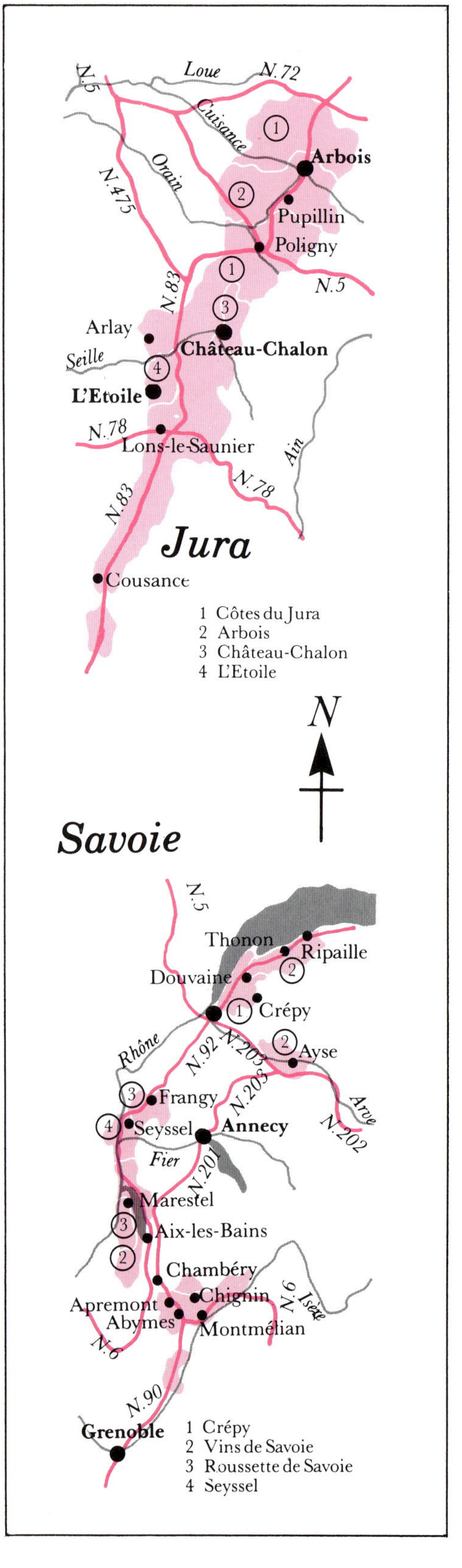

with trout freshly caught in Lake Bourget which is overlooked by the Roussette vines.

The Seyssel and Seyssel Mousseux dominate the *départements* of Savoy and Ain.

Great wines of Provence

Four wines have always stood out beyond and east of the Rhône corridor, namely Palette, Cassis, Bandol and Bellet.

Palette (R & W) Palette is the only one of the four not to have a piece of Mediterranean coastline, being situated close to the city of Aix-en-Provence. They are truly remarkable wines: the reds, based on the best Rhône grapes: Grenache, Cinsault and Mourvèdre, are highly coloured, tannic, full-bodied and keep well; the whites are made from the Clairette grape and are unusually sophisticated for this variety, a contradiction explained by their more northerly position.

Cassis (R, W and rosé) The whites are the best (Clairette, Marsanne, Ugni Blanc); these wines are floral and maintain their quality well, with good acidity.

Bandol (R, W and rosé) The reds are the best (60% minimum of Mourvèdre, Cinsault, Grenache), sometimes capable of rivalling the quality of some Bordeaux *crus classés*.

Bellet (R, W and rosé) The Bellet wines owe their quality to the fresh climate of the mountains overlooking Nice, planted with rare and original vines. The whites are dry and lively, the rosés are interesting and refined, while the firm, precise reds have none of the southern flabbiness. They are all perfectly suited to the very traditional and typical cuisine of Nice.

Provence

The four wines mentioned above are historically the finest in the region. However, a lot of progress has been made in Provence and the Languedoc-Rousillon (see page 106) in the past decade and even the epithet 'the California of France' is looking a little old-fashioned. Improvements in vinification have gone hand in hand with the introduction of classic grape varieties from other areas to produce wines that are quite different from the heavy southern style that used to be characteristic of the Provence region.

Côtes de Provence (R, W and rosé) Raised to *appellation* status in 1977 as a result of progress from the major producers. The reds are still mostly from the Grenache/Cinsault/Mourvèdre/Syrah grapes of the southern Rhône, with the Carignan being progressively reduced and Cabernet Sauvignon making an appearance. Rosés are becoming lighter and fruitier, while the whites are seeing their production increased from 10% to 15% to meet the international demand. This is a very mixed *appellation* where individual domaines are all looking for their own style.

Coteaux d'Aix-en-Provence/Coteaux des Baux-en-Provence Château Vignelaure, now a shadow of its former self, and Domaine de Trévallon have drawn attention to these joint *appellations*, whose quality rivals that of Côtes de Provence. Red, white, and rosés are made, of which the reds have the most potential.

Costières-du-Gard/Costières de Nimes The Roman province of the Gard produces wines that have as much in common with the Côtes du Rhone as with the Midi, while being a little lighter than both. The Costières de Nimes *appellation* was created in 1988. A fine white wine from the Gard is Clairette de Bellegarde.

Corsica

Corsican wines have made the same progress in the last decade as have those from the rest of Provence with the difference that thanks to a few enlightened producers, the classic Cabernet Sauvignon and Chardonnay have been very little planted, and the most striking wines are still made from the local Niellucio and Sciacarello grapes for the reds and rosés, and the Vermentino or Malvoisie de Corse for the whites. The finest *appellations* are Patrimonio and Porto-Vecchio.

Wine Producing Regions/France/Languedoc & the South-west

Languedoc

Between them, the plain of Aramon and the Carignan grape manage to produce one of the most mediocre wines of France and the world. This is the land of 'plonk', the kind of mouthwash that blenders try to 'improve' with Italian wines. These table wines are sold in bulk and do not concern us here.

Right *Picking white grapes in Languedoc.*

Nevertheless, the very same region does produce the Coteaux du Languedoc VDQS wines, most of them robust and red.

The three exclusively white AOCs are the Clairette de Bellegarde, the Clairette du Languedoc and the Blanquette de Limoux. These bear the name of their grape (Blanquette = Mauzac), the first two being rich and heady to the point of being heavy, while the third is full, round and nearly always sparkling. All three must be drunk young.

The three red AOCs are Fitou, Collioure and Côtes de Roussillon.

Fitou, the best wine from Carignan grapes planted *en coteau* (+ Grenache + Lladoner), is kept in the barrel for at least nine months. It is a dense, full and semi-refined wine that forms an excellent accompaniment to wild boar and cheese.

Collioure (Carignan, Grenache, Cinsault, Mourvèdre) is a strong red wine reminiscent of Fitou but often more sophisticated.

Côtes de Roussillon wines combine the grapes of the last two *appellations* (mainly Carignan). There are several light Côtes de Roussillon wines; some are drunk as *primeurs*, others are best after a few years.

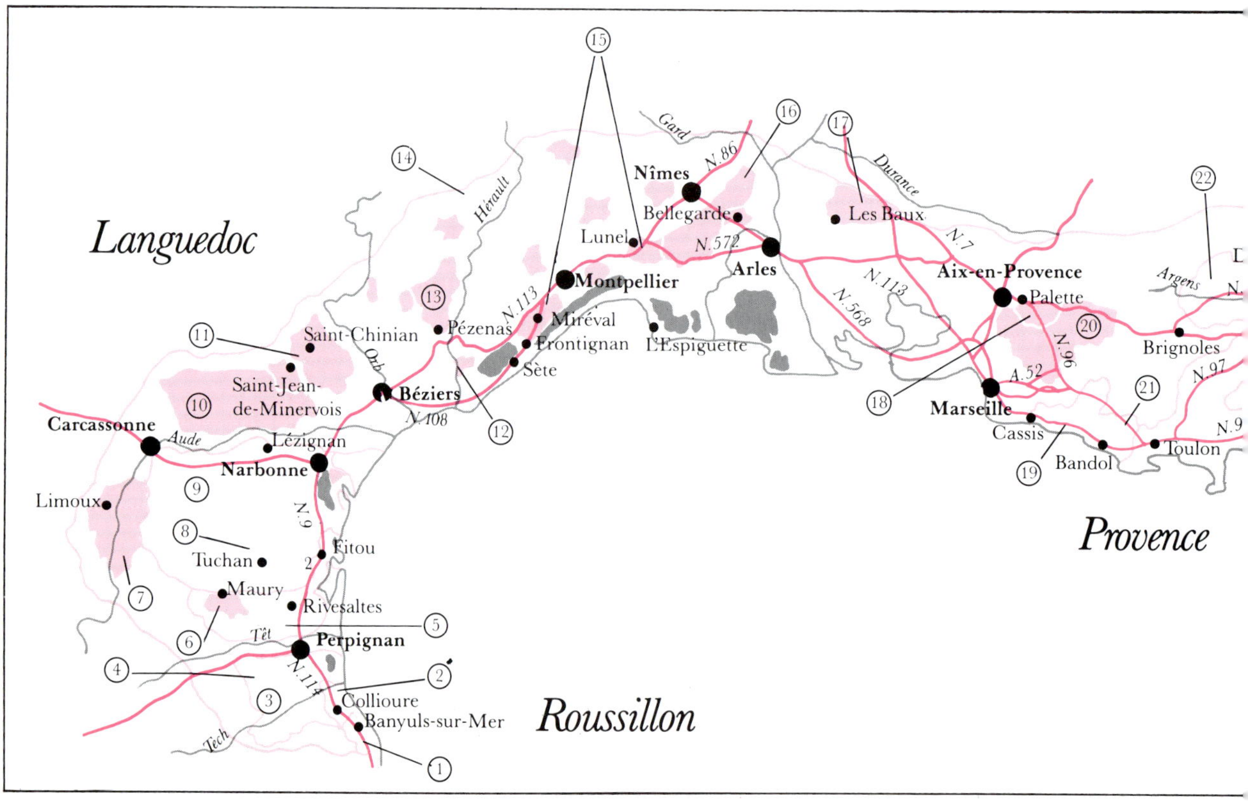

Their popularity is growing, and although they are light for the region, they have good body and fruit.

Corbières, Minervois and Costières du Gard are good quality VDQS wines, comprising three reds and an interesting white by virtue of its basic ingredient, the Folle Blanche grape (at least 70%), known locally as Picpoul de Pinet.

The South-west

A beautiful region of much interest to the student of wine because of its diversity of wines produced.

Cahors (R) An historic wine made with Malbec (at least 70%) known in the area as Auxerrois. This is the 'black wine' of the olden days, well-built, tannic and simple, ideal with goose *confit*.

Côtes de Buzet (R, W and rosé) Bordeaux varieties in good regional style.

Gaillac (R, W and rosé) Gaillac includes a vast range of wines: the Gamay red should be drunk young. There are other reds made from more local grape varieties (Braucol, Fer, Duras, etc.) which can be interestingly firm and balanced. The slightly sparkling Mauzac whites, best enjoyed when chilled and young, are fruity but sometimes low on acidity; the wines can be mellow and include a very interesting full sparkling wine made by the improved *méthode rurale*.

Côtes du Frontonnais (R, rosé) A soft red wine based on Négrette that is fruity, light and simple.

Madiran (R) Madiran is an impressive dark red Pyrenean wine which is lively yet keeps well, a suitable accompaniment to the strongest flavoured dishes.

Jurançon (W) An original wine made with special varieties of grape (Courbu, Manseng). This dry wine is lively with a firm clean flavour. The *liquoreux* wines show an amazingly spicy bouquet. In the mouth they offer a rewarding aromatic mixture of cinnamon, ginger, nutmeg and clove.

Pacherenc du Vic Bihl (W) Another Pyrenean wine similar to the dry Jurançon. Sometimes mellow.

Irouléguy (R, W and rosé) Hails from close to the border with Spain – the red is the best known of the three colours, not unlike the Madiran but less impressive.

Béarn (R, W and rosé) Bears the name of its home province. This is a simple and unpretentious wine, the rosé highly successful.

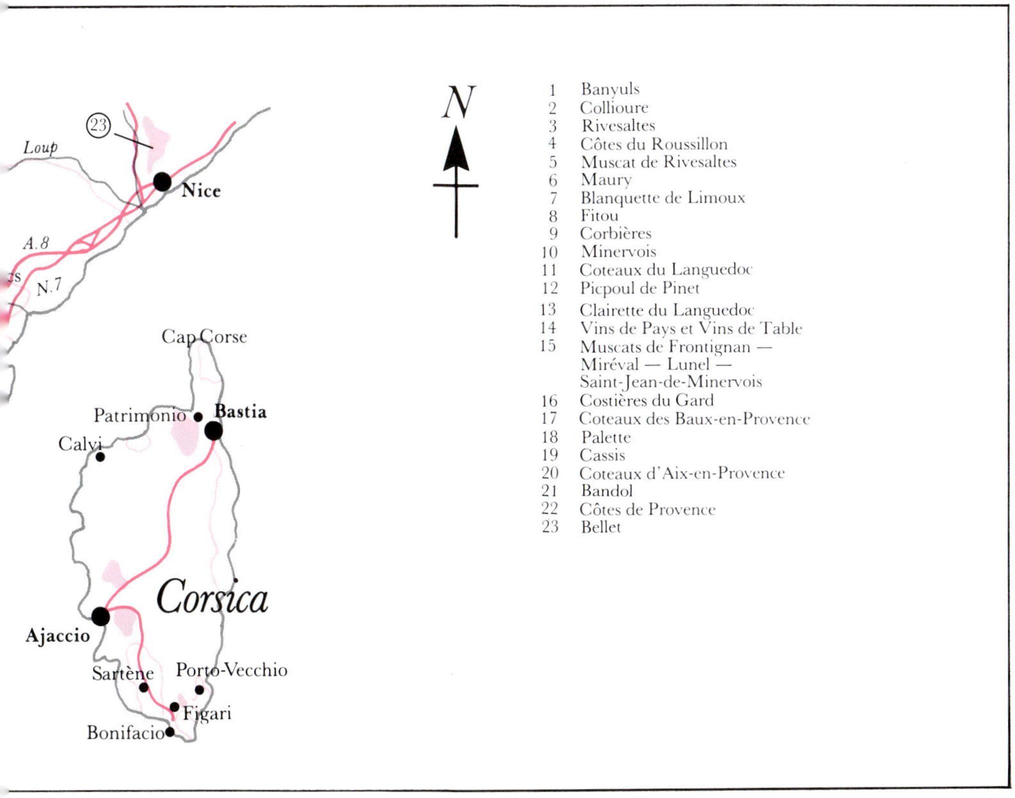

Wine Producing Regions/Germany 1

Of Germany's 99,335 hectares of vineyards, about 85% grow white grape varieties, that produce all qualities of wine, from the cheapest to the most distinguished and expensive. Some aspects of German wine making have changed radically in the last decade, and taste has moved away from refreshing, medium-sweet to drier wines. They are individual, and in a general way have some similarity with those of the northern French vineyards.

The Germans, more than anybody else, make use of the categories, from sweet to dry, established by EEC law. They are:

Trocken Dry wines, with a maximum of 9 gr/l of residual sugar, depending on the total acidity. The best have wonderful flavour, and sometimes 12% or more of natural alcohol, exclusively from the sugar in the grape. Recommended regions: Rheinpfalz, Rheinhessen, Baden, Franken.

Halbtrocken Medium-dry, with 10-18 gr/l of residual sugar, depending on the acidity. Not just a compromise but an excellent half-way house between the old medium-sweet and the modern dry wines. Recommended regions: Mosel-Saar-Ruwer, Rheingau, Nahe.

Lieblich Medium-sweet, 18-45 gr/l of residual sugar, typical for post World War II wines, until the late 1980s. At its best when balanced with fine Riesling acidity. Recommended regions: Mosel-Saar-Ruwer, Rheingau, Rheinhessen.

The definitions *trocken* and *halbtrocken* often appear on a wine label. Usually *lieblich* does not.

Quality categories

The quality categories of German wine are the result of a harvest that lasts from September to December, and is based initially on the sugar content of the grapes. However, the difference between the various categories is often more one of style than of quality. Besides a concentration of sugar, the grower also welcomes a high level of tartaric acid – a characteristic of good wines made in a cool climate.

The quality categories are defined in law and all German quality wines undergo a chemical analysis and bear a control ('AP') number. The categories are:

Deutscher Tafelwein (DTW) German Table Wines. Usually less than 5% of the harvest. Very basic wine with a superior category, *Landwein* – the equivalent of the French *vins du pays*. *Landwein* must be dry or medium-dry.

Qualitätswein eines bestimmten Anbaugebietes (QbA) Quality wine from a specified region. Often the largest part of a German vintage. Can vary from the basic and ordinary to the excellent.

Qualitätswein mit Prädikat (QmP) Superior quality wine. Here the finest German wines will be found. They are unsugared and therefore their alcohol content depends solely on the ripeness of the grape. The sub-categories of QmP are:

Kabinett Light (eg about 7-8% alcohol for a Mosel Kabinett). Charming, often most appealing when medium-dry or medium-sweet.

Spätlese Late picked, from grapes gathered at least seven days after the main harvest. Fuller than Kabinett in flavour and more alcoholic. Varying degrees of sweetness from dry to medium-sweet.

Auslese Usually pressed from selected bunches of grapes. The natural alcohol content varies according to vintage, grape variety and region, but can reach 13° or more. Impressive as a sweet or a dry wine.

Beerenauslese Produced from over-ripe grapes, probably attacked by 'noble rot'. Very rich and sweet wine. Riesling Beerenauslese only possible in great vintages, when the wine is superbly complex and lasting in flavour.

Eiswein The result of pressing grapes frozen naturally in the vineyard. Very concentrated acidity and sweetness, leading to wonderful, lively wines.

Trockenbeerenauslese A very rare wine only possible in the ripest vintages from over-ripe, individually picked grapes, dried on the vine, almost certainly attacked by 'noble rot'. Minute yield. Intensity, richness and length of flavour, defy adequate description.

The grape varieties

Together with the micro-climate, the vine variety has the greatest influence on the style and quality of German wine.

Müller-Thurgau Ripens early, producing light, fresh wines with relatively low acidity. When prevented from over-cropping can produce wines of depth and surprising quality (eg at Nierstein in the Rheinhessen or in eastern Franken).

White Riesling Very late ripening. Attrac-

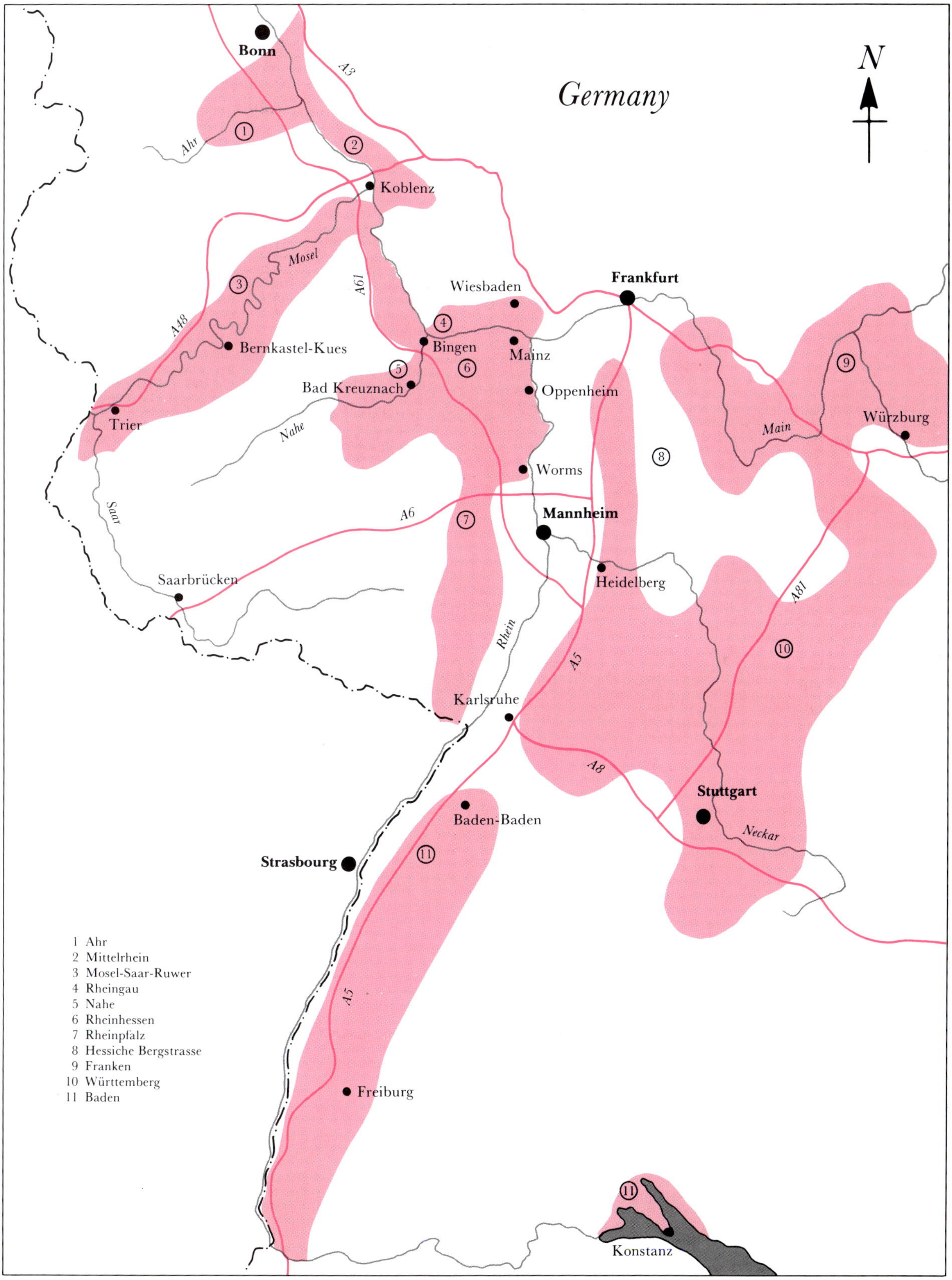
Germany
N
Bonn
Koblenz
Wiesbaden
Frankfurt
Bingen
Mainz
Bernkastel-Kues
Bad Kreuznach
Oppenheim
Trier
Worms
Mannheim
Heidelberg
Würzburg
Saarbrücken
Karlsruhe
Baden-Baden
Stuttgart
Strasbourg
Freiburg
Konstanz
Ahr
Mosel
Nahe
Saar
Rhein
Main
Neckar
A3
A61
A48
A6
A5
A81
A8
1 Ahr
2 Mittelrhein
3 Mosel-Saar-Ruwer
4 Rheingau
5 Nahe
6 Rheinhessen
7 Rheinpfalz
8 Hessiche Bergstrasse
9 Franken
10 Württemberg
11 Baden

Wine Producing Regions/Germany 2

Above The slate river banks of the Mosel provide the ideal conditions for the extensive cultivation of the Riesling grape.

tive wines, characterized by firm acidity at all levels of quality. Good at all degrees of sweetness. Arguably the finest white wine in the world, but at its best in the northern regions of Germany.

Green Silvaner Declining in popularity as a vine. Balanced clean wine with no excessive flavours. Can produce high quality in Franken, the Rheinhessen and in Kaiserstuhl – across the Rhein from Alsace.

Kerner The wine has good acidity without the finesse of Riesling. Sound, but often not very exciting wines, are produced in all quality categories. Grown throughout Germany.

Blauer Spätburgunder Known elsewhere as Pinot Noir. Increasing in Germany where some wine makers are producing wines of true Burgundian distinction. Widely planted in Baden.

About 100 other grape varieties occupy the remaining German vineyards. The most important are Scheurebe, Bacchus, Blauer Portugieser, Ruländer (Pinot Gris), and Trollinger.

Wine producing regions

Mosel-Saar-Ruwer A composite region following the Mosel and its tributaries, the Saar and the Ruwer, from the French border to Koblenz. The best known district is the Bereich Bernkastel, where top estates offer incomparably elegant, *spritzig*, individually made Riesling wines. Ruwer wines are very similar with variations in the flavour from the soil and microclimate. Those from the Saar are firm and steely – the best being of outstanding quality. The lower Mosel Rieslings from the Bereich Zell may be country cousins of the finest examples from the Bereich Bernkastel but can be excitingly positive and firm in flavour, particularly when made from a restricted yield.

Above *Burg Cochem, partly concealed by the burgeoning vines of the Mosel.*

Rheinhessen In the Rheinhessen villages on the Rheinterrasse between Bodenheim and Alsheim, some estates make marvellous wine, fuller in flavour than that of the better-known Rheingau. As usual, the best are Rieslings. Further north, wines from Ingelheim and Bingen are lighter, but elegant with a long flavour.

Rheinpfalz The best Rheinpfalz vineyards lie near the villages of Deidesheim, Forst and Wachenheim. In other parts of the region, some growers are also producing top-quality wines from limited yields – particularly from Riesling, Scheurebe, Weissburgunder (Pinot Blanc).

Rheingau Distinguished Riesling region. Many famous and ancient estates. Stylish, dry and medium-dry wines are in vogue – the latter, in particular, from the association of growers called 'Charta'. Rheingau wines are the best known on the export markets.

Franken Famous for its flagon-shaped 'Bocksbeutel' bottle, the wine region of Bavaria. The wines from the top estates benefit from an earthy, positive flavour from the soil.

Nahe A region with vineyards spread over a wide area. The central part from Bad Kreuznach to Schlossböckelheim and the Lower Nahe villages of Dorsheim and Münster-Sarmsheim produce 'zippy' Rieslings of good to outstanding quality.

Baden A region that largely follows the slopes of the Black Forest. Fuller wines, less acidic than those from further north, excellent Rieslings at Durbach and strong, full-flavoured wines in the Kaiserstuhl.

Some well-known wines

Although Germany produces fine wine, it is regrettably known abroad, mainly for its cheap, but undistinguished wines:

Liebfraumilch A quality wine (QbA), blended within one of four regions, predominantly from Riesling, Silvaner, Müller-Thurgau and Kerner. Most is medium-sweet, but can be cheap and of poor quality. More expensive, branded Liebfraumilch offers best value.

Niersteiner Gutes Domtal The Gutes Domtal, a large area of over 1,300 hectares with a minimal connection with the distinguished wine village of Nierstein, is the best known collective in the Rheinhessen.

Oppenheimer Krötenbrunnen Very similar to Niersteiner Gutes Domtal in all respects. Sometimes lighter in flavour.

Piesporter Michelsberg Overpriced wines compared with others of similar quality, from an oversold collective on the Mosel.

Bereich Bernkastel Although this district (*Bereich*) contains most of the best wine villages on the Mosel, a wine sold under the Bereich name, without the mention of Riesling, is unlikely to be exciting.

The wine makers

As a general rule the finest and the most exciting German wines are produced by private or state-owned properties. Standards of wine making are high and in regions such as the Rheinpfalz, Baden, and Württemberg the wines from the local cooperative cellars are equally as good.

A guide to the best wines is hardly possible but a badge or label bearing the initials 'DLG' is a useful indication of quality.

Wine Producing Regions/Italy 1

Italy is one of the oldest wine-producing regions in the world. The vine has been grown here for thousands of years – fossilized grape pips from the Stone Age have been unearthed near Venice – and wine has always played an important role in the life of the peninsula's inhabitants.

History

During the Greek Empire, the cultivation of the vine in Italy became increasingly important for both social and religious reasons. The cult of Dionysus, Greek god of wine, was particularly important in the south and in Sicily. There are still grapes growing in southern Italy with origins that date back to the Greeks (Greco di Tufo and Aglianico).

The Romans were accomplished vintners and the cultivation of the grape was encouraged both at home and in the outposts of the empire, notably in the Rhône and Burgundy areas of France and in Germany. Soldiers were rewarded with gifts of land on which they had to plant vines; since the vine takes four years to bear fruit, the emperor was thus guaranteed the loyalty of the new Roman territories while his soldier-farmers awaited their crops.

The pioneering spirit of modern Italians can still be found among its wine makers, many of whom have left their homeland to establish wineries in younger countries, notably in the United States, South America and Australia.

Geography and climate

The Greeks, who were the first to realize Italy's natural disposition as a wine-making area, named it Enotria or 'Land of Wine'. Apart from the flat, fertile, alluvial valley of the River Po, stretching from Turin in the north-west past Milan to Venice in the north-east, the terrain is broken by hills and mountains, making it ideal for wine grapes.

The Alps, forming the northern boundary of the country, slope gradually down to the Po Valley, criss-crossed by steep man-made terraces in the highest parts and carpeted with undulating vineyards on the gentler slopes. Italy's backbone is formed by the Apennine mountains which rise near Genoa in the west, and swing southwards near Bologna down to the tip of the boot-shaped peninsula. Apart from the highest, snow-covered peaks, these mountains, too, are covered with vineyards. Poor soil makes for good wine, and again Italy has an edge on other wine nations. Apart from the rich soil of the Po Valley, where rice and corn are the main crops, most of the country has fairly barren soil on which grapes thrive. The soil ranges from granite in the north-west with patches of clay and limestone in Trentino, to schistous clay and gravel in the centre, and volcanic soil in the south and in Sicily.

It is a popular misconception that the climate of Italy is perpetually sunny and warm. The truth is that there are several different types of climate: *continental* in the north and southward as far as Tuscany, giving bitter winters, hot summers and frequent rain and hail storms; *equable* in the central part with cool winters and warm summers; *Mediterranean* in the south and on the islands, with mild winters and hot dry summers in which drought can be a major

Right *The terrain of much of Italy – mountain and hill slopes – makes it an ideal wine-producing country and every region produces some wine.*

problem. The hills and valleys also give rise to individual microclimates which affect the wines made in these areas.

The tremendous variety of topographical, climatic and soil conditions in Italy result in a wider range of different types and styles of wine than in any other part of the world.

Italy's wine law

In 1963 the Italian government passed the DOC wine law. DOC stands for Denominazione di Origine Controllata or 'Controlled Place Name'. The law regulates the production of over 200 wines and controls the following:

- area of production;
- permitted grape varieties and percentage of each type;
- height above sea level and exposure of the vineyards;
- methods of training the vines;
- maximum yield of grapes per hectare;
- maximum yield of wine from grapes;
- ageing period in the winery before release;
- size of bottles or containers in which the wine may be sold;
- chemical analysis of the wine;
- organoleptic characteristics of the wine.

A step beyond DOC is DOCG – Denominazione di Origine Controllata e Garantita – which also guarantees the quality of a wine. Five wines (Barolo, Barbaresco, Vino Nobile di Montepulciano, Brunello di Montalcino and Albana di Romagna) are in this category. In addition to the controls for DOC wines, DOCG wines are tasted for quality at regular intervals by a panel of experts; if the wine of any producer is considered to be below standard all this wine is declassified to ordinary table wine. The DOCG law constitutes the strictest wine legislation in the world – for two reasons. In no other country is quality legally guaranteed, and nowhere else are so many aspects of wine production controlled by law. For example, if a wine maker makes more than the permitted quantity of wine from his vineyards, all his wine of that year is declassified to ordinary table wine. Compare this with France where over-production in Margaux is declassified to AOC Bordeaux.

Chaptalization, the adding of sugar to must in order to achieve higher alcohol, is illegal in Italy. Concentrated grape juice may be added instead to some wines.

Italian Wine Names

Wines may be named for:
1. *Geographical location* – e.g. Barolo (a village), Chianti (an area), Sangiovese *di Romagna* (a region). All DOC wines have a place name.
2. *Grape name* – *Barbera* d'Asti (grape + town), *Verdicchio* dei Castelli di Jesi (grape + area), *Pinot Grigio* delle Tre Venezie (grape + region).
3. *Brand or generic name* – Most non-DOC wines e.g. Corvo, Venegazzu'.

The wine regions of Italy

There are 20 autonomous regions in Italy – in the north, Valle d'Aosta, Piedmont, Lombardy, Liguria, Veneto, Trentino-Alto Adige and Friuli-Venezia Giulia; in the centre, Emilia-Romagna, Tuscany, Umbria, Marches and Latium; in the south, Campania, Abruzzi, Molise, Apulia, Basilicata and Calabria, plus Sicily and Sardinia.

Unlike other wine-producing nations, where wine is only made in certain areas, Italian wine is made in every single region. It is important to remember that Italy has been a united nation for little more than 100 years; before then the country was a conglomeration of kingdoms, duchies and city-states that were frequently at war with one another. Because they were separated geographically and politically, each region developed individual customs and traditions which can still be clearly identified today. These differences also extend to wine-making practices.

The easiest way to learn about Italian wines is to divide the country into five sections – the north-west, the north-east, the centre, the south, and the islands. Each section has broad similarities with regard to climate and grape varieties, though styles of the wines can vary.

Equally important to bear in mind is that because Italian wines are made from grapes rarely grown in other parts of the world they should never be compared with wines from other countries. Different grapes give different tastes so the only true way to understand Italian wines is to make an extensive tasting of the good examples. A little effort will be amply repaid since Italian wines can be outstanding and are generally slightly lower in price than wines from other countries.

Wine Producing Regions/Italy 2

1. North-west Italy

This section includes Valle d'Aosta, Piedmont, Liguria and Lombardy and is known for its full-bodied reds and for its excellent *brut spumante* which is often made by the champagne method.

Piedmont

One of the most important red wine areas in the world. Wines tend to be full-bodied and tannic and many require lengthy ageing to achieve their potential. About 90% of the production is of reds.

Barolo Full-bodied, tannic, made from the Nebbiolo grape grown near the village of Barolo in southern Piedmont. At its best after 10–15 years ageing, it possesses the typical garnet colour of wines from this grape and a rich bouquet which makes it one of the easiest wines to identify. DOCG.

Barbaresco Called Barolo's younger brother, also made from Nebbiolo, but the soil in Barbaresco produces a slightly more gentle, elegant wine. DOCG.

Barbera d'Asti and **Barbera d'Alba** The Barbera grape is the most widely planted variety in Piedmont, accounting for 50% of the region's reds. Best wines are from the south around Alba and Asti. Medium-bodied, fruity, good after 3–7 years. DOC.

Below Dégorgage, *refilling and corking of brut spumante, a sparkling wine made by the* méthode champenoise, *near Turin.*

Asti Most popular sparkling wine in the world. Made from Moscato di Canelli grapes around the town of Asti. Unlike other sparkling wines, Asti is only fermented once, in large tanks. After the harvest the must is refrigerated and stored at 0°C until fresh wines are needed. Then the must is brought to room temperature, inoculated with selected yeasts and fermented until an alcohol level of 7° is achieved. Fermentation is then arrested, the wine filtered and bottled. This method ensures that the fresh, fruity quality of the grape is captured in the wine. DOC.

Gattinara Also made from Nebbiolo, but in the north of Piedmont. Required ageing before release is 4 years and can be cellared for 10–15 years. DOC.

Carema, Ghemme Medium-bodied reds also from Nebbiolo grown in the north. Slightly lighter than other Piedmont Nebbiolos due to different soil. DOC.

Lombardy

Two main wine areas are Valtellina and Oltrepo' Pavese.

Valtellina Situated high in the mountains near Switzerland, has a tiny production of quality wines made from Chiavennasca grape (local name for Nebbiolo). All vineyards are on very steep, man-made terraces where all work has to be done by hand.

Sassella, Inferno, Valgella, Grumello The main wines made here. Lighter in style than Piedmont Nebbiolos and suited to only moderate ageing. DOC.

Sfursat From Nebbiolo grapes that have been dried for 2-3 months on special racks. A rich, lush wine with high (14-15°) alcohol and hint of residual sugar. DOC.

Oltrepo' Pavese The hilly area south of the Po Valley. Main grapes are Barbera and Bonarda for red wines (**Gutturnio dei Colli Piacentini** is one of the best), and Pinot and Chardonnay for whites, many of which are used as base wines for *brut spumante.*

2. North-east Italy

This section includes Veneto, Trentino-Alto Adige and Friuli-Venezia Giulia and is characterized by the fact that most of the wines are labelled for the grapes which make them (varietal wines). Many of the grapes were imported from France and Germany during the 19th century.

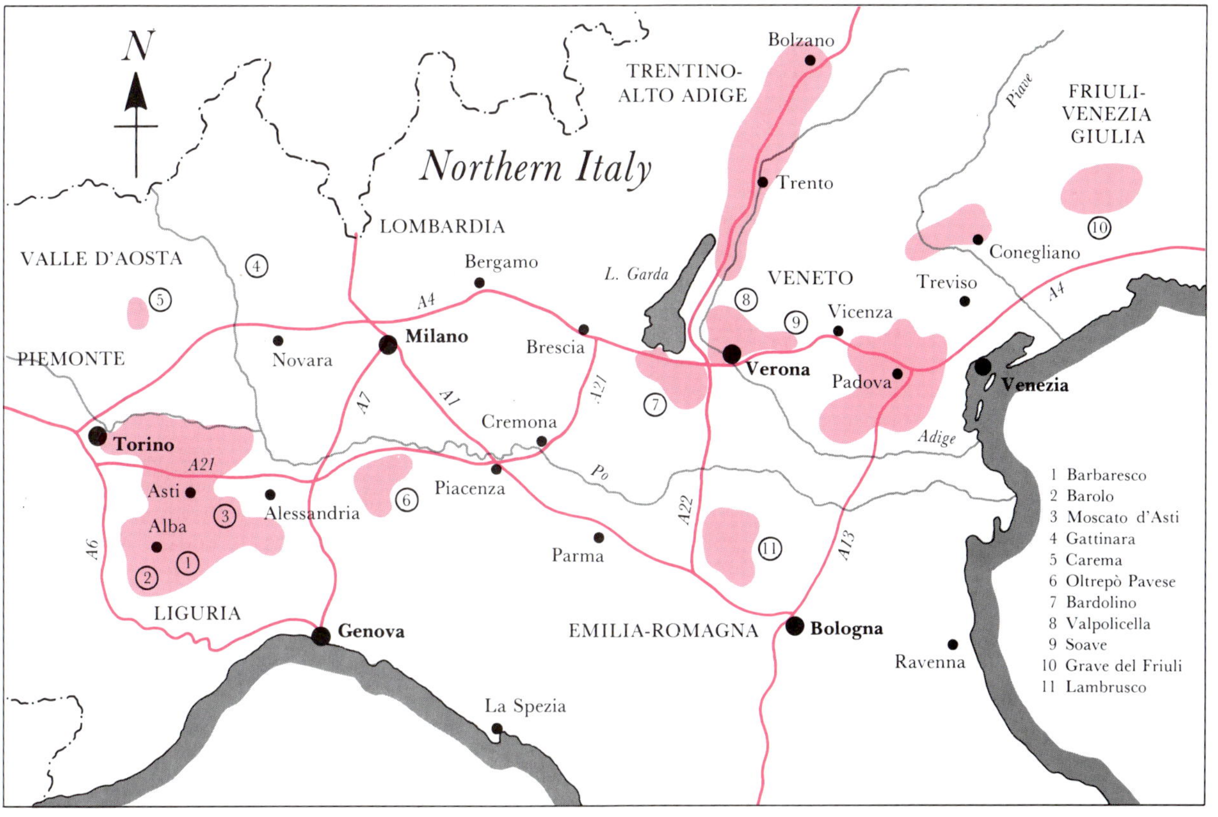

Veneto

The two main areas are the Veronese and the Piave Valley.

Veronese The area around the town of Verona and along the east shore of Lake Garda. Light, fresh wines are produced here.

Soave Perhaps Italy's best-known white wine, made from Garganega and Trebbiano grapes. DOC.

Bardolino and **Valpolicella** Light fruity reds to be drunk young. Smaller producers often make high-quality wines. DOC.

Amarone Made from the same grapes as Valpolicella which have been dried for 3 months on racks (cf. Sfursat from Lombardy). The wine is rich and lush and can stand lengthy ageing. DOC.

Piave A large area where four varieties are grown – Cabernet and Merlot for reds and Verduzzo and Tocai (both local varieties) for whites. Most of these wines are drunk locally.

Another area of quality wines is the countryside around the town of Treviso where **Prosecco di Conegliano**, a semi-dry, aromatic sparkling wine, and **Venegazzu'**, a proprietary label made from a blend of Cabernet, Merlot and Malbec, are made.

Trentino-Alto Adige

The northern half of this region, Alto Adige, is also known as Süd Tyrol and was ceded to Italy at the conclusion of World War I. Wines are made from Riesling, Müller-Thurgau, Sylvaner, Pinot Grigio, Chardonnay and Pinot Noir, and they tend to be clean, fruity and crisp. Quality is universally high. The DOC is called *Alto Adige* and controls a number of wines labelled for the grape variety from which they are made.

The southern half of the region is formed by the province of Trento where similar grapes are grown and the wines also labelled for the grape variety. The DOC is called *Trentino*. Chardonnay grapes are being planted increasingly and are used to make *brut spumante*.

Friuli-Venezia Giulia

Some of Italy's finest whites are made here from Riesling, Müller-Thurgau, Sauvignon, Sylvaner, Pinot Grigio, Tocai and Chardonnay grapes. Cabernet and Merlot make light, fruity reds for early consumption. The best DOC areas are *Collio* and *Grave del Friuli* and wines are labelled for their grape variety.

Wine Producing Regions/Italy 3

3. Central Italy

The third section is formed by Emilia-Romagna, Tuscany, Umbria, Marches and Latium. The main grapes are Sangiovese for reds and Trebbiano and Malvasia for whites.

Emilia-Romagna

Region known as the cellar of Italy due to its consistently abundant harvest.

Lambrusco A semi-sweet or semi-dry, low alcohol, effervescent red made from grapes of the same name. Extremely popular in the USA and Japan.

Sangiovese di Romagna A fruity red for early consumption. Ranges from fairly harsh and acidic to smooth and elegant.

Tuscany

Major red wine-producing area. Also famous for its olive oil, the typical Tuscan landscape comprising rows of vines separated by olive groves.

Chianti Perhaps Italy's most famous red wine and one of the most underestimated wines in the world. Made in two styles. The first produces a young wine, ready to drink by March following the harvest. This wine does not age well. The second style is intended for longer keeping and is called Riserva. It is aged for 3 years in wood in the winery, and good vintages can be held for 10–15 years. Wines labelled *Classico* come from the heart of the DOC area and are considered the best. The DOC area is the largest and has several geographical subdivisions. *Rufina* is regarded as second only to the Classico area.

Brunello di Montalcino Made from a clone of the Sangiovese grape, known as Brunello. A powerful, full red aged for 4 years in wood before release. One of the longest-lived wines, top vintages can take 25 years to reach their potential. DOCG.

Vino Nobile di Montepulciano Similar to Chianti, though with a little more finesse. Can be aged for 10 years in good vintages. DOCG.

Vernaccia di San Gimignano A quality white from the Vernaccia grape. Reputed to have been Michelangelo's favourite wine, it was also the first Italian wine to become DOC. The Riserva is aged in wood for one year.

Umbria

Known as the green heart of Italy and famous for its hill towns – Perugia, Assisi, etc.

Torgiano Rubesco Highly regarded red made from Sangiovese and other red grapes. The Riserva can age well for 10 years and becomes a very elegant, full wine.

Orvieto Two styles of this white are produced, *secco* and *abboccato* (dry and semi-sweet), both made from the Trebbiano and Malvasia grapes. The quality has improved during recent years thanks to newly introduced techniques for making white wines (cold fermentation, refrigeration). DOC.

Marches

Region famous for its Adriatic beaches and seafood.

Verdicchio A crisp, dry wine with high acidity suited to fish dishes. Made from grape of the same name and traditionally sold in green amphora-shaped bottle. DOC.

Latium

Rome is the capital of Italy and of the region of Latium. Wines from this area are generally light; most are drunk locally by tourists.

Frascati and **Marino** Best known whites of the area, similar in taste and style. Both are made from Trebbiano and Malvasia grapes. Recent vintages have benefited from the use of new white wine technology which results in crisper, cleaner, more stable wines. DOC.

4. Southern Italy

The south-eastern half of this section is responsible for the majority of wines produced in the south. The rest of the region tends to be very barren and rocky with a tendency to drought.

Regions in the south are Campania, Abruzzi-Molise, Basilicata, Apulia and Calabria.

Campania

Despite its southerly latitude, some of Italy's most elegant quality wines are made here, high up in the mountains where altitude offsets the effects of the southerly climate.

Taurasi A robust red made from the Aglianico grape (Aglianico = Hellenic, a grape of ancient Greek origins) grown inland from Naples on volcanic soil. Improves after 5–10 years ageing. DOC.

Fiano di Avellino One of the few Italian whites to improve with moderate ageing, made from Fiano grapes. A rich wine with a very agreeable, honeyed bouquet. DOC.

Greco di Tufo Another excellent white which can also withstand some ageing. Made from the Greco grape near the village of Tufo, named for its tufaceous (volcanic) soil, evidenced by the steely characteristic of the wine. DOC.

Basilicata

Aglianico del Vulture Similar in style to Taurasi, since it is made from the same grape, though slightly less elegant. DOC.

Apulia

Region which produces vast quantities of wine, much of it shipped in bulk to northern Italy and France. Recent experiments have yielded successful results with varieties such as Cabernet and Pinot Noir.

5. The Islands

Sicily

A region that produces large quantities of wine, much of which used to be shipped in bulk to France. Recently there has been an increase in the production of quality bottled wine, with heavy private and government investment. The finest wines are from Regaleali, near Palermo.

Sicily is also the home of Marsala, which is undergoing a deserved rennaissance as are other fortified wines (qv), particularly the lighter "vergine" style.

Sardinia

Although Sardinia produces some well-made and fruity DOC wines, they are mostly drunk on the island by tourists.

Vino da Tavola

Although originally a name for a table wine, or those wines which do not conform to the DOC rules in terms of the grape variety or the vinification method used. One of the main sources of interest lies in the high quality of some *vini da tavola*, eg Tuscan Sassicaia.

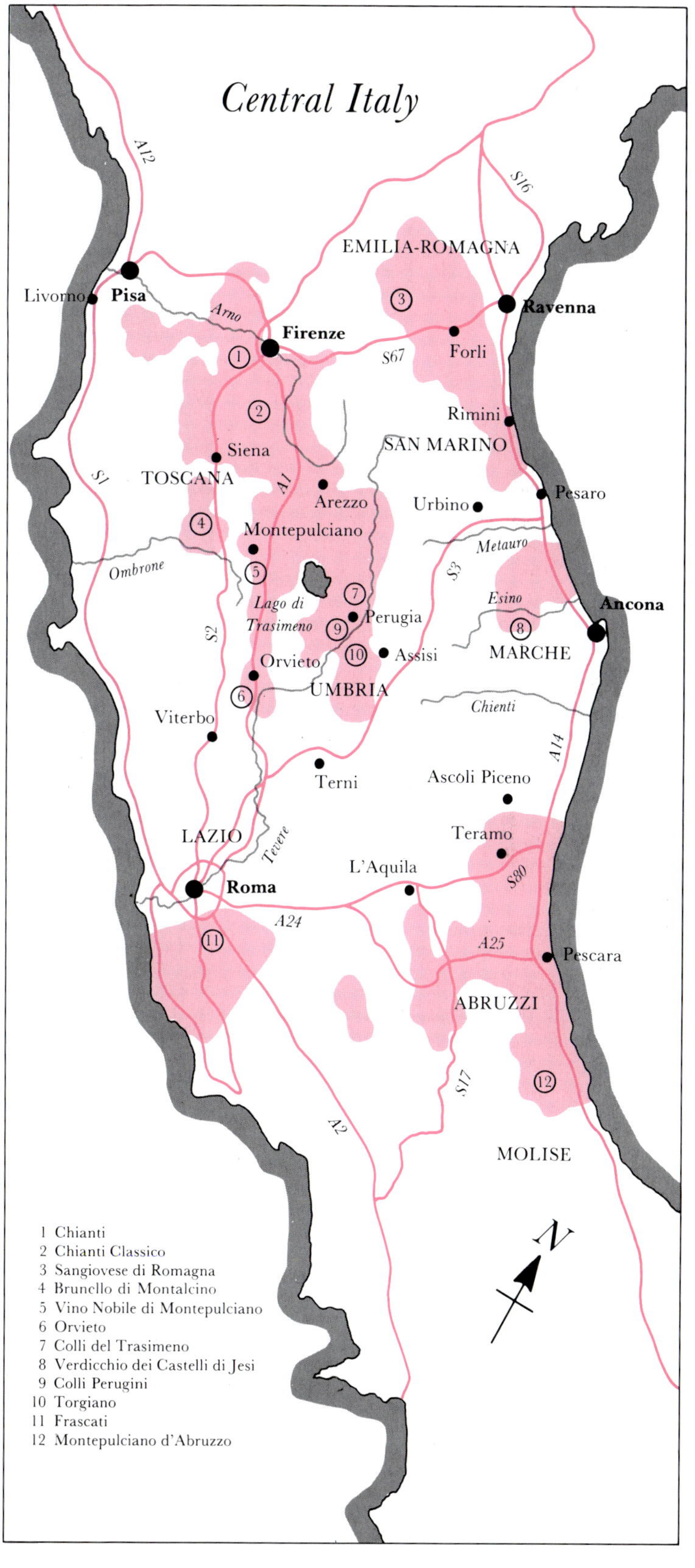

Wine Producing Regions/Spain & Portugal 1

Spain

Spain is the third largest wine producer in Europe, after France and Italy, although its vineyards cover a larger area than either of these countries. The history of Spanish vine-growing goes back well before the Christian era, but it is only in the last 20–30 years that high-quality table wines have been regularly produced. (The history of sherry is very different, fortified wines of the highest quality having been made in Andalusia for the past 200 years.)

In 1970, the Instituto Nacional de Denominaciónes de Origen was set up, similar to, although a little less strict than, the French AOC and Italian DOC systems. The fact that Spain, once known principally for its hearty but dull table wines, now has the reputation for producing some of the most interesting wines in Europe, is attributable to dramatic changes of policy: investment at vineyard level for higher yields of healthier grapes, much experimental planting of new grape varieties, installation of modern methods of vinification alongside the traditional wood-ageing, and constant commitment to quality by the producers.

Spanish table wines are produced in four major areas: Rioja, Catalonia, La Mancha and Levante, with scattered vineyards in the north-west and the south.

Above *Cement fermenting vats in the* bodega *of Valdepenas, one of the major wine producing towns of La Mancha in central Spain.*

Rioja

This region, named after the Rio Oja, a tributary of the Rio Ebro, which runs through the whole of this wine-producing district, is the best known for quality wine. While there are some quite exceptional wines from the Penedés region of Catalonia, these are better known under the names of the producers (Torrés, Jean León), than by their geographical appellation. The Rioja region has a quality ring to it, rather like Bordeaux. Indeed, the histories of the two regions are interlinked: in the 1870s and 1880s, many Bordelais growers left their phylloxera-ravaged vineyards for nearby Rioja, introducing their wine-making techniques. Although they departed again at the end of the century, when phylloxera eventually reached Spain, the Bordeaux influence remained.

In terms of geography and quality, the Rioja is divided into three distinct districts: Rioja Alta, of which the capital is Haro, with a temperate climate that produces the finest wines; Rioja Alavesa, centred on Logroño, producing fine wines under a similar climate; and Rioja Baja, on the south side of the Rio Ebro, where a hotter and drier climate produces heavy wines with low acidity. Wines from the Rioja Alta and Rioja Baja are often used together in commercial blends.

The production of the Rioja is mostly red, although more white grapes are being planted now that modern vinification techniques produce a lighter, crisper style. The principal grape for the better red Rioja is the local Tempranillo, to which may be added some Garnacho (the Grenache, from the Rhône Valley). In the Rioja Baja, Garnarcho is planted almost exclusively. White Rioja is made mainly from the Viura, while minor grapes used are the Malvasia and Garnacho Blanco.

Opposite below *Wine from the vineyards of Senorio de Sarría in Navarra can rival the best from Rioja in quality, although production is restricted.*

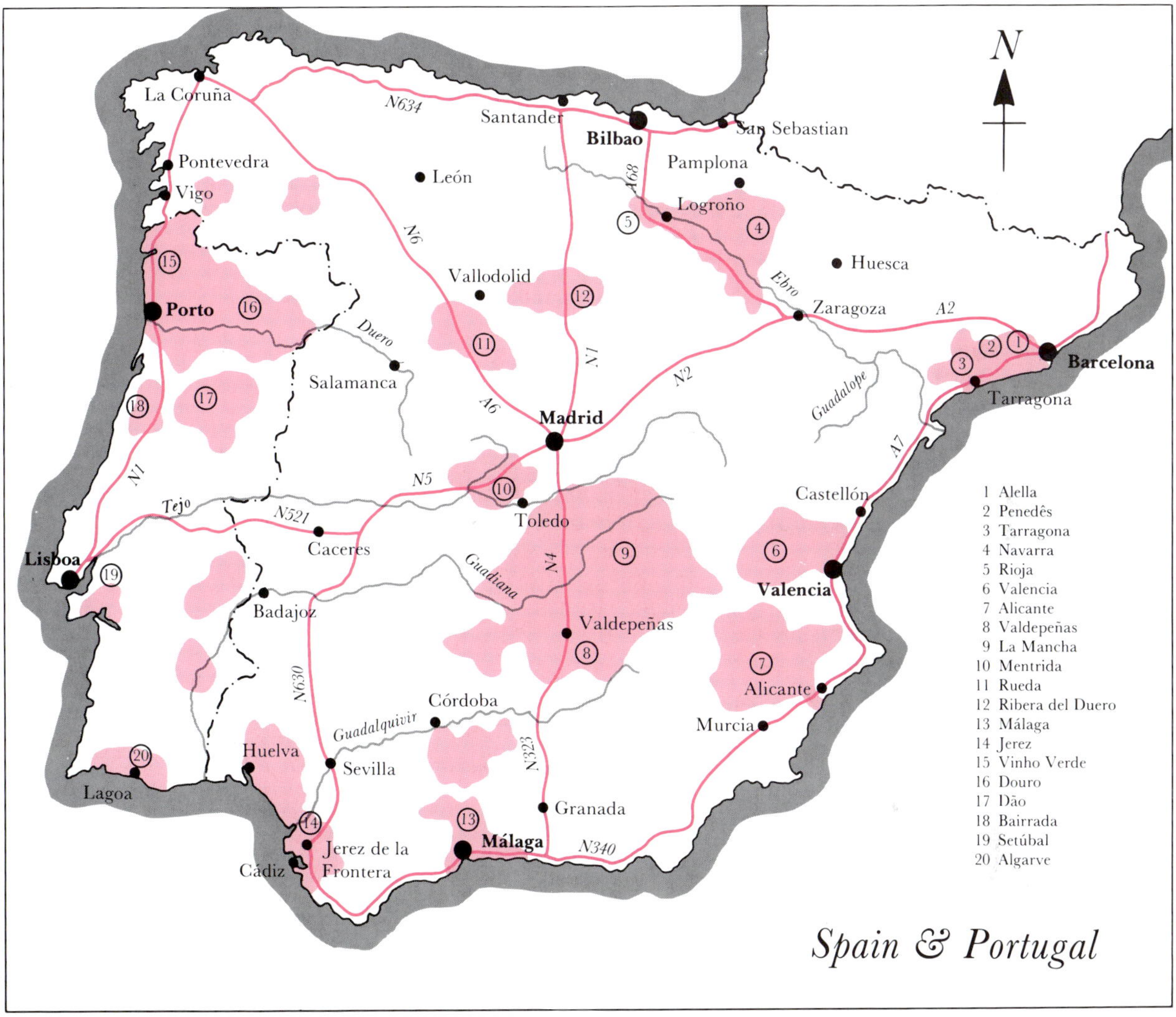

The style of wines from the Rioja region is very varied. The younger and cheaper are deep-coloured *tintos*; as they mature, particularly if aged traditionally in small oak barrels, they lose colour, take on a touch of vanilla from the wood, and become more complex and slightly drier. Vintage dates are more reliable than they used to be, and only the good years are vintaged. Riojas often state on the label the number of years after the date of the vintage that the wine was bottled – 3° ano, 4° ano – and may be drunk immediately. White wines are dry, and a clean, fruity, more 'modern' wine is taking over from the less fresh, more mature style. Whereas the image of a red Rioja seems quite well defined, that of a white Rioja is not. A little rosé is made, best consumed on the spot.

Wine Producing Regions/Spain & Portugal 2

Catalonia

The vines of Catalonia grow in the north-east of Spain, just down the coast and inland from Barcelona. If the Rioja region is known for quality, Catalonia, and more specifically the Penedés region, is known for the variety of its wines. North of Barcelona, the Denominación de Origen Alella produces fine white wine from the Farnacho Blanco, Picpoul, Malvasia and Maccabeo (the same as the Viura in the Rioja), and may either be dry or sweet. From around the port of Sitges comes the sweet, white Malvasia de Sitges, a fortified wine. Farther down the coast, the larger town of Tarragona has given its name to a rich sweet wine from the Garnacho, Maccabeo and Pedro Ximénez grapes, while above Tarragona a powerful dry red wine is made from the Garnacho and Cariñena grapes at Priorato.

These wines, however, are surpassed in quality and variety by the wines from the **Penedés** region. First in importance are the sparkling wines made by the *méthode champenoise*, which is distinguished from the *cuve close* process by the addition of the word 'Cava' to the label. These Cavas, especially the Brut Blanc de Blancs, can rival the best sparkling wines from other parts of the world. But perhaps the most innovative wines in Spain, certainly in Catalonia, are being made by the Torrés family. To the traditional white grape varieties of Parellada and Maccabeo, they have added Muscat, Riesling and Gewürztraminer from Alsace, and Chardonnay from Burgundy; alongside the classic reds, Ull de Llebre and Monastrel, they have planted Cabernet Sauvignon, Cabernet Franc and Merlot from Bordeaux and Pinot Noir from Burgundy. By matching these foreign grapes to the soil and climate, and allying ultra-modern methods of vinification to traditional wood-ageing, Torrés is making wines that break out of the Spanish mould. Another good grower in the Penedés, Jean León, has planted Chardonnay and Cabernet Sauvignon grapes.

La Mancha

The area of La Mancha, on the high plateau south of Madrid, produces the largest quantity per hectare in Spain. The wines of Valdepeñas are pleasant table wines, especially the reds. Much of the wine produced in the La Mancha region is used for blending or for distilling into brandy.

Levante

To the east of the La Mancha plateau, extending to the coast from Valencia to Alicante, the vine competes with other types of fruit in this Mediterranean climate. The districts of Valencia, Utiel-Requeña, Cheste, Almansa, Alicante, Jumilla and Yecla all benefit from Denominaciónes de Origen, but are seldom exported as such. The wines, produced mainly from the Monastrel grape, are high in alcohol and cannot rival in quality those from Rioja and Penedés.

Northern Spain

From Navarre, between the Rioja Baja and the Pyrenees, comes some solid red wine from the Garnacho grape, and from around Pamplona some firm but lighter reds and rosés from the Cerasol and Secano varieties. The region of León produces full-bodied reds and *claretes* (rosés), which have much in common with the wines of northern Portugal, while in the north-west corner of the country, Galicia produces rough, young wines, slightly acidic, even *spritzig*, in the Portuguese Vinho Verde style.

Southern Spain

The best known wine is Montilla-Moriles, a Denominación de Origen from south of Córdoba, which produces white wines more akin to sherry than to table wines. The principal grape is the Pedro Ximénes, grown on the same chalky soil as is found in the region of Jerez de la Frontera.

Below *The wines of Montilla are fermented in earthenware* tinajas *and then matured in a* solera *like those of Jerez.*

Portugal

Portuguese wines, with the exception of port, are not as well known as wines from Spain. Although wines from Portugal are exported all over the world, some 45% of this quantity comprises a handful of internationally known brands of slightly sweet rosé that are certainly better recognized by their brand name than for their origin.

In contrast to Spain and France, where the majority of vines are planted on the plain, Portugal is mainly mountainous, and the vineyards relatively scattered and divided.

Fine wine production is concentrated in the north. The coastal lowland vineyards give way to the terraced vineyards of the Sierras. Here the soil is rocky and schistous, excellent for the vines, but very hard to work. The climate is damp with very hot, dry summers.

Portugal has a system of regional Denominaçãos do Origem, under the control of the Junta Nacional do Vinho in Lisbon. There are already seven demarcated areas: Entre Minho e Douro, Douro/Tras os Montes, Dão, Colares, Carcavelos, Bucelas and Setúbal/Palmela. From these areas come the following wines:

Dão

Dão wines are the finest in Portugal. Vines are planted on hillside terraces in granite soil. The grapes used are Tourigo, Tinta Pinheira (related to the Pinot Noir) and Alvarelhão for the red wine; Arinto, Dona Branca and Barcelos for the white. The latter are straw-coloured and should be drunk young. The red wines have a deep ruby colour from long maceration of very ripe grapes, and a velvety richness on the palate.

Below *Springtime in the vineyards of Utiel-Requeña, in the hills west of Valencia. The region produces good red wines from the Monastrel grape and also a light and fragrant rosé.*

Douro

The Douro is better known for its port than for its table wines. Nonetheless, the latter are produced in large quantity in this region situated to the north of Dão and to the west of the Minho. The wines from the heart of the valley are more alcoholic and lower in acidity than those from the borders of the Douro, which are fresher and livelier.

Colares

Colares, in the Sintra region on the Atlantic coast opposite Lisbon, is famous for its vines which are resistant to phylloxera, due to being planted on sand-dunes. Red wines are made from the Ramisco grape, white wines from the Malvasia. They are light, with a refreshing acidity; both improve with age.

Bucelas

Bucelas comes from the valley of the river Trancão, inland and to the north-west of Colares. Only white wine is made from the Arinto grape. It is light and crisp and has a high natural acidity.

Moscatel de Setúbal

Moscatel de Setúbal is a dessert wine made to the south of Lisbon.

Vinhos Verdes

These come from the north-west corner of Portugal, roughly between the Minho and the Douro rivers. Vines are trained high to provide shade for the bunches of grapes. The word *verde* signifies 'green' or young wines, low in alcohol, high in malic and tartaric acids, slightly *pétillant*. Three-quarters of the wine produced is red, the rest white. Both should be drunk young.

Vinhos Rosados

Portugal's *vinhos rosados* have no Denominação do Origem, although their methods of production are controlled. The colour comes from a short maceration of red grapes. They may be dry or sweet, still or sparkling, the most popular style being slightly sparkling and slightly sweet.

Wine Producing Regions/Austria, Switzerland & Luxembourg

Austria

Wine-growing in Austria is concentrated in the eastern part of the country, the majority of table wines coming from near the Czechoslovak and Hungarian borders, and from the south, close to the Jugoslav frontier. One of the finest wine-growing regions of the old Austrian Empire, Tyrol, is now mainly Italian. Four-fifths of the wine produced is white, most of the remainder being red, with small quantities of rosé and sparkling wines.

The principal grape is the Grüner Veltliner, a variety particular to Austria, resembling a rather less aromatic version of the French Traminer, followed by the Müller-Thurgau, Wälschriesling (Italian Riesling), Rhein Riesling, Gewürztraminer, local versions of Pinot Blanc and Pinot Gris, a little Muscat Ottonel and the indigenous Rotgipfer. Red and rosé wines, almost all locally consumed, come from the Blauburgunder (Pinot Noir), Blauer Portugieser (Merlot) and Gamay.

Vines are planted in four main regions:

Lower Austria, in the north-east, is the most prolific, producing the country's finest white wines from the Rhein Riesling and the dominant Grüner Veltliner, as well as the charming and fruity Gumpoldskirchen from just south of Vienna.

Burgenland, in the south-east, produces some very fine dessert wine from botrytized grapes, and the only good Austrian red wines from the Eisenberg region.

Styria, on the Jugoslav border, produces attractive white wines from the Wälschriesling and the Müller-Thurgau, but in much smaller quantities than the other regions.

Vienna, the capital, would probably be merged with Lower Austria as a wine region were it not for the custom of serving *heurige*, the just fermented wine of the new vintage, direct from the grower's cellars or in the local Weinstuben.

With the exception of the dessert wines, white wines from Austria are generally drier than their counterparts from Germany.

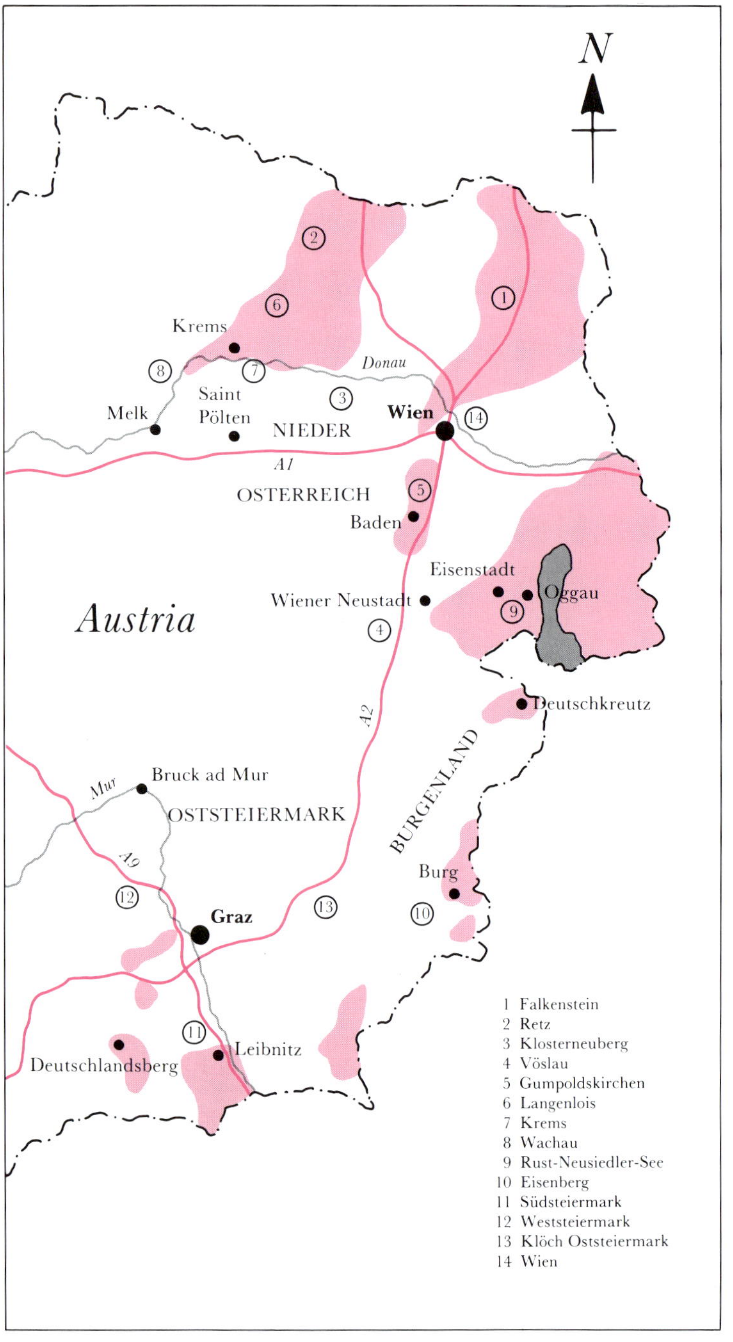

Switzerland

Switzerland, being part French, part German and part Italian, can be expected, as a wine-producing nation, to exhibit characteristics from each of these countries. Vines are planted principally on the foothills of the Alps, around Lakes Geneva and Neuchâtel, along the valley of the upper Rhône and in the canton of Ticino. French, German and Italian grapes, as well as many local varieties, produce over 200 different wines, two-thirds of them white. Most of the production is consumed domestically. Although there are no really great wines produced in Switzerland, the diversity of vines and the dedication of the growers are reflected in a wide range of

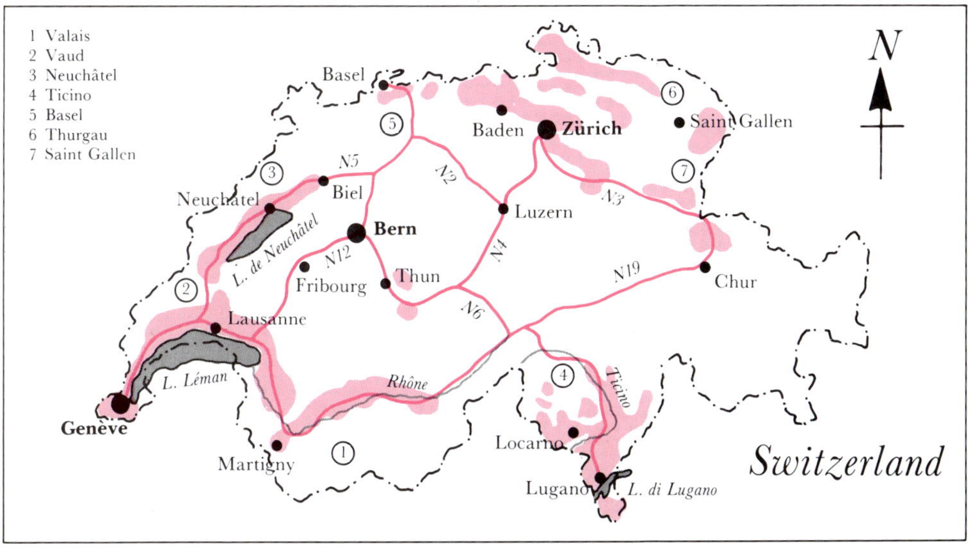

deliciously fruity wines of fine overall quality. The major wine-producing cantons are Valais, Vaud, Neuchâtel and Ticino.

Valais This is the most important canton for quality, producing Switzerland's best red wine, Dôle, made from the Pinot Noir or the Gamay, either separately or blended. Dôle has a rich ruby colour, some of the bouquet of a Burgundy and the body of a Côtes-du-Rhône. The dominant white wine is Fendant, made from the Chasselas grape; light and fruity, with low acidity, it should be drunk young and fresh. Other wines of note are Riesling, Johannisberg, Hermitage, the sweet Malvoisie and the very rare Glacier.

Vaud The leading canton for quantity, Vaud produces mainly white wines from the Chasselas. The principal vineyard areas are La Côte, on the northern slopes of Lake Geneva between Nyon and Lausanne, and Lavaux, from Lausanne east to Vevey, where the Dézaley wine combines body with finesse and distinction. From the Chablais region, farther east, come the firm, flinty whites of Yvorne and Aigle.

Neuchâtel From the north-west of Switzerland, along the northern side of Lake Neuchâtel, close to France, the Neuchâtel white wines are crisp and dry, yet although they are made from the Chasselas, they can be rather acid in poor years. These wines are often bottled *sur lie*, and also produced refreshingly *pétillant*. Some fine, light red wine is made from the Pinot Noir.

Italian- and German-speaking Switzerland Ticino, the Italian-speaking canton, produces mainly red *vins de table* from around Lugano and Locarno, the best coming from the Merlot grape. From the German part of Switzerland around Baden come some pleasantly fruity red wines from the Blauburgunder (Pinot Noir) and some everyday whites, mainly from the Müller-Thurgau.

Luxembourg

The wines of Luxembourg are of interest since they are produced along the river Moselle, as it winds its way from France into Germany, where, as the Mosel, it gives its name to some of the world's finest wines. In Luxembourg, as in Alsace, the type of wine is designated by the grape variety. The dominant local grape is the Ebling, which produces light, refreshingly crisp wines, while the Riesling-Sylvaner (Müller-Thurgau, known in Luxembourg as the Rivaner), is heavily planted. Other wines are made from the Pinot Blanc, the softer Auxerrois, the fruity Ruländer or Pinot Gris, the aromatic Traminer and the aristocratic Riesling. Almost all the total production is white, a little of which is made into sparkling wine.

Although Luxembourg wines tend to be overshadowed by those from Alsace and the Mosel, overall quality is high. An internal system of control awards the *appellation* 'Marque Nationale' to wines that have passed a rigorous series of quality controls and tastings. More than half the production comes into this category. Nearly three-quarters of all Luxembourg wine is consumed domestically.

Wine Producing Regions/California 1

The wines of California have made their presence felt on the international wine scene with such extraordinary suddenness that one would be forgiven for imagining that they are a very recent invention. In fact they have a history stretching back over 200 years.

As in many countries, it was the religious orders who first planted vines and made wine. In 1769 the Spanish Franciscans established the first mission in what is now San Diego. During the next 50 years 21 missions were created throughout California, stretching as far north as Sonoma. At each one vineyards were planted and wine produced for the benefit of the travellers who sought shelter for the night. In 1861, a Hungarian nobleman, Agoston Haraszthy, launched an expedition to Europe to bring back cuttings of *Vitis vinifera*. He gathered together over 100,000 different examples. Upon these the vineyards of California are founded.

Many of the famous names of California – Joseph Schram of Schramsberg, Georges de Latour of Beaulieu and Gustave Niebaum of Inglenook, to name but three – planted their first vines in the latter half of the 19th century and founded wineries which flourish to this day. However, their efforts suffered two serious setbacks; one a natural calamity and the other man-made.

As in Europe, *Vitis vinifera*'s worst enemy, phylloxera, attacked and virtually destroyed vineyards in and around the Napa Valley. Fortunately, it had already been discovered that the native American *Vitis labrusca* root stocks were resistant to the disease. The *Vitis vinifera* was thus grafted onto these roots and the vines were able to recover.

A much more serious setback was the passing of the Eighteenth Amendment to the Constitution prohibiting the sale of alcohol. Between 1919 and 1932 the wine industry came almost to a halt. Vineyards were uprooted or abandoned.

Below *Dry Creek Vineyard winery, Healdsburg, Sonoma County, California; founded in 1972 by David Stare, it now produces 80,000 cases a year.*

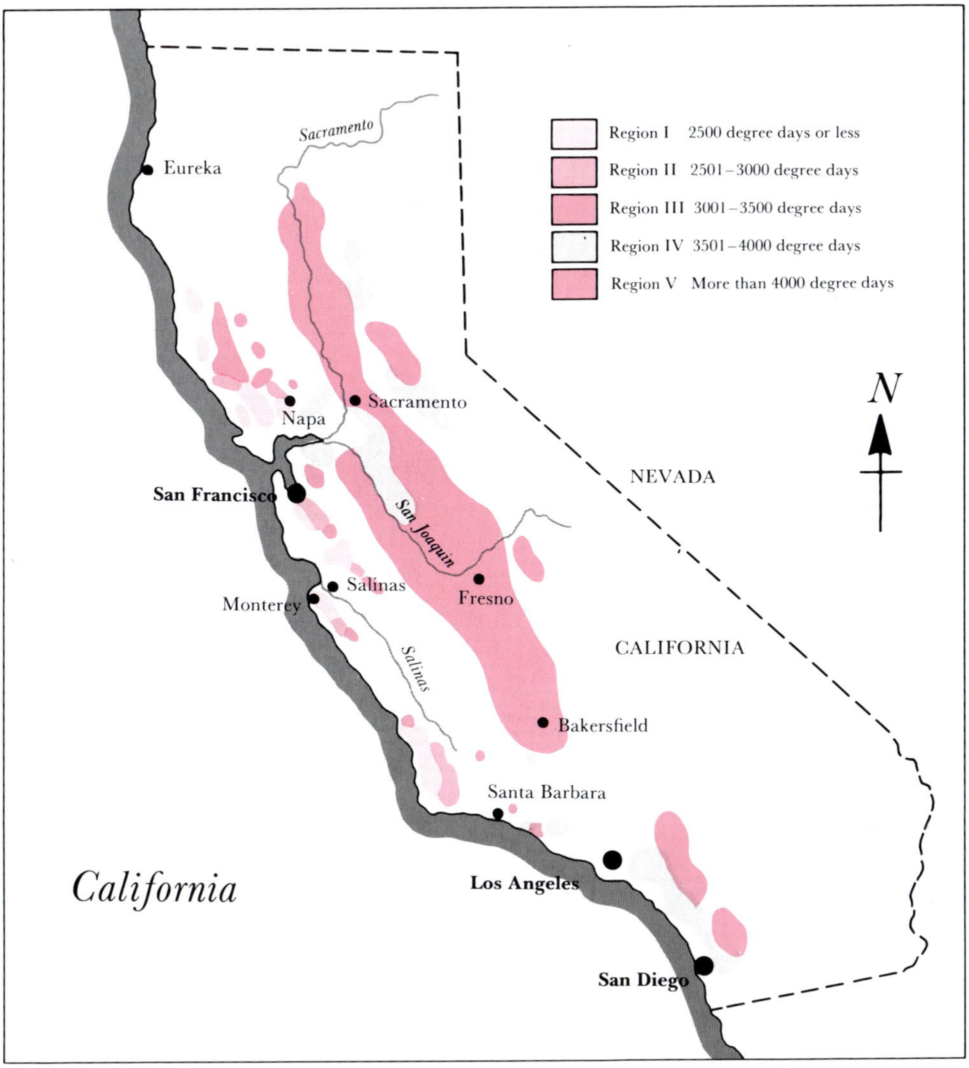

The American public lost the taste for wine and turned to making their own brews from low-quality grapes, or to patronizing whisky bootleggers. After the repeal of Prohibition, save for the religious orders who had been allowed to continue to make wine for sacramental purposes, few wineries were in a position to take up where they had left off. Stocks of mature wines were tiny and the cocktail craze spread through the country. World War II made life difficult for producer and consumer alike, so it was not until the late 1940s and early 1950s that California wine production was restarted.

Very slowly the American wine drinker began to demand both quantity and quality, and the modern era of production was established. In the early 1960s wineries such as Heitz and Ridge made their first wines and in 1966 Robert Mondavi broke away from the family-owned Charles Krug winery to found his now-famous winery in the Napa Valley. California wine had at last come of age and was on its way to making the state one of the most important and certainly the most exciting wine region in the world.

Wine Producing Regions/California 2

Above *Quantity vine growing for an ever-expanding American market.*

Current trends

The decade of the 1980s saw many important changes in the California wine industry. Some well-known names disappeared while others changed wine makers or on occasion ownership. Foreign investors from Europe and Japan eagerly paid millions of dollars for wineries with any sort of a track record.

Styles of wine changed too. The big, highly oaked, over alcoholic Chardonnays and Cabernets became few and far between. Instead we saw much leaner, higher acid wines known in some quarters as 'food wines'. These were wines where the emphasis was put on balance and elegance, sometimes it must be admitted to the detriment of flavour and character. Wine coolers, a blend of cheap white wine and fruit juice took America by storm, only to disappear almost without trace by the end of the decade.

Perhaps the most interesting new wine to

Far right *Barrel cleaning at a Californian winery.*

Above *Repairing barrels.*

come out of California during this period has been the white Zinfandel, a light rosé wine, slightly sweet, made from the once unloved red Zinfandel grape. This cheap summer wine gave the drinker a beverage which was pretty to look at and easy to drink. Its popularity shows signs of waning as we enter the 1990s but hopes are still high for this remarkable wine which made certain grape growers and wineries rich.

So what will the 1990s bring to California? Short harvests at the end of the previous decade have meant an overall shortage of grapes, particularly of Cabernet Sauvignon. This, together with a dollar which has weakened somewhat from past highs thus keeping imports off the bottom of the price scale, means prices will remain firm. This of course fits in with the domestic market which while not drinking more wine is all the time trading upwards in price. The American consumer has become accustomed to searching out top-quality wines and paying high prices for them.

Styles of wines continue to change. While the varietal labelled wine is still pre-eminent there is a movement towards blended wines of high quality, something the Europeans have been doing of course for hundreds of years. Such is the Californians' enthusiasm for these new wines, they have invented a name for them, 'Meritage'.

Different grapes to the traditional California varietals are beginning to appear up and down the State. Cabernet Franc, Syrah, Grenache, Mourvèdre for example in red and Viognier and Marsanne in white.

Like all things seemingly in California, the wine scene presents a constantly changing pattern. There is no sign that after four decades of modern wine making that California is sitting on its laurels.

Wine Producing Regions/California 3

Wine and wine making

The two most important pieces of information on a California wine label are the name of the predominant grape variety, if there is one, and who made it. If the wine is a blend of several varieties it will normally have a brand name, as, for example, Premium White or Valley Red. If it is made with 75% or more from one grape variety it will normally be called by that name. We shall examine the most common grape varieties, starting with the white ones and then moving on to the red.

One of the problems of writing about California wine is that within a few months the scene can change dramatically. A wine maker can leave, a winery acquire new owners, a hitherto unplanted region become a serious vineyard. New wineries appear with mind-boggling rapidity while the sudden influence of European investment is already being felt. The decade of the 1970s was a heady time to be in California wine but the 1980s will show just how far the Golden State can prove itself to the world.

The range of wines, the producers, the grape varieties, grow daily more confusing. The following are currently some of the best Californian wines:

Chardonnay
Acacia, Chalone, Edna Valley, Matanzas Creek, Robert Mondavi, Sonoma-Cutrer, Stony Hill, Trefethen.
Sauvignon Blanc (Fumé Blanc)
Dry Creek, Matanzas Creek, Robert Mondavi.
Riesling and Gewürztraminer
Firestone, Joseph Phelps, Mark West, Château St Jean.
Cabernet Sauvignon
Beaulieu Georges de Latour, Carmenet, Dominus, Heitz, Iron Horse, Robert Mondavi, Opus One, Joseph Phelps, Ridge, Stag's Leap.
Zinfandel
Lytton Springs, Ridge.
Pinot Noir
Acacia, Au Bon Climat, Calera, Chalone, Robert Mondavi, Sanford, Saintsbury.
Merlot
Clos du Bois, Duckhorn, Firestone.
Sparkling Wines
Iron Horse, Schramsberg.

Inevitably the list is incomplete. The joy of California wine is to experiment with it. To any wine drinker, rich, poor, novice or expert, California offers a plethora of fascinating experience.

The climatic regions

California is made up of a multitude of microclimates. Whereas in Europe great importance is paid to soils, subsoils and their variations within a very small area, in California more attention is given to the climate. The University of California at Davis has divided up the state into five climatic regions. The system is based upon the concept of 'degree days'. These are calculated between April 1 and October 31. One 'degree day' is if the average temperature over a period of 24 hours is one degree over 50°F. Therefore, if the average temperature is for example 70°F, 20 degree days are recorded. 50°F is taken as the starting temperature as below this no plant will grow satisfactorily.

Region 1
0–2500 degree days. The Rhine, Mosel and Champagne regions would fall into this category.
Region 2
2501–3000 degree days. This would be similar to Bordeaux.
Region 3
3001–3500 degree days. This would be similar to northern Italy and the Rhône Valley.
Region 4
3501–4000 degree days. This would be similar to central Spain.
Region 5
In excess of 4001 degree days. This would be similar to North Africa.

Far right *Trefethen vineyard, Napa Valley, one of California's most important producers of Chardonnay wines.*

The Grapes of California/Red

Alicante Bouschet A grape much loved by home wine makers for its colour and robustness. Now fallen out of fashion for most serious producers, there are still a few examples to be found. Big, heavy and usually high in alcohol on its own, it is also used in the blending of port-style wines.

Barbera Wine makers of Italian origin retain a fondness for this grape. At its best it can make a wine of rich depth and mellow fruitiness, but generally fails to rise to any great heights.

Cabernet Sauvignon The king of red wine grapes and a resounding success in California. The wines produced have been comparable to the great Bordeaux. Any wine maker wanting to make a name for himself will try to produce the finest Cabernet. Deep in colour and flavour, the wines are drinkable earlier than those made in Europe but there is nothing to suggest they will not last.

Cabernet Franc Very rarely found as a wine on its own, it is normally used as a blending grape with Cabernet Sauvignon.

Carignane One of the most widely planted red grapes, it is used mostly as a blending grape. A few examples of it as a simple variety are made but with no marked success.

Gamay or Napa Gamay The true grape of the Beaujolais, in California the wines seem to lack the freshness and 'gulpability' of their French cousins. Also used to make rosé.

Gamay Beaujolais Confusingly, nothing to do with the Beaujolais grape, but in fact a member of the Pinot Noir family. Somewhat reminiscent of a southern Burgundy, the wines often lack interest but are useful for picnics or barbecues.

Grenache Over 12,000 acres of this grape are planted though most of it goes towards the making of a rosé wine. Bonny Doon in Monterey are doing the best with it as full-bodied spicy red wine.

Grignolino Joe Heitz personally waves the banner for this variety. He makes an interesting spicy red wine from it and a rather more successful rosé

Merlot Some 4000 acres of this grape are planted. It is still primarily used as a blending grape, usually with Cabernet Sauvignon, although it can produce a delicious wine in its own right.

Petite Sirah Now established as the same as the Duriff grape of France, it produces dry red wines of robustness, depth and flavour. No great breeding or elegance are discernible, but the wines are honest and drinkable.

Pinot Noir More progress has been made with this grape than any other in California as wine makers have learnt where to plant it and how to handle it. Some superb examples can now be found along with a number of very ordinary ones. It is also widely used in sparkling wine production.

Ruby Cabernet A cross between Cabernet Sauvignon and Carignane, it is a high-class blending grape, which has proved most successful. Occasionally found on its own, it makes a drinkable low-priced wine of good colour, bouquet and flavour.

Syrah The true varietal of the Rhône Valley and not to be confused with Petite Sirah. Although there are under 200 acres planted, several small producers such as Joseph Phelps and Bonny Doon are doing interesting things with it.

Zinfandel Although often thought of as California's own unique grape, it did in fact come from Europe like most of the others. It is probably closely related to Italy's Primitivo grape. The old fashioned way of making a big heavy wine out of Zinfandel is dying out though a few producers loyally stick to it. Most Zinfandel now goes into making a 'blush' wine called White Zinfandel.

Some famous wineries make excellent medium-bodied wines which are similar in style to Cabernet Sauvignon but cost rather less. It is California's most widely planted red grape with over 30,000 acres.

Wine Producing Regions/California 4

The Napa Valley

The Napa Valley is to California what the Médoc is to Bordeaux. Quite simply, it is the best known and most prestigious wine-making region in California.

Running north-west for about 34 miles, its width varies between 1 and 5 miles. Flanked on either side by mountains, it lies about 50 miles north-east of San Francisco at its most southerly tip. The soil varies in composition but is mostly volcanic in origin.

The climate of the valley also varies and regions 1, 2 and 3 are all registered. The parts farthest away from San Francisco tend to be the hottest, while the southerly parts remain cooler, fanned as they are by the bay breezes. Almost every grape is to be found in the Napa Valley and most do well. In particular, Cabernet Sauvignon and Chardonnay stand out and many of the great Cabernets come from the Napa. Names like Robert Mondavi, Heitz, Mayacamas are among the many famous wineries that make up the 200 or so Napa producers.

Napa wines are invariably good though the area is now too famous to offer many bargains.

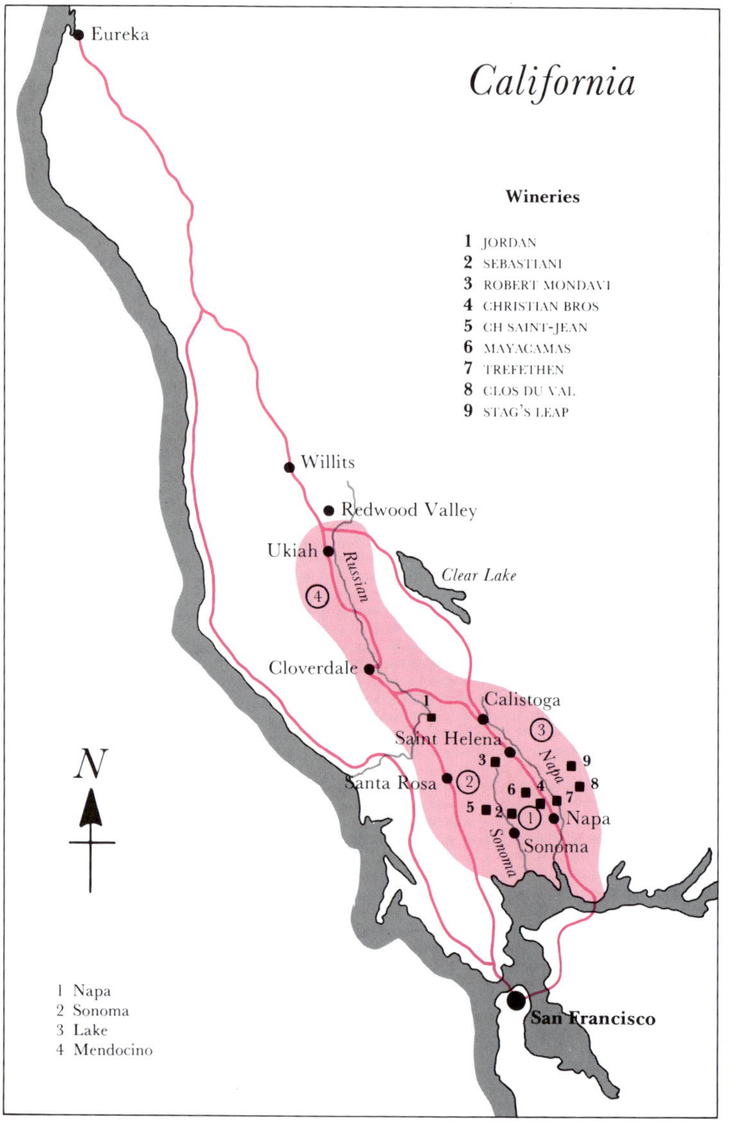

Sonoma County

Lying to the west and slightly to the south of the Napa Valley, Sonoma County is made up of three distinct valleys. These are Sonoma, Alexander and Dry Creek. A large array of microclimates means that regions 1, 2 and 3 are registered all over the county. Fog forms an important part of Sonoma's climatic conditions. It rolls off the Bay in the early morning and does not shift until mid-day at the earliest. This maintains a coolness even at the height of summer.

Soils range from clay loam to sandy brown and most are well drained and thus suitable as vineyards. Long felt to be in the shadow of the Napa, Sonoma is now establishing itself as a genuine alternative. Some of the better known wineries include Château St Jean, Jordan and Sebastiani.

Mendocino County

This is the most northern grape-growing area of California and until the late 1960s was not highly regarded for fine wine. During the 1970s a number of premium wineries began to produce wines of quality, even if not perhaps up to Napa or Sonoma standards.

There are three main parts of Mendocino County. The most important, and the largest, is the Ukiah Valley. Ukiah is a charming old town with an atmosphere of the wild west.

The valley is region 3 and such well-known producers as Parducci and Cresta Blanca can be found there.

Another part of Mendocino, also a region 3, is the Redwood Valley. Here the Fetzer Winery dominates the area and produces a wide range of wines of a very acceptable quality. Lastly, there is the least known part called the Anderson Valley. Perhaps the two most interesting wineries are Husch and Edmeades. Thanks to the cool climate (region 1) the area is rapidly getting a reputation for quality sparkling wines.

The Grapes of California/White

Chardonnay Undoubtedly the greatest success of them all. California Chardonnays are nearly always a delight to drink and the best will age well. Like their European cousins, particularly in Burgundy, the best ones are aged in wood to make a rich buttery wine with a lovely golden colour. However, unlike in France, most Chardonnays do not undergo malolactic fermentation, though barrel fermentation, which if anything is on the decrease in Burgundy, is again becoming popular. There are few modern wineries which do not produce Chardonnay. The less expensive ones are usually unwooded, light and fresh, with an apple flavour and green-gold colour. The better ones are perfectly balanced with a rich oaky flavour which does not dominate the fruit. There are over 40,000 acres planted with this adaptable grape and while California produces some of the best and most expensive Chardonnays in the world it is also now offering the consumer some excellent wines in the mid-price category.

Sauvignon Blanc Also known as Fumé Blanc, this grape variety is used to make a wine of many different styles in California. When blended with Sémillon and aged in oak, it can be a wonderfully rich wine with an elegant and appealingly complex style. On its own it makes a less subtle wine but deliciously fresh and best drunk young. California Sauvignons are quite different from those of the Loire and tend to be made akin to a white Bordeaux. Robert Mondavi, the most famous producer of Fumé Blanc, is now making small quantities of a sweet botrytis Sauvignon. About 14,000 acres of Sauvignon Blanc are planted in California.

Chenin Blanc In 1971 less than 9,000 acres of this grape were planted. Now there are almost 40,000. This is as a result of the great swing towards white wine. Chenin Blanc is a good yielder and can produce a reasonably priced wine with some style and complexity to it. Very often some residual sugar is left in the wine to give more character, and there are few which could be described as dry. Chenin is also used as a blending grape.

Pinot Blanc Although not widely planted, it is responsible for some excellent wines, mainly from the Monterey area. Not a prolific yielder, it is usually fermented dry and when aged in wood can make a wine similar in style to Chardonnay.

White Riesling While this is the correct name, it is widely known in California as Johannisberg Riesling in honour of the famous Schloss Johannisberg of Germany. This traditionally cool-climate grape has adapted in a remarkable way to the warm climate of California. The wines are full, fruity and complex, and quite delicious. They are different from their German counterparts in that they lack the subtlety of a Rheingau, but are mouth-filling and luscious. Dessert-style Rieslings which have been affected by botrytis are among the great sweet wines of the world. Rare as they are, they should be sought out and enjoyed.

Gewürztraminer The traditional spiciness of this grape is less apparent in California versions than, for example, in Alsace. Completely dry Gewürztraminers can be found in California but very often wine makers leave in a touch of residual sugar to give added character to the wine. Some 3000 acres of this early-ripening grape are planted. The wine is best drunk when young and fresh.

French Colombard Something approaching 60,000 acres of this grape are planted in California. It is at its best as a blending grape where its crisp acidity and floral bouquet enhance some of the lesser grapes. On its own it makes a pleasant enough quaffing wine but without any great distinction. It is a high yielder at between 8 to 12 tonnes per acre.

Sémillon Not often seen as a variety on its own, it is widely used to blend with Sauvignon Blanc. In Monterey and Santa Ynez it makes a dry wine of some interest. Sweet versions have so far shown no great distinction.

Emerald Riesling This is one of the better named *vinifera* hybrids produced by U. C. Davis. A cross between White Riesling and Muscadelle, it produces an off-dry wine which is crisp and fruity. Best drunk young and without too much scrutiny. Paul Masson produce a deservedly popular version.

Gray Riesling Known as Chauché Gris in France, it makes a pleasing quaffing wine of no great seriousness. The best examples come from the Livermore Valley.

Wine Producing Regions/California 5

The Central Coast

This is the name of a large area south of San Francisco embracing a number of small regions which are fighting to gain individual recognition. The wineries in these areas generally feel that the term 'Central Coast' denotes the hot central mass of California, not a place from which premium wines come. The region as a whole is very similar climatically to the north coast of California and can, in fact, even be cooler. Some very fine wines come from this area and it is worth a quick examination of the individual regions.

The Livermore Valley, region 3, has been producing grapes for more than 100 years. Its most famous winery, Wente Brothers, was founded in 1883. The white wines deserve particular attention though the reds, too, show signs of promise. The valley's soil is gravelly and well drained and is said to resemble that of the Graves in Bordeaux.

Santa Clara County has been a casualty of urban development. Before World War II there were approximately 60 wineries in this area but they have steadily been forced south by ever encroaching 'civilization'. However, several famous names remain – Almaden and San Martin are two of the largest, while Martin Ray and Mount Eden are smaller but even finer.

The Santa Cruz Mountains is a region which is busily trying to establish itself. In terms of area – only about 250 acres and a mere 100,000 cases produced – it might be thought insignificant. However, the quality of the wineries is very special. Ridge Vineyards, one of the finest producers in California is there, as are the David Bruce Winery, Felton-Empire Vineyards and Bonny Doon Vineyard, three producers well worth seeking out. The region and its wines maintain a strong identity.

Monterey County may well be the most important part of the Central Coast. It is certainly a most beautiful part of California. The county is the home of the huge Paul Masson winery and of the tiny and remote Chalone Vineyards. Two more opposite producers, in terms of output, could hardly be imagined. Other wineries worth noting are Jekel Vineyards, Mirassou, the Monterey Vineyard and Ventana.

San Louis Obispo County, perhaps the most interesting developments are happening in Edna Valley. The Edna Valley Vineyards lead the way with some wonderful

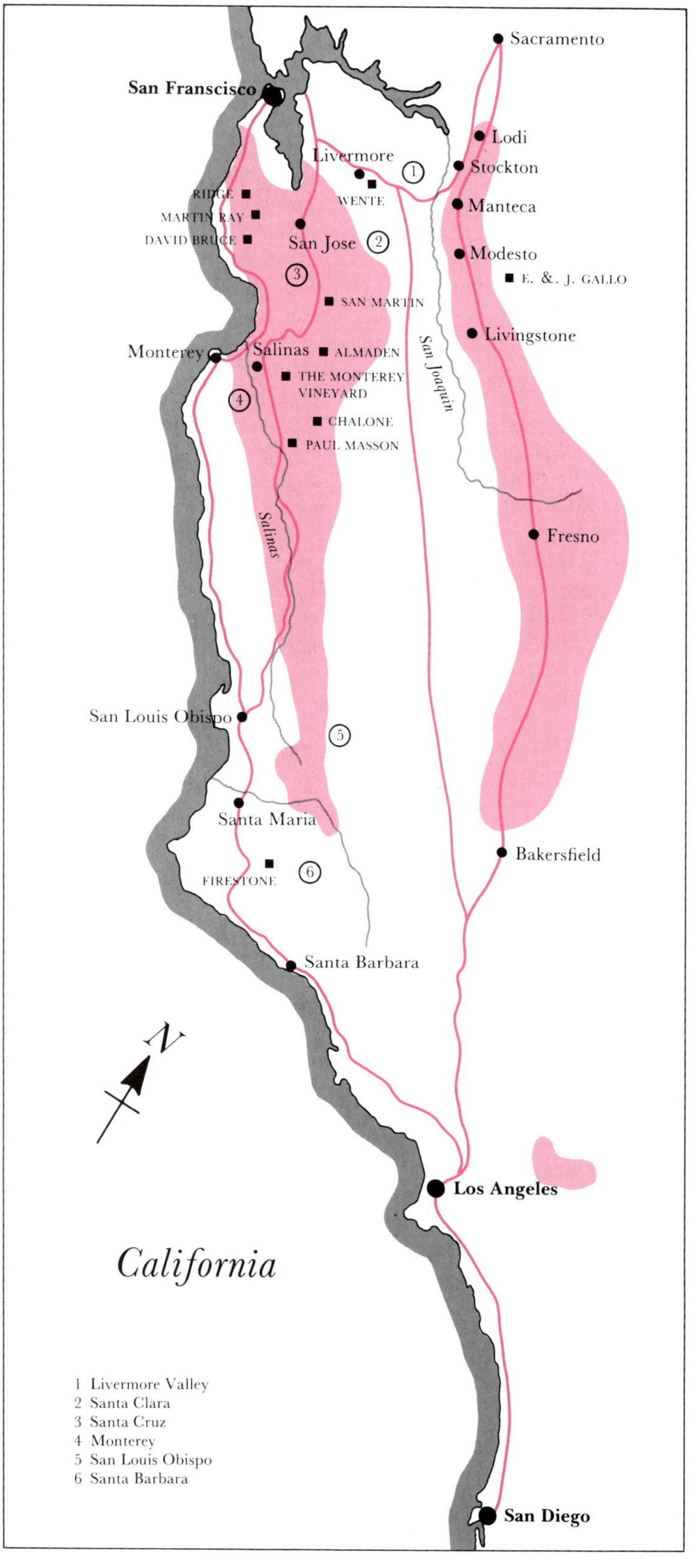

Chardonnays. Other new wineries are beginning to appear and this is clearly an area to watch. The champagne house of Deutz has bought land here.

Santa Barbara County is the most southerly part of the Central Coast and one of the coolest. It is a region 1, which perhaps explains why Pinot Noir and Riesling seem to do particularly well here. The Firestone Vineyard dominates the area and is making better and better wines, particularly Cabernet Sauvignon and Merlot. Smaller wineries such as Sanford and J. Carey are making some outstanding wines. All the signs are promising for this region.

The San Joaquin Valley

This is the home of the mass producers. In an area some 300 miles in length, stretching from Sacramento to south of Bakersfield, there are a mere 40 wineries; but from these comes almost 80% of California's wine.

More than half the state's grapes are grown here and the climate ranges from region 3 to about region 5 around Bakersfield.

The most famous producer and probably the largest in the world is the E. & J. Gallo Winery. Here is the great American dream come true: two brothers who, after Prohibition and with limited knowledge about wine, set themselves up as wine makers. They brought to the American consumer wines at irresistibly low prices. In terms of range and quality they have been successful at almost every level. Their production is approaching 60 million cases of wine a year; almost all of it is extremely drinkable and offers excellent value for money.

North of San Diego is the San Pasqual Valley containing three wineries. The most interesting is San Pasqual. Their Chenin Blanc and Fumé Blanc are respectable, while their Gamay is above the average California version.

The southernmost end of California is not the ideal place for grape-growing, as in general the climate is too hot. However, the wineries which have discovered the cooler microclimates are worth noting.

South of Los Angeles

In 1769, a Bordelais by the appropriate name of Jean Louis Vignes planted a vineyard on what is now the Los Angeles main rail station. For a century this part of California remained the most important grape-growing region and it was not until towards the end of the 19th century that Northern California took over as the dominant wine-making area.

Today pollution and urbanization have all but put an end to wine production in Los Angeles County. The one remaining winery, San Antonio, has been designated as a Cultural Historical Monument.

Farther south near Temecula a rash of wineries has appeared taking advantage of the cool sea breezes. Foremost among these is the Callaway Vineyard now owned by the giant Allied group. They produce only white wines with their dryish Chenin Blanc being the best and their botrytized Chenin Blanc called 'Sweet Nancy' being the best known. They also have an excellent Chardonnay called 'Callalees'. Other wineries in this up and coming area include the sparkling wine producer, John Culbertson.

Above *Massive investment has been made in modern plant for the Californian vineyards: here, a steel vat is undergoing cleaning.*

Wine Producing Regions/Rest of United States

The Pacific North-West

The mounting challenge of Oregon and Washington State, the vast land mass running north of California up to the Canadian border, for the title of America's premier wine producing state has been gaining ground recently. However, there is no doubt that California still enjoys a comfortable lead. That is not to say that the Pacific North-West is not producing some very fine wines for it is. The fact is that at the moment it lacks the consistency of California.

Oregon

Oregon has proclaimed itself, with some justification, to be the Pinot Noir capital of America. Certainly Pinot Noir is the most successful varietal currently produced. Wineries such as Amity, Eyrie, Ponzi and Adelsheim have all made some excellent wines. However, Pinot Noir is as difficult to make here as anywhere else and there are still far too many mediocre ones being made by wine makers who are merely experimenting at the expense of the consumer.

Chardonnay is successful, though too often the wines have been clumsily made without the finesse or elegance that is found in the best of California. Eyrie, Ponzi and Tualatin are some of the best producers.

Oregon's grape growing history goes back to the 19th century, though Prohibition put an end to wine production until the 1960s. Most of the best known wineries are situated in the Willamette Valley area south-west of Portland. Here the climate is cool and grapes achieve the naturally high acidity which is often missing in California wines. This climate is of course particularly suited to the growing of grapes for sparkling wines and it may well be in this direction that Oregon's future lies. Some famous names such as Laurent Perrier and Brian Croser from Australia have bought land in the Dundee area with a view to making high-quality sparkling wine.

Of all the states outside California, Oregon shows the most potential. Now that more top-quality wine makers are coming into the area, that potential may be realised before very long.

Washington State

The first *vinifera* grapes were planted in 1950 in a part of eastern Washington called the Yakima Valley. This valley is 120 miles long and runs eastwards along the Yakima River.

Many of the best producers are to be found in this area and in particular Château St Michelle, the largest and best known winery in Washington State.

Château Ste Michelle made its reputation from the high quality of its white wines but is also now producing some fine Merlots and Cabernets which show well against similar varietals from California. There is a second label called Colombia Crest which offers sound wines at reasonable prices.

Other wineries that merit attention include the Associated Vintners operation where an English Master of Wine, David Lake, continues to make a selection of fine wines such as Chardonnay, Sauvignon Blanc, and Sémillon in white and Cabernet in red. One of the best smaller wineries is Arbor Crest, situated near the Spokane River in north-east Washington. Chardon-

Above *High technology: new steel vats in a New York State winery.*

nay and Fumé Blanc are particularly successful here.

New York State

The quality of wines from this area have changed beyond all recognition in the last few years and are now some of the most exciting in America. There are more wineries here than in any other state apart from California and Oregon, and they are even doing well with red as well as white wines.

There are two main viticultural areas where most of the wineries are situated, the Finger Lakes region and Long Island.

Wine making around the Finger Lakes can be traced back to the 1820s but recently has been particularly noted for its sparkling wines. The climate is cool, often to extreme, so provides a good location for sparkling wine producers and one of the best known names, Great Western, is situated here.

Some good still wines are now also being made in this area. Wagner Vineyards make a full buttery Chardonnay which is regarded as one of the top Chardonnays in America. Other good producers include Glenora and Hermann J. Wiemer.

Long Island is a very recent arrival on the New York State wine scene and until the late 1970s there was only one serious estate making wine. Now Hargrave Vineyards have been joined by other wineries such as Pindar, Bridgehampton, Lenz and Bidwell. Hargrave are still making the best wine in the state including one of the few really good Cabernets. And as Long Island is on a similar latitude to Bordeaux, with gravelly well-drained soil and temperatures lower than the West Coast, there is every reason to be optimistic for the future.

The Rest of the United States

Alaska is probably the only American state not claiming to have a winery within its borders, but knowing the ingenuity of the Americans this last bastion will fall before long. However few of the remaining states really warrant attention except perhaps for reasons of curiosity.

The best of the rest are certainly Idaho with its Ste Chapelle Winery, and Texas with the Pleasant Ridge Winery and the Llano Winery.

Of the other states, Connecticut, Maryland, Massachusetts, Missouri, New Jersey, Ohio, Pennsylvania, Rhode Island and Virginia all produce wines of varying quality.

Wine Producing Regions/Australia & New Zealand

Australia has been a wine-making country for more than 150 years and is now recognized as the most important producer in the Southern Hemisphere.

In the 19th century much of the wine made was of the fortified variety. Hefty 'ports' and 'sherries' found favour not only with the immigrant population but also with the people of Victorian England who were naturally well disposed towards a product of the Empire. Australia had an export boom.

It was the early settlers, although they were principally farmers, who established the first vineyards. The British settled north of Sydney and planted grapes in the rich soil of the Hunter Valley, while it was left to the Germans to populate the Barossa Valley just outside Adelaide.

Since that time these two valleys have been the backbone of the Australian wine industry. The Hunter Valley is famous for its big earthy red wines made from the Shiraz grape, known also as Syrah or Hermitage. These wines have a distinctive 'barn-yard' bouquet to them and the best benefit enormously from bottle maturation.

Traditionally the Sémillon grape was planted in the Hunter Valley and made a wine unique in the world. Dry and crisply refreshing when very young, and the ideal accompaniment to Sydney's delicious rock oysters, it then closes up in mid-life only to develop after eight or nine years into a quite extraordinarily flavourful wine. More recently however the ever fashionable Chardonnay has been widely planted and has produced some really wonderful wines in a style and at a price which have made Australia famous. Rich and buttery, these Chardonnays are made on the whole to drink young. Rosemount, the Rothbury Estate and Lindemans are among the best known producers. Other grapes are found in the Hunter Valley but do not achieve very high quality.

The Barossa Valley in South Australia is where many of the large producers are to be found. As well as Shiraz, some very fine Cabernet Sauvignons are made, or sometimes a blend of the two. Chardonnay and Rhine Riesling account for most of the white wine production. Penfold's, Orlando, Yalumba and Wolf Blass are some of the best known and most highly rated larger producers. Other areas of South Australia to note include Coonawarra famous for its 'terra rossa' and the Adelaide Hills area made famous by the top-quality producer, Petaluma, now partly owned by the champagne house of Bollinger.

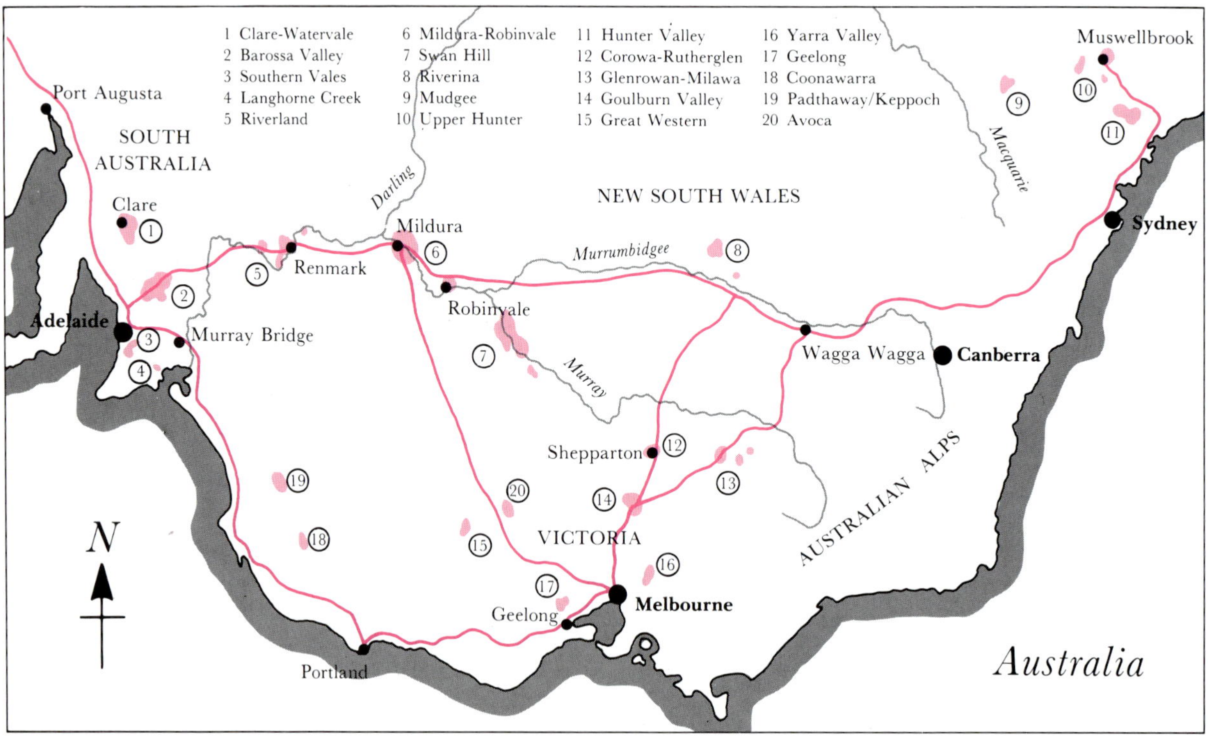

Victoria also has some high-quality producers, notably Brown Brothers in Milawa and Château Tahbilk in Central Victoria. Nearer the coast in the Geelong area are two small wineries with great potential for making very fine wines and in particular Chardonnay and Pinot Noir, Bannockburn and Anakie.

One of the coolest parts of Victoria is the Yarra Valley which has a climate more akin to the classic regions of France. Lilydale, Yarra Yering and Coldstream Hills are making great wines here although in small quantities.

Over in Western Australia things move almost as fast as they do in California. New wineries emerge and new vineyards are planted, all with the result that we are seeing a rash of new and exciting wines, albeit at high prices. Swan Valley and the Margaret River area are where it's all happening. Wineries such as Houghton and Evans and Tate in Swan Valley, and Leeuwin Estate, Vasse Felix and Cullens in the Margaret River have made this hitherto unknown part of Australia world famous.

There are of course pockets of wine production in other parts of Australia – there are even vineyards around Alice Springs, one of the hottest parts of the country – including the cool island of Tasmania.

There are now around 550 wineries in Australia and very few poor wines being made. However, unlike other parts of the world a very large part of the production is in the hands of a relatively few wineries. At the last count 43 wineries accounted for 93% of Australia's wine production. But although exports have more than doubled in recent years they only account for 11% of output. Over half of the wine produced remains in cask and flagon, ie the low end of the market.

Australia's bursting onto the world wine scene was probably the most exciting thing to happen to the international market in the latter half of the 1980s. The potential remains enormous as new areas are planted and modern wine making is put to its best use. This has not meant however that traditional Australian styles such as liqueur muscats or Hunter Sémillons have been forgotten but merely that grapes such as Chardonnay and Pinot Noir have been introduced. Sparkling wines are now being made to rival the world's best.

Australian wines have come to represent all that's best in the wine world, quality, enterprise and value for money.

New Zealand

Even by the standards of the New World, the history of serious wine-making in New Zealand is very short. For although the records show that grapes were planted in 1819 by the Reverend Samuel Marsden at Keri Keri, and that wine was first made in 1840 by James Busby (the father of the country's wine industry), real wine production was not started until the early 1970s.

In 1974 the vineyard area was increased by 75%, mainly around Blenheim at the north end of South Island and near Gisborne in the western part of North Island. Müller-Thurgau is the most widely planted white grape though there are increasing amounts of Chardonnay, Pinot Gris, Chenin Blanc and Gewürztraminer. Cabernet Sauvignon is also commonly found and makes a pleasant medium-bodied wine. Pinotage is grown with some success, as are Pinot Meunier and Pinot Noir. All in all there are now 12,000 acres under cultivation and more new plantings coming on apace.

Most of the wineries are to be found in the North Island. There are four main areas. Around the city of Auckland, Gisborne and Hawkes Bay on the east coast and Martinborough, just north of Wellington. Famous names from these areas include Delegat's, Babich, Nobilo and Matua Valley.

In the South Island, the Marlborough area is now perhaps the most famous of all regions, and it is hard to believe that the first grapes were only planted in 1973. Two wineries in particular have been responsible for bringing the Marlborough region to the attention of the world: the huge Montana Winery, by far and away New Zealand's biggest producer, and Cloudy Bay the legendary maker of the finest Sauvignon Blanc, Chardonnay and now Cabernet and Merlot. The soil is gravelly and free-draining and this combined with long hours of sunshine makes for some spectacular wines.

For a small country, in production terms, New Zealand has achieved a great deal in a short time. Wine is becoming New Zealand's most important export and there is no doubt that their wines will continue to increase in quality.

Wine Producing Regions/South America

The continent of South America is one of the world's major wine-producing areas. The wines come from four countries: Argentina, Chile, Brazil and Uruguay (in order of volume), and in terms of bulk the first two rank in the top ten throughout the world. Most South American wine is consumed domestically but as quality continues to improve, more and more is exported.

Above *Vineyards near Cafayate, Salta Province, northern Argentina.*

Argentina

Argentina is at present the fifth largest wine-producing nation in the world. Almost three-quarters of this very considerable quantity is made in the province of Mendoza, where the vines grow in near-desert country on the Andes plain. Most of the rest comes from the province of San Juan, to the north, from grapes grown in similar circumstances. With a maximum of 10 inches of rainfall annually, irrigation is essential, and this is provided by a system of canals complemented by deep water holes. Since Argentina has virtually no laws of *appellation*, the names on the bottles originally bore little relationship to the actual taste of the wine. However, with the planting of French and other European grapes, the varietal name nowadays appears on the label, instead of 'Chablis', 'Champagne' or 'Margaux'. There are now more acres under European vines than under the indigenous Criolla grape. Sémillon, Chardonnay and Riesling are used for white wine, while for red wine the principal grape is the Malbec from Bordeaux, alongside Cabernet Sauvignon, Merlot and Pinot Noir, the Tempranillo from Spain and the Barbera from Italy. The style of Argentinian wine is decidedly more 'modern'; the whites, less markedly oxidized, are becoming fresh and fruity, while the full-bodied reds benefit from the sun without becoming enslaved to it.

Chile

Chile is the tenth biggest wine-producer in the world; and, in contrast to Argentina, its wine is subject to strict government controls. Perhaps the unique characteristic of Chilean wine is that the vines have never been attacked by phylloxera. The high Andes mountains, the arid Atacama Desert to the north and the cold Humboldt current along the Pacific coast have combined to keep the insect pest out of the country.

Chile has three main vineyard areas: north, central and south. The northern region, from the Atacama Desert to 100 miles north of Valparaiso, produces mostly fortified wines from the Muscat grape. The climate of the Central Valley zone, with cool breezes from the Pacific, has much in common with Northern California, but although the predominant varieties here are from Bordeaux, Burgundy and Germany, the red wine perhaps has more in common with a Rioja than a Médoc, because of the heat. The southern region is notable mainly for table wine from the local Pais grape, although the current trend, backed by heavy investment, is for the planting of European varieties, notably Cabernet Sauvignon and Merlot. Chile already produces the finest red wines in South America, and this influence will only enhance their reputation.

Brazil

Wine is made in the southern tip of Brazil, most of it from hybrid grapes that do well in the humid climate. Whereas there is a French influence in Chile, the keynote in Brazil is Italian, with the Barbera producing fruity red wines and the Trebbiano, Moscato and Malvasia dominating the *vinifera* whites. The overall quality, however, is not up to that of Chile or Argentina.

Uruguay

The wines of Uruguay resemble those of Brazil. American hybrids are planted to resist the climate, but experiments are being made with *vinifera* grapes, with some good results from the Cabernet Sauvignon.

South Africa

South Africa has one of the oldest histories of wine-growing in the world. Vines were first planted in the middle of the 17th century in the south-west of Cape Province by the Dutch settlers. By the early part of the 18th century, the famous Constantia – a rich, dessert wine to rival Madeira and Tokay – had already been exported to Europe, and the French Huguenot settlers were expanding the vineyards. The possession of the Cape from 1805 by the British caused a flourishing trade to develop with Great Britain, aided by preferential tariffs. The removal of these tariffs, however, combined with the ravages of phylloxera, led to the collapse of the wine industry at the end of the century. Reconstruction came with the formation, in 1918, of the KWV (Co-operative Wine Growers' Association of South Africa), and in 1931 of the SAWFA (South African Wine Farmers' Association), which began to ensure standards of quality. In 1972 the government introduced control for 'Wines of Origin', designating 14 regional areas and imposing a government seal of identification certifying the origin, the vintage and the grape variety. Control also extended to the terms 'Superior', for which the wine must consist 100% of the named variety, and the 'Estate', which is limited to properties bottling their own wine.

The wines of South Africa come from two major regions: the Coastal Plain, comprising Constantia, Durbanville, Malmesbury, Stellenbosch and Paarl; and, to the east, the Klein Karoo, embracing Robertson, Worcester and Tulbagh. The soil in the plain is sandstone with granite elements, in the Klein Karoo it is more schistous. The climate is very Mediterranean, mild and warm, with twice as much rainfall in the coastal areas than inland.

Grape varieties are mainly European, with local grafting. The major red grape is the Cinsault from the southern Rhône, known here as the Hermitage, which makes an even finer wine under the name of Pinotage, when it is crossed with the Pinot Noir. The Pinot Noir is planted on its own, as is the Shiraz, a variation of the Syrah, the Merlot and the Cabernet Sauvignon. The general style is for full, fruity wines with great warmth and sometimes too much alcohol. The most 'typical' are the Pinotage wines, but some people think the finest comes from the Cabernet Sauvignon-Merlot blends from the Stellenbosch region. For white wine, the most popular grape is the Chenin Blanc, called the Steen, which makes soft, fruity wines and rare botrytized wines like the Nederburg Edelkeur. The Sémillon, Clairette and Ugni Blanc all produce attractive wines rather low in acidity, while the Riesling is very successful in the German style, especially at Nederburg. Also planted is the Palomino, from Andalusia, and – for rich dessert wines – the Muscat d'Alexandrie.

The largest wine-producing area in the country is Stellenbosch, which also makes the finest wines of South Africa. Paarl, second only to Stellenbosch, is known for the well-made wines of the KWV, as well as for the very high quality sherry-style wines, certainly the finest outside Spain, and some very successful ruby, tawny and vintage 'ports'. Where irrigation is necessary, in the Klein Karoo, a large amount of table wine is made.

Below *Vines growing on a Cape Dutch homestead near Franschhoek.*

3
Advanced Course

The purpose of the Advanced Course is to put into practice what we have seen in theory. It is all very well to discuss soil, climate, grape varieties, methods of vinification, vintage years and so on; but to describe the actual taste of a wine is something different, and there is no substitute for the direct *verre en main* approach. Indeed, the whole purpose of a wine-tasting course at the Académie du Vin is to let the wines themselves illustrate (or if need be, disprove) the points we wish to make. Although we seldom taste more than eight wines per session, the number of wines in these tastings has been increased to give a wider spread. Because comparison is probably the most important element in wine-tasting, we have attempted to describe the wines themselves, to see how they correspond to their *appellation* or style, and to compare them with wines tasted in the same group. We have also cross-referenced back to the text in Courses 1 and 2, and to other tastings of comparable wines in the Advanced Course.

We have already discussed the actual method of wine-tasting and what points to look for. (The standard work on the subject is Michael Broadbent's *Winetasting*, first published in 1968, which has been expanded and reprinted many times (see Bibliography on page 223). Perhaps the most technical and impressive from France is Professeur Emile Peynaud's *Le goût du vin*, but Broadbent's book remains the essential reading on the subject.) There is no need to repeat this information. Instead we shall now concentrate on the taste of the wines themselves. The Advanced Course is divided into four sections:

1. Basic wine tasting

We treat wines as ranging from dry to sweet, light to heavy. The choice is accentuated towards France, with six wines from each twelve, since the system of *appellation contrôlée* has resulted in recognizable styles of wine, and in many cases these styles are used as reference points by international wine makers. While some wines are unquestionably dry, sweet, light or heavy, most wines that are made to be drunk with food fit into a middle category. At the same time, the acidity and weight of a wine is perceived differently by different people. A Frenchman from Paris, for example, will find a Muscadet less dry than his counterpart in Nice; and the latter, in turn, would judge a Châteauneuf-du-Pape to be fruity and pleasant whereas the Parisian tends to regard it as heavy and sleep-inducing. We have chosen wines of all categories, noting variations in style. The three white wine tastings and the three red wine tastings should be studied independently.

2. Different grape varieties

This section focuses on the major grape varieties planted throughout the world, and once again the bias is towards France, since, with the exception of Riesling, the internationally planted varieties tend to be French in origin. The purpose is to show how the same grape performs in different soils, climates and with different styles of winemaking. The characteristic tastes of the grape varieties themselves tend to be strongly marked in young wines. (This is distinct from the overall 'grapey' taste often possessed by young wines.) As a wine ages, the grape loses its dominance as secondary and tertiary aromas and flavours appear, yet the style can still be traced to the variety from which it is made. French wines tend to be judged more from their *appellations* (Meursault, Hermitage), than from their grape varieties (Chardonnay, Syrah), because both are interrelated. Such geographical *appellations* are well developed in other European countries, but when such 'French' or international varietals are dominant, the *appellation* is usually forfeited, such wines being deemed 'untypical'. This should not prevent the taster from considering them as regional as well as varietal examples, as we have shown.

3. The influence of vintage and appellation

In these four tastings, we have two 'vertical' tastings (a single Château or Domaine wine through a series of vintages), and two 'horizontal' tastings (a series of different *appellations* from the same region in the same year). The purpose in the vertical tastings is to isolate the vintage factor, everything being constant except the climatic conditions; and in the horizontal tastings to show up the influence of soil, microclimate, grape selection and vinification through comparable wines in a single year. Once again, we have used only French wines, and have concentrated on Burgundy and Bordeaux, the two most important and homogeneous wine regions. The section concludes with a comparative tasting of fortified wines.

4. The colour of wine

It is easier to describe colour than to describe smell or taste. Wines never, with the exception of Muscat, smell of grapes: when young, they have floral or fruity aromas, which develop into a bouquet of herbs, spices and types of wood – an infinite range of sensations. The taste of a wine follows the same pattern. Wines conform to certain styles (a Médoc is austere, an Alsace fruity, for example), and these depend on many factors, notably where the wine is made and what it is made from. But although the style may be easy to recognize, the taste is hard to describe. Even so, it is instructive to look at different wines from different areas, grapes and vintages, to study the variations in colour and to know why they occur. The series of robes reproduced on pages 180–185 are graded in tone from light to full, young or mature.

We have attempted to reproduce in writing actual tastings at the Académie du Vin. If the tasting notes seem fanciful or long-winded, it is only because we have tried to describe the wines as fully as possible.

Tasting/Very Dry Whites

In this tasting we look at wines that are relatively light in body and relatively high in acidity. Dryness should not, however, be equated with acidity. All wines have acidity, even the very sweetest, such as Château d'Yquem. What we are considering here is the total absence of sweetness. If the acidity is pronounced, it should be a crisp, mouth-watering acidity, in harmony with the wine's fruit and character. A wine that has too much acidity either comes from unripe grapes or from poor vinification.

The majority of very dry white wines are young as well as light. This is because wines appear to lose acidity with age. In fact, acidity remains constant, the wine either gaining in body and fruit, or losing its youthful freshness, both factors combining to make the wine appear less tart. Some of the wines for this tasting are made to be drunk very young, some may be drunk or kept, according to taste, while others are included simply because they *are* very young.

APPEARANCE	BOUQUET	PALATE	COMMENTS
Muscadet de Sèvre et Maine sur lie 'Carte d'Or' Sauvion et fils			Loire, France
Clear, very pale yellow, very fresh and youthful, slight CO_2 presence to keep the freshness.	Fresh, clean, sprightly aroma, not really fruity, more straightforwardly refreshing with a lively acidity.	Lively, crisp flavour, good (highish) acidity, almost all in the attack. Clean, refreshing finish.	Well-made, noted for freshness not for richness of flavour. Classic, crisp Muscadet, drink young.
Vinho Verde NV Quinta da Aveleda Penafiel			Portugal
Clean, clear very pale yellow, plenty of CO_2 but not sparkling.	Fruity, spring-like aromas, not much depth but fresh and lively.	Clean, dry, good crisp finish, quite floral with a refreshing lift from the CO_2.	Overall clean and fresh, no real complexity, but a straightforward, lively, refreshing wine for quaffing as an aperitif or with light meals.
Castello di Neive 1988 Vino da Tavola			Italy/*Arneis della Langhe*
Very pale, almost white yellow, paler if anything than the first two, very slight CO_2.	Discreet fruit aromas, softer than above, more subtle than assertive.	Clean, straightforward fruit, a hint of fresh almonds, smooth and lively at the same time, a pretty wine with a lovely balance. Dry finish.	Very fine vinification, no great depth, but good quality and length, light and fresh but stylish and smooth.
Pouilly-Fumé 1988 Jean-Claude Chatelain			Loire, France
Clean, pale yellow with greenish tints, more presence than the Muscadet.	Youthful, crisp style, dominantly fruity (redcurrants) and faintly herbaceous but restrained and elegant Sauvignon style.	Lively, fruity flavour, blackcurrant leaf at first, excellent fruit/acid balance, stylish and elegant, less assertive than Sancerre (see page 157).	An excellent example, good acidity balancing the high level of alcohol at 13°, quality wine making, classic Pouilly-Fumé.
Delegat's Hawkes Bay Sauvignon Blanc 1988			New Zealand
Clean, medium yellow, with no green tints, quite rich.	Fruity, sappy, slightly grassy Sauvignon aromas, light touch of new oak, well blended in.	Dry but not aggressive, clean fruit with a touch of pineapple/exotic character, but not too pronounced, well balanced.	Good example, fine depth of fruit, less complex than the Pouilly-Fumé, but with a straightforward, fruity attack and good follow through.
Pinot Blanc d'Alsace 1988 Cave d'Eguisheim			Alsace, France
Clean, palish yellow, but much fuller and more rich looking than the first four wines, very attractive.	Fruity, almost explosively so in the Alsace style, but retaining a refreshing lightness, very attractive and grapey.	Excellent fruit flavours, slight green apple acidity to give balance, good grapey-fruit extract and length. A lovely style of wine.	Quite delicious as an aperitif, but really made for food. Good body and distinct fruit flavours rather than just crisp dryness; a very good alternative to Mâcon blanc (see page 160).

APPEARANCE	BOUQUET	PALATE	COMMENTS
Bourgogne-Aligoté de Bouzeron 1988 A. & P. de Villaine			Burgundy, France
Pale youthful yellow with greenish tints, quite rich on the glass. Fine and quite striking.	Discreet fruitiness with a hint of flowers and fresh almonds, persistent. Complex with more depth than expected from the Aligoté.	Racy, fruity (white peaches, appley acidity), very well-balanced and distinctive. Lively but with depth and length, quite Burgundian.	An extremely stylish wine, lovely fruit/acid balance but above all a fine expression of *terroir* and wine making surpassing the grape variety. The Pinot Blanc is simple in comparison.
Lenz Moser Grüner Veltliner 1987			Austria
Fine pale yellow, clean and fresh looking, lovely appearance.	Lively, fruity nose, fresh, herbaceously fruity. Mouthwatering.	Fine lively, zesty flavour, crisp acidity on the finish. Clean, very dry, almost invigorating.	Well-balanced, an excellent wine for aperitif or light meals. Resembles a fullish Muscadet or a good dry Chenin Blanc.
CVNE 1987 Rioja			Spain/*Blanco Viura*
Very pale, almost white/yellow, light and fresh.	Clean, faintly Riesling/light petrol aroma, very lively and mouthwatering.	Straightforwardly fruity, more weight and smoothness than the Muscadet, but less persistent flavour. Unpretentious.	A clean, crisp wine, good either as aperitif or with food, to be drunk young. Good example of early-picked grapes, well-vinified.
Ch. Roquetaillade-la-Grange 1987 Graves Sec			Graves, France
Clean, pale yellow, faint green tinge, but more buttery and slightly fuller than the Pouilly-Fumé.	Lively impression, but fruit still a little discreet, needs time.	Clean, fruity, smoother and more suave in style than the Pouilly-Fumé, with a touch of new oak. Good acidity, no greenness, good balance.	Definitely a food wine, the proportion of Sémillon (80%) to Sauvignon plus the Graves *terroir* provides a more subtle wine that will still improve.
Chablis ler Cru les Montmains 1986 Louis Michel			Chablis, France
Lovely, fullish greeny-yellow, the pure colour of Chablis. A clear, firm looking wine.	Rather grassy, green, still rather lean and hard.	No obvious fruit on the attack, impression of youthful leanness and firm acidity, but fine edge of fruit waiting to emerge.	Overall lean finish, not unbalanced, but with the vegetal/herbaceous characteristics to the fore, needs another year at least. Shows the inherent 'steeliness' of a certain style of Chablis.
Colombia Crest Winery Chardonnay 1986			Washington State, USA
Fine clean colour, lemony-yellow, quite rich looking.	Good clean fruit, herbaceous rather than floral, but quite soft.	Fruity, smooth flavours with a touch of vegetal acidity, cold fermentation leading to a slight lack of fullness.	A good wine, but more importance placed on clean fruit than varietal flavour and complexity, also the result of young vines.

Tasting/Dry Whites

This tasting category covers the majority of white wines for drinking with food. They have no or very little residual sugar after fermentation and are therefore dry. The wines in this tasting are fuller-bodied than the very dry white wines, overall more complex, showing the different international styles and also the influence of vintage years, vinification and ageing.

If we have been more critical in the commentaries in this tasting than in the previous one, it is because these wines have a greater potential character than very light dry white wines. Most of these dry whites are drinkable young, right after bottling, but it is not then that they are at their best. The extra levels of alcohol, fruit sugar, acidity and extract need time to develop their inherent style and character. When developed, they are the perfect accompaniment to food, often transcending the meal.

APPEARANCE	BOUQUET	PALATE	COMMENTS
Hunters Chardonnay Marlborough 1988			New Zealand
Lovely, fullish yellow with greeny tints, even oily, striking.	Fruity, rather grassy Chardonnay, a cool country wine. Oak present, but already well blended in.	Fine extract of fruit flavours, quite rich with a lemony acidity to balance this. Citric/fruity/ oaky finish, still too young.	Good example of a herbaceous rather than floral or buttery Chardonnay. Perhaps re-acidified to balance the alcohol of 13.5°. Well made.
Santa Rita Chardonnay 1987 Medalla Real			Maipo Valley, Chile
Very pale colour, almost white-yellow, slight CO_2.	Discreetly fruity, slightly exotic, pineappley, evidence of grapes picked early to retain acidity and cold fermentation.	Fuller and fruitier than the aroma would suggest, hint of oak in attack, clean finish, good acidity.	Overall light and 'zippy' style, clean and fruity but more impression of youth than flavour.
Soave Classico Monte Carbonare, Viticola Suavia 1987			Italy
Lively, clean pale yellow, touch of CO_2, a brisk-looking wine.	Clean, crisp acidity and fruit, lively, mouthwatering.	Similar lively fruit/acidity, but softer and more floral on the middle palate, still very young.	Currently belongs more in the 'very dry' category, but will soften with bottle age and broaden out.
Tokay-Pinot Gris 1987 Domaine Weinbach			Alsace, France
Clean, lively pale yellow, slight CO_2, fresh and youthful but more rich-looking than the Soave.	Soft, musky fruit, ripe grapes, very perfumed Alsace style.	Quite broad in flavour, fruit very present, fine. Balanced with reticent sweetness and good acidity.	A lovely, complete wine, fruity, soft but lively, perfect balance. Can be drunk or kept.
Meursault-Blagny ler Cru 1987			Côte de Beaune, Burgundy, France
Clean, limpid medium yellow with hint of green, quite rich: a really lovely colour.	Touch of new wood, ripe Chardonnay fruit, very stylish and fine expression of Blagny *terroir* (rather lean for Meursault, see Clos de la Barre, page 161).	Fine floral, honeysuckle fruit, hazelnut overtones, firm, good acidity, extremely elegant.	Very good for 1987, wonderful example of grape variety dominated by *terroir*. Perfect balance, great persistence.
Chimney Rock Chardonnay 1986			Napa Valley, California, USA
Fine light yellow-gold, quite full and rich, ripe.	Touch of oak, exotic fruit aromas with attractive lemony edge, not restrained but not overblown either.	Good, clean fruit, less wood on the palate than the nose, positive, ripe flavours with good acidity. Well balanced.	A very good wine, complete contrast to the Meursault, whose firmness and potential over-shadows this more open example (see Chardonnay, page 161).

APPEARANCE	BOUQUET	PALATE	COMMENTS
Vouvray Sec 1986 Clos Naudin (A. Foreau)			Touraine, Loire, France
Lovely fullish greeny-yellow, a very good colour showing the acidity of the Chenin Blanc and the ripeness of the year.	Clean, vibrant fruit, redcurrants and quince, rather lean but fine.	Floral, honey, flowers and fruit on attack, but still rather subdued with a slightly aggressive, green finish that will soften with age.	A pure example of Vouvray and Chenin Blanc (see page 162). Plainly not a hot country wine, natural ripeness and high natural acidity, classic.
Sandstone Sémillon 1986			Margaret River, Western Australia
Fine, striking, fullish yellow with some green tints.	Lovely, soft yet persistent, waxy, fruity and smooth.	Excellent attack, clean fruit, suave texture, quite full but with edge of acidity, toasty oak touches. Very good finesse and length.	Fine example of Sémillon (particularly successful in Australia) from healthy, ripe grapes, beautifully vinified. Can be drunk or kept.
Ch. Smith-Haut-Lafitte 1986 Graves Grand Cru Classé			Graves, France
Brilliant, pale yellow, youthful, slight greeny edge.	Fruity, slightly waxy bouquet, with the liveliness of the Sauvignon (100%) and the more complex fruit from the Cru Classé.	Complex, elegant flavours, direct fruitiness, subtle use of oak. Lovely balance.	Firm and clean, less expressive than the Sandstone, but more polished and stylish, excellent fruit/acid balance. Will improve for 2-3 years and last for more.
Hermitage 1984 Jean-Louis Chave			Mauves, Rhône, France
Clear medium/full yellow, clean and fresh, no hint of age for the year.	Complex, fruity, nutty (almond and peach kernels), very fine for a difficult year.	Fine fruit, straw-like, lengthy acidity, complex flavours. Not at all an obvious wine, but one of high quality. Weighty, unctuous but dry.	Very fine, great length and and structure but not heavy. Pure expression of the *appellation.* Repays close attention.
CVNE Blanco Seco 1983 Rioja			Haro la Rioja, Spain
Clean and lively, medium yellow, quite rich but not sweet looking. Very young for a 1983.	Fruity, waxy, with maturity and above all oak showing, but still fresh and well balanced.	Smooth, suave fruit, with oak/vanilla present but less than on the nose.	Well-balanced, clean and complex, hints of Sémillon in its character, good length. At its best.
Riesling Osterberg 1983 Bernard Heydt			Ribeauvillé, Alsace, France
Clean pale yellow, slight green tint to show acidity, no real age.	Strikingly 'zippy', fruity, lemony bouquet; typical 'petrol'-like Riesling overtones.	Quite a broad fruit flavour (ripeness of the 1983s), very floral and lively, dry but with an almost honeyed finish. Very long and positive flavour.	Classic Riesling (see page 158), length and persistence from a noble variety in a great year, with a firm backbone for future ageing.

Tasting/Sweet & Aromatic Whites

This tasting concerns wines that finish sweet, or at least off-dry, and wines that are so headily aromatic that they cannot be fitted into the dry white wine category. Nor do these highly perfumed, full-bodied wines go particularly well with food.

The degree of sweetness of the *demi-sec* and *moelleux* wines varies with the type of wine and the vintage. Wines that are sweet by definition, like Sauternes, will be sweeter and richer in a year with a lot of sun, since there is a higher level of natural sugar in the grapes to be converted into alcohol and residual sugar. Wines that are sweet by the choice of the wine maker, such as those from Vouvray, Anjou and Alsace, will only appear in years when there is enough over-ripeness in the grapes to produce the desired concentration and richness. The over-ripening of the grapes is the key factor, and given the right climatic conditions, most noble grape varieties will achieve a high concentration of sugar. In specialized climates, this will be achieved through *pourriture noble* or botrytis. Attempts to make a well-balanced sweet wine in years when the grapes do not ripen sufficiently, or when there is no botrytis, are not generally very successful.

Fine sweet wines, however rich, should not be too cloying. They should *look* sweet, just as very dry wines *look* dry. Unlike medium-bodied dry wines, they are often best drunk on their own.

APPEARANCE	BOUQUET	PALATE	COMMENTS
Condrieu 1988 E. Guigal			Ampuis, Rhône, France
Striking, clear, brilliant youthful pale yellow, so rich as to be clinging to the glass.	Explosive, exotic aromas of ripe peaches, apricots, with citrus elements, marvellous extraction.	Similar pure explosion of pleasure: rich, unctuous, racy, superb fruit extract, brilliant wine making. Delicious.	The epitome of Condrieu, exotic and sensual, rich from a very ripe year, mouthfilling lively fruit, but still a balanced, great wine.
Bonnezeaux 1986 Ch. de Fesles (J. Boivin)			Anjou, Loire, France
Clean, pale yellow, quite pale for 1986, no richness yet.	Still a touch of SO_2 (partially the cause of the pale colour), but a honeyed, floral, waxy fruit showing through.	Good acidity, fullish and vibrant with medium sweetness. SO_2 still faintly present to mask the smoothness; floral, honeyed, lively finish.	A fine wine, still too young but a good example of Loire Chenin Blanc with its balance of richness and fruit. Needs five years.
Gewürztraminer Bollenberg 1986 Théo Cattin			Alsace, France
Clean, light to medium yellow, touches of green, very rich and oily.	Unctuous exotic and persistent, full of lychees/pineapple fruitiness.	Mouthfilling, rich and oily, with a spicy unctuous flavour and slightly honeyed finish.	Rich, finishes a little short after an impressive attack, fullish (13°) classic Gewürztraminer of the rich style, hugely aromatic and persistent.
Burgmeister Nachfolder 1985 Scheurebe Auslese			Langehlonsheim, Germany
Palish yellow (for 1985) with greenish tints denoting northern climate and good acidity.	Fine, mouthwatering, fruity aromas, dominated by citric, grapefruity style.	Quite rich and honeyed, summery fruit. Good balance with freshness and clean acidity.	A lovely wine, not overly long on the finish, with flowery, medium sweetness and full of 'joie de vivre'. Best drunk on its own.
Jurançon 1987 Domaine Cahupé			Monein, Pyrenees, France
Full, medium yellow, still youthful with slight green tints, but veering towards pale gold. Very rich.	Extremely persistent, rich, honeyed with spice and lemony overtones, a wonderful concentration of pure fruit.	Rich, unctuous, honey and flowers fruit, full and luscious but balanced by a keen acidity. Impressive length, concentrated but not too heavy.	A marvellous example of a rare *appellation* now deservedly recognized again. Easily the equal of fine sweet wines across the world.
Ch. Lafaurie-Peyraguey 1985 1er Grand Cru Classé			Sauternes, France
Full yellow, verging on gold, but still with a hint of green. Luscious.	Very floral, hot-house, honeyed bouquet, with an impression of great sweetness but not over-heady.	Rich, honey and lanolin flavours, barley sugar sweetness. Great fruit extract, high in alcohol but good acidity. Luscious, classy finish.	Fully sweet Sauternes from a fine year, has none of the lemony acidity of the Jurançon or the Ch. Climens, but good use of oak. A wine to keep.

APPEARANCE	BOUQUET	PALATE	COMMENTS
Ch. Climens 1983 1er Grand Cru Classé			Barsac/Sauternes, France
Medium yellow, slight greeny tints, beginning to turn yellow-gold, but paler than Lafaurie-Peyraguey.	Honeyed, waxy, very ripe Sémillon fruit, great persistence, musky from botrytis, rich and complex.	Marvellous honeyed attack, beautifully balanced despite heavy concentration and naturally high alcohol by a perfect lemony acidity. A powerful wine, but completely harmonious.	A classic wine from a fine vineyard in a very good year where meticulous attention to detail produces top quality. Outclasses the very good previous wine.
Lindemans Griffith Botrytis Selection Sémillon 1987			NSW, Australia
Full medium gold with a touch of amber, very rich and full.	Powerful, concentrated, honeyed, peachy-apricot aromas, very fruity, masses of extract.	Very rich barley sugar fruit, fully sweet, exotic apricot fruit. Almost too honeyed in the middle but saved by a lively acidity.	Marvellously rich, luscious with lemony zest. Lower in alcohol and more intensely sweet than the Sauternes.
Beringer 'Nightingale' Botrytised Sauvignon Blanc 1983			Napa, USA
Full yellow-gold, very rich and luscious.	Faint hint of blackcurrant leaves followed by honeyed fruit with an excellent acidity that bounces the fruit back.	Very sweet indeed, fully honeyed, apricot unctuousness. A little massive compared to the Climens, but very successful, great length.	A really grapey (Sauvignon) sweetness compared to the Lindemans which is more complex with a higher concentration. Very fine.
Isola e Olena Vin Santo			Tuscany, Italy
Clear, pale amber, no real gold aspects, colour of an old amontillado.	Nutty, concentrated walnut and almond aromas. More the impression of a malmsey than a non-fortified wine.	Same richness in flavour, with a spicy, fruit-cake style and elements of marzipan. Long lingering flavour without needing weight to carry it.	A lovely, reposing wine. Its pure, slightly burnt flavour, obtains richness from a concentration of grapes and as a result finishes drier than the previous five wines.
Tokai Aszú 5 Puttonyos Tokaji Wine Trust			Hungary
Amber, pale mahogany, amontillado or madeira colour.	Honeyed, nutty but also fruit-acid bouquet, intense and concentrated, very persistent.	Great concentration of fruit combined with high natural acidity, burnt caramel flavours backed up by quince-like fruit. Very fine and long.	Not a fortified wine, but gives the impression of one. Slightly richer than the Vin Santo, but a concentrated rather than luscious finish. Will last many years.
Icewine 1987 Inniskillin			Niagara Peninsula, Canada
Palish amber gold, fully rich and luscious, very attractive.	Massive concentration of sugar and heady aroma of apricots, followed by the impression of a clean, searing acidity.	Richly sweet, more concentration of sugar even than a German TBA and high acidity to balance. Powerful, impressive, not overly complex.	Extraordinary wine from Canada, more of a blockbuster than the German style. The most concentrated wine of the tasting.

Tasting/Light Reds

In this tasting we look at wines that are at their best drunk young. Light red wines, like very dry white wines (pages 142–3), may be kept, but their main attraction is their freshness and fruit. What we are looking for is a lively fruit, fresh acidity and little or no tannin. We have excluded the basic everyday table wines, since these are blended for immediate consumption anyway, and whether light, medium or heavy, are not meant to be kept. We have also included in this tasting wines that should perhaps be in the following tasting of medium reds in order to show a more interesting range. At the same time, we have excluded wines such as Corbières and Minervois from France, for although these are generally drunk young, they are not really very light. The key to wines in this tasting is their drinkability: although some may have further ageing potential, they are at their best now. All of these wines have a definite and recognizable style.

APPEARANCE	BOUQUET	PALATE	COMMENTS
Beaujolais-Villages 1988 Georges Duboeuf			Beaujolais, France
Vibrantly youthful clean carmine-red with pronounced violetty edge.	Attractive, ripe crushed fruit aromas, flowery, violetty hints, pretty.	Immediate, fruity attack, clear progression of fruit over the palate, same impression of crushed, ripe fruits as on the nose.	Good balance, fruit, acidity and length. Beaujolais and Gamay styles evident. Good example from a firm, fruity year.
Chinon 1988 Domaine de Roncée			Panzoult, Loire, France
Quite full, youthful, violet/carmine-red, very attractive.	Lively, immediate fruit, slightly floral and herbaceous, softer than the Beaujolais, less aggressive.	Youthful, juicy, raspberry-scented fruit, faintly earthy softness in the middle with a lively finish.	A lively, quaffable wine, but with enough depth of fruit and trueness of style (the Cabernet Franc a good contrast to the Gamay) to keep for a year or two.
Dry River Pinot Noir 1988			Marlborough, New Zealand
Lovely pale carmine with light violetty edge. Attractive.	Fruity, blackcurrant aromas in a clean, simple style.	Immediate soft Pinot, strawberry/blackcurrant fruit, straightforward with a light acidity.	Pleasantly fruity, easily recognizable Pinot Noir. Lightness much due to young vines. Future vintages should be more complex.
Sancerre Rouge 1987 Domaine de Montigny			Sancerre, France
Full rich carmine-red, youthful and vibrant but no violet left.	Fullish, quite concentrated Pinot Noir aromas, strawberry fruit, enhanced by a touch of wood, surprisingly good depth.	Quite intense fruit extract, still with a touch of wood, fairly complex and not at all in the 'primeur' easy fruity style.	Could be mistaken for a lesser Côte du Nuits rather than a Pinot Noir from the upper Loire, excellent extract, especially for the year.
Malteser Blauer Zweigelt 1987 Trocken Souveräner Malteser Ritterorden			Kommende Mailberg, Austria
Fresh, youthful, fullish ruby with violet edge. Quite rich.	Fruity, cherry-like aromas, slight hints of Pinot Noir or Gamay.	Pretty, youthful, grapey flavours, slight earthiness but very much a quaffing wine, attractive acidity.	Pleasant, straightforward light, fruity red wine. Should be served cool. An excellent alternative to Beaujolais.
Côtes du Rhône 1987 Domaine Rabasse-Charavin			Cairanne, Rhône, France
Medium red, quite rich, grenadine colour, light edge.	Spicy, peppery aromas, with hints of ripe fruits and flowers, definitely a warm southern France bouquet.	Firm fruit on attack, followed by soft, warm, slightly licorice fruit. Good balance, a softer, richer fruit than the sometimes edgy Gamay.	Very well-made wine from a light vintage, showing the soft fruit of the Côtes du Rhône, without the tannin (see Full-bodied Reds, page 152).

APPEARANCE	BOUQUET	PALATE	COMMENTS
Chianti Classico 1986 Podere Capaccia			Radda, Chianti, Italy
Fullish rich ruby-red, showing a slight brick-red rim, warm-looking.	Dried fruit, spice aromas, hints of tea, ripish fruit but not over-ripe nor over-rich.	Firm, clear fruit on the palate, rather lean and leathery at the finish, with the typical Chianti acidity, personality well defined.	A well-made and well-balanced Chianti from a medium year, made to be drunk with food. A complete contrast in style to the fruitiness of the first three wines.
Valpolicella Classico Superiore 1985 Allegrini			Veneto, Italy
Medium, even palish brick-red, very clean and still youthful looking.	Fine, rose-like bouquet, some sweetness in attack, drier on second nose.	Clean, cherry-like fruit flavours, a hint of wood and a touch of bitter almonds. Good balance. Quite long, dry finish.	Fine long flavour despite the light colour, balanced and complex. Like the Chianti, a wine for food. At its best.
Mercurey 1985 Ier Cru Clos du Roy Faiveley			Nuits-Saint-Georges, France
Medium red, grenadine colour, quite rich, firm edge, not fading at all.	Lovely, lightly concentrated Pinot Noir bouquet: mixed fruits, strawberries, then earthy, vegetal and animal overtones. Classic.	Fine Pinot attack, pure ripe fruit plus *terroir*, good acidity through wood ageing. Tannin beginning to fade, but keeping the wine balanced.	A very fine example of the Côte Chalonnaise reds, and bench-mark lightish Pinot Noir (see page 166). Delicious now but will keep.
Ch. Patache d'Aux 1985 Cru Bourgeois			Médoc, France
Very fine deep crimson, quite rich and full of fruit. Good depth of colour from Cabernet Sauvignon in a ripe year.	Bouquet of ripe fruits, dried fruits, spices, nuts, even leather, clear and persistent.	Good attack, with the slightly lean finish of wines from the northern Médoc. Not too much oak, ready now but will keep 5 years.	A classic medium quality Médoc, perfect contrast Burgundy/Bordeaux with the previous wine. Neither are strictly speaking 'light', but they have a balanced, approachable style.
Rioja Crianza 1984 Gran Condal Bodegas Rioja			Santiago, Spain
Clean medium red, beginning to take a slight mahogany tinge.	Discreet fruit, dominant redcurrants, quite lean, wood evident.	Straightforward, fruit and wood well balanced but lacks the vibrancy of other wines in this tasting. Still a hint of vanilla in the finish.	A light Rioja from a medium year, probably going past its best, but balanced and clear cut.
Quinta de Camarete 1984 J-M da Fonseca			Portugal
Firm youthful red, as young looking as the Patache d'Aux, but not as full.	Concentrated, fruity bouquet, slightly earthy, rich but not heavy.	Slightly vanilla/oaky attack, sweet concentrated fruit followed by dried fruit on the finish, quite high tone due possibly to an excess of volatile acidity.	Lovely, satisfying dry wine with sweet fruit attack. Good example, at its best.

Tasting/Medium Reds

This tasting should cover most red table wines. The lighter wines are seldom less than 11° alcohol and even the fullest stay under 14°. The average is probably around 12.5°. However, we are not looking merely for medium weight, but also for added depth, complexity and balance: wines with potential.

We have chosen an international selection of wines, repeating many of the *appellations* or regions from the light red wine tasting. These come either from better vintages, older vines or finer parts of the *appellation*. The same principle is followed in the next tasting.

We have taken 'medium' to be neither too light, nor too heavy and certainly not 'medium quality'. Light wines should be drunk young; full intense wines generally age very well; the interesting factor here is balance, complexity and potential.

APPEARANCE	BOUQUET	PALATE	COMMENTS
Fleurie 1988 Domaine des Quatre Vents Georges Duboeuf			Beaujolais, France
Fabulous, rich, fruity violet-red, very striking, typical of a very good year.	Fruity but firm. Ripe fruits: grenadine, raspberry, firmed up by wood ageing.	Stylish up-front fruit with an intensity and depth quite different to the Beaujolais-Villages (see page 148). Elegant, minerally and woody characteristics.	Can be drunk, but the polish, depth and *terroir* of Fleurie prove that it should be kept. About as good as Gamay can get.
Ch. Smith-Haut-Lafitte 1986 Graves Grand Cru Classé			Graves, France
Rich, deep carmine-red, very young (still with purple tinges), superb.	Touch of new oak, clear persistent fruit, classy and clean. A 'modern' style Graves, fresh and attractive.	Persistent, smooth rose-like rich fruit, still a touch of oak in attack, less on finish; falls a little short, could have more extract.	Good quality Graves, lacking a little intensity on the palate, made more for stylishness and to be drunk relatively young.
Santa Rita Cabernet Sauvignon 1986 Riserva			Maipo Valley, Chile
Fine deep, youthful carmine-red, deep cherry tones. Vibrant.	Youthful, fragrant and bouncy fruit: blackcurrant leaves, raspberries, very attractive, faintly sweet.	Smoky, firm fruit with still quite a hard tannin from the oak. Fresh and fragrant on attack, leaner and more raw on the finish. Needs time to balance out.	Good extract, lovely fragrant fruit, good potential from a vineyard still almost in the experimental stage (see the 1985, page 164).
Orlando Cabernet Sauvignon 1986			Coonawarra, South Australia
Very rich plummy, full young colour, no age at all, still almost opaque.	Solid, foursquare crushed bouquet, blackcurrants and blackberries.	Same sweet, crushed fruit impression on palate, very fruity with good acidity despite the vanilla-oak, blackcurrant fruit dominates.	Quite well-balanced, but the varietal character suffers from the over-fruitiness. With no definition of *terroir* it is easy to drink, but simple compared to drier wines.
Crozes-Hermitage 1986 Domaine de Thalabert Paul Jaboulet Aîné			Rhône, France
Quite extraordinary colour, rich, almost black, so intense as to be almost impenetrable.	Intense, smoky, animally aromas, very concentrated. Obviously very strict selection and vinification.	Masses of extract, still very tannic, a big, almost old-fashioned wine, intense, smoky-spicy fruit, high natural acidity.	A tough wine, more a full-bodied than a medium red, but still less powerful than the Hermitage 1983 (see page 153). Needs at least three years to become elegant.

APPEARANCE	BOUQUET	PALATE	COMMENTS
Chinon 1985 Château de la Grille			Chinon, Loire, France
Full, deep carmine/ruby colour, still very young and quite intense.	Masses of extract, a sort of briary fruit with leathery, woody overtones. Dry bouquet, Pauillac-style.	Long maceration on the skins and long wood ageing have brought lots of extract, but the fruit of the Cabernet Franc and *terroir* of Chinon just dominate. Needs time.	A serious, complex wine, the opposite to Chinon 1988 (see page 148). Aimed clearly at the Bordeaux Cru Classé style with a certain loss of attractive fruit on the way. Will age very well.
Chambolle-Musigny 1985 Domaine Roumier			Côte d'Or, France
Medium, clear cherry-red, quite rich, but could perhaps be deeper for the year.	Ripe fruit bouquet, more stewed fruits than the crushed fruit of younger wines, especially Gamays. Finesse rather than intensity.	Sweet, red fruits flavour, strawberry dominant, a touch of oak (not new), attractive, balanced, all in finesse.	A good example of the elegance of Chambolle-Musigny, but could have more persistence. About the same weight as the Mercurey 1985 (see page 149).
Quinta da Cotta 1985 Grande Escolha			Douro, Portugal
Very rich colour, full blackcurranty red, no ageing. Contrast with Chambolle shows the vast difference that comes from grape variety etc.	Vibrant, briary fruit bouquet. Spiciness, woodiness and fruit combined.	Full, earthy, solidly fruity flavour, good lean finish, definite hint of *terroir* from the granite soil, still very young.	A robust but lean, tough wine, a complete contrast to the Smith-Haut-Lafitte style, bigger than most in this tasting.
Bandol 1984 Domaine de Pibarnon			La Cadière d'Azur, Provence, France
Rich, full meaty red, very young for a 1984, quite intense.	Spicy, earthy, almost leathery impression with warm fruit.	Quite full-bodied for a medium year in Bandol, a polished, spicy wine with good fruit, consistent, lean but not hard.	Less good than the excellent 1983 and 1985, but shows the lean power of the Mouvrèdre grape.
Trefethen Cabernet Sauvignon 1984			Napa Valley, USA
Very fine deep carmine/ruby red, young and quite rich.	Pronounced blackberry/blackcurrant nose, lingering sweet fruit.	Minty, spicy flavours, slight vanilla hint from the oak, blackberry and green pepper together in a sweetish attack, lively finish.	Well-made California Cabernet, perhaps a little sweet in the attack, but with a clean tannic finish. To compare to a good Médoc Cru Bourgeois.
Ch. Le Bon-Pasteur 1983			Pomerol, France
Full colour, deep brick-red, very solid and not showing much age.	Concentrated fruit nose, followed by licorice, tarry, slightly burnt aspects and exotic spices, a fine rich Pomerol.	Soft, intense, rich fruit, smoky, truffly, earthy flavours, rich and firm at the same time.	Beautifully balanced wine, great extract and length, a very fine wine nearing its best. The best wine of this tasting.
CVNE Viña Real Gran Reserva 1976			Spain
Medium red, but fading tawny edge, definitely mature and not surprising for the vintage.	Mature fruits, rosehip, redcurrants, attractively sweet and still very young.	Lovely silky texture, some acidity and tannin still in the finish, but good balance and sweet, lingering fruit.	The fruit gives it a mature Côte de Beaune aspect, still a touch of wood. Very good with food. Excellent example of a 13-year-old wine.

Tasting/Full-bodied Reds

Light red wines can, and should, be drunk young; medium-bodied red wines can, but should not, be drunk too young; full-bodied red wines should not be drunk young. This said, we are not looking in this tasting at wines that are merely high in alcohol, but those with great depth and great ageing potential.

We have spread the net fairly wide, with France represented especially by the sturdy wines of the Rhône valley. Some full-bodied Burgundies and Bordeaux appear in the Pinot Noir and Cabernet Sauvignon tastings. The non-French wines are balanced between classic and indigenous grape varieties.

The potential here is in the grapes and the soil, compounded by good vintages and skilful wine making.

APPEARANCE	BOUQUET	PALATE	COMMENTS
Ridge Zinfandel 1986			Geyserville, USA
Fine, deep rich fruit, plummy youthful colour, still with a violet edge.	Pronounced primary fruit aromas: blackcurrants and blackberries, soft and spicy.	Rich flavours, very plummy, blackberries dominant, slight briary fruit edge from small percentage of Petite Syrah and Carignan in the blend.	A lively plummy Zinfandel, still needing 1-2 years. Lighter in style than the Crozes-Hermitage Thalabert (see page 150) but still in the full-bodied category.
Bonnes-Mares 1985 Roumier			Côte d'Or, France
Full, black-cherry dark red, velvety and rich, no sign of ageing. A beautiful colour, ten times darker than the Chambolle-Musigny.	Concentrated, rich, 'multi-tiered' fruit. No new wood to mask the pure fruit, but wood present. Wonderfully deep Pinot Burgundy bouquet.	Firm but sensuous; well-knit, silky but solid, beginning to develop a gamey hint. Firm acidity, marvellous extract and balance.	A very fine example of Côte de Nuits, with less fat than many 1985s. Excellent extract, tannins. Great vineyard, great wine making. A benchmark.
Wynns Cabernet Sauvignon 1985 John Riddock Coonawarra Estate			South Australia
Huge, intense colour, deep crimson, velvety red, still very youthful. Rich and fat.	Concentrated red fruits, touch of cedar, hint of eucalyptus, persistent with a lovely complexity appearing.	Intense, ripe fruit, concentrated blackcurrants and spice. Good (light) use of oak, better balanced than most Australian Cabernets. Impressive finish.	Rich fruit, but firm Cabernet finish, excellent balance: weight and finesse. A world classic.
Beringer Cabernet Sauvignon 1985 Knight's Valley Vineyard			Sonoma, California, USA
Rich, vibrant purple red, still very young and dense, more rich on the glass than the previous wine.	Concentrated blackcurrant leaf and green pepper aroma, very rich, deep extraction, a touch vegetal, muscular and powerful.	Big wine, lots of extract and intensity of ripe fruit, but still very tannic and at the moment, lacks finesse. Needs many years.	More aggressive, in extract and tannin, than the Wynns. A big teeth-coating old-style Napa Cabernet, a 'blockbuster' that needs time.
Châteauneuf-du-Pape 1985 Ch. Rayas			Rhône, France
Full, vibrant concentrated rich crimson, showing no age, but has lost its youthful violet edge.	Incredibly intense, almost spirity impression, high in alcohol, followed by the sweet, farmyardy fruit of very ripe Grenache.	Full and sweet with masses of presence, at the moment all in the attack, with the long wood ageing leaving a degree of volatile acidity and a firm tannin.	A great wine, still overly rich and not the most stable in modern terms, but will turn out to be a superb Châteauneuf in time.
Barolo Monprivato 1984			Piedmont, Italy
Full, youthful deep crimson, deeper and more rich and powerful looking than the Ch. Rayas.	Spicy, rather lean and still woody, but with a good extract of tarry fruit waiting to come through.	Tannic, lean, muscular, old fashioned (ie no soft plummy tannins), an austere and almost a stand-offish wine; great depth and reserve, needs time.	Still very tannic (wood ageing plus natural extract), high natural acidity. Will be very good indeed, if always rather massive.

APPEARANCE	BOUQUET	PALATE	COMMENTS
Torres Gran Coronas Reserva 1982 (Black Label)			Penedès, Spain
Very full-bodied, rich deep red, resembles ruby port, showing no age at all.	Mixture of rich fruits and woody, spicy (nutmeg), minty and even leathery aromas, still evolving.	Full, spicy fruit, rich plum cake impressions, still firm and slightly tannic, but soft on the middle palate due to the ripe fruit. Good acid/tannic balance.	Very well-balanced, complex wine, beginning to open up. The Cabernet Sauvignon (100%) blends in well with the plummy Torres style.
Hermitage 'La Chapelle' 1983 Jaboulet Aîné			Tain l'Hermitage, Rhône, France
Very intense, deep carmine-ruby, clear but still almost impenetrably solid, no hint of age.	Concentrated blackcurranty, blackberry, briary aromas, intense and only just beginning to open up.	Masses of extract, lots of flavour and tannin, most of it from wood ageing, leaving an edgy, vegetal impression that guarantees longevity.	Intense and close knit, does not have the aromatic fruit of the Crozes-Hermitage Thalabert 1986 (see page 150) yet surpasses it in structure and potential.
Châteauneuf-du-Pape 1981 Ch. de Beaucastel			Courthezon, Rhône, France
Rich, deep crimson ruby, a firm leathery/ mahogany hue, vibrant and youthful for the vintage.	Pungent, gamey with concentrated fruits, ripeness and richness and a touch of wood. Mature and opening up.	Impressive balance between sweetness of Châteauneuf-du-Pape fruit and complex leanness, with the different grapes playing their part. Very fine fruit/wood balance.	A very individual wine, low in Grenache for a Châteauneuf, high in Mourvèdre, more structure than fat, more depth than alcohol. A contrast to Ch. Rayas (cf).
Côte-Rôtie 'La Landonne' 1981 E. Guigal			Ampuis, Rhône, France
Very deep, black cherry full-bodied red, the colour extract clinging to the sides of the glass.	Rich, even port-like concentrated fruit, heightened by a touch of volatile acidity, showing blackberries and spices.	Big, almost thick taste, a lovely impression of completely ripe fruit, fine use of wood to balance the richness. Smooth, unctuous, with a firm structure.	An exceptional wine from a medium vintage in the northern Rhône. Great balance and persistence of flavour, powerful and elegant at the same time.
Jean Leon Cabernet Sauvignon 1978			Penedès, Spain
Full, rich, plummy, blackcurranty red, an extremely young colour for a 1978, with a richness that clings to the glass.	Rich, spicy, above all minty bouquet, youthful, ripe fruit.	Spicy, blackcurrants and mint, marked impression of oak, leaving a lean, tannic edge despite the plummy fruit.	Good concentration of fruit, typical 'hot country' Cabernet Sauvignon, possibly over-oaked before bottling, but impressive.
Ch. La Mission Haut Brion 1978 Graves Grand Cru Classé			Pessac, France
Splendid youthful colour: deep ruby, almost black, no signs of maturity, so rich as to be almost oily.	Intense and spicy, with earthy, mineral elements, concentrated ripe fruit.	Mouthfilling fruit, high in fruit, wood and acidity. A big *dry* wine, still very tannic and foursquare.	An old-fashioned wine (cf Barolo) almost more Pauillac than Graves, except for the bouquet. Some (too much?) *vin de presse.* A la Mission classic.

Tasting/Sparkling Wines

This tasting shows a range of different styles of sparkling wine. The best known, most celebrated, sparkling wine is, of course, champagne and the *méthode champenoise* is regarded as being the finest, and for many wine makers and wine drinkers the only way to induce bubbles into still wine.

Since sparkling wines are generally blended and certainly 'manipulated', the taste of the grape is less present than in still wines, with the exception of the Moscato d'Asti. Whereas the wine maker can assume his still wines will be generally drunk with food, sparkling wines are more usually drunk as an aperitif. While champagne no longer has the monopoly of this style of wine, most countries are looking for the same balance of flavour and finesse that has made champagne's reputation.

APPEARANCE	BOUQUET	PALATE	COMMENTS
Crémant de Bourgogne Brut NV Cave de Viré			Mâconnais, France
Attractive pale yellow, good *mousse*, small persistent bubbles.	Green apples aroma, touch of hazelnuts but overall refreshingly green.	Lively, good attack, persistent *mousse* on the palate, better as an aperitif than with a meal.	Rather short finish and highish acidity (Aligoté grape), will soften a little with cellaring, but remain very *brut*.
Asti Spumante NV La Brenta d'Oro			Piedmont, Italy
Pretty, lightish pale yellow, fine persistent *mousse.*	Lovely grapey aroma from the Moscato, pure 'joie de vivre', with the bouquet pushed up by the bubbles.	Light, frothy, fruity, with a sweet attack but good balance through a slight lemony acidity. Very quaffable, only 7° alcohol.	A lovely, well-made Asti, pure and fruity and as different as can be imagined to the Crémant de Bourgogne.
Freixenet Cordon Negro Brut NV Cava			Spain
Pale, very light yellow, brilliant, fine *mousse.*	Very lively, almost Riesling (lemony/petrol edge) in style due to the Parellada grape.	Zesty and lively, with a rather frothy *mousse* that dies away quickly, no great depth.	Lively and with an attractive sweet/fruity flavour. Good as an aperitif, to be drunk young.
Raimat Chardonnay Brut Nature NV Cava			Spain
Fullish yellow, a fine mature colour, quite different to the Freixenet, fine persistent *mousse* with small bubbles.	Floral, honeyed but dry, a lovely waxy Chardonnay fruit.	Full and quite rich in attack with a clean, dry finish, a ripe wine with a good *mousse.* Much better balanced than the Crémant de Bourgogne.	Smooth, lanolin texture through top-quality ripe grapes and bottle age. A very fine example indeed.
Omar Khayyam 1986 Brut			Maharasta, India
Clean, lemony yellow, fine, persistent bubbles.	Clean fruit, slightly nutty Chardonnay bouquet, hints of wood.	Clean, dry flavour and finish, good *mousse* and texture, much in the *cava* style, well-made wine.	Fine balance of fruit/acidity, good length, not much sense of *terroir* but a better quality sparkling wine than many lesser champagnes.
Blanquette de Limoux 'Laurens' Brut 1986 Cave de Chenevrières			Languedoc, France
Pale, soft, pale straw yellow, very fine, lively *mousse.*	Soft, faintly honeysuckle, ripe fruit and no edge of acidity.	Full of grapey flavour, but less obvious and summery than the Asti, fully sparkling, but not aggressive, very well made, good length.	A very fine sparkling wine from one of the oldest *appellations* in France. Such wines are in no way copying champagne. Stylish, natural fruit, *brut* finish.

APPEARANCE	BOUQUET	PALATE	COMMENTS
Croser 1986 Brut			Petaluma, South Australia
Fine pale yellow with lemony edge, very fine *mousse*, persistent, an impressive appearance.	Lovely, mature fruit, impression of white grapes dominant, stylish and lingering.	More aggressive on palate than expected, biscuity, winey flavour, showing presence of black grapes. Good length, structure and especially a fine creamy texture.	Lovely balance, Blanc de Blancs on the nose, more Pinot on the palate, perfect wine making, better than anything else from Australia and a good deal from France. Quality from attention to detail.
Vouvray Petillant 1985 Brut Clos Naudin			Vouvray, Loire, France
Medium fullish yellow, touch of gold, mature, persistent fine *mousse*.	Floral, fruity but discreet, honeysuckle, soft fruit.	Clear, balance fruit, *mousse* persistent but not aggressive, fine Chenin flavour. Sparkle beautifully blended in through long bottle ageing.	Very dry finish to complete the honeysuckle grapeyness on the palate. A discreet sparkling wine, perfect with food.
Veuve Clicquot Yellow Label Brut NV			Reims, Champagne, France
Clean, medium yellow, fine persistent *mousse*, classic.	Nutty, biscuity bouquet, rather creamy, fine balance and fruit.	Fine flavour and length of fruit, plainly red grapes dominant, almost a meaty flavour, but still elegant. Shows bottle ageing. Very good.	A 'plump', winey champagne, showing style and *terroir* producing quality. A benchmark non-vintage champagne.
Schramsberg Blanc de Noirs 1982 Brut			Napa Valley, California
Lovely pale yellow, only a hint of gold, still very young for a 1982, fine persistent *mousse*.	Very attractive toasted bouquet, combination of black grapes and oak casks. A very successful style.	Rich, almost soft, the toastiness remains, but dominated by winey flavour, persistent *mousse* and good depth.	Excellent balance, a complete contrast to the Croser, combines meatiness and elegance. A classic, superlative quality *méthode champenoise*, follows on well from the Veuve Clicquot.
Bollinger 1979 RD Extra Brut (Disgorged 21.10.1988)			Ay, Champagne, France
Medium yellow, slight hints of gold, mature colour. Superb *mousse*, persistent and really tiny bubbles.	Fabulous, yeasty, winey bouquet, great depth and complexity.	Rich, winey, fully mature but will last for years. Can almost taste the barrels the wine was aged in, weighty but elegant, very long.	Winey and mature, but still full of youth, high acidity, almost the pure essence of Champagne. Has to be drunk with a meal. A triumph.
Langlois Crémant Rosé Brut			Saumur, Loire, France
Very pretty salmon pink, good *mousse*, lovely to look at.	Pure fruit, raspberries/ strawberries from the Cabernet Franc, but pleasantly discreet.	Soft and slightly sweet fruit on attack in keeping with a rosé wine that is lightly effervescent, rather than a sparkling rosé.	Fine fruit flavours with a soft, charming finish. Not a serious wine, but a pleasurable one.

Tasting/Rosés

In this tasting we compare the different styles of rosé. There are very few wines that are specifically rosé, that is to say that the *appellation* is for a vin rosé alone. In France, Tavel is one, Rosé des Riceys from Champagne is another. Otherwise, the production of a rosé is up to the wine maker. While *appellation contrôlée* wines do not admit the mixing of red and white wine, they do accept the addition of white grapes to red, generally to a maximum of 20%. Basically, a rosé is a light red wine, the pretty pink colour coming from a much shorter contact of the skins with the must than for true red wines. The style of vinification and ageing will determine the taste of the wine as much as will the region from which it comes.

One conclusion from this tasting is that a rosé should be fresh and appealing, and that, with very rare exceptions, they lose their point if they are not. Another aspect is that rosés have much less bouquet than either a white or a red wine, and that where the bouquet is pronounced, it is generally from a wine made with a single grape variety (Pinot Noir, Cabernet Franc), than from a selection of grapes.

APPEARANCE	BOUQUET	PALATE	COMMENTS
White Zinfandel 1988 Robert Mondavi			Napa Valley, California, USA
Very pale pink, a 'blush' wine, with just an edge of colour.	Light, fruity, floral, refreshing, summery.	Clean fruity attack, soft, sweetish finish, reminiscent of rosehips. Fine appley acidity.	A delightful light rosé, almost a *blanc de noirs*, more for drinking on its own than with food.
Capezzana 1988 'Vin Ruspo' Rosato di Carmignano			Italy
Lovely violetty rosé, almost very pale red, rose-pink, a very summery colour.	Deliciously fruity, pure grapey fruit with floral overtones.	Clean, straightforwardly fruity on palate, slight edge of fruit tannin, quite full on aftertaste (13°).	A *saignée* rosé, lively and fresh, but underlining the presence of red grapes. Very well made, more serious than the Mondavi.
Chinon Rosé 1988 Ch. de la Grille			Loire, France
Pale, rose pink with lovely violetty tones, almost a perfect rosé colour, more lively and fresh than the Bandol (cf).	French fruit aromas, raspberry, bouncy, lively fruit.	Zesty, almost Sauvignon Blanc attack, lively fruit with clean vegetal acidity: direct fruit with a distinct bite.	Clean finish, very dry for a Cabernet Franc rosé, obviously a northern wine, complete contrast to the Bandol.
Tavel 1988 Domaine de la Mordorée			Rhône, France
Brilliant violetty pink, lively, but fuller and richer than the Chinon.	Explosive fruit aromas, very grapey but with a fleshiness from the Grenache grape balanced by superb fruit acidity.	Same impression on the palate of lively and fleshy fruit with no heaviness while maintaining a strong style. A fine mouthful of wine.	An exceptional rosé to combine a fresh grapey attack and long fruit flavours with elegance and verve. A real benchmark for Tavel.
Bandol 1986 Domaine Tempier			Provence, France
Pale, salmon pink, pretty and still young for 1986, a soft, fading silky pink.	Perfumed, spicy, almost resinous, fine and complex, has lost the primary fruit of the Tavel.	High quality, soft, spicy fruit, slight presence of wood, a firm rosé with plenty of flavour.	Lovely, subdued (compared to the Tavel) concentration of flavour for a rosé, winey, serious. A classic style.
Ostenberg Schlossberg Spätburgunduer Weissherbst Spätlese Trocken 1983			Germany
Pale, partridge-eye rosé, a yellowish pink, in fact 'gris', but very pretty.	Attractive, floral bouquet, still youthful, especially for a 1983.	Soft on attack, quite rich Pinot fruit, hints of strawberries, rather aggressive finish due to highish alcohol.	Clean finish, good fruit, now passing its best, the opposite end of the spectrum to the Mondavi Zinfandel.

Tasting/Grape Varieties/Riesling

In an attempt to show how the classic French varieties behave in differing soils and climates, we have set up eight tastings. French wines have been used as the criterion in all these tastings with the exception of the Rieslings, where we have used wines from Germany. We have tried to be as broad as possible with the selection of wines, and have used those in which the characteristics of each variety are plainly to be seen.

The *cépages* have already been discussed earlier (pages 70–85), and they have all appeared in earlier tastings.

It can forcefully be argued that the Riesling grape makes the finest white wine in the world. It is a low-yielding grape and is very slow-ripening in cool climates, yet it is this ability to ripen over a long sunny autumn and into winter that produces the concentration of sugar and flavour that makes these wines so extraordinary.

In Europe, the Riesling thrives only on slopes fully exposed to the sun, and only works well if planted in the right conditions. If the exposition is wrong, the soil unsuitable or the vintage poor, the resulting wine will be hard and acid. The basic Riesling style is dry, lively, with delicate, floral aromas and a smooth, perfumed, clean taste. It is relatively low in alcohol and high in acidity, but it has a youthful lemony acidity that balances beautifully the fruit of the wine on the palate.

The Riesling grape is planted all over the world, more so than any other fine grape variety. This tasting uses German Rieslings as the benchmark, for it is they that set the criterion for these wines. With the varying degrees of origin and sweetness, the style of the grape comes through every time: the high quality, positive attack, the great freshness, delicacy and length of flavour.

APPEARANCE	BOUQUET	PALATE	COMMENTS
Rhine Riesling Leeuwin Estate 1987			Margaret River, Western Australia
Brilliant pale yellow with greeny tints, quite rich looking.	Pronounced floral aromas, honeysuckle, with fruity sweetness.	Clean, soft fruit on attack, crisp lime finish, very attractive flavour and fruit, slight residual sugar, good length.	Pretty, floral wine with fine citric overtones, both classic Riesling elements. Well made, to be drunk young.
Petaluma Rhine Riesling 1987			Piccadilly, South Australia
Brilliant pale yellow, with slightly firmer green tints than the Leeuwin, and a firmer colour.	Concentrated, floral, rich, even oily: complexity and persistence from ripe grapes and fine wine making.	Ripe, floral attack, a softer peach-like fruit in the middle and a firm Riesling finish. Complex, with good length and presence.	A beautifully made wine (see Croser 1986, page 155) harmonious and persistent with the clean bite of Riesling acidity. High class.
Riesling 1985 Cuvée Frederick Emile			Trimbach, Ribeauville, Alsace, France
Clean, very pale whitish yellow, just beginning to take on more colour, paler than the first two.	Classic Alsace Riesling 'floral/petrol' bouquet, followed by a lemony fruit, persistent and penetrating.	Lively and packed with restrained (ie not obvious) fruit, beginning to show complexity and length, excellent acidity.	A fine and pure example of textbook Riesling. The dry Alsatian style is underlined by the Trimbach vinification, lean wines that age to perfection.
Wehlener-Sonnenuhr 1986 Riesling Kabinett Deinhard			Mosel, Germany
Clean, brilliant, limpid, very pale yellow.	Delicately floral bouquet, slightly honeyed/apricot overtones, but forecasting a a dry or off-dry wine.	Lively, floral/fruity, summery flavour with a fine lemony acidity in the finish. Fine and balanced, a lovely wine.	A classic Mosel German Riesling from a very good but not a great year. Delicacy, finesse and length from the grape and the northern *terroir*.
Mittelheimer Edelmann Riesling Kabinett 1986 Weingut Hupfeld Erben			Rheingau, Germany
Clear, brilliant palish yellow with slight green tints, young and fresh.	Beautiful Riesling bouquet, floral with mineral/ petrol tones. Stylish, racy, hints of fruit from ripe grapes.	Drier than expected after the nose, but quite broad flavour, especially compared to the preceding wine. Good concentration of fruit and crisp acidity. Almost bone dry.	Still very young, will become more complex and penetrating with age. Drier but bigger than the Mosel wine.

APPEARANCE	BOUQUET	PALATE	COMMENTS
Firestone Johannisberg Riesling 1986			California, USA
Medium to full yellow with green tints, really quite rich and giving the impression of a sweet wine.	Concentrated, very floral, honeyed style: peaches and apricots with the clear Riesling 'zip' of acidity.	Floral and intensely aromatic on the palate, a full Riesling, high in residual sugar, a broad fruity sweetness and definite concentration.	A full, fruity wine with the Germanic persistence of fruit, the Alsatian broadness and the full ripeness from California. Very good Riesling.
Snowqualmie White Riesling 1987 Reserve Late Harvest			Washington State, USA
Medium full yellow, slight greeny tinge, rich, the colour of a young Sauternes.	Concentrated hot-house fruit aromas: peaches, apricots, fine and penetrating.	Rich concentration on palate, honeyed, almost barley sugar fruit, but still the Riesling acidity present. Good length.	A juicy, lively wine, really delicious in the dessert wine (see page 178) category, concentrated ripe fruit, high residual sugar, fine balance.
Traben-Trabacher Goldgrübe 1976 Riesling Auslese Deinhard			Mosel, Germany
Lovely mature medium yellow, beginning to show gold, but still with a hint of green. Rich.	Ripe fruits, apricots and peaches, with lanolin and barley sugar overtones. A beautiful, arresting and complex bouquet.	Perfect balance between sugar and fruit with a lovely purity of texture and flavour, finishes clean and youthful, despite its 13 years.	A classic Auslese from the Mosel, with more underlying acidity than the rather broader Rheingaus. Benchmark aged (but not old) Riesling.
Nelson Late Harvest Rhine Riesling 1988			Redwood Valley Estate, New Zealand
Full yellow straw-gold, very rich indeed, clinging and cloying. Impressive.	Marvellously concentrated apricot and honeyed aromas, very, very rich, extraordinary extract, over-ripe, even raisiny.	Wonderful, sweet, intensely rich flavours, with the vigorous acidity of the Riesling grape. Almost an Eiswein in weight and style.	Superb finish, cloying perhaps, but with vivid flavours and not tiring. Great extraction of fruit blossoming out across the palate.
Joseph Phelps Johannisberg Riesling 1985 Special Select Late Harvest			Napa Valley, California, USA
Full straw amber-gold, just losing its yellowness. Exceptionally rich.	Massively concentrated bouquet, almost marmaladey, pure concentration of apricots and quinces, intense fruit.	A continuation of the bouquet, rich extract of apricots for fruit and quinces for acidity, quite extraordinary weight and length. Residual sugar 24%, bigger than a German TBA.	The epitome of richness and concentration, viscous, heady, really the essence of the grape, more a liqueur than a wine.
Riesling Hugel 1976 Sélection de Grains Nobles			Riquewihr, Alsace, France
Rich, yellowy gold/ amber, showing a little age, vibrant, oily.	Richly honeyed, concentrated, floral, with a farmyardy *terroir* edge and petrol-like Riesling character.	Concentrated honeyed, apricotty fruit, younger on the palate than on the nose, massive sweetness but very good acidity. Easier to digest than the Phelps, with a much firmer structure.	Quite different to the Phelps and the TBA, as this has 16.2° alcohol (Phelps under half at 7.2°) and was still fermenting in July 1977. A work of art.
Oestricher Lenchen Riesling 1971 TBA Deinhard			Rheingau, Germany
Clear, bright amber-gold, colour of a light amontillado, very rich.	Hugely rich, apricotty, sugary, even syrupy bouquet, more of an essence than a wine, even more so than the Phelps, due to concentration through age.	Rich, unctuous, oily, massively concentrated fruit backed by a crackling acidity. Perfect balance, sweet but not cloying. Incredible persistence.	A fabulous comparison between these last two, both the perfect essence of the Riesling grape. Many more dimensions than the Canadian Icewine (see page 147), even more than the Phelps. A very great wine from a great year. Only pure dedication can create wines like these.

Tasting/Grape Varieties/Sauvignon Blanc

The Sauvignon Blanc cannot claim the same complexity and depth as the Chardonnay or the Riesling, or (in France) the Chenin Blanc, but it is still one of the world's major white wine grape varieties. Its dominant characteristics are: an explosive bouquet of gooseberry or redcurrant fruit, often with grassy or leafy overtones, an immediate fruit on the palate and a slightly tart finish. The Sauvignon is at its most typical, or most obviously Sauvignon, in the centre of the Loire Valley, where it is solely responsible for the wines of Sancerre, Pouilly-Fumé, Quincy, Reuilly and Ménétou-Salon, as well as the popular Sauvignon de Touraine. Recently New Zealand has been producing some fine Sauvignon of which the most remarkable is Cloudy Bay.

When transplanted to the south-west of France, however, and the region of Bordeaux in particular, the young assertive style is softened. In the Graves *appellation*, where it is planted on poor, gravelly soil and blended principally with the Sémillon, the Sauvignon produces a wine of great finesse, firmness and longevity. The Sauvignon also plays a minor but essential rôle in the Sauternes, Barsac and other sweet white wines.

An aspect that the Sauvignon Blanc shares with its cousin the Cabernet Sauvignon is that it thrives in warm climates. It is now being planted across the south of France, in the north of Spain, in Italy and in the USA, South America and Australia. It has done particularly well in California, where the style seems to be divided between the Loire Valley 'Blanc Fumés' and the Graves, which is due more to the decision of the wine maker than the grape itself.

This tasting, along with the Sauvignon-based wines in the first three tastings, shows some of the classic examples of the grape variety.

APPEARANCE	BOUQUET	PALATE	COMMENTS
Sancerre 1988 Henry Natter, Domaine de Montigny			France
Brilliant, very pale, almost white yellow, but not wishy-washy.	Striking aroma of blackcurrant leaves, crisp and refreshing.	Lovely balance of fruit and acidity. Definite impression of *terroir* and more finesse than is usual in Sancerre.	A very fine example, made more to show the *terroir* than the grape, thus less obvious, more complex than most.
Cloudy Bay 1988			Cape Mentelle, Blenheim, New Zealand
Brilliant palish yellow, slight green tints, firm and consistent.	Immediate fruit aromas, redcurrants, rhubarb, blackcurrants, and also a great sense of class.	Similar impression on the palate, with a fine balance between the slightly aggressive Sauvignon/blackcurrant attack and the lively, polished finish.	An elegant, mouthfilling wine with a lively concentration of aromatic fruit, length and elegance. Very fine, a little more punch than the Sancerre.
Katnook Estate 1987			Coonawarra, South Australia
Brilliant pale yellow, lively, clean and still fresh.	Faintly aggressive, slightly vegetal Sauvignon aromas, also a touch exotic.	Softer, less aggressive on the palate, full of ripe, citrusy fruit, good acidity on the finish, but not much length.	An attractive wine, light and lively for a Sauvignon from Australia, but not in the class of the Cloudy Bay.
Neil Ellis 1987 Vineyard Selection			Stellenbosch, South Africa
Clean, pale to medium yellow, no green tints, lively.	Rather discreet bouquet of ripe fruits but with toasty/charred oak still dominant.	Smooth fruit on the palate, not an aggressive Sauvignon, much helped in this respect by the toasty French oak.	Less stylish than Cloudy Bay, rather richer and more of a food wine, and a fine example of the use of oak on young Sauvignon.
Dry Creek 1987 Fumé Blanc			Sonoma County, California, USA
Quite light, lively, clean pale yellow, pretty and youthful.	Immediate Sauvignon fruit, slight 'catty' grassy aromas in the Dry Creek style, but not too marked to be out of balance.	Clean, crisp fruit with just a touch of oak (not discernible on the nose), good intensity of fruit and quite full (13.5°), dry but not acid finish.	A well-made, complex wine from an established winery for the Fumé style. Fruit/oak/acidity all in balance. Different in approach to the previous wine.
Ch. Malartic-Lagraviere 1984 Graves Grand Cru Classé			France
Pale yellow, almost white/lemony yellow, very pale for a 5-year-old wine, but not light.	Slightly resinous, piney and oaky aromas dominate a clean, lively Sauvignon bouquet.	Fruity, floral flavours over a smooth, lanolin texture. The presence of oak and the *terroir* dominates the grape variety.	Excellent balance, beginning to mature when other wines would have been past their best. A subtle wine.

Note: All these are *dry* wines. Sweet and botrytis affected Sauvignons are to be found on pages 146-7.

Tasting/Grape Varieties/Chardonnay

The Chardonnay grape makes the world's finest dry white wine. This is not to decry the qualities of the other fine varieties, but if the emphasis is on *dry* white wine, the Chardonnay has no equal. In character it is not so definitive as, say, the Riesling, which tastes quite plainly Riesling wherever it is grown and however it is vinified, and therefore it is less easy to cast as a type.

There are classic Chardonnay styles from France: Blanc de Blancs from Champagne, Chablis, Meursault, the Montrachet family, Pouilly-Fuissé, Mâcon Blanc – yet these wines are so different that at first sight they might not even be made from the same grape. But, in fact, what other grape could they come from? Certainly not the Riesling, the Chenin Blanc, the Sauvignon or the Sémillon. It is the idea of *terroir* that leads one to recognize certain styles of Chardonnay: Chablis is different from Meursault, Coteaux Champenois very different from Pouilly-Fuissé. The character of these basic *appellations* comes from their soil and climate, enhanced by the generally accepted methods of wine-making. Thus, a tank-fermented Meursault that has not seen oak will differ from what might be expected, as will a Mâcon Blanc that has been barrel-fermented and aged in wood. Even outside France, where the principles of *appellations* are less strict with regard to where grape varieties may be planted, the style still evolves from the soil, climate, vinification and ageing.

Common to all these wines is the taste of the Chardonnay itself: fresh yellow in colour, ranging from pale to golden, sometimes with green tints; fruity on the nose, sometimes appley, flowery, buttery, nutty, oaky; much the same on the palate, well-balanced, never sweet and seldom tart. Chardonnay is the perfect wine to drink with a meal.

This tasting shows the great adaptability of the Chardonnay to different regions and styles of wine-making.

APPEARANCE	BOUQUET	PALATE	COMMENTS
Tiefenbrünner Chardonnay dell'Alto Adige 1988			Italy
Clean, lively, very pale, youthful, light.	Floral, lively, slightly 'pear drop' aromas (cold fermentation), vivacious and mouthwatering.	Same impression on palate, grapefruity/melon fruit, fresh acidity, good balance.	Delicious summery Chardonnay showing stylish fruit. Perfect for the very dry white wine category.
Mâcon-Prissé 1988 Georges Duboeuf			Mâconnais, France
Clear, brilliant pale yellow, lively and fresh, richer than the Tiefenbrünner.	Floral fruity aromas, hints of grapefruit and pineapple, quite rich but with a lively acidity.	Fine, grapey Chardonnay, no wood, all up-front lively fruit, ripeness tempered by good acidity.	Straightforward zestful Mâcon. Other Mâcon-Villages – Viré, Clessé, Loché – would have more depth, as would Saint-Véran. More for youthful quaffing.
Chablis 1987 ler Cru les Butteaux Jean-Marie Raveneau			France
Clear, very pale yellow, green tints, light, almost Muscadet colour.	Slight straw-like aromas, hints of wood, vegetal, firm, fruit just beginning to show.	Firm and more positive fruit on palate. Lean, good structure, has none of the honeyed, fleshy charm of the 1986; a vintage which needs time to show the fruit.	Completely opposite in style to the easy openness of the Mâcon, and to the richer Chardonnays from the New World. Lean and tough, but will improve.
Ngatarawa 1987			Hawkes Bay, New Zealand
Fullish yellow, no green tints, rich and full-bodied.	Immediate impression of oak and exotic fruits, full and rich, with slightly vegetal undertones, still immature.	Full, fruity, oaky, buttery with a grapefruity richness showing fruit and acidity. A big wine (over 13°), but not overpowering.	Rather massive and forthright at the moment, needs a year to lose its aggression, very good fruit extract, big for a New Zealand Chardonnay.
Jim Barry 1987			Clare Valley, South Australia
Clean, medium-pale, buttery yellow, quite rich.	Very floral, honeysuckle plus ripe, exotic fruits.	Rich and floral on the palate, fruity, almost sweet attack, with citrus fruit finish, has almost the richness and fruit of a Gewürztraminer.	An Alsatian-style Chardonnay with rich citrusy fruits and only just a touch of wood. Fruity rather than complex.

APPEARANCE	BOUQUET	PALATE	COMMENTS
Phelps 1987			Saint Helena, Napa Valley, California, USA
Clear, brilliant pale yellow, fresh, lively, well balanced.	Very fine on the nose: fruity, grapefruit, with a touch of almonds. Much more elegant than the last two, with a lovely extract.	Really fine, fruity and floral attack with a hidden touch of oak. Quite high in extract and alcohol, but no heaviness, very good length.	A lovely style of wine, akin to Puligny-Montrachet. Perfect, confident wine making, even the impression of *terroir*.
Acacia 1987			Carneros, Napa Valley, California, USA
Clean, pale yellow, greeny edge, lively, quite rich and complete.	Attractive oak and fruit aromas well balanced, elegant, in the new 'restrained' California style.	Fine clean fruit, slightly minerally overtones and lemony acidity. Evidence of the cool Carneros climate, honeyed fruit beginning to appear, very well balanced, still young.	Another French-style California Chardonnay (complete contrast to a weighty Beringer Chardonnay also tasted), showing the Chardonnay influenced by climate, soil and wine making.
Covey Rise 1986			Idaho, Washington State, USA
Clean, pale yellow, youthful greeny edge, a little lighter than Acacia.	Lively, floral Chardonnay fruit, a touch of vanilla/oak.	Attractive, lively fruit, relatively light, but subtle, backed by oak and minerally tones. Balanced and stylish. On the light side.	Plainly young vines. Very good example of an emerging vineyard area, fine wine making, looking for polish and style rather than weight.
Meursault 1986 Clos de la Barre Comtes Lafon			Côte d'Or, France
Full yellow, even slightly gold hints, no green tints, very rich and unctuous, full even for a 1986.	Honeyed, buttery, even slightly resinous, still rich and oaky and needs time.	Complex, rather sweet fruit on attack, backed by slightly charred oak. Good extract, alcohol/acid balance, great presence and weight, but not heavy.	Still young, but carries a faint over-ripe quality due to late picked grapes. Has the rich nuttiness of a fine Meursault and the fleshy fruit of a ripe Chardonnay.
Chassagne-Montrachet 1986 Ier Cru Morgeot Jean-Noel Gagnard			Côte d'Or, France
Really fine full medium yellow with green tints. An exciting, firm colour.	Still discreet, floral, oaky aromas, sense of class and *terroir*.	Fine, slightly subdued fruit, faintly honeyed with a touch of oak for ageing and backbone. A fine, polished wine with purity of style.	Still a little over-oaked, but will be superb. Shows the quality of *terroir* and wine making, which dominates the varietal. Classic white Burgundy, thus a benchmark Chardonnay.
Puligny-Montrachet 1986 Ier Cru les Referts Louis Jadot			Côte d'Or, France
Very fine pale straw yellow with green tints, firm, quite rich.	Pronounced floral May blossom bouquets, slight nuttiness, elegant.	Beautiful expression of fruit on palate, with the new oak blending in well, quite rich in alcohol, but has the subtlety and polish of the best Pulignys.	In contrast to the Chassagne, a fraction more fleshy and more forward. Good example.
Corton-Charlemagne 1985 Louis Jadot			Côte d'Or, France
Fabulously rich, oily yellow-green colour with a wonderful weight and presence.	Floral and nutty, great persistence, masses of fruit and extract waiting to blossom out, great quality, no heaviness.	Intensely fruity, almost sweet, nutty, lean and rich at the same time. Terrific length and persistence, still not at its best. Carries extra weight of the very ripe 1985 vintage.	No doubt about being a 'Grand Vin'. Shows power, extract, elegance, a formidable presence, perfectly balanced and can only improve. Overwhelms the other Chardonnays in this tasting.

Tasting/Grape Varieties/Chenin Blanc

The Chenin Blanc, also known in France as the Pineau de la Loire (no relation to the Pinot family of Burgundy, Alsace and Champagne), is a most versatile grape variety. In France it produces all the great wines in Touraine and Anjou, wines on a par with the finest whites that the country can produce. Montlouis, Vouvray, Saumur, Savennières, Bonnezeaux and Coteaux du Layon all share the honeyed fruit and lemony acidity that rivals the Riesling grape, and in the years when the grapes are attacked by botrytis, the results are wines in the class of the finest Sauternes. The Chenin Blanc, like the Riesling, has the quality of making fruity, crisply acidic wines from an early harvest or a light year, semi-sweet wines from a later picking, and luscious dessert wines from grapes sometimes picked well into November. It is also one of the classic grapes for the *méthode champenoise* sparkling wines, as is proved by the well-established sparkling wine production around Saumur.

Outside France, however, the Chenin loses some of its acidity, and produces softer wines with an easy charm. It is one of the most successful varietals in South Africa and this tasting features two examples. See also the two Chenin Blancs from Touraine and Anjou in the tastings on pages 144-147.

APPEARANCE	BOUQUET	PALATE	COMMENTS
Dry Creek 1988 Dry Chenin Blanc			Sonoma County, California, USA
Pale, crisp, lively yellow, light and fresh looking.	Floral fruity – melons – with citrus overtones, mouthwatering.	Quite full and fruity, has the up-front fruit and profile of a young Sauvignon, just a hint of sweetness, good acidity showing the Chenin Blanc.	A lively, pleasant wine for easy drinking. Well made, a good alternative to the Sauvignon, fruity and fresh, no great complexity.
KWV Steen 1987			Coastal Region, South Africa
Pale, lively, light yellow with a certain richness.	Pretty, herbaceous aromas with light fruit and pleasant acidity.	Clean flavours, rather lean after the bouquet, crisp dry finish.	Correct, clean Chenin/Steen style, but lacks a little charm. A little overwhelmed by the fruity freshness of the Dry Creek.
Savennières 1986 Clos de la Coulée de Serrant			Anjou, Loire, France
Clear, medium yellow, quite full-bodied, lively, a fine colour.	Faintly honeyed and slightly earthy bouquet, pure Anjou Chenin, only just beginning to show its complexity.	Lively rather than overtly fruity, minerally overtones, acidity dominates the fruit now, but there is great aromatic potential.	This rare wine needs at least five years to open out. At the moment the firmness and persistence show a sense of *terroir* and potential, little else.
Vouvray 1986 Ch. Gaudrelle			Touraine, Loire, France
Full medium yellow, green tints, quite rich and full-bodied.	Lively citrus fruit aromas, marked by honeysuckle overtones, floral and honeyed, persistent, high quality.	Delicious impact of floral fruit, striking balance of honeyed richness and acidity. Definite impression of *appellation*, which dominates the grape variety.	Very fine example of *demi-sec* Vouvray, with rich sugars and high natural acidity. More approachable than the Coulée de Serrant, and leaner than the Vouvray sec (see page 145).
Vouvray 'Moelleux' 1985 Le Haut Lieu Domaine Huet			Loire, France
Clean, palish yellow, paler than the Ch. Gaudrelle, pale for the year and for a 'moelleux' (due perhaps to some SO_2), yet very rich.	Soft, fruity, floral bouquet, slight earthiness, impression of honey and flowers, fine and delicate.	Same delicious delicacy on palate, with a lovely attack, sweet but not oversweet, less weight than the Ch. Gaudrelle, but more persistence and finesse.	Beautiful now, but should be kept to fill out, take on colour and richness for 15-20 years. A beautifully poised, harmonious wine.
Nederburg 1978 Edelkuer			Paarl, South Africa
Fabulous, brilliant bright amber, a burnt amontillado colour, very rich.	Intense, golden syrup, bitter oranges bouquet with toffee and raisins. Concentrated and heady, wonderful extract.	Excessively sweet, raisiny flavour. Extremely rich, impression of botrytis, but good acidity on the finish and not at all cloying. Very long.	An exceptional wine, (see Sweet Wines page 146), on a par with the best of dessert wines with its rich/bitter taste.

Tasting/Grape Varieties/Sémillon

Although recognised as the basis of the finest sweet wines from Sauternes, Barsac and other Bordeaux *appellations*, as well as some of the most individual dry Graves, the Sémillon has only recently been considered as a major grape variety. Australia has been the country most responsible for this and Sémillons from the Hunter Valley remain the finest examples of this grape used on its own. In the Gironde, blended with 10-20% Sauvignon (and a little Muscadelle for floral aroma), the Sémillon provides the soft fleshy fruit base for the 'zip' of the Sauvignon.

The Sémillon is more sensitive to climate than the more hardy Sauvignon and Chardonnay, and has to be severely controlled to avoid the blandness of over-production or clumsiness of too much alcohol. It is naturally low in immediate aroma and has a lack of acidity which gives the impression of softness. Picked early it has a smooth lemony flavour in contrast to the assertiveness of the Sauvignon, and this smoothness can be enhanced by wood ageing to achieve the mature, waxy or lanolin style which is Sémillon at its most expressive.

For this tasting we have chosen a selection of dry wines. See also the Lindeman's Sémillon and the two Sauternes in the sweet wines tasting.

APPEARANCE	BOUQUET	PALATE	COMMENTS
Rothbury Estate 1988	Brokenback Vineyard		Hunter Valley, NSW, Australia
Really lovely brilliant pale greeny-yellow. Vibrant and fresh.	Stunning, almost explosive floral, appley, herbaceous aromas, clean and lively extract of fruit, no oak used, hence pure grapey fruit.	Fine, crisp, elegant flavour, floral and fresh, quite long, despite low alcohol at 10.5°, perfect now but will keep.	A beautifully-made wine, a classic of its grape variety, blending long, aromatic flavour, depth and good acidity without aggression.
Moss Wood 1986			Margaret River, Western Australia
Full, brilliant yellowy-green, rich-looking and still very fresh.	Smooth, waxy, ripe fruit, very Sémillon, with hints of grapefruit.	Smooth and very fruity, mouthfilling, excellent use of oak as a support which adds weight and complexity; long, exciting flavour.	A classic in the international sense: the grape is very present on the attack, elegance, length and balance thereafter. Even Domaine Benoit (cf) tastes short in comparison.
'R'. de Ch. Rieussec 1986	**Bordeaux Supérieur**		Sauternes, France
Brilliant pale yellow, quite rich but still bright and fresh.	Not over-powerful, but soft waxy fruit.	Big flavour across the palate with a dry finish. Has the slightly waxy Sémillon style, quite honeyed and floral with a good bite at the end, but a touch heavy.	Rather forthright compared to the other wines, perhaps not really at ease being a dry Sauternes.
Mercurey Bay 1985			Waikoukou, New Zealand
Lovely colour, fullish but clean yellow with green tints, impressive.	Immediate impact of fruit, rich at first, more acidic and firm (nettles, minerals) after.	Firm fruity attack, leading to a markedly herbaceous finish, probably due to young vines. Almost more Sauvignon than Sémillon.	A sense of *terroir* – herby, spicy, even citric – dominates the grape. An individual wine, still very fresh and young.
Domaine Benoit 1985			Graves, France
Very fresh and youthful pale yellow, beginning to deepen, quite rich.	Very fine soft, ripe fruit, waxy, slightly smoky, lovely balance.	Clean and quite full, oak still present but only as a background, has the weight of a Meursault, soft fruit and good length.	A fairly new departure for Graves to use 100% Sémillon, now being imitated. Complete contrast to the Smith-Haut-Lafitte (see page 145).
The Rothbury Estate 1976	Individual Paddock		Hunter Valley, NSW, Australia
Full, rich, greeny-yellow, taking on a faint touch of gold, but still incredibly young for a 13-year-old Sémillon.	Waxy, slightly earthy and 'farmyardy' bouquet, a hint of oak, lovely ripe mature fruit.	Same soft, suave fruit across the palate, buttery texture with an edge of acidity. Perfect maturity with no loss of vivacity, difficult to find in a 13 y.o. dry white.	A rounded, complete, vivacious wine, with the wood showing through. A tribute to selected, healthy ripe grapes and dedicated wine making.

Tasting/Grape Varieties/Cabernet Sauvignon

When considering the character of different grape varieties, the basic style is usually found to be inseparable from that of a particular type of wine made in France. Thus, Chardonnay equals white Burgundy, Gamay equals Beaujolais, Syrah equals Hermitage, and so on. On these lines, Cabernet Sauvignon equals Médoc. Although Médoc is very, very rarely 100% Cabernet Sauvignon, and is never intended to be so, it is to the wines of this region, and to Pauillac and Saint-Julien in particular, that the Cabernet is most often compared. Wherever planted, however, the characteristics are the same: a very full, intense red colour (almost inky black when young), a pungent aroma of blackcurrants, peppers, with a touch of cinnamon or cedar, great depth of flavour, austere, chewy, often rough and always tannic when young, but with a clear fruit throughout. Except when very young, when it is forbiddingly tannic, the Cabernet Sauvignon is firm and refreshing; red wines do not normally cloy on the palate, but none of them are as delightfully clean as the Cabernet, as we shall see below.

The Cabernet Sauvignon is a most consistent grape variety and is planted (at least where red grapes can ripen) throughout the world. In France, where its northern limit is the Loire Valley, it is grown throughout the south-west, and has found its way into vineyards across southern France that are anxious to improve their quality. In Italy, the raspberry-scented Cabernet Franc is more popular, yet the Cabernet Sauvignon is producing a handful of exceptional wines. Throughout eastern Europe, South Africa, Australia and the Americas, the Cabernet Sauvignon is looked on as the classic red grape, even if other varieties are indigenous or more successful.

When unblended, the Cabernet Sauvignon style is four-square and uncompromising; with the addition of suitable varieties like the Merlot or the Cabernet Franc (according to the soil and climate), the inherent finesse is only enhanced, while as a blender grape in itself, it adds structure, fruit and elegance. The Cabernet Sauvignon grape is a thoroughbred, as these wines, and others from previous tastings, should prove.

APPEARANCE	BOUQUET	PALATE	COMMENTS
Stonyridge 1987			Waiheke Island, New Zealand
		Cabernet Sauvignon 79%, Merlot 15%, Cabernet Franc 4%, Malbec 2%	
Huge colour, intense, plummy, purple/black-red, very full, the intensity of a young Hermitage.	Spicy, ripe, blackcurranty, peppery fruit, still very young and shut in; oak very present.	Masses of ripe fruit on attack, followed by masses of quite hard tannins that are balanced by the fruit, but a wine of more intensity than subtlety.	A serious example of concentration of extract and fruit, needs at least five years.
Vasse Felix 1987			Margaret River, Western Australia
Lovely, deep, full, rich blackcurranty red, still very young, attractive.	Rich, almost heady, very blackcurranty/blackberry aromas, lovely warm extract of fruit, less hard than the Stonyridge.	Wood (oak) and natural tannin evident after a very fruity attack. Still young, but with a lovely aromatic development beginning.	Excellent example of rich Cabernet Sauvignon fruit backed by natural tannin and wood. Better balanced and less intense than the Stonyridge.
Santa Rita 1985 Medalla Real			Maipo Valley, Chile
Full, rich, youthful, purply red, a fine warm vibrant hue.	Very ripe, red berry fruit aromas, rich and firm, excellent extract and impression of depth.	Smoky (oak), earthy flavour overlying firm and ripe fruit. Good structure and length from ripe grapes and good wine making. Classic Cabernet.	Fine tannin/fruit balance, ready now but will improve. Much better than the Riserva (see page 150), more French in style than the first two.
Orlando Saint Hugo 1985			Coonawarra, South Australia
Very full colour, rich and meaty, looks a little more mature than Santa Rita, but still intense.	Rich, concentrated blackcurrant bouquet, full of ripe, briary fruit, almost fleshy.	Rich, almost sweet fruit, its maturity and natural richness makes it very attractive. Opposite in style to the drier, European Cabernets.	A lovely and impressive mouthful with a ripe sweetness, with more class than the Orlando 1986 Cabernet (see page 150).

APPEARANCE	BOUQUET	PALATE	COMMENTS
Ch. Haut-Bages-Liberal 1985 Pauillac 5ème cru classé			Bordeaux, France
Full, still intense deep carmine-ruby red, not beginning to age, an impressive colour.	Briary fruit, blackcurrant leaf bouquet, complete contrast to the concentrated sweetness of the Orlando, pure Cabernet, clean and refreshing.	Clean, straightforward fruit, fine tannin balance. An elegant, supple wine, in contrast to the more weighty wines from hotter vineyards.	Very Cabernet Sauvignon, obviously very skilled wine making to extract the rich fruit with just an edge of tannin. Could be drunk, but will improve.
Sassicaia 1985 Vino da Tavola Tenuta San Guido			Tuscany, Italy
Very concentrated, deep carmine-ruby, still with a violet edge, almost impenetrable for a 1985.	Concentrated but very fine fruit aromas, pure blackcurrant Cabernet with just the right touch of new oak.	Same impression of superb balance between fruit and oak, a smoky, lissom, vibrant fruit, pure harmony. Much too young, will last 20 years.	A classic wine by any standards and a beautifully balanced Cabernet Sauvignon with an almost feminine charm despite the firmness of fruit.
Rose Creek 1985			Washington State, USA
Very deep, intense, rich black-cherry red, masses of extract, no age at all.	Intense aromas of wood and ripe fruit.	Smoky, firm concentrated fruit, very tannic and very young, but plainly Cabernet.	Very young vines, planted 1980. The 1985 has too much tannin but a lovely base of fruit. The balance will improve as the vineyard ages.
Marqués de Griñon 1984 Vino da Mesa			Toldeo, Spain *Cabernet Sauvignon 90%, Merlot 10%*
Very fine, young for 1984, intense almost black ruby, firm but not heavy.	Good clear briary blackcurranty fruit with smoky, vanilla overtones. Quite lean compared to the Orlando, plummy compared to the Haut-Bages.	Firm elegant fruit, slight smoked bacon flavour, intense but restrained fruit extract giving a fine supple wine with an edge of tannin.	Excellent balance of ripe fruit but no sweetness, well aged in wood to add a tobacco-cedary polish. Not yet at its best.
Ridge 1984 York Creek			Santa Clara County, California, USA *Cabernet Sauvignon 89%, Merlot 9%, Cabernet Franc 2%*
Full, deep carmine, less intense than the range of 1985s, but fine and rich and still young.	Ripe fruit, but a rawish green pepper aroma gives an edge of aggression.	Rich, more rounded on palate, fine Cabernet fruit, complete but still with a firm edge of tannin.	A lean, almost tough Cabernet in the Pauillac style, but more muscular than the Haut-Bages. Needs 3-4 years.
Ch. Desmirail 1983 2ème Cru Classé Margaux			France
Full, deep vermillion, rich, still very young, an exciting, intense colour.	Lovely, quite intense, redcurranty bouquet, blackcurrant leaf, fragrant fruit showing the directness of the Cabernet and the charm of Margaux.	Wonderful fragrant, sweet fruit, cedary balance from the oak, even a little fleshiness from the Merlot. A lovely example of Margaux, pure finesse and balance.	Lovely sweet ripe fruit finish, but not heaviness and a dry finish, a perfect wine for food. Could be drunk, due to the balance, but will improve.
Ch. Branaire-Ducru 1979 4ème Cru Classé Saint-Julien			France
Full colour, firm deep red, only very faint tawny edge, young.	Beautifully fragrant, cedary Médoc bouquet, where elegance and harmony deplace the primary fruits of the younger wines.	Classic Médoc, dry finish preceded by clean, ripe fruit. Poised and balanced, a fine expression of *terroir* where the grape is much less in evidence.	Classic claret from a very good if large vintage. Now perfect to drink, the Cabernet softening with age, but retaining all its firmness.
Ch. Montrose 1970 2ème Cru Classé Saint-Estèphe			France
Intense, very deep red with a brick-red edge, still vibrant and full after 18 years.	Intense 'heat on stones' bouquet, austere Cabernet tannins, but a ripe year, complex.	Still very austere, full of fruit, masses of extract, not at all in the current style of soft tannin Médocs. Very long.	Will remain very tannic, but the fruit is there. A very intense wine, comparable to La Mission 1978 (see page 153), very serious, needs decanting.

Tasting/Grape Varieties/Pinot Noir

The Pinot Noir is the only grape from which red Burgundy may be made, and it is inextricably connected with wines from this region. Although it is also the major grape in Champagne, and is found in other areas of France, as is the Chardonnay, it is not so adaptable as the white grape variety. While the Chardonnay has many styles, the Pinot Noir has a narrower definition. The colour, with few exceptions, is never too heavy or too dark; young, it should have an aroma of crushed fruit, principally of strawberries or wild cherries, while in ageing it evolves towards a bouquet of faded fruit or even animal. The taste should be clean and refreshing, however voluptuous the wine, for, despite the popular image of Burgundy as a rich, full wine, the best wines from the Pinot are elegant, with a lingering fruit. Furthermore, unlike the Cabernet family, the Merlot or the Syrah, it does not blend well with other grapes, its finesse and breed being lost in the process. The Pinot Noir fares best in a cool growing climate and, more than any other grape variety, it tends to reflect the soil and the climate in which it is grown.

In France the Pinot is grown in many different places: Champagne, the Loire, Burgundy, Jura and Alsace. It produces a distinctively different wine from each region, even from each microclimate; but outside France, it is the Burgundy style that is sought. Not possessing the same growing conditions, the wines will be very different. Perhaps because wines with a true Pinot Noir bouquet and flavour are rare, both from France and elsewhere, a comparative tasting is apt to be less balanced than, for example, a tasting of Cabernet Sauvignons. In this tasting we tried to select Pinots that have kept their varietal character, while giving an indication of their regional origin.

APPEARANCE	BOUQUET	PALATE	COMMENTS
Gevrey-Chambertin 1987 1er Cru 'les Fonteneys'		Joseph Roty	Côte d'Or, France
Beautiful, vibrant deep cherry-red, young, quite full.	Market presence of new wood, still dominating a fine rich crushed fruits aroma.	Minerally and licorice flavours, wood dominant, but clean, pure fruit coming through, showing the complexity that will evolve. Good length, acidity and balance.	Classic Gevrey-Chambertin – firm, slightly spicy fruit – and classic Pinot Noir, if over-oaked at the moment. Long and persistent, needs at least five years.
Hunter's Marlborough Pinot Noir 1987			New Zealand
Medium colour, slight touch of orangey-red, much less intensity than the previous wine.	Good Pinot fruit, but of the 'stewed' rather than the fresher 'crushed' style, less up front. Slightly peppery and spicy.	Similar fruit on the palate, with oak present, good balance, still a little edgy on the finish, but nearly mature.	A goodish Pinot from young vines, subsequent vintages should have a firmer definition of fruit.
Ponzi 1986			Willamette Valley, Oregon, USA
Clean, medium full cherry-red, slight fading to brick-red.	Spicy, herby bouquet (nettles) but good Pinot fruit overall.	Similar impression on palate, good (high) acidity and natural extract, slight leanness and wood tannin on the finish, but good balance.	More of a vegetal Pinot than a strawberry-fruity Pinot. Young vines prevent a fuller dimension that is found in the Gevrey Chambertin, or even the soft fruit of the Arbois.
Arbois 1986 Rolet Père et fils			Jura, France
Clear, youthful medium full cherry-red with light edge.	Pure Pinot fruit – strawberries, cherries – with a touch of oak, the same impression as a light Côte de Beaune, delicious.	Pinot fruit continues to dominate the *terroir*, a lovely rounded fruit with a firmness added by the wood. Straightforward, very well made.	A modern, fruity Pinot, in contrast to the less direct varietals from Arbois, the Trousseau and the Poulsard. Harmonious, can be drunk or kept.
Au Bon Climat 1986			Santa Barbara County, California, USA
Fine, deep black cherry-red, full and youthful, an exciting rich colour.	Immediately fruity, lightly concentrated, good extract, touch of oak, elegant and lingering.	Fine lively fruit across the palate and excellent use of oak, not masking the vibrant Pinot flavour and the *terroir*. Excellent fruit/acid balance.	Excellent flavour and length, one of the better Pinots from California from low yielding vines with intelligent wine making.

APPEARANCE	BOUQUET	PALATE	COMMENTS
Calera Jensen 1986			San Benito County, California, USA
Rich, vibrant, youthful colour, fuller and deeper than the already firm Au Bon Climat.	Rich, concentrated licorice aromas, full of fruits with a blackberry richness, hints of wood, a lively complex wine.	Very fine extract of mature *ripe* fruit, a beautiful follow-on from the nose, great persistence and balance and length. Excellent.	One of the very best California Pinots from a dedicated wine maker. Outclasses the Au Bon Climat for depth, intensity and complexity. Easily 1er Cru Côtes de Nuits standard.
Pinot Noir d'Alsace 1985	Cuvée à l'Ancienne	Cave de Turkheim	France
Pale red, but much more of a red than a rosé, which is unusual for a Pinot Noir d'Alsace, slightly tawny edge.	Pure Pinot bouquet: chocolaty, vegetal, smoky, sweet, slightly edgy.	Pure Pinot flavours, quite high in alcohol, but balanced with good extract. A little tough and minerally on the finish, in the Côte de Nuits style.	Very good example of Pinot Noir, from a particularly good year in Alsace. Full silky texture with an edge of tannin.
Mount Mary Vineyards 1985	Lilydale		Victoria, Australia
Medium to quite deep cherry-carmine red, still youthful and quite rich.	Rich, with the typical high tone and 'farmyardy' aspect of some Côte de Nuits, with elements of wood to back it up.	Rich, fruity, 'stewed' fruit flavours, good depth and balance; at its peak but will last.	A very elegant and stylish Pinot Noir, particularly from Australia. Not as fine as the California wines, but with lovely balance and fruit.
Moss Wood 1985			Margaret River, Western Australia
Full, deep cherry-red, robust, good extract, deeper than Mount Mary.	Concentrated fruity, strawberry Pinot aromas, dominated by new oak, still very young.	Rather sweet but lovely rich Pinot attack with smoky, oaky tones, highish acidity on the finish, almost 1er Cru Burgundy in style with opulence and finesse, but a little too sweet.	Fine, polished wine, delicious in attack, finely grained, open and supple: a very good Pinot Noir.
Hamilton Russell Vineyards 'Grand Vin Noir'			Cape of Good Hope, South Africa
Aged brick/mahogany red, slight browning and paling at edges, rich.	Complex fruit, sweet strawberry on attack and stewed fruit thereafter, good acidity.	Warm, full-bodied wines, sweet flavoured fruit, faintly earthy finish. Spicy (camphor, cinnamon), quite mature.	Excellent balance. Not a vintage-dated wine, but at least five years old. Good fruit and typical Pinot acidity, sweet flavours and balance.
Mondavi Pinot Noir 1984			Napa Valley, California, USA
Medium colour, slightly fuller, probably younger than the previous wine, richer and more consistent.	Sweet spicy fruit with strong eucalyptus hints, but still very Pinot. Good extract of fruit.	Fully fruity, even licoricey: warm ripe fruit, quite persistent if not complex, good forthright attack. Well made.	Has the fruit, vegetal character and sweetness of the Pinot, but not the polish and depth of Au Bon Climat or Calera.
Clos Saint-Denis 1978	**Grand Cru**	Georges Lignier	Côte d'Or, France
Fully mature warm colour, mahogany-red, definite browning at edges, but no real age.	Rich, animally, 'gamey' Pinot, heady, hints of compost, deep fruit, definite Côte de Nuits.	Falls a bit short after the bouquet, showing some age, but has kept the sweet Pinot fruit and minerally Côte de Nuits character.	Midway from mature to old, could have been more vibrant, more youthful, but a beautifully balanced wine. The Roumier Bonnes-Mares 1985 (see page 152) will certainly outclass this.

Tasting/Grape Varieties/Merlot

The principal characteristic of wines made from the Merlot grape is their soft fruit. In contrast to the Cabernet Sauvignon, with which it is often blended, it is less austere and intense, more rich and fruity. It also has less tannin, although the Cabernet Sauvignon on its own often has too much, and needs the softness of the Merlot to balance this. Except in great years (1961, 1982), or from vineyards with plenty of sun (Australia, California), the Merlot will not have the deep concentration of colour of the Cabernet Sauvignon, but rather a soft, welcoming ruby tone. Being an early budder, it is often subject to spring frosts, and during a cool, wet harvest is very prone to rot. However, it ripens early, and in good years the wines acquire a sweetness of fruit and great intensity of flavour.

The Merlot is best known in France in the region of Bordeaux, especially in Pomerol and Saint-Emilion. Here it is the dominant grape variety, and one has only to consider the reputation of wines such as Châteaux Pétrus and Trotanoy to see the potential of the grape. In the Médoc and Graves regions, the Merlot is secondary to the Cabernet Sauvignon but is a vital part of the makeup of these wines. It is planted throughout south-western France, and there have been experimental plantings along the Mediterranean coast. In Northern Italy it makes lovely, soft, fruity wines, while the hotter the climate, the more robust it becomes. It is extremely successful in California and Oregon, where the Cabernet Sauvignon can be a little massive and unyielding.

APPEARANCE	BOUQUET	PALATE	COMMENTS
Vin du Pays de l'Aude 1988			Chantovent, France
Rich, plummy, purply-red, very young of course, fruity.	Plummy fruit aromas, clean grapey fruit but some complexity.	Soft fruity plummy attack, just an edge of firmness to stop it being too soft.	A well-made, very inexpensive Merlot, good fruit, good extract and some length, typical Merlot easy fruitiness.
Clos du Bois 1986			Sonoma County, California, USA *76% Merlot, 24% Cabernet Sauvignon*
Fine, rich youthful deep ruby, full and vibrantly fruity.	Rich, plummy bouquet, touch of new oak still, soft and suave.	Same rich fruit on palate, rather firmer finish due to the presence of Cabernet Sauvignon, good balance, not overly complex.	Attractive, rich, smooth wine, just a touch of oak, made for pleasant drinking over the next year or two, not for ageing.
Rosemount Estate 1985			Hunter Valley, NSW, Australia
Full, deep, black cherry, velvety red, smooth and suave looking.	Fruity, smooth, hints of fresh almonds, milky bouquet, well-pronounced fruit, no tannin.	Oak very present, but adds a suaveness rather than a charred taste. Ripe, fruity, smooth, mellow, supple, lacks great depth.	Very supple, well made, the Merlot evident in the fruity smoothness rather than in the intensity of flavour of the La Grave Trignant de Boisset.
Newton 1985			Napa Valley, California, USA
Fine, vibrant, rich, deep carmine, fine youthful aspect.	Lovely blend of fruit and oak with slight tobacco, fruity aromas.	Good fruit and acidity, excellent balance. Not an over-rich or over fruity Merlot, but all the fruit brought out by fine wine making.	Beautifully conceived wine, with good ripeness, fine grained fruit and excellent use of oak. A classic, restrained Merlot, for ageing.
Sainte-Michelle River Ridge Vineyards 1983			Washington State, USA
Huge colour, intense, inky purple, incredibly young for a 1983.	Spicy, concentrated blackberries, almost Zinfandel bouquet, fat and fleshy fruit on attack, but leaner finish.	Rich, briary, blackcurranty fruit, lots of extract, but the impression of *vin de presse* underlines the power at the expense of finesse. Tough.	Impressive, rather massive, still very tannic, finally shows more tannin than inherent fruit.
Ch. La Grave Trignant de Boisset 1982			Pomerol, France
Full-bodied, deep red with mahogany-brick edge, showing only a little maturity.	Rich, soft, earthy, truffly Merlot; soft, almost sweet, hints of stewed prunes.	Rich, fruit, same hints of stewed fruit but moving to spicy dried fruit, a rich, warm generous wine with a firm edge.	Very polished, almost exotic spicy fruit, still a touch of oak, opulent but still firm. Very complex, showing the best of Merlot and Pomerol.

Tasting/Grape Varieties/Syrah

The Syrah grape flourishes in a sunny climate: in France it is at its best in the Rhône Valley, particularly the northern part, and is now heavily planted throughout Provence. It is very successful in Australia, where it is known as the Shiraz or the Hermitage (to underline the French parentage), in South Africa and in California, where it should not be confused with the Petite Sirah. Wines made from the Syrah have a deep purple colour, an intense aroma of blackcurrants and spices, are rich and robust on the palate with a rough fruit that often needs several years to smoothen out and show the complexity behind the power. Professor Saintsbury called Hermitage 'the manliest of wines', which seems a fitting description. There can be no doubt that Hermitage and Côte-Rôtie, where vines planted on the steeply terraced slopes above the Rhône river produce wines of incomparably concentrated bouquet and flavour, show the Syrah at its peak.

The Syrah is the sole grape responsible for Hermitage, Cornas, St Joseph, and Crozes-Hermitage, is generally so for Côte-Rôtie (which may add up to 20% of the Viognier white grape), and plays a significant rôle in the wines of Châteauneuf-du-Pape, of southern Côtes-du-Rhône and of Provence, where its firm spicy fruit balances the rich fullness of the Grenache. Despite its reputation as a big wine, it is seldom heavy, and it has a natural acidity that, except in very hot climates, prevents it from becoming over-ripe. The true Syrah style is consistent and quite easy to recognize, as this and previous tastings show.

APPEARANCE	BOUQUET	PALATE	COMMENTS
Rosemount Hunter Valley 1987			NSW, Australia
Rich, intense, youthful and almost impenetrable, very full bodied.	Leathery, muscular fruit, but giving way to a softer blackberry and blackcurrant aroma.	Rich, plummy and briary fruit, clear blackberry fruit, ample, fleshy, rich with an almost sorbet-like concentration.	Very rich and fruity, all in the attack, plummy and mouthfilling, very much in the rich Australian Syrah style.
Cornas 1986			Rhône, France
Fabulous colour, intense, purply-red, rich but not heavy.	Still quite shut-in, but hidden power, just showing a blackberry, peppery, smoky fruit, very fine.	A serious, classic Syrah, packed with understated fruit, highish in tannin and lowish in alcohol, almost Médoc-style in comparison to Rosemount.	A finely balanced wine from a medium vintage: the 1985 has double the fruit, grip and tannin. Classic Syrah, but more Cornas (*terroir*) than Syrah.
The Armagh 1985 Jim Barry			Clare, South Australia
Huge colour, deep, black-red, intense but clean-cut, very rich. A marvellous-looking wine.	Rich, concentrated blackberry fruit and strong impression of high-quality oak, in the Sassicaia style. Aspects of volatile acidity help to lift the bouquet.	Velvety, spicy, mouthfilling flavour, very generous and heady, blackcurrants and oak with a minty/eucalyptus finish. Floral and intense.	A wine of great class and potential, intense Syrah spicy fruit, mouthfilling but not clumsy.
Ch. Le Amon 1985			Bendigo, Australia
Almost black, completely youthful colour (could be a 1988), very rich, similar to The Armagh.	Spicy, minty aromas, more Napa Cabernet Sauvignon than Shiraz, clean briary fruit.	Rich, firm fruit, with personality and depth, lean tannins, but not too lean for the fruit, good balance.	Lots of extract, a clean muscular wine, firmer and less flamboyant than The Armagh. A very good example.
Joseph Phelps 1980			Napa Valley, California, USA
Full, fairly intense, deep mahogany-red, slight paling and browning at edge and a contrast to the younger wines.	Spicy, ripe fruit, slightly sweaty/leathery-earthy/gamey, almost Burgundian, good concentration.	Similar impression on palate, good sweet fruit attack and still an edge of acidity, good balance.	Completely mature, showing complexity rather than up-front fruit, but keeping the typical peppery-spicy flavour. Good balanced wine.
Côte-Rotie 'Côte Brune' 1978 Gentax-Dervieux			Rhône, France
Rich, youthful, dark vermilion, vibrant garnet colour, very little ageing for a 10-year-old wine.	Complex, spicy, vegetal, smoky compost-like bouquet, deep fruit, still lively and spicy.	Perfect balance of intense fruit, still slightly blackberry and youthful, hints of wood, great concentration and elegance. A very polished yet unpretentious wine.	Really fine, firm wine, roasted, concentrated fruit, great length, less rich than the Landonne (see page 153), but perhaps more classic. A perfect example.

Horizontal Tasting/Red Burgundy 1978

The purpose of this tasting is similar to the horizontal tasting of 1983 Bordeaux on pages 172–3, namely to show the difference between the *appellations* in the Côte de Beaune and the Côte de Nuits. With one single grape variety, the Pinot Noir, differences in style and character are caused by the geographical siting of the vineyards, soil, subsoil and microclimate. Since the Burgundy vineyards are so fragmented, the differences in wine making often either exaggerate or blur the intrinsic character of the various *appellations*. For this tasting, therefore, we decided to choose all the wines from one highly respected *négociant-éleveur*, Leroy. The wines were purchased from individual *propriétaires* and bottled unblended. They tend to reflect Madame Bize-Leroy's personal preference for well-structured long-lived wines as much as they do the style of the various *villages*, and we feel that this sort of homogeneity serves to underline the differences between them.

1978 is known in France, but especially in Burgundy as 'the miracle vintage'. The flowering in June had been late and already a small crop was on the cards. July was cold and August was so wet that some of the growers in Burgundy did not think they would have a vintage to pick. Then in the first week of September the weather changed, the sun came out and it remained sunny and dry with hardly a break until the middle of October. The result was wines of great structure, not sun-concentrated as in the drought year of 1976, or rather diffuse in the following high yield of 1979. Both the Côte de Beaune and the Côte de Nuits produced wines with a deep colour with a depth of serious fruit that demands and repays long cellaring. At 11 years after the vintage the Villages wines are their best, the Premier and Grand Cru have a promising future ahead.

APPEARANCE	BOUQUET	PALATE	COMMENTS
Côte de Beaune-Villages			
Fine solid brick-red, still young, clear edge, no browning.	Rich fruit with spicy, licorice, gamey aspects, very ripe and mature, sense of *terroir*.	Supple, good fruit and good length, well-balanced acidity, smoothness, structure and finesse.	Very good example of a Côte de Beaune: smoothness but firm fruit, with the balanced concentration of 1978.
Chassagne-Montrachet			
Solid mahogany-red, fuller and more consistent than the first wine.	Floral Pinot fruit, musky, hints of leather and game, ephemeral.	Very good attack, stewed, spicy fruit, hint of leather, clean length of flavour, good acidity, some tannin but a rich base of fruit.	Excellent balance, showing more class than the first wine without being a major *appellation*.
Auxey-Duresses			
Superbly concentrated youthful dark mahogany, velvety, rich, very impressive and very young.	Same concentration, slightly burnt, roasted aromas (cocoa, coffee), even a touch of violets, very rich and deep, obviously from very old vines.	Marvellously young, velvety multi-layered floral fruit, even an unlikely hint of new wood, extraordinarily sensuous but firm wine.	A superb wine, with the force and attack of a Côte de Nuits, but richly suave on the finish, wonderful extraction, will last another ten years.
Savigny-lès-Beaune 'les Narbentons' 1er Cru			
Full, young and rich, less concentration than the Auxey-Duresses, but very satisfying.	Mixed bouquet of fruit and torrefaction, wonderful warm fruit on attack.	Smooth fruit and more than a hint of chocolate, lovely impression of sweet Pinot fruit with the delicacy of wines from the Beaune side of the Savigny.	Finely balanced, very good length and finesse. A Savigny-lès-Beaune 'Les Serpentières' was more serious, but with less charm, more Aloxe-Corton than Beaune.
Volnay-Santenots 1er Cru			
Fine solid velvety red, rich on the glass, not fading.	Rather concentrated mixed red fruits, quite rich, straightforward.	Fine, polished furniture wax, fruit, quite rich, good balance, ripe, lacks a little complexity.	Rich, ripe, solid, full for a Volnay (this is from the Meursault commune), a little less lively than the Savignys.

APPEARANCE	BOUQUET	PALATE	COMMENTS
Volnay-Caillerets 1er Cru			
Very fine colour, much younger and more vibrant than the Santenots, with the same velvety aspect.	Concentrated floral fruit, hints of wild violets, elegant and showing obvious 1er Cru class.	Lively, almost youthful fruit, touch of violets, even irises, good extract but above all wonderful finesse.	Lovely breed, delicacy and persistence of fruit. Fascinating contrast to the Santenots, which is satisfying, but not of the same quality.
Pommard 'Les Vignots'			
Fine youthful colour, firm, deep mahogany, hardly any ageing.	Rather discreet fruit, plainly a firm wine with good fruit, but does not have the aromatic bouquet of the Volnay-Caillerets.	Wonderful explosion of aromatic fruit on the palate, concentrated crushed fruit, slightly leathery, very good structure, length and finesse.	Excellent length, a classic firm, but not heavy Pommard, still youthful, a fine contrast to the floral elegance of the Volnay-Caillerets. Still a long way to go.
Chambolle-Musigny			
Fine medium red, but lacks the depth of the last five. Perhaps from young vines.	Stewed, mature Pinot fruit, slightly woody, beginning to show a little age.	Straightforward, lacks the complexity and excitement of the previous wines, fruit rather dominated by wood and natural acidity.	At a disadvantage after the Volnays and the Pommard. Perhaps still too young, but more likely the lack of complexity from a *villages* wine as compared to a *cru*.
Nuits-Saint-Georges 'Les Boudots' 1er Cru			
Rich, solid deep red, deep and consistent, velvety.	Rich fruit, slightly musky, still rather closed-in, firm.	Striking volume of fruit on the palate, a rich, animally fruit, powerful but with length and breed.	A classic firm Nuits-Saint-Georges, highish acidity from the vintage, almost aggressive, opposite in style to the Volnay-Caillerets, needs to be kept.
Nuits-Saint-Georges 'Les Perdrix' 1er Cru			
Fabulous colour, very young and very rich, wonderful deep warm red.	Striking, almost explosive fruit, exotic, spicy elements, lively, great depth and lingering aromas.	Magnificent expression of fruit and *terroir*, rich, chewy, smooth, velvety. Much more grip than the Boudots, quite excellent.	A wine of Grand cru quality, has the finesse of a Bonnes-Mares (see Roumier, page 152) with the firmness of Nuits-Saint-Georges.
Gevrey-Chambertin La Combe aux Moines			
Very deep colour, as deep as the Perdrix, full, firm and velvety, no age.	Extraordinary mix of floral (violets, irises), gamey aromas, with rich chocolate overtones, concentrated but elegant.	Superb attack: chocolate, cocoa, dried fruit, rich and almost thick with extract, but great elegance and presence. A superb wine.	Very fine example of Gevrey-Chambertin at about its best, wonderful extract and *terroir*, massive yet lingering. Grand cru standard.
Mazis-Chambertin			
Lovely colour, less rich and dense than the Gevrey-Chambertin, but perhaps more lively and vibrant, really fine.	Perfect expression of fruit, silky yet powerful, pure elegance, incredible aromatic length.	Chocolate, coffee, rich fruits, a great sense of *terroir*, leaving the Mazis more lissom and even longer than the Gevrey-Chambertin. Less assertive, more finesse.	Difficult to describe the transition from grape to glass with this kind of wine: the quality and mystery of fine Burgundy. Perfection.

Horizontal Tasting/Red Bordeaux 1983

The purpose of this tasting is to illustrate the differences in style between the major *appellations* in Bordeaux, showing the influence of soil and climate, and especially grape varietal mix and the individual style of the châteaux. We have selected the 1983 vintage which, after six years, is beginning to open up. Of the preceding vintages: 1982 was certainly more opulent, probably the richest vintage since 1961; 1981 was very fine, with classic wines of a lean style; 1980 rather light; 1979 was a year of large production which is now drinking very well, illustrating the fact that Cabernet Sauvignon can sustain heavy cropping better than Pinot Noir; 1978 was a classic year as the wines tasted on pages 170–171 illustrate. However, rather than choose a vintage very near maturity, as in the Burgundy tasting, we have chosen a vintage in evolution, where the differences in *terroir* are perhaps more marked.

Meteorologically, 1983 was an almost perfect year, with a fine flowering and only a little too much rain in the first part of September. The crop was big, not so concentrated as 1982 (with the notable exception of Margaux), producing classic wines with depth and regional character. The minor wines are now very drinkable, those in this tasting still a few years from their best.

APPEARANCE	BOUQUET	PALATE	COMMENTS
Ch. Prieuré-Lichine 3ème Cru Classé Margaux			*Cabernet Sauvignon 52%, Merlot 31%, Cabernet Franc 12%, Petit Verdot 5%*
Rich, deep mahogany red, no real age, dense and warm.	Rich, spicy even faintly burnt, lots of extract and elegance.	Fine attack, more power than usual from Prieuré-Lichine, more concentration. A fleshy, firm wine, but clearly Margaux from the finesse.	A ripe 1983, aromas of violets, rich fruit, fine and long. Ready in three years.
Ch. Palmer 3ème Cru Classé Margaux			*Cabernet Sauvignon 55%, Merlot 40%, Cabernet Franc 3%, Petit Verdot 2%*
Full, meaty colour, oily viscosity clinging to the glass, rich and fine.	Rich, fruity, spicy 'Christmas pudding' aromas, big and good extract.	Masses of fruit and flavour, fleshy, spicy and supple in comparison to some leaner Margaux (see Ch. Desmirail 1983, page 165), almost voluptuous.	Wonderful extract of fruit and superb balance, a typical fleshy Palmer from a vintage where Margaux outshone the other Médocs.
Ch. La Lagune 3ème Cru Classé Ludon, Haut-Médoc			*Cabernet Sauvignon 55%, Merlot 20%, Cabernet Franc 20%, Petit Verdot 5%*
Very full colour, as full as the Palmer, not quite so rich.	Plummy, vanilla oak, sweet concentrated fruit with tannin present.	Rich, plummy, less spicy and intense than the Palmer, ripe blackcurranty fruit balanced by new wood. Needs 2-3 years.	A fine, densely fruity, smoky wine, still firm from the wood.
Ch. Léoville-Poyferré 2ème Cru Classé Saint-Julien			*Cabernet Sauvignon 65%, Merlot 35%*
Very, very big colour, denser than Palmer and La Lagune, due to long extract of ripe Cabernet Sauvignon.	Spicy, dense fruit, dominated by Cabernet, some wood, not all new as in La Lagune.	Still solid and shut-in, power and depth from the Cabernet leaves a slight stalky impression, but good extract and will age well.	One of the best vintages from a château beginning to match its classification. Lacks polish and elegance at the moment.
Ch. Lynch-Bages 5ème Cru Classé Pauillac			*Cabernet Sauvignon 70%, Merlot 18%, Cabernet Franc 10%, Petit Verdot 2%*
Very fine colour, plummy, intense ruby, very rich and dense.	Lovely spicy aromas, crushed fruit and cedar wood overtones, faint leatheriness, showing a tough, firm fruit.	Superb fruit, full of spicy Cabernet concentration, fine and clean, not the massive richness of 1982, but excellent vinification. Long and full of potential.	Classic Médoc, as usual from Lynch-Bages, full and rich, but firm.

APPEARANCE	BOUQUET	PALATE	COMMENTS
Ch. Duhart-Milon-Rothschild 4ème Cru Classé Pauillac			*Cabernet Sauvignon 70%, Merlot 20%, Cabernet Franc 5%, Petit Verdot 5%*
Fine, deep concentrated carmine, quite rich, but less intense than Lynch-Bages.	Firmly concentrated red berry fruits, firm edge, none of the smoky fat of Lynch-Bages, more restrained fruit.	Firm fruit with cedary, woody tannin, a fine grained Pauillac, will need 4-5 years for the fruit to re-emerge from the wood ageing.	Opposite in style to the voluptuous Lynch-Bages, a firm, close-knit wine that shows up the slight hardness of most 1983 Pauillacs.
Ch. Cos d'Estournel 2ème Cru Classé Saint-Estèphe			*Cabernet Sauvignon 60%, Merlot 40%*
Massive colour, no ageing at all from a solid meaty red, but perhaps less vibrantly young than Lynch-Bages and Palmer.	Rather sturdy, 'sweaty' fruit, midway between a more mature bouquet and prime fruit aromas, shut-in compared to the others.	More expression on the palate, a full, firm wine, with smoky overtones and richness from the Merlot. Beginning to mature.	1983 was less successful in the northern Médoc and the contrast with the Palmer is evident. Good but not great.
Ch. Haut-Bailly Cru Classé Graves			*Cabernet Sauvignon 36%, Merlot 30%, Cabernet Franc 10%, old vines 24%*
Firm, fruity deep brick-red, showing slight maturation on rim, more advanced than the others in this tasting.	Mixed fruit aromas, redcurrants, slightly rosehip, still woody, but overall beginning to ripen out.	Firm fruit, lost the fleshy fruit of youth while still keeping the tannins. Good balance, needs two years to show well, still a little edgy.	Fragrant, rather understated Graves, less successful than in 1979 and 1982, but will emerge from its awkward stage, arrived at earlier than most 1983s.
Ch. La Mission Haut-Brion Cru Classé Graves			*Cabernet Sauvignon 60%, Merlot 35%, Cabernet Franc 5%*
Very big, rich colour, lots of extract, only a faint hint of maturity.	Meaty, spicy, licorice fruit, but with a fragrant, rose-like floral aspect. Very fine indeed.	Very fine depth of fruit, beginning to mature with wood evident, but not all new, marvellous concentration, vibrant, rivals the Palmer and the Lynch Bages.	Concentrated, almost old-fashioned, but compared to the 1978 not so tannic. A very fine, balanced wine, quite different to the Haut-Bailly, needs five years.
Ch. Larmande Grand Cru Classé Saint-Emilion			*Merlot 65%, Cabernet Franc 30%, Cabernet Sauvignon 5%*
Very big, dense, rich colour, full, young and velvety.	Smoky, concentrated rich Merlot fruit, plummy and exciting.	Superb, meaty, rich fruit flavours with just the right amount of wood. A ripe wine, lots of extract, very well made, just beginning to mature.	A very fine Saint-Emilion, avoiding the sickly fruitiness of many wines, on a par with Palmer and Lynch-Bages for 1983, if not for absolute quality.
Ch. Magdelaine 1er Grand Cru Classé Saint-Emilion			*Merlot 80%, Cabernet Franc 20%*
Deep, concentrated colour, perhaps less rich than Larmande, but very fine and perfect timbre.	Much lighter on the attack than Larmande, but more depth of fragrance, the vineyard position on the high Saint-Emilion slopes showing through.	Very fragrant fruit, Cabernet Franc dominant, with smoky aspects from the wood, rich but extremely elegant. Almost ready to drink.	Fabulous balance, an impression of the finesse of a Volnay in Saint-Emilion, less meaty than Larmande, very fine.
Ch. Latour à Pomerol	**Pomerol**		*Merlot 80%, Cabernet Franc 20%*
Marvellous deep mahogany, vermilion, dark, intense and rich.	Rich, velvety, earthy, gamey aromas, very full and heady.	Spicy, full-bodied serious fruit, firm edge of tannin and rich fruit extract, greath depth of flavour.	Same grape balance as Ch. Magdelaine, the Pomerol more resembles a Corton-Rugiens, meaty and earthy. Very successful, as good as the 1982.

Vertical Tasting/Red Burgundy

The purpose of this tasting is to show the difference between 12 vintages in Burgundy through the 1960s, 1970s and 1980s. We have chosen a single vineyard Volnay, the Clos de la Bousse d'Or, where the wine has been made by the same person (Gérard Potel) in each vintage, so as to best isolate the vintage factor. Volnay is considered to produce the archetypical Côte de Beaune.

Clos de la Bousse d'Or, Volnay

The domaine possesses 13 hectares of vines, with vineyards in Pommard and Santenay as well as Volnay. The vineyard of the Clos de la Bousse d'Or (which reverted in 1967 to its original name from that of Clos de la Pousse d'Or) is a *monopole.* With the estates of the Marquis d'Angerville and Mme Hubert de Montille, the domaine is the finest estate in Volnay, and Gérard Potel is one of the most skilful wine makers in the Côte d'Or.

Except in cold years, when the stalks will give an astringent taste to the wine instead of a tannin support, M. Potel does not *égrappe* before fermentation. Fermentation takes place in glass-lined enamel vats and usually lasts 12–14 days. The wine spends an average of 14 months in cask, of which 50% are renewed each year. In the 1960s, M. Potel did not filter his wines before bottling, but the lack of star-brightness was not understood on the export markets, and now the wines receive a very light filtering. He chaptalizes as little as possible, and when the natural sugar levels permit (1971, 1985), he does not chaptalize at all. The yield is average to low, owing to the rare practice of *ébourgeonage* in the spring, preceded by a very severe pruning. The vines have an average age of 27 years.

In style, the Clos de la Bousse d'Or is firm and assertive, with a constant level of tannin that allows the fruit to develop slowly. It is perhaps a Pauillac amongst Volnays.

APPEARANCE	BOUQUET	PALATE	COMMENTS
1986			
Firm, deep carmine red, with the rim still youthful and pink.	Good extract, clean fruit, wood present, beginning to lose its fruity young Pinot aromas.	Firm, quite solid fruit, wood giving added firmness, but good balance and length. Needs five years.	1986 was a vintage split between those who picked early, making light pleasant wines, and those who waited out the rain and picked late, making superb wines, mostly in the Côte de Nuits. This is midway.
1985			
Full, vibrant colour, fuller than the 1986, more velvety and rich.	Rich fruit, red berries and plums, with a certain earthy/animal density.	Very fine flavour, rich extract, a firm but fleshy Volnay with ripe, smooth fruit, no heaviness, perfect balance and length.	A vintage of perfect ripeness with healthy grapes producing a harmonious wine. The extra quality here is due to concentration of flavour through low yields and good wine making.
1984			
Full, deep mahogany red, very good for a 1984, only a slight paling at the edge.	Quite ripe, stewed fruit bouquet, hint of acidity, but good fruit.	Quite big on attack, but still an edge of acidity and wood. Good concentration of fruit for an 'off' vintage due to selection. Needs two years to lose the acidity.	A cold, wet summer, producing grapes with not enough mature ripeness. This is a very good example, which will age better than most, ending up dry, but not dried out.
1983			
Medium-full colour, more red than expected from a year where many wines have lost their colour.	Good concentration of fruit: red berries, plums, an extract of fruit rather than natural ripeness.	High extract, highish acidity and high tannin, still quite hard and lacks the charm of Volnay, but a fine, serious, complex wine for 5-10 years. One of the best 1983s.	A fast spreading rot from the third week in September forced most domaines to pick quickly. Only those who eliminated rotten grapes and gave the rest a long fermentation made fine wine.

APPEARANCE	BOUQUET	PALATE	COMMENTS
1982			
Medium colour, quite mature, slight browning at the edge and rather diffuse.	Pleasant, some fruit, lightly concentrated, still some wood.	Lightish, especially after the concentration of the 1983, lacks follow-through. At its best and will not improve.	A year of great over-production, where even the Bousse d'Or lacks stuffing and presence. Less good than the 1984.
1980			
Good colour, youthful for a nine-year-old wine, more depth than the 1982.	Quite rich, expansive bouquet, red fruit, hints of tobacco and chocolate.	Well-balanced fruit, smooth, with firmness and finesse, chocolate overtones, quite mature but will hold.	An underrated vintage, better in the Côte de Nuits (perhaps the equivalent of 1986). Lacks length, but has balance.
1979			
Very fine ruby mahogany red, more youthful and velvety than the 1980.	Lovely fruit, still reminiscent of the Pinot grape, with a blend of earthiness and suaveness.	Very fine, a really lovely Côte de Beaune, lissom, harmonious, aged very well and will keep. The balance one looks for in Volnay, not a great wine, but perfect at ten years old.	Late, but good flowering, a moderate summer and fine weather during the vintage produced a large crop of supple wines, with enough body to last a decade. A minor classic.
1978			
Still quite big, deeper than the 1979, but beginning to brown at the edge.	Rich, concentrated fruit, a slight earthiness, more length and depth than the 1979.	Fine concentration of flavours to denote a great wine, mature fruit, almost velvety extract with the firmness of the Bousse d'Or, great length. A textbook Burgundy, approaching its peak and will last ten years.	Cold spring, late, reduced flowering, very poor summer, but constant sunny weather from September produced a 'miracle' vintage. Small crop of firm, balanced wines, the best of the 1970s.
1976			
Deep, almost powerful colour, deeper than the two previous wines.	Concentrated, robust bouquet, showing a four-square style in contrast to that of Volnay or the Bousse d'Or.	Beginning to lose the hard tannin, with the extract of fruit appearing. Still too hard edged to show at its best, great concentration with balance.	Small to average crop of grapes over-concentrated by an exceptionally hot, dry summer. Careful wine making was needed to keep the finesse of the Pinot.
1971			
More tawny than mahogany red in complete contrast to the 1976.	Sweetness and ripeness despite its age, but beginning to fade.	Good fruit and still quite rich, evidence of previous high concentration of rather over-ripe fruit. Very good for a vintage which was most unequal, but past its peak.	After a patchy flowering, violent hailstorms in mid-August further reduced the crop, giving the grapes a greater concentration, but also a *goût de grêle*. Many wines were unbalanced.
1966			
Fine, clean palish tawny with yellow cognac rim.	Lissom, sweet fruit, evidence of concentration, still very much alive.	Soft, fading roses, strawberry fruit, beautiful balance, beginning to go but more harmonious than the 1971, and will hold for some years. A lovely wine.	A cold spring, warm June, poor July and August and then lovely weather for the vintage produced racy, distinguished wines, not very assertive at first, but beautifully balanced.
1964			
Quite firm tawny red, fuller than the 1966, more vibrant.	More assertive and concentrated than the 1966, chocolate overtones, slight earthiness from a rich, intense vintage.	Firm structure with a rich but not sweet presence in the mouth, very different in style to the 1966, a remarkable contrast.	Good weather in June produced a correct flowering, but a hot dry summer (like 1976) reduced the crop and thickened the skins of grapes to yield solid wines of great character and potential.

Vertical Tasting/Red Bordeaux

The aim of this tasting is to show the differences in the character of a vintage and its state of maturity at a particular time. To illustrate this, we have chosen a top class château from the Médoc which has been in the same family since its purchase in 1826.

Château Léoville-Barton 2ème Cru Classé Saint-Julien

Château Léoville-Barton covers 45 hectares of gravelly soil with clay sub-soil which is planted with the following grape varieties: 70% Cabernet Sauvignon, 20% Merlot, 8% Cabernet Franc, 2% Petit Verdot. The average age of the vines is a little over 25 years. Fermentation is carried out in the traditional wooden vats and the wine spends 24 months in small oak, less for lighter years such as 1980 and 1984. Anthony Barton succeeded his uncle Ronald Barton in 1986, but had already been the main influence in wine making since the early 1980s. The wines of Léoville-Barton have a fragrance and balance that is the hallmark of the finest claret.

APPEARANCE	BOUQUET	PALATE	COMMENTS
1986			
Very fine deep royal carmine, striking, full, still very young but already looks balanced, classic.	Concentrated red fruits, blackcurrant leaf, definite and positive elements of wood, solid Cabernet fruit, lean and ripe, great style.	Positive and persistent fruit, excellent extract, structure and balance, not too fat like many modern Médocs. A very fine Léoville to keep until 1993.	From a very large, record harvest, the ripeness of the Cabernet and superb wine making result in a superbly balanced wine.
1985			
Rich, full, meaty, deep velvety red, no youthful purple, but still very young, lots of body but less striking than 1986.	Richly concentrated, seems more backward than the 1986, but actually bigger and less stylish. Lots of extract.	Very broad, overall a bigger wine than 1986, fruit tannin and wood tannin in balance, richer and more fleshy, but less elegant length.	A heatwave vintage, this is firmer and less obvious than expected, just beginning to show the first signs of maturity. At its best in 1995.
1984			
Medium red, not yet showing much age, but not full and vibrant, correct for the year.	Fragrant, pleasant bouquet, clean fruit, not rich and concentrated, but elegant and light, pleasant hint of wood.	Fragrant Cabernet fruit, not fleshy, slight edge of green acidity and more wood than on the nose. Needs a little more time to soften.	Well balanced, the lack of total ripeness showing clearly in a lack of glycerine and dense fruit, but typical Médoc flavours. Drink 1990–93.
1983			
Firm, solid deep red, a slightly pale edge, not as much extract and concentration as the first two, but much fuller than the 1984.	Elegant, spicy, cedar/cigar box nose, markedly Cabernet with green peppers from the Cabernet Sauvignon and fragrance from the Cabernet Franc, followed by rich fruit.	Very well balanced from a positive attack to a long follow through, good curranty fruit and firm tannic edge to back it up, elegant.	Fine balance and well made, but not the striking success of 1986. Needs to wait until 1991-92 and will last until 2000.
1982			
Very big, intense colour indeed, rich, concentrated, very ripe wine, very impressive for a 7-year-old wine, opulent but firm.	Concentration and finesse at once, almost the tar-like quality of Barolo with the violetty fragrance of the Médoc, a hint of volatile acidity gives the fruit more 'bounce'.	Intense, warm fruit, an edge of tannin from the wood, an almost earthy, leafy fruit, perfect balance despite the 'bigness' of the year, still very youthful.	The most exceptional heatwave year. The late Ronald Barton said that this was one of the best wines he had ever made. Shows the possibility of great years (1961, 1970), with almost too much concentration, though remaining elegant.

APPEARANCE	BOUQUET	PALATE	COMMENTS
1981			
Fullish brick-red, slight paling at edge but still youthful and quite rich, although a lesser hue than the extraordinary 1982.	Fragrant, Cabernet bouquet, quity meaty, but the leafy, firm fruit of Cabernet is evident.	Good direct attack, still some clear remnants of sweet fruit, positive 'clarety' flavour, firm finish, relatively lean, elegant, almost ready.	Described as a 'claret lovers' vintage', 1981 had its ripeness diluted by rain, leaving a firm, precise fruit but lacking richness and opulence.
1979			
Medium full, mahogany-red, quite firm and good for a 10-year-old wine, at mid-life.	Lovely leafy Cabernet fragrance married to meaty, even leathery overtones, with fragrance dominating, elegance rather than power.	Well balanced fruit, just an edge of greenness on the finish, will only slightly improve and last for five years.	Certain 1979 Médocs had more concentration, perhaps the abundance of the crop affected the intensity.
1978			
Rich, deep mahogany colour, tawny rim, older than 1979 but much more vibrant, more viscous and more presence.	Very fine, fragrant, leafy bouquet, typical to Léoville-Barton, lovely mature balance of fruit, lingering and clear.	Marvellous presence of fruit on the attack, followed by a firm edge of tannin that will allow it to last ten years or more. Very high quality.	A much lower yield in 1978, higher concentration and classic Léoville balance place this wine much higher than the 1979. Fragrance and delicacy on the nose and firm Médoc fruit.
1976			
Rich, full mahogany red, warm and mature. Very fine. Not really old.	Quite rich, plummy fruit, evident ripeness from this very hot year, but none of the burnt or cooked aromas of some wines, a lovely bouquet.	Rich, warm fruit with a softness in complete contrast to the 1978. Quite mouthfilling, if not intense, good balance if not very long.	A deliciously elegant wine from an excessively dry and hot summer. Lowish in natural acidity, quite mature and will last until the mid-1990s. The stylishness of a fine Saint-Julien shows through.
1975			
Very fine colour, slightly burnt, dark mahogany-red, tawny edge, but firm, vibrant, rich impression.	Typical fragrant Léoville-Barton/Cabernet bouquet, much more openly floral than expected from the reputation of the year, impressive, fine.	Fine balance between fruit and natural tannins, not as full as the wines of the 1980s, certainly less high in alcohol. A rather restrained, old-fashioned wine in comparison.	A really lovely wine, almost charming for the year, classic lack of pretension, just very fine quality. Now ready, but will last 15 years.
1970			
Deep, still dense, but plainly mature burnt red. Tawny edge, but no sign of fading.	Lovely richness, ripe fruit, Léoville fragrance, quite mature, Cabernet very evident, cedar wood finish. Classic claret bouquet from a great year.	Beautiful fruit on the attack, slight volatile acidity enhances the fruit which has already attained patina of age. Ready, but will hold.	A vintage combining large quantity and very high quality. At almost 20 years, this is a benchmark Saint-Julien.
1966			
Fine, clear, deep brick-red, fading to tawny edge, still firm for the vintage.	Lovely, fragrant bouquet, even slight chocolate tones, balanced and persistent.	Fine, persistent, still ripe fruit, with cedary and resinous hints, even chocolate from the bouquet, balanced and multi-faceted.	Lovely fruit, fine balance, acidity finally showing through and will begin to dominate the fine, lingering, fragrant fruit in a few years.

Tasting/Fortified and Dessert Wines

Fortified wines are generally drunk on their own, either as an aperitif or after meals. There is no reason, however, why they should not be drunk at certain times during a meal: sherry or madeira with the soup, port with the cheese, for instance, but these customs vary from country to country. This tasting is therefore a comparison of some of the basic styles of fortified wine (see page 200). An interesting comparison in concentration of sweetness and flavours may be made with the richer wines in the tasting of Sweet and Aromatic Wines.

Coming from so many different regions, these wines are not easily compared. The natural wine is fortified at different stages during vinification, some being bone dry, some being naturally sweet and others having sweetness added. Sherry and madeira are basically white wines that become darker (maderize) with age, while port and Banyuls are red wines that lose colour with age. Unless they are sweetened during the ageing process, they all have a tendency to become progressively drier, until the alcohol dominates the fruit.

APPEARANCE	BOUQUET	PALATE	COMMENTS
Sherry Fino San Patricio Garvey			Spain
Pale, straw-yellow, slight greenish, youthful tinge, fresh and crisp. The colour of a dry white wine.	Yeasty, fresh hay aromas, zesty, tangy, slightly salty.	Bone dry, mouthwatering clean, tangy flavour, good structure, faintly malty, floral but firm, good crisp acidity.	A fino par excellence, the perfect aperitif, a dry, tangy white wine, lightly fortified to add backbone but not heaviness. Serve chilled.
Sherry Fine Dry Oloroso Sandeman			Spain
Lovely pale amber, light golden brown, a slightly burnt and warm colour. More glycerine than the fino.	Nutty, malty, high-toned with hints of caramel richness, quite full but lively.	Nutty, fullish flavour, tangy, spicy, almost brandy-like finish. Definite wood elements adding firmness, dry, aged (12 years average) finish with a hint of rancio.	Beautifully balanced, as dry as the fino, but richer textured and more complex: nuttiness through wood ageing and the dry oloroso style.
Madeira Cossart's Duo Centenary Sercial			Madeira/Portugal
Marvellous amber hue, fuller than the oloroso, hints of orange, the colour of Armagnac with a greeny edge. Quite rich.	Rich, rancio bouquet, nutty, Armagnac hints, high acidity, lots of wood through long ageing.	Rich tangy flavour balanced by firm acidity: an almost sweet attack, full, nutty flavour and biting finish, very long, more depth and burnt flavour than the oloroso.	The searing acidity of a fine Sercial cuts through the richness to finish dry and very long. A perfect aperitif or with soup.
Madeira Finest Old Verdelho, Solera 1851 (Bottled 1973)			Madeira
Burnt amber, almost yellow-brown, colour of aged pale Cognac, wonderful clarity.	Superb rancio bouquet, almost more Cognac than Madeira, very clear-cut, long wood ageing evident, typical high acidity.	Sweet, ripe attack, incredible balance between woody/caramel, burnt flavours, direct and intense.	Impression of great length, a wine that has dried out but lost none of its vigour, almost the epitome of a fortified wine. Very rare.
Port Graham's 1985 (Bottled 1987)			Portugal
Huge, intense, almost opaque black cherry colour, very high in viscosity.	Plummy, spicy, Christmas pudding aromas, alcohol, sweetness very present, but basically dry behind the the plumminess.	Sweet, raisiny attack, with blackcurrants, figs, mixed dried fruits, soft, plummy tannin, rich and vibrant.	A very young vintage port, could be drunk since the sweetness covers the tannin, but needs ten years to balance out. It will become drier and last a further 15 years.
Banyuls 1975 'Vieilles Vignes' Domaine du Mas Blanc (Bottled 1989)			France
Full, deep mahogany, aged mature red, with brick-tawny rim.	Concentrated, burnt dried fruit bouquet, impression of sun-cooked grapes, over-ripeness, and touch of rancio through ageing.	Warm, almost chocolaty flavours, spicy, concentrated, fine rancio dry finish.	A marvellous balance with richness, concentration, extract and dryness. 'A wine grower's port', aged beautifully.

APPEARANCE	BOUQUET	PALATE	COMMENTS
Port Taylor's 20-year-old Tawny (Bottled 1989)			Portugal
Aged, burnt red-amber, a really brilliant, rich hue, with a tawny-yellow edge.	Rich, burnt, spicy, minerally, peppery, nutty and lightly caramelly. Wonderfully warm, complex and penetrating bouquet.	Rich, vibrant, sweet but spicy, dried fruits, an almost refreshing touch of rancio, wood aged finish. A very polished wine.	A perfect tawny port, lovely concentration of sweetness with a firm walnutty fruit. High-quality blending and ageing.
Port Graham's 1966 (Bottled 1968)			Portugal
Fine solid deep carmine-ruby, very rich, no hint of being 23 years old, except that vintage port keeps such a youthful colour.	Concentrated sweetness, followed by a peppery, dried fruit, fig and tea-like bouquet. But overall sweet, ripe fruit.	Rich, warm, spicy, very grapey for a 1966, raisiny. All the extract and warmth of a fine vintage port.	Well balanced, sweet style (Graham's), does not have the tannic grip of a really great vintage (1977, 1963). A complete contrast in style to the Taylor's 20-year-old Tawny, both very fine.
Muscat de Beaumes de Venise 1987 Domaine Coyeux			France
Clean, palish yellow, slight gold touch, quite rich.	Pretty, floral, apricot and ripe melons, pure summery fruits.	Rich and musky, young and floral, ripe from sugar-filled grapes.	Alcohol just discernible through the fruit, but obviously a very great contrast after the port. Pure summery Muscat explosion of fruit. Not too heavy.
Pineau de Charentes Ch. de Beaulon 10-years-old			France
Medium, slightly straw-yellow, very rich, a fine aged colour but not yet amber.	Floral, raisiny bouquet, faintly straw-like from the alcohol, but fine balance.	Rich, raisiny but not cloying, wood ageing adds a depth and complexity which sets it apart from the exuberant but simple fruit of the Muscat.	A very interesting wine typical of Cognac. Weighty but much finesse. Excellent as an aperitif.
Setubal Moscatel J-M da Fonseca 20-years-old			Portugal
Very fine light mahogany, burnt amber colour, brilliantly clear.	Very rich, slightly rancio bouquet, not unlike the Taylor's showing the definite effect of wood ageing, but more rich and sweet than spicy.	Very old tawny port style, fully rich, slightly burnt with a sweet raisiny concentration and good acidity. Full of Muscat fruit, complex.	A beautifully made wine, great concentration of flavour through selection of grapes and wood ageing. A classic amongst sweet fortified wines.
Sherry Very, Very Old Oloroso Sandeman			Spain
Very deep polished mahogany with hints of gold, yellow-amber rim, intense, rich and warm-looking.	Intense, rich, nutty bouquet, hints of molasses, dried fruit, ripeness and richness.	Marvellous rich sweetness, full opulent flavours, very big and unctuous, but with a fine acidity. The weight of a German TBA or Grains Nobles dessert wine, and the presence.	From a solera with an average age of 24 years, this has all the richness of the finest dessert wines. The added alcohol during fortification adds length to the flavour without heaviness.

Tasting/Colour of Wine/Whites

Muscadet de Sèvre et Maine *One year old Loire white*
This light Loire white is very pale, almost colourless, fresh and mouthwatering. A Muscadet may be a little fuller from very sunny years, but in comparison to other dry whites will always be amongst the palest.

Pouilly Fumé *One year old Loire white*
Slightly fuller than the Muscadet, this young wine from the Sauvignon grape has the light colour of a crisp, dry white. Once the colour loses its freshness, after 3-4 years, the wine will have as well.

Riesling *One year old Alsatian white*
Much the same tone as the Pouilly Fumé, but a little firmer with a touch of green. The colour is young as expected, will fill out as the wine matures, the acidity keeping it fresh for many years.

Meursault *Four year old Côte de Beaune white*
A softer, more buttery colour, deeper and richer than the Riesling. The high quality of this wine, a Premier Cru, with good acidity to balance the rich fruit, has kept the colour young and fresh.

Napa Valley Chardonnay *Four years old*
Very similar to the Meursault, both Chardonnays, but no green tints and slightly softer. This is one of the 'French-style' Napa Chardonnays, and is fresh for a California white.

Arbois *Three year old Arbois white*
More full and mature looking than the older Chardonnays. Part of the colour comes from the local Savagnin grape, part from the time spent in wood, aiming at the dry, nutty Arbois style.

Vouvray demi-sec *Sixteen year old semi-sweet Loire white*
Remarkably fresh, though intense, colour for a wine of this age, due to the acidity of the Chenin Blanc. Now a very complete straw, honey-yellow.

Sauternes 1er Cru *Ten years old*
Full, rich golden yellow of a *very* sweet wine from a top vintage, now approaching maturity. From this point the colour will mature quite quickly to an amber gold, and after many more years to burnt amber.

Tasting/Colour of Wine/Rosés

Bourgueil Rosé *One year old Touraine rosé*
A very light Loire rosé from the Cabernet Franc grape. The 'blush' comes from the *saignée* process, whereby the colour is slowly bled out of the skins. These wines should be drunk as young as they look.

Bandol Rosé *One year old Provence rosé*
The best rosé in Provence, the pale salmon colour is due to short skin contact and the soft oranginess from wood ageing. Although the colour is light, the wine is firm and will hold well.

Côtes de Provence Rosé *One year old Provence rosé*
This is the other style of Provence rosé, where a longer skin contact gives more colour and flesh, but the wine is kept in stainless steel to avoid oxidation. Should be treated like a light red wine.

Arbois Rosé *One year old Arbois rosé*
This is a rosé which is vinified like a red wine, the rosé colour due to the low level of pigment in the Poulsard grape. The slight brown edge sets it apart from the others, and in flavour it is closer to a red than a rosé.

Tasting/Colour of Wine/Volnay Premier Cru

Three year old Volnay *Medium vintage*
Shows the fresh young colour of Pinot Noir, seldom rich and intense like a Cabernet or Syrah, from a large vintage. A fruity looking wine, but the fading at the rim suggests a relatively quick maturing future.

Four year old Volnay *Very good vintage*
From a much smaller crop, the colour is more intense, richer looking and less mature than the previous wine. The deep oxblood hue suggests that it is no longer *very* young, but it is showing no signs of age.

Six year old Volnay *Very good, hot vintage*
From a year when the skins were exceptionally dark and thick, and the colour accordingly concentrated. Another intense Pinot, with the hints of mahogany showing the extra two years of age. Will mature well.

Eleven year old Volnay *Good, very ripe vintage*
A perfectly mature Burgundy, where the intense red of the younger wines has matured to a full mahogany richness. The yellow edge suggests that the wine is now at its peak and that it will lose colour from now on.

Tasting/Colour of Wine/Reds

Brouilly *One year old Beaujolais*
The full, violetty, youthful red of a young Beaujolais. The Gamay grape should always have this look, neither too heavy nor too light, but appealingly fruity. In two years the colour will have lost its youth, as will the wine.

Chinon 'Vieilles Vignes' *One year old Touraine red*
A very fine colour from old Cabernet Franc vines, a rich carmine with a young purple edge. This edge will fade, but the firmness and intensity of the red will hold for many years.

Crozes-Hermitage *Three year old Côtes-du-Rhône*
Very deep, blackberry red, to be expected from a young Syrah from a good vineyard and vintage. Just losing the opaque purple of youth, the huge extract shows concentration of fruit. Will mature slowly.

California Zinfandel *Four years old*
As intense as the Crozes-Hermitage, rich, blackcurranty red with no sign of age. The plumminess on the palate and even tannin can be sensed from the colour, which will age, losing fruit as well, very slowly.

Saint Emilion Grand Cru Classé *Four years old*
Full, rich red, beginning to mature. The Merlot does not usually have the same intensity as the Cabernet Sauvignon, Syrah or Zinfandel. This will begin to show mahogany tints in about five years.

Margaux Cru Classé *Three year old Médoc*
Very deep, vibrant colour from a very successful Haut-Médoc; the Cabernet Sauvignon holds the firmness for longer than other Bordeaux grapes. This shows no sign of maturing and will still be an intense ruby in five years.

Margaux Cru Classé *Eleven year old Médoc*
A fully mature Bordeaux, the same château as above, from a good but not great vintage. The colour, a firm oxblood to brick-red with a tawny, slightly paling rim suggests that this wine is at its peak.

Vacqueyras *Fifteen year old Côtes-du-Rhône*
This is a fully mature red from the southern Rhône from a very good vintage. The yellow-tawny rim shows that the wine is beginning to lose colour and fruit, with a potential to last, but not improve.

4
SPECIAL STUDIES

Wine and Food

Serving Wine

Fortified and Distilled Wines

Oak

Wine and Health

Tasting Cards

Tasting Terms

Vintage Table

Wine & Food 1

The four primary flavours

The interplay between food and wine, offering a wealth of potential combinations, is a complex matter. Although there are only four basic flavours – salty, acidic, sweet and bitter – the taste buds do not perceive these four elements simultaneously, nor do the flavour components linger equally long in the mouth. Sweet flavours, for instance, are perceived almost instantaneously but hardly last for more than ten seconds in the mouth. Acidity and saltiness are also quickly savoured but their impression lasts longer on the tongue. Bitterness, on the other hand, takes a time to build up, but once fully developed, it persists for much longer than the other three.

Laboratory research has shown that these primary flavours act on one another in the following ways:

Saltiness reinforces bitterness.

Acidity conceals bitterness, though only temporarily, and enhances the perception of sweetness.

Sweetness reduces the impression of saltiness, bitterness and acidity.

Bitterness reduces acidity.

Great wines are of course created to be drunk during meals, and so food and wine ought always to complement each other perfectly.

The right sequence

The sequence in which food dishes should be served is governed by a number of specific rules. Here are some:

Never begin with spicy dishes; flavours should grow progressively.

Always serve salty dishes before sweet ones.

Never garnish with too many starchy foods.

Do not serve too many dishes in heavy sauces.

Wines too should obey certain principles:

Start with the youngest and go on to the oldest (which does not mean those that are 'tired').

Proceed from the lightest to the most full-bodied; from the coolest to the most *chambré*; from the weakest in alcohol to the most potent; and from dry to sweet.

Drink whites before reds.

If you do not vary the wine, at least vary the year.

Matching wines with food is a tricky business and it is not always possible to follow each of these rules to the letter; nevertheless it is important to ensure that a new wine never overshadows the one that has just been drunk.

Above *Lobster and trout dishes with a bottle of Sancerre.*

Tradition usually demands that like matches like: a delicate dish goes with a delicate wine, while a full-flavoured course requires a full-bodied, robust wine. More adventurous combinations may succeed in bringing out unexpected and delightful contrasts, although regional specialities will probably clash with non-local wines. Finally, a dish cooked in wine should be enjoyed with the same wine or a slightly superior one.

One-wine menus

A whole meal with just one type of wine may be easier to organize, but beware of pitfalls!

Red wines leave a fair amount of room for manoeuvre; with rosés, however, the sequence of dishes is less easy to plan, and should be restricted to simple, flavourful Mediterranean cooking.

An all-white menu will revolve around fish, white meats and goat's cheese.

A classic meal with champagne offers the opportunity to select between ordinary and top-of-the-range grades, and wines with different proportions of white and black grapes. Red Bouzy should be drunk with cheese, but naturally *fromage des Riceys* is best enjoyed with Rosé des Riceys.

Even a meal accompanied only by fortified wines or ports can be an unqualified success, but it does require oenological and culinary skill and imagination.

Left *Brie with green peppers and a white cheese with paprika, accompanied by a Gewürztraminer.*

Wine & Food 2

Aperitifs

Dry white wines are traditionally used as aperitifs, but there are a number of alternatives. These do not, however, include spirits, which spoil the palate for the wines to come.

Aperitifs can be drunk by themselves or accompanied by peanuts, savoury biscuits, caviar or salmon fingers, cocktail sausages, cheese straws, anchovies and so on. Such snacks will not affect the taste of the wine, but beware of olives and pickles. Dry whites, sparkling whites and dry champagne (Blanc de Blancs) make excellent aperitifs, as do certain rosés, while the dry-before-sweet rule might occasionally be broken by serving sherries and other fortified wines before the meal. Sweet wines and *vins doux naturels* are, of course, generally associated with desserts, but as we shall see, the combination of sugared desserts and sweet wines is not necessarily a happy one; besides, by the end of the meal one's guests may well be quite satisfied and will balk at the thought of a rich, heavy wine.

The choice of menu will affect the choice of aperitif, and a melon offered as a starter should be preceded by a fortified wine which the guests can use to pour over the cool, refreshing fruit. A meal that starts with *foie gras* might well commence with one of the great sherries instead of a mature white or red wine.

Hors d'oeuvre, cold meats

Wine should never be served with soup, of course, and *sauce vinaigrette* should also be avoided since vinegar is the sworn enemy of wine. Lemon dressings are likewise undesirable, and so the problem can be solved simply by using white wine instead, as, for instance, in a potato salad.

Egg-based starters should be avoided, unless the eggs are actually prepared in wine. Cold meats, however, go well with a rosé, a light red or possibly an Alsace white. Here again though, caution is needed, since cooked ham gives wine (especially red) a metallic side-taste.

Rillettes and some pâtés have a softness and richness that is excellently enhanced by a Coteaux du Layon, the sweetness of which is offset by acidity to lend it plenty of vitality.

One final word of warning – snails and

Right Jambon persillé *with Mâcon-Viré.*

wine do not go together! The garlic used in the preparation of snails will ruin the taste of any wine.

As a general rule, fish and seafood should never be served with good red wines, though there are certain exceptions.

Shellfish

Oysters are generally eaten with dry whites, but because seawater salt adds unpleasantly to the wine's acidity some people prefer light reds instead, especially those from the Graves. Tannins are incompatible with the proteins present in shellfish and an over-exuberant fruity wine will certainly clash with the strong odour of seafood.

If you still insist on a white wine, choose wines that are both dry and well-rounded (Chablis) or slightly more gentle (Côte de Beaune). A Manzanilla or Fino is also perfect with seafood.

Crustaceans

Most crustaceans – lobster, crayfish, scallops, etc. – are too costly to be treated lightly and deserve to be accompanied by the great whites of Bordeaux, Burgundy or the Rhône.

Fish

Most fish goes well with white wine, and the more complex the preparation the more subtle the wine should be. Fish served cold with mayonnaise is best eaten with ordinary whites that are young and lively, while fish soufflés or terrines (unless there is a strong presence of dill) go best with complex wines.

For fried or grilled fish, a moderately good dry white will suffice, or a rosé if the fish is strong-tasting (sardines, anchovies).

Smoked fish is best enjoyed with dry whites of pronounced character, or even with sherry.

The great white Burgundies, mature Loire wines (Vouvray) and the better class champagnes are still the best choice to accompany baked or steamed fish such as pike, fresh salmon or turbot, whether or not they are served with a rich sauce.

With any fish cooked in red wine (eel, trout or sole), serve the same wine or one slightly better. Bouillabaisse has to be served with unambitious rosés or dry whites, since the saffron will overwhelm any more complex or subtle vintage. Finally, caviar calls for a dry white of some distinction, such as a Burgundy or champagne.

Below left Ecrevisses à la nage *with Seyssel.*
Below *A seafood quiche with Listel Gris.*

Wine & Food 3

Poultry

At one time poultry was served before red meat, followed by game, and this called for a light red wine. Nowadays, however, poultry is itself the main dish of a meal and so can command a superior vintage of Bourgueil or Chinon in the case of white poultry (chicken) or a fuller-bodied red (Cahors, Madiran) if the flesh is dark (duck).

Local customs should always be respected: the area around Sauternes and Barsac, for example, is the home of roast chicken served with sweet, rich wines, while in the Champagne region, baked poultry is eaten with 'bubbly'.

Tannic red wines should accompany *confit d'oie* and *confit de canard* (Médoc, Saint-Emilion, Madiran); *coq au vin jaune* or *au Chambertin* of course call for the wine in which they are prepared.

White meats

Since roast white meats – veal, pork and lamb – have no very pronounced flavours, they prefer the company of delicate red wines; lamb and Médoc are a legendary combination, while if you prefer a Burgundy, choose a Côte de Beaune for the best results.

Veal sweetbreads and kidneys demand sophisticated culinary treatment and hence their table companions should also be wines of breeding and distinction: Médoc, Graves, Pomerol or first growths of Volnay, Pernand-Vergelesses from Burgundy.

Pasta dishes and vegetables

Vegetables do not as a rule complement wines to good effect. Asparagus, artichokes, spinach and sorrel possess a degree of acidity that never accords well with wines; fennel's aniseed flavour is too strong, but cabbage in the form of sauerkraut has found a firm friend in the wine of Alsace.

The mushroom is one vegetable that definitely goes with either reds or whites, and the truffle in particular represents the perfect complement to the better vintages of Pomerol, mature Jurançon, champagne, Côte Rôtie and others. Morels and *vin jaune* are yet another classical match, as are *cèpes* (boletus) and Saint-Emilion or Pomerol.

Finally, pasta, rice and noodle dishes are often incapable of setting off a wine in spite of their relative neutrality, and go quite well with light reds especially, of course, Italian reds.

Left Coq au vin jaune aux morilles *with a* vin jaune *from the Jura.*

Below Volaille au vinaigre *with Beaujolais-Villages.*

Red meats

Beef is a strong aromatic meat which of course loves the company of red wines. In its more modest form – beef stews – it goes well with Beaujolais and wines from the Mâcon region. For grilled beef, the better growths of Beaujolais, Burgundies or the minor *appellations* are perfect escorts, as is Saint-Emilion.

Roast beef calls for wines that are vigorous and forthcoming, such as good Burgundy AOC's and Rhône Valley wines. Beef dishes cooked in wine should of course be eaten together with a bottle of the same style of wine but generally of better quality.

Game

Any game should be accompanied by wines that are warm and full-bodied to bring out the meat's own pronounced flavours. For feathered game, go for a classified growth of Graves or Médoc, a first growth of Côte d'Or, or one of the better years of Côte Chalonnaise.

All other game is perfectly enhanced by the great reds from the northern (Côte Rôtie) or southern (Châteauneuf-du-Pape) Rhône valley. To follow this up when the cheese is served, choose a good Côte de Nuits or possibly a Saint-Emilion or Pomerol of distinction (Château Canon, Vieux-Château Certan).

Spicy dishes

Dishes which are heavily spiced, whether Indian, North African, South American, etc., pose real problems since a good bottle would certainly be wasted. Instead, choose a wine that is first and foremost 'gulpable' and thirst-quenching – a light fresh red or rosé, or even a white provided it is not over-acidic, otherwise it will taste harsh in the presence of certain spices and seasonings.

A Gewürztraminer may accompany a fairly subtle curry, while a full-bodied robust red (a Rioja, for instance) will stand up to a medium-strong chilli con carne.

Left Tarte aux cailles *with a Pinot Noir from Alsace.*

Wine & Food 4

Wine and Cheese

Although they combine perfectly, it is undeniable that cheese tends to benefit more from the accompaniment of wine than vice-versa.

Of course, there is cheese and cheese, and there are all too few really good makers. What is more, the same label often graces a variety of products that have little in common as regards taste and texture. There are all too many pasty concoctions that pass for the real thing, and once they start to run it is too late to eat them because of their excessively salty or ammonia-like flavour. A cheese of distinction, however, deserves a good vintage wine, and many local and regional wines and cheeses go naturally together: Munster with the wine of Alsace (Gewürztraminer), Epoisses and Burgundy (Côte d'Or), Banon and Côtes de Provence, Crottin de Chavignol and Sancerre, Morbier and Arbois Rouge, to name but a few.

As a rule, the choice of wine should be based on the cheese's actual raw materials and

Right *Cheeses from north Burgundy (Montrachet, Langres, Gratte-Paille and Charolais* mi-chèvre*) with Côte de Beaune-Villages.*

Left *Roquefort, delicious with full-bodied red wines from the Rhône Valley.*

method of manufacture. There are some guidelines:

All fresh cheeses: dry whites, rosés or light reds.

Goat's cheese: dry, fruity whites.

Soft blue cheeses: (e.g. Bleu d'Auvergne, des Causses, de Bressa, etc. made from cow's milk, or Roquefort from ewe's milk) wines with plenty of *sève*, robust, full-bodied wines from the Rhône Valley, or fortified wines. The traditional combination of Roquefort with Sauternes in south-western France originally derived from the British custom of eating Stilton with port.

Soft cheese in a wax crust (Brie, Camembert). The fruitiness of these cheeses often clashes with that of wines, but well-rounded, vigorous reds (local Côte d'Or *appellations*) are good accompaniments.

Soft cheeses with light crusts (Pont l'Evêque, Livarot). These should be enjoyed with wines that are robust (Madiran, Bandol) and rich (Côte de Nuits *premiers crus*).

Pressed hard cheeses (Gruyère, Emmentaler), hard cheeses from skimmed milk (Reblochon, St Nectaire, Edam, etc.). These cheeses go with a wide range of wines, although Cantal poses a problem because of its bitterness. Most hard cheeses go well with red wines from the Loire, Bordeaux, Burgundy or the Rhône; a Beaufort, for instance, will form an excellent complement to a mature Bordeaux, no matter how distinctive.

Wines and Desserts

Chocolate desserts, whether in the form of a mousse, a gâteau or hot sauce poured over fresh fruit, always rule out a wine accompaniment since the taste of chocolate fills the mouth, drowning the wine's aromas before they have a chance to develop. Lemon goes equally poorly with wine – its acidity kills any other flavour, as do most fruits (oranges, apricots, gooseberries, etc.).

Heavy, creamy desserts will cloy the mouth; the presence of alcohol in fruit salads or soufflés will overwhelm the flavour of a good vintage unless it is very discreet indeed. The same goes for too much sugar.

Among the desserts that can be enjoyed with wine are the following: Madeira cake or almond-based pastries, nuts, walnut gâteaux, light flaky pastries, plain pancakes, chestnut desserts, petits fours without cream, apple tarts, pear flans, etc. Such moderately sweet desserts should be eaten with medium-dry champagnes or a sweet wine from the Loire or south-western France. The *vins doux naturels* (Muscat, Rasteau, etc.) or sparkling wines made from aromatic grape varieties (Clairette de Die) may also be suitable.

Ices and sorbets are best enjoyed by themselves, but may be successfully followed by a demi-sec white wine or champagne.

Finally, fresh fruit in red wine should never be accompanied by any wine at all, and certainly not by red.

Serving Wine 1

The right time to fetch the bottle

If you are fortunate enough to have your own cellar, the bottle should be brought up one or more hours before the meal depending on whether or not it is to be uncorked and/or decanted. A young wine should be carried and uncorked in the upright position, while an older vintage likely to throw off a deposit should be placed gently in a serving basket and poured from this near-horizontal position.

If you have no cellar and are therefore compelled to buy your wine from a retailer, you should make your purchase as late as possible on the day before consumption and leave it upright in a cool dark place overnight. Never allow a wine to stand for too long in a refrigerator, even if it is to be drunk chilled.

The right time to uncork

The reason why a wine should be uncorked in advance of a meal is to let the wine breathe and oxygenate, and to eliminate any foreign odours (sulphur dioxide, mercaptans, etc.). Since all air changes are minimal, oxidation is not a problem, except with particularly sensitive wines. The well-known Bordeaux oenologist Emile Peynaud even disregards this factor altogether, claiming that it makes little difference whether a bottle is opened three hours or three minutes before a meal, so that it might as well be done at the last minute.

Perhaps the best solution to the problem is simply to uncork the bottle, taste the wine and decide either to replace the cork (healthy young wines, very aged wines with subtle, volatile esters), leave the bottle open (to eliminate foreign odours), or decant it.

The right time to decant

Decanting enables the wine to throw off its deposit, an operation which necessarily brings the wine into contact with oxygen. Not all wines should be decanted; those that benefit most by such treatment are the wines of Bordeaux and occasionally certain red wines from the northern Rhône Valley, since their otherwise restrained aromas can be released more fully in this way. Whites, rosés and the more fragile reds, on the other hand, do not derive any benefit from decantation.

Some people, nevertheless, believe in decanting irrespective of bottle, and at Château Palmer, with its classified Médoc growths, they never serve a bottle, whatever the year, that has not been decanted well in advance.

Temperature

Generally speaking, wines that should be drunk chilled are usually too cold and those that must be consumed at room temperature (*chambré*) are too warm. In fact, the term *chambrer* has become somewhat redundant now that homes are centrally heated to as much as 24°C in winter, very much warmer than our grandparents' dining-rooms, which never went above 17 or 18°C.

Each type of wine of course needs an optimum tasting temperature, although this is always relative since a glass of wine at 18°C will taste different according to the season and outside conditions. Most white wines should be chilled, but this does not mean 'frozen', and anything much below 6°C is below the taste threshold. Always beware of labels requiring you to drink the wine 'well

Below *Corkscrews should have wide coils free from sharp edges and be long enough to ensure good purchase on even the longest corks; l. to r.: wooden counterscrew, butterfly lever, screwpull, waiter's friend (above) and butler's friend (below).*

Left Decanting a wine helps to release the more restrained aromas.

chilled' – the contents will probably have defects that will be concealed by a very low temperature. The temperature of the wine should also be reduced *gradually*. Place the bottle in an ice bucket half filled with water, then add ice cubes; once poured, the wine will quickly warm up by one or two degrees.

Sweet white wines Unless you specifically wish to accentuate the sweetness of the wine, it should be cooled to around 6°, bearing in mind what has already been said.

Champagnes and sparkling wines A good rule of thumb is 6° in the glass; one or two degrees more can suit sparkling wines that have matured for some years.

Dry white wines With these wines, the temperature will depend largely on the quality of the vintage. 'Little' dry whites be consumed very cool (8°), while more complex whites, yet with a decidedly dry character (Graves, Alsace) are best enjoyed at 10–12°. The rich white wines that leave the merest hint of sweetness (the great Burgundies, white Châteauneuf-du-Pape, Condrieu, etc.) will not suffer from being drunk at 13–14° in the glass.

Vin jaune This is the only white that can be drunk relatively *chambré* (16°).

Rosés These are by their very nature young, fresh and fruity wines that should be served at cellar temperature, i.e. 9–10°.

Red wines Light reds drunk young or very young should also be enjoyed slightly chilled, since their fruitiness is damaged by too much warmth (Beaujolais, all Gamays, etc.).

Loire reds such as Bourgueil, and all wines from the Cabernet Franc are better structured and capable of withstanding one or two more degrees when drunk fairly young (13–14°). The great wines of the Rhône valley and Burgundy give of their best at 15–16°, while the more tannic Bordeaux prefer top-of-the-range temperatures around 16–18°, the upper threshold (18°) being reserved for the older vintages.

Serving Wine 2

Right *Stages in the correct uncorking of a wine bottle.*

The right way to uncork

Start by cutting away the capsule about a quarter of an inch below the neck to prevent the wine coming into contact with metal.

The corkscrew should have wide coils that are free from any sharp edges and preferably long enough to withdraw corks of any size (screwpull, wine-waiter's friend, etc.). Never shake the bottle when opening – no good wine deserves rough treatment. Never 'pop' a champagne cork since a rapid release of gas will actually harm the quality of the contents.

A bottle that has been placed in a basket to allow the deposit to settle should always be opened in the same position. Just lift the bottle slightly, inserting a spare cork between the neck and the edge of the basket. This will slightly increase the slant of the bottle and so avoid the risk of losing any of the precious liquid.

Wine glasses

Wine should be poured gently into the glass – but not just any glass. Both the shape and the

Below *The suitability of the glass to the wine is of prime importance; l. to r.: ISO tasting glass, Burgundy, Bordeaux, Paris goblet (reds); tulip, goblet, Alsace (whites).*

thickness are of prime importance. Generally speaking, a good wine glass is one that is colourless, uncut and with a stem and foot. At the Académie du Vin we use AFNOR (French standard) glasses which are adequate for whites, reds and sparkling wines, excellent for wine-tasting but not ideal for everyday drinking at the dinner table. For this there are others, such as the Bordeaux glass in the shape of a tulip, the bulbous Burgundy glass that is slightly narrower at the lip, the Alsace glass and the familiar champagne flute. A word of warning, however: never use the shallow *coupe* for sparkling wines; its lack of depth will not show the bubbles rising and its wide rim will let all the bouquet escape.

Whatever the shape of your wine glasses, the diameters of the foot and rim should be less than that of the body at its widest point, in order to hold in the wine's aromas. Glasses should be filled to half or three-quarters, never full. Finally, a clean white tablecloth is really the only acceptable background to set off the colour of any good vintage.

Below *L. to r.: sherry, port, port/madeira, champagne flutes, cognac balloon and cognac recommended.*

Fortified Wines/Vin Doux Naturels & Vins de Liqueur

These two styles of fortified wine are made in the same way as all fortified wine: alcohol is added to the must during fermentation, so that the fermenting process is stopped, leaving a lower degree of natural alcohol and an accordingly higher degree of natural sugar. The addition of alcohol can vary from 6° to 10° by volume. Only grapes possessing a minimum of 250 grams per litre of natural sugar (the equivalent of 14° alcohol) may undergo this operation, and they are thus specially selected varieties, grown in specific regions. The French word for this process is *mutage*, from *muet*, meaning 'dumb', since alcohol 'silences' the fermentation.

The difference between *vins de liqueur* and *vins doux naturels* in France is purely administrative, the former being taxed as spirits and the latter as wines. They are all dissimilar in taste, because they are made in different regions from different grapes, but the methods of production are the same.

The best known French *vin de liqueur* is Pineau des Charentes (see Fortified Tasting, page 179), made from grapes picked in the Cognac region, with the addition of Cognac. It may be served either as an aperitif or a dessert wine – ice-cold – the alcoholic content varying from 16.5° to 22°. In Champagne a similar fortified wine, made from champagne grapes, is called Ratafia; and the allied Floc de Gascogne consists of grape juice and Armagnac. All three merit an AOC *appellation*.

The *vins doux naturels* are sweet wines produced in the Roussillon across the Languedoc to Marseille and in the Rhône valley. The wines are naturally sweet, but fortified, and must not be confused with *vins liquoreux* which are wines naturally sweet from overmaturity or botrytized grapes. The principal grapes are the Grenache and the Muscat, with a little Malvoisie and Maccabeo. VDNs may be white, rosé, or red and the

Sweet Muscats are made in centres along the Mediterranean coast: at Lunel, Rivesaltes, Frontignan and also at Beaumes-de-Venise in the Vaucluse.

alcohol should give no sense of burning or roughness. VDNs may be sold at two or three months, while those made from the Grenache become more complex and may undergo and benefit from many years in wood. Such wines take on an aged or 'maderized' flavour, known as 'rancio', a flavour that also appears in old Cognacs and Armagnacs. Wines of 10 and 20 years old will have a magnificent concentration of flavour while remaining lively and spirited on the palate.

The finest of these wines are Banyuls and the Muscats. The former are always red, the latter always white. Banyuls is undoubtedly the finest VDN in France, grown in the Roussillon, almost on the Spanish frontier (also the home of Maury and Rivesaltes), from steeply terraced schistous vineyards. The addition of alcohol may come early or late in the fermentation; the later the *mutage*, the drier the wine. To benefit from the *appellation* Banyuls Grand Cru, the must should ferment for at least five days before the addition of alcohol, and the wine must be aged in wood. A good Banyuls may rival a fine port (see Fortified Tasting, page 178).

The sweet Muscats (not to be confused with the Muscat d'Alsace, which is very aromatic but bone-dry) are found along the Mediterranean coast, at Lunel, Rivesaltes, Frontignan, and in the southern Côtes-du-Rhône at Beaumes-de-Venise (see Fortified Tasting, page 179). They have a wonderful golden colour, an explosive, richly aromatic bouquet, and a concentrated, sunny flavour. They must be served very cold, and they do not improve with age.

Ratafia is a fortified wine made in Champagne from champagne grapes.

Fortified Wines/Sherry, Port & Madeira

Fortified wines are produced, as we have seen, by adding alcohol to the must during fermentation. The best known wines in this category, far surpassing in international repute those made in France, are sherry, port and madeira.

Sherry

Sherry is different from other fortified wines in that it is fermented out to complete dryness, and the alcohol is added later. Since, in the usual fashion, the must is fortified during fermentation, leaving residual sugar in the wine, fortified wines are generally sweet. Sherry is dry, the sweetness in the richer blends arriving from the addition of wines specially selected for this purpose.

Sherry comes from vineyards to the south of Andalusia, between Cadiz and Seville, the best being grouped around the town of Jerez de la Frontera. The determinant factor of quality, however, is the nature of the soil, and the white, chalky *albariza* soil gives to sherry the finest breed and bouquet. On this soil, it is the Palomino grape that is universally planted, from which all types of the finer sherries are made. Several other grape varieties are planted for use in blending, especially the Pedro Ximénez; bunches of these grapes are dried in the sun for several days before fermentation to make a powerful, sweet wine to be used for the richer sherries.

After fermentation, the key to making sherry lies in selection and blending. A first selection will take place in December, following the vintage in September. The lighter, finer wines will be set aside to make finos or amontillados, and will be fortified up to 15.5°; fuller wines, with less finesse, will be more heavily fortified to 17–18°, and will be destined for the oloroso family. The wine is still bone-dry. After fortification, the different wines are stocked in separate *criaderas* or wine-nurseries. The finos will develop a sort of milky skim (*flor*) on the surface of the wine (as is also found in the wines of Château-Chalon) in casks that have been left one-quarter empty. They will be bottled after one or two years, the result being a pale, clean, dry sherry. Amontillado is classically an aged fino, taking on colour and, curiously enough, alcohol through ageing in wood. The oloroso family may be aged and unsweetened, resulting in a complex, nutty wine, or be sweetened with PX (Pedro Ximénez) to be sold as a cream sherry. Throughout its life in cask, sherries are blended from butt to butt (the so-called solera system), which is also found in the making of madeira.

At Sanlucar de Barrameda, not far along the coast from Jerez, a sherry-style fino called manzanilla is made from the same grapes as sherry, but is said to get its very dry, tangy character from the salty sea breezes blowing in from the Atlantic.

Port

Port is probably the best known of the fortified wines. It comes from the Cima Corgo and Baixo Corgo regions of the Douro Valley

Right *L. to r.: lighter, finer wines are used for the preparation of finos and amontillados; manzanilla is a sherry-style fino made exclusively at Sanlucar de Barrameda.*

in north-east Portugal. Because of the schistous rock 'soil' and the steeply terraced vineyards, this is perhaps the most arduous wine-growing region in the world. There are many grape varieties, both red and white, but their character is of less importance than the soil, the climate and the human factor. The vintage takes place in mid-September, the red grapes having the maximum amount of colour extracted during the short period of fermentation, before the addition of alcohol – local *eau de vie* – to a minimum level of 16.5°. This will raise the 4–6° of natural alcohol to a total of 22.5–24.5°, incorporating a high level of residual sugar which gives port its sweetness. In the following spring the wine is brought down to the port lodges (as the above ground cellars are called), in Vila Nova de Gaia where it matures in preparation for its final blending.

There are two basic types of port: vintage port and wood port. The former is the product of a single year – and sometimes of a single domaine or *Quinta* – kept in cask until two years after the vintage, bottled and continuing to mature in bottle. Not all port shippers declare the same year as a vintage, some specialize in 'off'-vintages from their estates, and many offer a late-bottled vintage, bottled after longer in wood than the classic vintage. Wood port can be white, ruby or tawny. White port is generally fermented much drier than red port, but only the finest are very dry from several years in cask. Ruby is bottled after three to five years in wood, after which it tends to lose its full colour and become progressively more tawny and less sweet with age. Port shippers do not use the solera system, but keep large reserves of older vintages and blend to match their house style. An old tawny will be a blend of several years, and if it carries a date – say 20 years old – the average age of the blend will not be less than 20 years. Ruby and white ports are less expensive than tawny port, as they are bottled earlier. A fine tawny is as good as, but different from, a mature vintage port. These styles are examined in the tasting on page 179.

Madeira

Madeira wine comes from the Portuguese island of the same name, and is almost as well known as port. It is, however, better known for its use in sauces and cakes, and not significantly appreciated as a fortified wine. The fame of madeira began when ships stopping off at Funchal on their way to the Americas for fresh water took on casks of the local wine as ballast. The lengthy sea voyage, during which the wine was kept at a high temperature, imparted a 'burnt' flavour that was much appreciated. Today, the same effect is achieved through the vinification process called *estafugem*.

Madeira grapes are grown on a volcanic soil infused with potash, and make four main styles of wine. Sercial, the palest and driest, is excellent as an aperitif. If it is aged in cask for many years it darkens in colour, develops an intense nuttiness, but never loses its acidity.

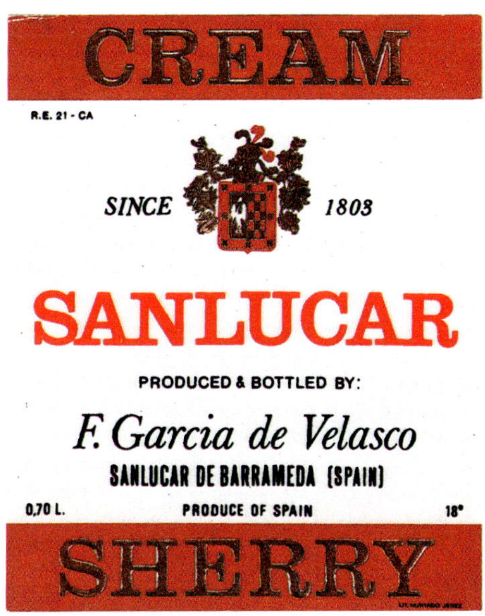

Left *Oloroso sherries may be sweetened with the Pedro Ximénez grape to produce cream sherry.*

Distilled Wines/Cognac

Distilled Wines

In France the right to distil wines or their by-products into brandies is being increasingly restricted to the major commercial distilleries. The great wine brandies – Cognac and Armagnac – enjoy AOC distinction, while others are entitled to display regulated *appellations*, for example the brandies of Burgundy, Champagne and other areas.

Distillation conditions are strictly enforced, with stills carrying out one run or more; they may be heated directly or by means of the water bath technique (*bain-marie*), with the *marc* being heated directly or indirectly by the steam which absorbs the alcohol vapour. The still's condenser must be cooled efficiently or some of the precious aroma is lost, and distillation is carried out slowly for the same reason. Hourly output and the specification of the raw material are also governed by official rules.

The distiller's art is to select the right apparatus for the distillation process itself, then to mature correctly in wooden casks; the timber, age and capacity of these casks all play as important a part as the ageing period itself.

Cognac

Distillation has been going on in the Charente region since the 18th century, and during that time the Ugni Blanc, known locally as 'Saint-Emilion', has taken over from the less reliable Folle Blanche which once went into the making of the finest Cognacs.

Vines planted in wide rows – two or three metres apart – and machine harvested produce a modest, sourish wine of 7–8° of alcohol which is never chaptalized or sulphured. Although the hectare yield is unlimited, the plants are pruned to give around 60,000 buds to the hectare. The area of production is divided into six different zones corresponding to six grades of Cognac, and in most instances these brandies are in fact a blend of the various grades.

Grande Champagne In the very heart of the region are some 13,000 hectares of crumbly limestone soil that yield the most delicate brandies with the most persistent aftertaste.

The **Petite Champagne** area is adjacent to that of the Grande Champagne, its limestone soil covering 16,000 hectares which produce fine brandies that mature more rapidly than those from the heart of the region.

Les Borderies This comprises 5000 hectares of silica-clay soil located to the north of the Grande Champagne which yield a Cognac notable for its roundness.

Les Fins Bois This huge area, some 40,000 hectares in all, encircles the preceding three. Its soil is silica-clay, and the Fins Bois Cognacs are well-balanced, elegant brandies which mature quickly.

Right *Checking the specific gravity of Cognac.*

Les Bons Bois Les Bons Bois in their turn enclose the preceding area, extending over 21,000 hectares of clay soil that yields a less balanced and less sophisticated brandy.

Les Bois Ordinaires These consist of 4000 hectares of Quaternary alluvial soil close to the Atlantic Ocean, yielding a more everyday type of brandy – said to taste of the salt sea.

The term *Fine champagne* does not indicate a region but denotes a blend of at least 50% of Grande Champagne with Petite Champagne.

Cognac is always obtained by double distillation: the first *chauffe* gives the *brouilli* which is collected at an alcohol content of around 30°. This is then re-distilled to give a final Cognac strength of 60–70°. It is placed in aged oak casks, during which operation some volume and alcohol content is lost. Estimates put the annual loss due to evaporation as high as 50,000 hectolitres, equivalent to seventeen million bottles!

The Cognac that is finally bottled will be blended from various different regions and different ages, while the alcohol content is reduced by watering. Caramel extract lends the brandy its characteristic hue and softness.

Cognac is never labelled by year, but its age can nevertheless be told by other distinctive markings. Three stars, for example, indicate that the contents are at least 2 years old, while VSOP, VO and Réserve denote 4 years. The designations Vieille Réserve, Extra and Napoléon are guarantees of over 5 years maturing in cask, while the average age of a blend is usually much greater.

Left *Stoking the stove under a Cognac still.*

Distilled Wines/Armagnac

Historically, Armagnac is at least as old as Cognac, though only about one-tenth as much is produced. Additionally, its quality is less consistent and it is therefore more difficult to market. The region of *appellation* relates only partially to Armagnac itself, and this in turn can be divided into three zones, each with its own *appellation*. The Bas Armagnac covers more than 11,000 hectares of vines planted in a Tertiary topsoil of sand and pebbles, covering a silica-clay subsoil. This zone includes the Grand Bas Armagnac, close to Labastide d'Armagnac, where the very best Armagnac brandy is produced.

Le Bas Armagnac This Armagnac requires long maturing: at least five years and often up to 30 (in casks) before it can rival the finest Cognacs.

Le Tenarèze Over 8000 hectares of vineyards to the east of Bas Armagnac, covering limestone and clay soils, produce a brandy that is more flavoured and rustic than the Bas Armagnac, with a plum aroma.

Le Haut Armagnac This covers a vast area to the south and east of the two preceding zones, although only a mere 500 hectares are actually planted for the production of Armagnac, the rest being devoted to table wines. The soil is mostly limestone and as a region is undistinguished.

Grape varieties include the Folle Blanche (the best), and one of the most widespread is named after its inventor, Baco (22 A); others include the Colombard and the Ugni Blanc.

Distillation methods are by no means uniform, although lovers of true Armagnac

Right *An Armagnac still; distillation methods vary from producer to producer.*

prefer the brandy from the actual Armagnac stills. The brandy is not rectified, and has an alcohol strength of 50–55°.

The reduction in strength to 40–45° alcohol is done naturally, without watering, in casks made from local oak, each containing 400 litres. The brandy is never transferred from cask to cask, so each one is said to have 'its' Armagnac, and vice-versa, making for a unique marriage of oak and brandy.

The old original Armagnac stills are now hard to find, but each has its distinctive personality, and two different stills have been known to produce an identical brandy. The more modern stills are designed to produce brandies of around 60–65° alcohol. It is obvious that the lower the alcohol content, the more important the rôle played by other components, giving richness and character to the Armagnacs, which should be left in their casks for a very long time. After 40 years in the wood, however, the brandy 'dries out' and has to be bottled or transferred to smaller *bonbonnes*.

There is another method of distilling Armagnac similar to that used for Cognac (double distillation), but the finished product has less character and matures more quickly.

Unlike Cognac, the great Armagnacs may carry a vintage date. Those that are not so good may bear three stars or the word Monopole, etc. to indicate they are over one year old; VO, VSOP and Réserve denote a brandy that is over four years of age, while XO, Napoléon, Vieille Réserve and Hors d'âge are older than five years.

Left *Blending casks; the strength of Armagnac is reduced in the cask, but the brandy is never transferred from cask to cask.*

Oak

A number of experiments have been carried out in Burgundy and the Bordeaux region to assess the importance of wood during the maturing of wine in casks. In Burgundy a *cuvée* of red Mercurey and one of Chassagne-Montrachet were systematically investigated in 1978, with tests done on a variety of different oaks: Limousin, Nièvre, Bourgogne, Tronçais, Vosges, etc., different sizes of pores and different tannin levels.

The way in which the staves are cut (split or sawn) is also important, and the timber may be seasoned naturally or artificially. The staves can then be bent with the use of steam or over a fire.

Wood is, of course, a permeable material and so permits the exchange of gases which alter the make-up of a wine's component parts; and wines that have matured in new oak casks will have different properties to those aged in old casks, or to wines that mature in enamelled metal vats.

During the above-mentioned tests, chemical and sensory tests were carried out at four-monthly intervals, with the following results:

There was a greater loss of alcohol from casks made from semi-split, steam-shaped Burgundy oak staves and from casks of Tronçais oak that had been sawn and split.

Volatile acidity was lower in used casks.

Malolactic fermentation took longer in worn casks.

Total acidity and dry extract was more or less the same in all types of container.

Wines kept in new woods were richest in colour and tannins; apart from tannin, the new wood also gave the wine polysaccharides (sugars).

Three tastings were held by 20 experts over the 16 months of maturing, the final tasting coming just before bottling. The overall decision was in favour of the new oak casks and against the old oak casks and metal vats. Yet that was not all. There were differences between the various new casks as well. Those with staves that had been shaped over steam were not as good for the wine as those with fire-formed staves. During the burning process the destruction of the lignin in the wood gives rise to a vanilla odour, while the sugars present in the hemicellulose molecules lend an aroma of caramel. Sawing of the staves, as opposed to splitting, did not seem to have any harmful effect on the wine.

In the case of red wines, the 'woody' character inherent in casks made from oak from the Tronçais, Nièvre and Bourgogne regions was superior in quality, while for white wines, the Burgundy oaks from around Mercurey and Cîteaux gave the best flavour. It was interesting to note that sawn oak from the Tronçais forests did more for the young wine than split oak from the same area.

These initial experiments will of course be complemented by further tastings once the samples have undergone several years of bottle-ageing. Clearly, more work needs to be done on the nature of the effect of oak.

Above *Forcing the hoops on to a new oak barrel, which will eventually modify the character of the wine stored in it.*

Wine & Health

It is quite untrue to say that wine is bad for the health; but obviously there is a distinction between use and abuse. Like any other food, wine becomes toxic if taken in excess, and too high a concentration of alcohol in the body cannot be eliminated without some damage being done, since in order to expel the excess alcohol whole body cells have to be burned up, and this means a waste of vitamins and proteins.

Levels of alcohol tolerance naturally vary from one person to another, and, more particularly, according to sex, owing to a weight difference. They also vary depending on the context in which the wine is consumed, i.e. whether it is drunk by itself, during a meal or with one food rather than another. Alcohol is more dangerous when the diet is lacking in meats, dairy foods and fish, while diets that are over-lean or excessively fat can reduce its elimination from the body by up to 20%.

Wine can benefit the health if taken slowly and in moderation. The French Academy of Medicine has fixed the daily intake at 1 gram of alcohol per kilogram of body weight, which means that a person weighing 155 pounds can quite safely drink one bottle of wine a day – in stages.

Wine as a foodstuff can provide up to one-quarter of our calorific needs; it is not rich in vitamins or mineral salts, but its alcohol is a source of calories that economize on lipids, glucids and amino-acids which are thus available for extra physical or mental effort. There is no better drink at table than wine – it is a source of water (85%) and many of its components actually aid digestion. The acids contained help the stomach muscles to flex and contract, assisting the natural stomach acids to digest starchy and albuminoid substances. The tannins present in wine stimulate the muscular fibres and promote the rate of metabolism; they also seem to be good carriers of vitamin C.

Wine is of course a depressant and as such has a calming, euphoric effect. Studies have shown that in old people's homes the atmosphere is considerably relaxed when a glass of wine is served with the meal.

The Wine Institute of San Francisco has even asserted that moderate wine drinkers live longer than teetotallers, and Dr Arthur L. Klasty believes this to be due in part to the beneficial effects of alcohol on the heart and circulation. Dr John P. Kane of the Cardiovascular Research Institute of the University of California, San Francisco, claims that alcohol has beneficial effects on high density lipoprotein (HDL) levels in plasma, since high levels of HDL afford protection against hardening of the arteries.

Finally, it should be stressed that cirrhosis of the liver, caused by wine alone, is nowadays an extremely rare complaint. Indeed, like most other things taken in excess, wine can be harmful; but taken in reasonable quantity, it would seem to be more beneficial than otherwise.

Above *Levels of wine tolerance vary from person to person, but it is generally agreed that wine drinking in moderation can actually benefit the health.*

Tasting Cards

Tasting cards can take a number of different forms, of greater or lesser complexity. The card below is adapted from a form commonly used in France; its major advantage is that it compels the taster to make a precise examination of the various elements which will go into forming his final judgement of a given wine.

Wine Type (White/Rosé/Red)			**Appellation:** **Type:**
Laboratory observations and conclusion			**Date of Analysis**
Specific Gravity Alcohol Residual Sugar Potential Alcohol Total SO_2 Free SO_2	pH colour index P/x Index of permanganate		Total Acidity Fixed Acidity Volatile Acidity (corrected for sulphuric acid)
Method of Vinification			
Visual Examination	**Surface of the liquid**		Brilliant – dull Clean – iridescent – oily
	Colour	**White Wine**	Pale with green or yellow tints – pale yellow – straw yellow – canary yellow – gold – amber
		Rosé Wine	Pale with violet or rose tints – grey – light rose – deep rose – partridge eye – onion skin
		Red Wine	Red with crimson or violet tints – cherry red – ruby – garnet red – red brown – tile red – mahogany – tawny
		Colour Hue	Frank – oxidized – cloudy
	Aspect	Crystalline – brilliant – limpid – hazy – cloudy – turgid – lead – grey/white – opaque, with or without deposit	
	Legs/Tears	Quick or slow to form – non-existent – slight – heavy	
Temperature of the Wine			**Any factor hindering the tasting**
Olfactory Examination	**First Impression**		Pleasant – ordinary – unpleasant
	Aroma	**Intensity**	Powerful – adequate – feeble – non-existent
		Quality	Very fine – racy – distinguished – fine – ordinary – common – not very pleasant – unpleasant
		Character	Primary – secondary – tertiary – floral – fruity – vegetal – spicy – animal – oxidized
		Length	Long – average – short
	Abnormal odours		CO_2 – SO_2 – H_2S – mercaptan – strongly oxidized – woody – lactic acid acescence – phenolic – corky flaw { temporary – permanent / slight – serious }
	Details		
Any factor hindering or stopping the continuation of the tasting			

Gustatory Examination	**First impression**			
	Flavours and sensations	**Sweetness**	Sugar	Heavy – very sweet – sweet – dry – brut
			Glycerine and alcohol	Soft – unctuous – velvety – smooth – rough – dried out
		Acidity	Excessive	Acid – green – tart – nervy – acidulous
			Balanced	Fresh – lively – supple – smooth
			Insufficient	Flat – flabby
		Body	Alcoholic strength	Light – sufficient – generous – heady – hot
			Flesh	Fat – round – full – thin – meagre
			Tannin	Rich – balanced – insufficient – astringent – bitter
		Aromas in the mouth	Intensity	Powerful – average – weak – long – short
			Quality	Very fine – elegant – pleasant – common – faded
			Nature	Floral – fruity – vegetable – spicy – wood – chemical – animal – other young – developed – complex
	Inherent or abnormal flavours	**'Terroir'**		Marked – noticeable – faint – non-existent
		Sickness		Grease – turned – aldehydes – sweet – sour – rancid – acetic acid – lactic acid
		Accident		Stagnant – mould – lees – woody – cork – metallic – H_2S – herbaceous – acrid
	Final impression	**Balance**		Harmonious – bold – correct – unbalanced Xs acid, Xs sugar, Xs tannin, Xs alcohol
		After taste		Straightforward – unpleasant
		Resistance of taste and aroma		〉8 sec Very long; 5–7 sec long; 4–5 sec medium; 〈 3 sec short
Conclusions	**Conformity to appellation or type**			
	Score out of 20			
	Summary of tasting (character of wine – future, readiness for drinking)			

Wine-tasting terms 1

(As formulated and defined by the Departmental Testing and Research Laboratory at Tours.)

In addition to long experience, keen sensibility and thorough knowledge, a wine taster must possess a specialized vocabulary so that he can express his exact feelings and conclusions.

We have therefore thought it worthwhile to include here a simple list of standard wine-tasting terms. These terms are used in the trade to define a wine's positive qualities and weaknesses, thus enabling the taster, whether amateur or professional, to describe it in some detail and with the greatest possible precision.

Sight

The wine's appearance

Bourbeux: miry; heavy cloudiness of a young wine that has not yet been racked.

Brillant: brilliant; great limpidity, associated with white wines.

Clair: see *limpide.*

Crémant: slight sparkle; sparkling wines in which the pressure is equal to 3.5 atmospheres. The 'Crémant de Loire' is a wine that can only be made in Touraine.

Cristallin: crystal-clear; perfect transparency and as bright as crystal.

Disque: disc; curved upper surface of the wine in the glass. The disc should usually be brilliant. When the wine has deteriorated, the disc presents a matt surface where various particles are to be seen.

Jambes: legs, also known as 'tears'; when the wine is swirled round the glass, it leaves a ringlet with an oily, colourless outline. This ringlet may be very noticeable or almost non-existent. The 'tears' which run down the inside of the glass from this ringlet and have an oily aspect are known as *jambes.* These 'legs' can be either thick or thin, form more or less quickly and vary in number. They are an indication of the richness of the wine in alcohol, sugar and glycerol.

Limpide: clear; perfect transparency with a complete absence of particles in suspension.

Louche: shady; cloudy of wine in which transparency and brilliance are slightly lacking.

Mousseux: fully sparkling, as with champagne; the bubbles rising to the surface are fine and persistent, with a pressure of from 4 to 5 atmospheres at its strongest. The bubbles leave a thin froth over the surface disc and then run away from the centre to the side of the glass where they form a ring round the inside known as the *cordon, collier* or *collerette.*

Perlant: beady, slightly gaseous; generally applies to young wines, wines that are kept on lees (Muscadet), sold straight from the barrel, or to those wines which are undergoing malolactic permentation or a slight alcoholic fermentation.

Pétillant: slightly sparkling wine, made by the champagne method with a pressure of from 2 to 3 atmospheres. Carbonic gas is revealed by the fine but relatively few bubbles which rise to the surface to create a slight covering of froth, which quickly disappears. It is more noticeable on the palate because of its light tingling sensation.

Tranquille: still, non-sparkling; complete absence of bubbles.

Trouble: 'troubled', cloudy wine; wine lacking in clarity because of gel or particles in suspension.

The wine's colour

Robe: colour and clarity of the wine, taken together, as seen through its transparency. A wine is said to have a fine colour *(une belle robe)* when it is bright and clear.

Robe chatoyante: a glistening colour.

Red wines

Clairet: red wine that has a weak colour because of its short maceration period (Bordeaux region). Not to be confused with Claret.

Rouge grenat: garnet-red; colour that is taken on by certain wines as they age.

Rouge pelure d'oignon: onion-skin red; strong tawny-pink.

Rouge pourpré: crimson-red; dark red with a violet shade.

Rouge rubis: ruby-red; bright, firm colour of wines that are still young with good, steady acidity.

Rouge tuilé: tile-red; red with a shade of orange; colour taken on by wines as they age, similar to brick-red.

Rouge violacé: purplish-red; shade that is particular to certain wines lacking in acidity.

Rosé wines

Rose pelure d'oignon: onion-skin pink; dark, coppery-pink (rosé d'Arbois, Tavel, etc.).

Rose 'œil de perdrix': partridge-eye pink; clear, bright ruby-pink.

Rose saumoné ou ambré: salmon or amber-pink; pink with a yellow shade.

Rose vif: bright pink; a pink with great luminosity.

Gris rosé wines

Vins gris rosés: very pale rosé wines with a shade that lies between the white and rosé wines produced from direct pressing of red or grey grapes (Pineau d'Aunis).

White wines

Jaune ambré: amber-yellow; resembling the colour of yellow amber (fossil resin).

Jaune beige: beige-yellow; pale yellow with a shade of grey (dull colour).

Jaune citron: lemon-yellow; bright yellow like the colour of a lemon.
Jaune doré: golden-yellow; bright yellow similar to that of gold.
Jaune miel: honey-yellow; pale golden yellow with a slight tawny shade.
Jaune paille: straw-yellow; slightly pronounced yellow resembling the colour of straw.
Jaune plombé: lead-yellow; greyish yellow, noticeable in wine that has had tannin added.
Jaune vert: greenish-yellow; pale brilliant yellow with a green shade.
Vieil or: old gold; golden yellow with a sustained warm shade (found in old wines).

Smell

General terms of appreciation

Vins aromatiques: aromatic wines; wines with a very pronounced scent, such as wines from the Sauvignon grape.
Bouquet: the complex rich smell that develops during ageing (the wine is said to be *bouqueté*, having a bouquet).
Fumet: word used by some wine experts to describe the tertiary smells. (See *Odeurs tertiaires.*)
Nez: nose; the complex smell given off by the wine. A wine is said to have 'nose' when it is rich in scents.
Nez fleuri: flowery nose; a term used to describe a wine that has the scent of a flower.
Nez fruité: fruity nose; used to describe a wine that has a fruity smell. It is particularly used of young wine which still retains the smell of the grape from which it was made.
Nez subtil: subtle nose; used to describe a wine that has a fine, delicate smell.
Odeurs primaires: primary smells (sometimes referred to as 'natural' smells or original smells); describes those smells which come from the grape itself, found in young wines.
Odeurs secondaires: secondary smells (or fermentation smells); smells which appear during fermentation, caused by the yeasts.
Odeurs tertiaires: tertiary smells (or ageing smells); they develop as the wine ages in the bottle, guarding its secret of those subtle processes of oxidation and reduction. These are very complex scents, more abstract and richer than the afore-mentioned ones. They make up the real 'bouquet' of a wine (such as old Chinon or Bourgueil).
Perspective odorante: aromatic perspective (or convergence of smells); used to describe the complex smell of primary, secondary and tertiary scents given off by an outstanding wine, which in certain cases coexist and complement one another.

Smells by groups

Odeurs animales: animal smells; musk, ambergris, venison, game, fur, leather.
Odeurs balsamiques: balsamic smells; incense, vanilla, camphor.
Odeurs boisées: wood smells; cedar, liquorice, resin.
Odeurs empyreumatiques: smells of fiery origin; toast, grilled almonds, coffee, smoke, tobacco, tea, grilled herbs, hay.
Odeurs épicées: spicy smells; pepper, sandalwood, cloves, cinnamon.
Odeurs florales: floral scents; rose, violet, mignonette, jasmine, orange-blossom, iris, carnation, lime-tree, wallflower, primrose, verbena, hawthorn, acacia, syringa, honeysuckle, bluebell, peony, etc.
Odeurs fruitées: fruity smells; apple, raspberry, cherry, peach, quince, plum, blackcurrant, banana, hazelnut, lemon, strawberry, walnut, apricot, redcurrant, almond, etc.

There are, obviously, many other smells which do not fall into these groups. For example:
Odeur d'iode: iodine smell; can be found in those wines coming from maritime regions, or those made from grapes affected by 'noble rot', such as Vouvray or Montlouis. If this smell is too pronounced, it must be considered a defect.
Odeur de suie, de fumée: sooty, smoky smell; characteristic of certain wines.
Odeur de 'pierre à fusil': gun-flint smell; smell which recalls that obtained when two pieces of flint are rubbed together (characteristic of the white AOC wine of Jasnières).
Odeur de résine: resin smell; smell taken on by wine kept in conifer-wood barrels or found in certain Greek wines treated with pine resin.

Unpleasant smells

Odeurs dues à la vendange: smells which have their origin in the harvesting; earthy smell (presence of earth on the grapes), rambergue (presence of the *Aristolochia* plant at harvest-time), iodine smell (excess of 'noble rot'), foxy smell (characteristic of the native American vine).
Odeurs dues à une maladie: smells originating from an illness *ou à un mauvais traitement du vin:* or poor wine treatment; acescent smells (sour or stinging wine), stale or musty smells (formation of ethyl alcohol reminiscent of the smell of apples, wine that has been neglected and left open to the air), geranium smell (change in the ascorbic acid content), sulphuric hydrogen smell (SH_2, smell of rotten eggs, due to late sulphur spraying of the vine, or to sulphite treatment of the wine during fermentation).
Odeurs dues aux contenants: smells coming from containers; the smell of the cask, of dry wood, cement, plastic; stagnant, mouldy, corky smells.

Wine-tasting terms 2

Terms of taste and palate

Acerbe: sour; unpleasant, disagreeable, e.g. too much acidity.

Acre: bitter; wine with an excess of tannin, of volatile acidity – stinging, burning.

Agressif: aggressive; unpleasant, too much acidity (excess of alcohol).

Aimable: pleasant; agreeable and nicely balanced.

Alcalin: alkaline; wine rich in sodium chloride and potassium.

Altéré: wine that has deteriorated, having lost its normal characteristics as a result of illness or misuse of chemicals.

Amaigri: thin; wine whose natural colour and strength is exhausted (said of red wine, for example, that is too old).

Amer: bitter; bitterness coming from colouring matter or imparted by tannic acids – bitterness, disease coming from decomposition of glycerol (acrolein).

Apre: disagreeable, rough, harsh, due to an excess of tannin or acidity.

Aqueux: watery; flat, diluted appearance, characteristics of a wine that has been 'watered down' or suffering from the disease known as *fleur* ('flower'), advanced stage of mould.

Austère: austere or harsh; hard wine with too much natural strength and unpleasant to drink (as with ordinary red table wine produced from certain hybrid vines).

Bien en bouche: a rich, well-balanced wine.

Bouchonné: corky; smell of cork mainly perceived by the nose.

Bref: short; leaving no pleasant or lingering aftertaste.

Brûlant: burning sensation given by an excess of alcohol in the wine; warm sensation.

Brut: very dry; applied to those sparkling wines with little sugar content (total absence of sugar gives Extra-Dry).

Capiteux: heady; high in alcohol, going to the head, intoxicating.

Charnu: fleshy; fills the mouth well, leaving a strong sensation on the taste-buds – full-bodied.

Charpenté: well constituted; rich constitution and high in alcohol.

Chaud: warm, rich in alcohol.

Corsé: full-bodied; wine with high alcoholic content and well-constituted; wine is said to have 'body' when it gives a sensation of fullness and rich consistency.

Coulant: pleasant, supple, not too high in alcohol, easy to drink.

Creux: hollow; lacking in body, unbalanced, excess acidity.

Cru: raw or coarse; used to describe a thin or young wine, under-developed, fairly acid, lacking in fullness.

Décharné: fleshless, thin of body; having lost its original qualities.

Délicat: delicate; fine, graceful, light wine.

Dépouillé: stripped; weakening of some of its substances as the wine ages (found in old red wines).

Déséquilibré: unbalanced; poor body, badly constituted and lacking in harmony, e.g. with a pronounced dominance of acidity.

Distingué: distinguished; fine quality wine with its own character.

Doucereux: sweetish; having an insipid, somewhat unpleasant sweetness.

Doux: sweet; having a certain richness in sugar which does not shock the palate.

Dur: hard; lacking in suppleness, rough to swallow due to an excess of volatile tartaric acid or tannin.

Edulcoré: artificially sweetened.

Elégant: elegant; distinguished and superb, as with wines from the great vineyards *(vins de cru)*.

Epais: thick; common, heavy wines without distinction.

Epanoui: well-developed; wines that wrap themselves round the palate.

Equilibré: well-balanced; well constituted in the right proportions (characteristic of all great wines).

Etoffé: full; well constituted, linked also with the rich colour of a wine.

Exubérant: exuberant; sparkling.

Fade: tasteless; weak, thin wine, lacking in character and taste.

Ferme: firm; lacks suppleness – rich in tannins and extracts.

Filant: ropy; forming viscous or gelatinous threads, suffering from *graisse* (grease or ropy) disease, or wine rich in dextran.

Fin: fine; describes wine of superb quality, well-balanced and harmonious (such as the *vins de cru* – the great wines).

Fini court: short-finish; short-lived taste.

Fondu: well-blended; well-matured, constituents in complete harmony.

Fort: strong; alcohol content predominant.

Frais: fresh; with a fair amount of acid, but not to excess; refreshing character; pleasant; thirst-quenching.

Franc: honest; natural, clean, sound wine without any faults.

Friand: delicious; wine with an agreeable taste, and pleasant to drink.

Fruité: fruity; still having the fresh, natural flavour of the grape.

Gazeux: gaseous; fizzy because of excess carbonic gas following refermentation in the bottle, or due to a disease.

Généreux: generous; noble, rich in alcohol, well constituted, full-bodied, rich in ester.

Gouleyant: easy to drink; light and pleasant.

Grain: excellent consistency; used to describe a first-class wine of superb quality, when it is said to have *du grain*.

Gras: rich in content; fleshy, full-bodied, sweet; rich in alcohol and glycerine (qualities associated with a truly great wine).

Grossier: vulgar; coarse, heavy wine, lacking in quality.

Harmonieux: harmonious; wine whose constituents are well balanced and in perfect harmony.

Jeune: young; new wine or wine that has kept its young character.

Joyeux: joyous; happy; a wine that cheers.

Léger: light; well-balanced wine, low in alcohol and extracts, but pleasant to drink (*vins rosés*, for example).

Liquoreux: liqueur-like; sweet wine, with rich sugar content and heady.

Long: long; wine whose taste lingers in the mouth with intense aromatic flavour. White wines have a more persistent flavour than reds. As a guide, the following time-scale gives some indication of the persistency of this 'aftertaste':

— *vin ordinaire:* ordinary wine; 1 to 3 sec.
— *vin de qualité:* good quality wine; 4 to 5 sec.
— *grand vin:* superb wine; 6 to 8 sec.
— *vin blanc sec:* dry white wine; 8 to 11 sec.
— *très grand vin:* superlative wine; 11 to 15 sec.
— *vin blanc liquoreux:* sweet white wine; 18 sec.
— *Grands Vouvray:* the great wines of Vouvray; 20 to 25 sec.

The term *caudalies* (caudals) is also used instead of seconds to describe the length of time.

Loyal: faithful; loyal; a natural wine that has been made following all the legal processes, without cheating, and having no hidden vices.

Mâche: chewy; full-bodied, filling the mouth well (when it is said to be 'chewy').

Mâché: chewed up; said of a wine where slight oxidation is present, a momentary deterioration after bottling.

Maigre: thin; lacking in alcohol and extracts, does not fill the mouth (opposite of *charnu*, full bodied). A large amount of volatile acidity makes a wine 'thin'.

Marchand: marketable; wine that has those characteristics required by all local commercial laws and regulations.

Mielleux: honey-like; wine in which the sugar content is predominant, throwing it out of balance with the other constituents.

Moelleux: mellow; full, well-rounded wine, with a certain amount of richness in sugar and glycerine, with little acidity. (Great dry white wine can be *moelleux*, e.g. Meursault.)

Mou: flabby, weak; lacking in body and freshness.

Muet: dumb; lacking in character and unattractive.

Mur: ripe, mellow; wine that has matured.

Nerveux: nervy; vigorous, with good body, a certain amount of acidity, and ageing well. These characteristics can stem from the soil from which the wine was produced.

Neutre: neutral; common and without any particular characteristics (a wine not capable of changing other wines with which it is blended).

Normal: without fault.

Onctueux: unctuous; mellow wine with good viscosity, having a full-bodied feeling about it (rich in sugar and glycerine).

Pâteux: pasty; thick pasty consistency, rich in extracts, clinging to the palate.

Petit: little, in the sense of poor in alcohol and other constituents.

Piquant: sharp; tart, prickly, sensation on the tongue and palate, coming from carbonic gas (sparkling wines).

Plat: flat, lacking in body, alcohol and acidity.

Plein: full; well-balanced; wine with good body, rich in all its constituents, filling the mouth well.

Pommadé: falsified; thick, rich in sugar.

Puissant: powerful; rich, well-balanced wine.

Pulpeux: pulpy; thick in the mouth (having *mâche*, q.v.).

Qualité: quality; a good-quality wine is one that is above average, thanks to the grape and soil from which it was produced.

Raide: stiff; lacking in suppleness, acid.

Rance: rancid; defective wine (contact with air).

Râpeux: rough; raspy feeling on the tongue coming from the tannin in the wine.

Rassis: settled, well-balanced; wine that has finished ageing.

Riche: rich; high in alcohol and colour.

Rond: well-rounded and full; well-balanced, supple and mellow, generally full-bodied.

Savoureux: tasty; very pleasant on the palate.

Sec: dry; lacking in sugar. Applied to red wines, it means lacking in thickness (dry taste coming from deterioration of grapes at harvest-time).

Solide: solid; well constituted, keeping well.

Souple: supple; pleasant to drink, low tannin and acid content, soft on the palate.

Soyeux: silky texture; supple, recalls the feel of silk.

Tannique: tannic; wine having an excess of tannin.

Tendre: delicate; wine containing little acid, supple, light, slightly sweet.

Terne: dull; lacking vivacity and character; uninteresting.

Usé: worn-out; wine that is over-the-hill, too old, having lost its original qualities, keeping badly.

Velouté: velvety texture; supple, mellow, slipping easily over the tongue and palate, recalls the feel of velvet, soft in the mouth.

Vert: green in the sense of unripe; acid and young (excess of malic acid derived from picking of unripe grapes at harvest-time).

Vieux: old; characteristic adopted by the wine as it ages in the bottle. May be used in a pejorative sense when applied to a wine that is *usé* (q.v.).

Vif: lively; fresh, light wine, with average alcohol and acid content.

Vineux: having good vinosity; high alcohol content dominating other characteristics; warm to the taste.

Vintage Chart

Vintage charts are a guide to the quality of the wine from a given region in a given year, but they can provide only the simplest indication of relative quality on the broadest possible scale. The Académie du Vin vintage chart is based on information from growers and *négociants* in the different wine districts, tempered by our own tastings.

All vintage charts should be reviewed once a year. Older vintages become of academic interest, particularly for white wines, and wines from younger vintages gain or lose quality. Some charts advise when a wine should be drunk, but they obviously cannot take into account who is drinking the wine, where it is drunk and how it has been stored. The French tend to enjoy their wines young; the British prefer them with more age; European wines in America or Australia may be drunk earlier than in, say, Belgium, to compensate for the sea voyage. Storage is the vital element for anything but the youngest wines, for it determines the eventual condition of the wine. No amount of fine service

VINTAGES		'45	'47	'48	'49	'52	'53	'55	'57	'59	'61
RED BORDEAUX	Médoc/Graves	20	18	15	19	16	19	17	12	16	20
	Saint-Emilion/Pomerol	19	20	14	19	16	19	18	10	16	20
WHITE BORDEAUX	Sauternes/Barsac	19	19	14	18	16	18	18	15	18	17
RED BURGUNDY	Côte de Nuits	19	17	16	20	18	17	16	14	18	19
	Côte de Beaune	19	17	16	20	17	18	16	14	18	19
WHITE BURGUNDY		16	15	15	16	14	14	16	13	16	15
BEAUJOLAIS		18	19	12	18	16	19	17	16	17	19
RHÔNE	North, Côtes-du-Rhône	18	16		16	16	18	16	14	16	20
	South, Côtes-du-Rhône	18	16		18	15	18	18	16	16	17
LOIRE	Muscadet/Touraine/Anjou	19	20	13	14	14	13	15	13	19	16
	Pouilly-Fumé/Sancerre		19	15	14	14	13	14	15	19	14
ALSACE		19	18	16	19	13	18	18	16	20	18
VINTAGE CHAMPAGNE						17	16	19		15	16
GERMANY	Rhine						19	11		18	11
	Mosel						19	11		18	11
ITALY	Tuscany										
	Piedmont										
PORTUGAL	Vintage Port	20	17	18				18			
SPAIN	Rioja										12
CALIFORNIA	Red										18
NORTH COAST	White										18
		'45	'47	'48	'49	'52	'53	'55	'57	'59	'61

can bring a wine back from the grave.

For the Académie du Vin vintage chart, we have used a 20-point scale:

0–9 Bad, very poor, poor.
10–11 Acceptable.
12–13 Quite good.
14–15 Good.
16–18 Very good.
19–20 Exceptional.

We have chosen to start in 1945 and have shown every vintage from 1969. Prior to this, we have omitted the generally accepted poor years, even though in some regions (1950 in the Médoc and 1968 in Tuscany, for example) the wines were very good. With improvements in viticulture and vinification as a result of continuing research and investment, there are fewer 'bad' vintages, as the chart illustrates. Indeed the decade of the 1980s has been quite exceptional. Although natural disasters such as the 1956 frost in Saint-Emilion, will always be with us, growers and wine makers are now better prepared for what nature imposes on them.

2	'64	'66	'67	'69	'70	'71	'74	'75	'76	'77	'78	'79	'80	'81	'82	'83	'84	'85	'86	'87	'88	'89	'90	'91	'92
7	16	18	14	11	19	17	13	18	15	11	18	17	13	17	19	17	15	18	18	12	17	16	18	13	13
7	18	18	13	11	19	18	13	18	16	11	17	17	13	16	18	17	11	17	15	11	17	16	18	10	12
5	12	15	19	12	18	15	11	18	16	12	14	16	15	15	13	17	13	15	19	11	18	19	18	12	10
7	16	17	14	17	14	17	13	5	18	9	18	14	15	12	13	16	12	18	14	15	17	16	19	14	16
6	17	17	14	18	14	16	12	7	18	9	18	16	13	14	14	17	13	19	14	15	17	16	19	14	17
8	16	16	14	18	16	16	13	14	16	13	17	17	12	18	18	18	14	17	18	16	16	19	16	15	16
7	16	17	14	17	16	16	12	13	17	8	19	15	12	16	14	17	14	16	17	12	19	18	14	18	16
6	15	15	14	17	16	14	12	10	16	12	19	16	15	13	14	19	14	19	16	17	18	18	19	16	14
6	14	15	18	16	14	16	12	10	16	11	18	16	15	15	12	16	13	18	17	13	16	20	20	13	14
4	15	13	11	15	14	15	10	16	16	11	16	14	13	15	14	17	14	18	16	14	18	18	18	15	16
6	16	14	14	14	14	19	14	16	18	12	17	15	15	16	13	15	14	17	16	15	16	18	18	15	16
4	19	13	15	14	15	19	14	16	18	12	17	16	13	17	14	20	13	18	16	15	17	19	17	14	16
7	15	16	12	17	17	15		18	16		15	16	14	15	17		13	18	16	14	16	16	16		
	15	15	16	16	11	19	5	14	18	8	9	15	8	15	11	18	10	17	15	12	18	19	20	15	18
	18	16	12	16	11	19	5	17	18	8	9	15	8	15	11	18	10	17	16	12	18	19	20	16	17
		12	15	16	16	20	14	16	8	16	20	16	16	12	18	19	13	19	17	13	15	13	20	15	12
		4	16	14	16	20	18	10	10	10	20	16	14	12	20	17	12	19	16	13	15	18	18	12	12
	20	18			17			13		19			15		15	17		18					14	16	
3	20	16	14	13	20	11	13	15	14	8	19	13	15	17	16	15	14	19	16	16	17	12	14	16	16
4	19	16	16	17	20	18	20	18	18	16	19	18	18	17	15	13	13	19	17	17	16	13	17	18	17
4	19	16	16	17	18	18	18	18	18	16	17	18	19	17	15	14	15	18	18	17	16	13	17	18	17
2	'64	'66	'67	'69	'70	'71	'74	'75	'76	'77	'78	'79	'80	'81	'82	'83	'84	'85	'86	'87	'88	'89	'90	'91	'92

ores for the vintages 1991 and 1992 are only provisional – many of the wines are too young to tell exactly how they will develop.

Glossary of Wine Terms

Alcool acquis The actual alcoholic degree of a wine

Alcool en puissance A wine's potential alcoholic strength

ampelography The science of grape varieties

Anthocyane A polyphenol that lends colour to young red wines

AOC Appellation d'Origine Contrôlée. Better than VQPRD

Appellation The name that guarantees a wine's origin and grape variety, but not necessarily its quality

Assemblage The blending of wines of the same origin

Blanc de Blancs White wine made from pressing white grapes

Blanc de Noirs A white wine made from pressing black grapes

Bourbes Solid substances (waste matter) that are separated from the (white) must

Carbonic maceration Maceration preceding the fermentation of light wines and wines made for quick consumption (*vins de primeur*)

Caudalie Unit of measurement of aromatic persistence, equal to one second

Cépage Variety of grape

Cépage teinturier Ordinary variety that produces a red 'plonk', the chief characteristic of which is its colouring power

Chapeau Cap of solids forming at the surface of the wine during fermentation

Chaptalization Adding sugar to the grape-must to raise its alcohol content

Clone A vine plant whose genetic make-up will be reproduced (cloned) over an entire vineyard

Coller (un vin) Fining

Coupage The blending of wines of different origins

Cuvée In Champagne, 1. the first ten casks (205 litres) from pressing; 2. wine-blending

Débourbage Separation of solids from fermenting grape juice or must

Dégorgement Removal of deposit formed during the second fermentation stage of sparkling wines

Ecoulage Emptying a fermenting tank

Egrappoir/Erafloir Machine that separates the grape berries from their stalks

Extract Collective term for all solids found in a wine

Flash pasteurization Pasteurization at 70°C

Fleur du vin Skin of yeasts or mycoderma that forms at the wine's surface

Fouloir A machine for crushing grapes

Fouloir/érafloir Machine that combines crushing with de-stalking

Franche de pied A term used in reference to a non-grafted vine, i.e. native to the country in which it grows

Liqueur de dosage (or liqueur d'expédition) Sugared liquid added to sparkling wines prior to corking

Liqueur de tirage A liquor added to the wine to induce the *prise de mousse (méthode champenoise)*

Malolactic fermentation Process in which the malic acid is turned into lactic acid under the action of malic ferments

Moût de goutte Unfermented grape juice which runs off naturally

Moût de presse Unfermented grape juice from pressings

Mutage Artificially halting the fermenting process

Oenologue Anyone versed in the science of oenology

Oenologie The science of wine; oenology

Palissage Method of training vines on wires and canes

Passerillé Desiccated (grapes)

Pasteurization Heating the wine to 70°C in order to kill off the biological components (e.g. ferments)

Phylloxera Aphid which attacked and destroyed European vines from around 1865

Pigeage Stamping down the 'cap' by hand (or foot)

Porte-greffe Vine stock, or root on to which the *greffon* or aerial branches are grafted

Pourriture noble 'Noble rot', a brown mould on the grape caused by *Botrytis cinerea* (fortified wines)

Première taille The wine from the second pressing in the *méthode champenoise*

Primary aroma Aroma of the fruit

Prise de mousse Corresponds to second in-bottle fermentation (*méthode champenoise*)

Rafle Vine stalk or stem

Remontage Immersion of the 'cap' by pumping up wine in the fermenting tank

Secondary aroma Post-fermentation aroma

Seconde taille The juice from the third pressing in the *méthode champenoise*, never used for quality sparkling wines

Sélection clonale Combination of characteristics

Soutirage Tapping the wine from a vat or barrel

Sur lattes Horizontal storage of wine bottles

Sur pointe Vertical storage of bottles, neck down, in the *méthode champenoise*

Tannin A bitter and astringent phenol compound

Tertiary aroma Aroma after maturing

Tri, trie Selective picking or harvesting of the grape (for fortified wines)

Ullage, ullaging Replenishment of wine in bottles lost due to natural contraction, evaporation, etc.

VDQS Vin de Qualité Supérieure. Not as good as VQPRD

Véraison Moment when the berries start to take on colour

Vin de goutte Wine drawn off from the fermenting tank

Vin de pays Legal designation for *vins ordinaires* governed by certain rules

Vin de presse Wine from the pressing of the skins after fermentation.

Vin de table Literally 'table wine', below *vin de pays* in the French system of *appellation*, but seen often in Italy and Spain to describe fine wines whose grape varieties do not match the legal requirements.

Vin viné A wine muted by the addition of alcohol, as an aperitif (cf. 'mutage')

Vin marchand A wine that is reasonably saleable

Vinage Addition of alcohol to a wine or grape-must

VQPRD Vin de Qualité Produit dans des Régions Délimitées, i.e. a quality wine produced only in specific areas but complying with European quality regulations

Index

Page numbers in *italics* refer to captions to illustrations.
Abbreviations: Ch. = Château.

A

Abruzzi-Molise 113, 116
ageing: bottle 43, 136, 203, 208; wood (casks etc.) *41*, *43*, 48, *48*, *49*, 96, 118, 119, 127, 131, 174, 176, 201, 203, 204, 205, 207, 208, *208*
Aglianico 112, 116, 117; del Vulture 117
Alella 120
Alicante Bouschet grape 19, 129
Aligoté grape 84, 90
Almaden 129, 132
Alsace 24, 72, 76, 80, 81, 82, 83, 84, 100–1, *100*, 120, 123, 143, 144, 146, 158, 159, 180, *193*; classification 100; cooperatives 100; rosé 75
Altesse *see* Roussette de Savoie
Alvarelhão grape 121
America *see* United States, California etc.
American vine stocks 34, *35*, 124
Anjou 44, *62*, 85, 146, 162; Coteaux de la Loire Gamay 103; red 74; rosé 44, 74, 79; white 146
aperitifs *see* wine and food
appellations d'origine contrôlée (AOC) 14, 16, 30, 56, 70, 94, 100–1, 141
Apremont 85
Apulia 113, 116, 117
Aramon du Val de Loire *see* Grolleau grape
Arbois 80, 104; Pupillin 104; rosé 182; *vin jaune* 104; white 104, 181
Argentina 138, *138*
Arinto grape 121
Armagnac 80, 82, 84, 200, 204, 206–7, *206*, *207*
Associated Vintners 134
Asti 114
Asti Spumante 51, 83
Aude 84; Pays d'Aude *72*
Aude-Pyrénées Orientales 83
Auslese 108
Ausone, Ch. 32, 86
Australia 77, 80, 112, 136–7, 169; rosé 78; South Australia 136, 158, 160
Austria 81, 83, 122; Lower Austria 122
Auvernat *see* Pinot grape
Auxerrois *see* Malbec grape
Auxey-Duresses 92

B

Baco 24 grape 80, 84
Bandol 105, 152; rosé 182
Banyuls 53, 201
Barbaresco 113, 114
Barbera d'Alba 114; d'Asti 113, 114
Barbera grape 114, 129, 138; wines 50
Barcelona 120
Barcelos grape 121
Bardolino 115
Barolo 113, 114
Baroque grape 85
Barossa Valley 136
Barsac 53, 88, 147
Basilicata 113, 116, 117
Béarn 79, 107
Beaucastel, Ch. de 55
Beaujolais 31, *38*, *71*, 76, 90, 150 184; Primeur 93; Supérieur 93; -Villages 93, 148, *192*, vinification 54, *55*
Beaulieu winery 124
Beaumes-de-Venise 83, *200*, 201
Beaune 92, 93; Hospices de *93*
Beaunois *see* Chardonnay grape
Beaurenard, Ch. 54
Beerenauslese 108
Benmarl 135
Bergerac 62, 89, *89*; Côtes de Saussignac 89
Bergeron *see* Roussanne grape
Blanc de Blancs 94, 96; Blanc de Noirs 94
Blanc Fumé *see* Sauvignon grape
Blanquette de Limoux 50, 84, 104
Blauer Portugieser *see* Merlot
blending methods 72–3, *73*, 75, 94
Bois, Clos du 128
Bollinger 34, 155
Bonarda grape 114
Bonnes Mares 90, 152
Bonnezeaux 103, 146
Bordeaux 19, 29, 30, 31, 34, *38*, 40, 42, 46, 49, 61, 74, 75, 76, 77, 79, 80, 86–9, *86*, 100, 118, 120, 141; classification 86, 87; Côtes de Castillon 89; Côtes de Francs 89; red 19, 172–3; Supérieur 87, 89; white 52, 83, 84
botrytis 31, 131, 133, 139; *see also pourriture noble*
bottling 48, 49, 51, 64, *64*, *65*
Bouchy *see* Cabernet Franc grape
Bourboulenc grape 85
Bourgogne: Aligoté 84, 90, 143; Passetoutgrains 75
Bourgueil 74, 102–3; rosé 182
Bousse d'Or, Clos de la 174–5
Bouzy 96, 188
Brazil 138
Breton *see* Cabernet Franc grape
Broadbent, Michael 140
Brouilly 93, 184
Brown Bros 137
Brunello de Monalcino 113, 116
brut spumante 114, *114*, 115
Burgenland 122
Burgunder, Blauburgunder *see* Pinot Noir grape
Burgundy 21, 31, 40, 46, 72, 75, 82, 84, 85, 90–3, *91*, 110, 112, 120, 141, 162, 165, 170–1
Busby, James 137
buying wine 62, *62*; German wines 111

C

Cabernet grapes 42, 44, 70, 74, 75, 76, 115, 117, 164
Cabernet d'Anjou 103
Cabernet Franc (Bouchy, Breton) grapes 74, *74*, 79, 86, 103, 120, 129
Cabernet Sauvignon grape 61, 74, *74*, 76, 86, 120, 128, 129, 130, 136, 137, 138, 139, 164–5
Cahors *37*, 76, 107; vine stocks 76
Caillerets 92
Calabria 113, 116
California *29*, *41*, 75, 77, 78, 82, 83, 124–33, *124*, 129, 131, *134*, 168; climatic regions 128, 130, 133
California, University of 128
Callaway Vineyard 133
Campania 113, 116
Cantenac 86
Carignan grape 42, 78, 105, 106
Carignane grape 129
Carcavelos 121
Cariñena 78; grape 120
Catalonia 118, 120
Chablis 29, 31, 80, 90, *91*, 143, 160
Chalon, Château- 55, 85, 100, 104, 202
Chalone 128; Vineyards 132
Chambertin 90
Chambolle-Musigny 171
Champagne 21, 29, 31, *31*, 34, 37, 42, 46, 50, *50*, *65*, *73*, 75, 94–7, *96*, *97*, 142, 154–5, 160, 200; Crémant 21, *46*; rosé 44, 96; vintage 94
chaptalization 42, 77, 113, 174, 204
Chardonnay grape *46*, 70, 80, 90, 93, 94, 96, 110, 114, 115, 120, 130, 131, 135, 136, 137, 138, 143, 160–1, 164; wines 80, 104, 128, *128*, 132, 134, 160–1, 181
Chassagne-Montrachet 92
Chasselas grape 46, 83, 84, 102, 104
Châteauneuf-du-Pape *30*, *32*, 33, 42, 54, 55, 99, *99*, 141; red 72, 78; white 85
cheese and wine *see* wine and food
Chenin Blanc grape 81, 102, 103, 131, 137, 139, 162; wines 81, 133, 162
Chenin Noir *see* Pineau d'Aunis
Cheste 120
Cheval Blanc, Ch. 74, 86, 88
Chianti 42, 82, 113, 116
Chile 138
Chinon *63*, 74, 102, 148, 184
Cinsault grape 78, 99, 105, 106, 139
Clairette: de Bellegarde 85, 106; de Die 83, 85; du Languedoc 85, 106; grape 85, 105, 139
Clevner (Klevner) *see* Pinot Blanc grape
closed vat (*cuve close*) method 50, 51, 120
Cognac 80, 82, 84, 200, 204–5, *204*, *205*
Colares 127
Collio 115
Colombard grape 80, 206; brandies 80
colour 19, 21, 141. *See also* robe
Condrieu 85, 99, 146
Cook's Wine Company 137
Coonawarra winery 136–7
Constantia 139
corks 64
Cornas 99, 169
Corsica 82, 105
Corton 92; -Charlemagne 92
Coteaux Champenois 96, 160
Coteaux de l'Aubance 103
Coteaux du Languedoc 106
Coteaux du Layon 103
Côte Chalonnaise 90, 93
Côte de Beaune 90, 92, 144, 170, 180, 183; -Villages 93, 170, *194*
Côte de Brouilly 93
Côte de Nuits 90, 91, 152, 167, 170; -Villages 93
Côte d'Or 76, 77, 90
Côte Rotie 98, *99*
Côtes de Bergerac 89
Côtes de Blaye 80, 89
Côtes de Provence 78, 105
Côtes-du-Rhône *44*, *58*, 78, 98–9, 148, 151, 184, 185; -Villages 99
Côtes de Roussillon 106–7
Côtes de Saint Mont 79
Courbu grape 107
Crépy 84, 104
Crozes-Hermitage 54, 99, 184

D

Dactylosphera vitifolii 34, *34*
Dão 121
Denominazione di Origine Controllata (e Garantiti) (DOC; DOCG) 113
Deutz 133
Dézaley 123
Dillon, Ch. 74
disc 19, *19*
distilled wines 204–7
Dona Branca grape 121
Dordogne 86, 88, 89
Dorin *see* Chasselas grape

Douro river 121, 202; Douro/Tras os Montes 121
dressing 31; mechanized 37
Dry Creek Vineyard 124, 128, 162; valley 130
Durbanville 139

E
Echézeaux 90
Edelzwicker 101
Edna Valley Vineyard 132
Eisenberg 122
Eiswein 108
Elbling grape 123
Emilia-Romagna 113, 116
Entre-Deux-Mers *49*, 80, 89, 142
Entre Minho e Douro 121
Epenots 92
Eyrie Vineyards 135

F
Felton-Empire Vineyards 132
Fendant 123; *see also* Chasselas grape
fermentation 22, 24, 40, 44, 46, *47*, 50, 53, 54, 55, 72, 73, 114, 131, 160; enzyme 54; fortified wines 200, 201, 202; malolactic 41, 42, 44, 46, 54, 208; red wine 44; rosé wine 44; second 51, *51*, *73*, 97; white wine 46
Fiano di Avellina 116; grapes 116
Figeac, Ch. 88
fining (clarification) 48–9
Firestone Vineyard 128, 133
Fitou 106
Fixin 90
fleur du vin (*flor*), 55, 202
'fliers' 18
Folle Blanche (Gros Plant, Picpoul) grape 80, 84, 107, 204, 206; brandies 80
fortified wines 24, 52, 53, 61, 120, 137, 138, 141, 178–9, 190, 200–3, *200*, *201*
France 68, 74, 75, 78, 80, 82, 85, 86–107, 112, 118; *see also* under regional names
France, south-west 74, 79, 83, 84, 85, 107, 153
Franconia 111
Franschhoek *139*
Frascati 116
French Colombard grape 131
Friuli-Venezia Giulia 113, 114, 115
Frontignan 83, *200*, 201
frost 58, *58*, 75, 76, 78, 168

G
Gaillac 50, 76, 84, 107
Galicia 120
Gamay grape *71*, 75, 76–7, *76*, 79, 90, 93, 96, 107, 122, 123, 129, 184
Gamay-Beaujolais grape 76, 129
Gardère, Jean-Paul 31
Garnacho grape 118, 120
Garonne river 79, 86, 88, 89
Gattinara 114
Germany 24, 46, 71, 72, 75, 80, 81, 82, 83, 108–11, 112; classification 108; cooperatives 111; *see also* under district names
Gevrey-Chambertin 90
Gewürztraminer grape 72, 81, *81*, 120, 122, 131, 137; wine 72, 81, 101, 128, 131, 134, 146, 189
Gigondas 78, 99
Gironde *département* 86
Giscours, Ch. 185
Givry 93
Glacier wine 123
Gousset, Maurice 62
grafting 34–5, *34*, *35*, 71, 78
Grands Echézeaux 90
grape harvest *16*, 29, *52*, 73, 88; machine harvesting 31, 37, *37*; *see also* vintage
grape varieties 19, 42, *44*, 61, 68, 70–85, 90, 140, 141, 157–69
Graves 61, 74, 75, 84, 86, 88, 168; red 88, 153, 173; white 84, 143, 145, 163
Great Western Champagne 135
Greco: di Tufo 112, 117; grape 117
Greece 83
Grenache grape 61, 78, 79, 99, 105, 115, 129, 201; Blanc 78; Gris 78; Noir 78; *see also* Garnacho grape
Grignolino grape 129
Grillet, Ch. 85, 99
Grolleau grape 79
Gros Plant du Pays Nantais 84, 103
Grüner Veltliner grape 122
Gumpoldskirchen 122
Gutedel *see* Chasselas grape

H
Haraszthy, Baron Agoston 76, 124
Haut-Bailly, Ch. 61
Haut-Brion, Ch. 86, 100
Heidsieck *97*
Heitz, Joe 129; Heitz winery 126, 128, 130
Hermitage 78, 99; red 77; white 85, 99, 145
Hermitage (Swiss) 123
heurige 122
Hungary 53, 80, 129
Hunter Valley 136, 163, 168
Hunter Riesling *see* Sémillon grape

I
Inferno 114
Inglenook winery 124, 129
Institut National des Appellations d'Origine Contrôlée (INAO) 70
Instituto Nacional de Denominaciónes de Origen 118
Iron Horse winery 128
Irouléguy 79, 107
Italy 72, 75, 80, 82, 112–17, *112*, 118; DOC wine law 113; names 113; *see also* under regional names

J
Jacquère grape 85
Jasnières 103
Jekel Vineyards 132
Jerez de la Frontera 120, *120*, 202
Jordan Winery 130
Joseph Phelps Vineyards 128, 129, 159
Journal Officiel 70
Juliénas 93
Jumilla 120
Junta Nacional de Vinho 121
Jura 53, 76, 80, 85, 104, 166; red 104; rosé 79
Jurançon 30, 107; grape 79; wine 146

K
Kabinett wines 102, 111
Kaiser Stuhl winery 136
Keri Keri 137
Klein Karoo 139

L
Lafite Rothschild 86
Lake, David 134
La Mancha 118, *118*, 120
Languedoc 78, 84, 106–7, *106*, *200*
Latium 113, 116
Latour, Ch. 31, 77, 86
Latour, Georges de 124
Laville-Haut-Brion 84
Le goût du vin (Emile Peynaud) 27, 140
'legs' 19, 21, *21*
León 120
León, Jean 118, 120
Levante 118, 120
Liguria 113, 114
liqueur: de dosage, de tirage, d'expédition 97
Livermore Valley 131, 132
Logroño 118
Loire Valley 61, *62*, 72, 74, 76, 79, 81, 83, 102–3, 142, 151, 162, 164, 166, 180, 181; red 76; rosé 76
Loire Atlantique 85
Lombardy 113, 114
Lunel 83, *200*, 201
Luxembourg 80, 123
Lyonnais, Lyons 76, 90, 98

M
Maccabeu (Maccabeo) grape 85, 120
maceration 44, 54, 55; carbonic 54, 99, 133
Mâcon 93; Blanc 160; Supérieur 93; -Villages 160; -Viré 190
Mâconnais 80, 90, 93, *93*, 160
madeira 202, 203; Sercial 203
maderization 85, 178
Malbec (Auxerrois) grape 76, 107, 115, 123, 138
Malvasia grape 116, 118, 121, 138
Malvasia de Sitges 120
Malvoisie 123
Malvoisie de Corse (Vernentino) grape 105
manzanilla 202, *202*
marc 40–1, *55*
Marches 113, 116
Margaux 48, 113; Ch. *38*, *86*
Marne *département* 94
Marsanne grape 85, 99, 105
maturation *47*, 48, *49*; *see also* ageing
Mauzac (Blanquette) grape 84–5, 107
mechanical cultivation 31, 36–7, *36*
Médoc 32, *40*, 74, 75, 86, 168; Bas-Médoc 86; Haut-Médoc 86, 87, 172, 173; wines 74, 185
Melon Blanc *see* Chardonnay grape
Melon de Bourgogne *see* Muscadet grape
Ménétou Salon 102
Merlot grape 42, 64, *70*, 75, 76, 86, 88, 115, 120, 129, 138, 139, 164, 168; wine 75, 128
méthode champenoise 50, 51, 84, 85, 99, 114, *114*, 120, 162
méthode rurale 50, 51, 84, 107
Meursault 92, 160, 161, 180
Midi 76, 78
mildew 31
Moët & Chandon *73*, *94*
Monastrel 120, *121*
Mondavi, Robert 126–7; Winery 128, 130, 131
Monterey: County 131, 132; Vineyard 132
Monthélie 92
Montlouis 102
Montrachet 80, 92, 160
Morey Saint-Denis 90
Morgon 93
Mosel (Moselle) *108*, 110, *110*, *111*, 123, 158, 159
Mosel-Saar-Ruwer 111
Mourvèdre grape 78–9, 99, 105, 106
Mouton-Rothschild, Ch. 86
Müller-Thurgau grape 71, 110, 111, 115, 122, 123, 137

Muscadelle grape 84, 86, 131
Muscadet (Melon de Bourgogne) grape 85, 103; wine 85, 140
Muscadet des Coteaux de la Loire 103
Muscadet de Sèvre-et-Maine 103, 142, 180
Muscat *200*, 201
Muscat d'Alexandrie 83, 139
Muscat d'Alsace 83, 101
Muscat grape 83, 85, 120, 138
Muscat Ottonel grape 83, 122
mutage 53, 200, 201

N
Nahe 110
Napa Valley *29*, *33*, 76, 127, *128*, 130, 165, 168, 169, 181
Navarre (Navarra) *118*, 120
Négrette grape 79, 107
Neuchâtel 122, 123
New York State 135, *135*
New Zealand 137, *137*, 164, 166
Noirien *see* Pinot Noir grape

O
oidium 31
Oltrepo' Pavese 114
Oregon 134, 135, 166
Orléans 102

P
Pais grape 138
Palatinate (Pfalz) 81, 100, 110, 111
Palette 105
Palmer, Ch. 40, 42
Palomino grape 139, 202
Pauillac 86, 87, 88
Pedro Ximénez grape 120, 202, *203*
Penedés 118, 120; Brut Blanc de Blancs 120
Pérignon, Dom 50, 73, 94, *94*
Pernand-Vergelesses 92, 93
Petite-Sirah (Duriff) grape 129
Pétrus, Ch. 86
Peynaud, Emile 27, 140, 196
Petit Verdot grape 74
phylloxera 30, 31, 34, 78, 118, 121, 124, 138, 139
Picpoul de Pinet 84; Picpoul grape 120
Piedmont 113, 114
Pineau d'Aunis (Chenin Noir) grape 79, 103
Pineau de la Loire *see* Chenin Blanc
Pineau de Saumur *see* Grolleau grape
Pinotage grape 137, 139
Pinot Beurot *see* Pinot Gris
Pinot Blanc grape 70, 82, 93; wine 82, 101, 122, 123, 137
Pinot grapes 42, 70, 76, 80, 92, 94, 114
Pinot Grigio 115
Pinot Gris (Ruländer) 82, *82*, 101, 122, 123
Pinot-Meunier 75, 94, 102, 137
Pinot Noir grape 34, 75, *75*, 79, 82, 93, 94, 96, 104, 115, 120, 121, 123, 129, 133, 136, 137, 138, 139, 166-7, 170; wine 75, 90, 101, 102, 128, 166-7
Pomerol 75, 86, 88–9, 168
Pommard 92, 171
port 53, 121, 133, 202–3; ruby 203; tawny 203; vintage 203; white 203; wood 203
Portugal 34, 120, 121, 203; classification 120
Pouilly-Fuissé 93, *93*, 160
Pouilly Fumé 83, 102, 142, 163, 180
Pouilly-Loché 93
Pouilly-sur-Loire 83, 84, 102
Pouilly-Vinzelle 93
Poulsard grapes 44, 79, 104
pourriture gris (grey rot) 58, 85
pourriture noble (*Botrytis cinerea*) 80, 81, 84, 88, 146
Po Valley 112, 114
Premières Côtes de Bordeaux *52*, 89
Pressac *see* Malbec grape
pressing 42, 44, 46, *47*, 94
Prohibition 124–6, 133, 135
Provence 105, 149, 152, 166, 182
pruning 31, *31*
Puligny-Montrachet 92

Q
Qualitätswein eines bestimmten Anbaugebietes (QbA) 108
Qualitätswein mit Prädikat (QmP) 108
Quart de Chaumes 103
Quincy 83, 102, 163

R
Ratfia 200, *201*
Reuilly 83, 102, 163
Rheingau 100, 110, 111, 131, 159
Rheinhessen 83, 110
Rhine river 80, 100, *100*
Rhône Valley 31, 42, 54, 72, 73, 76, 77, 85, 98–9, *98*, 104, 112, 118, 122, 143, 154, 169, *195*, 201
Richebourg 90
Ridge Vineyards 126, 128, 132, 167, 184
Riesling grape 71, 72, 80–1, *80*, 83, 110, *110*, 111, 115, 120, 122, 123, 131, 133, 135, 138, 139, 159, 180; wine 72, 81, 101, 111, 128, 134, 141, 145; Clare Riesling 136; Emerald Riesling 131; Gray Riesling (Chauché Gris) 131; Rhein Riesling *122*; Rhine Riesling 136, 159; Wälschriesling 122; White (Johannisberg) Riesling 131
Rioja (Alta, Baia) 118–119, *118*, 120
Rivaner *see* Müller-Thurgau grape
Rivesaltes 83, *200*, 201
robe 19, *19*, 21, 141, 180–5; *see also* colour
Romanée 90
Romanée-Conti 34, 90
Romanée-Saint-Vivant 90
Rosé d'Anjou 44, 103
Rosé des Riceys 96, 188
Rothbury Estate 136
Roussanne grape 85, 99
Roussette de Savoie 104
Roussillon 78, 85, 201
Ruländer *see* Pinot Gris grape
Rully 93

S
Saint-Emilion 32, 34, 74, 75, 76, 80, 82, 88, 89, 189; classification 86; Saint-Georges-Saint-Emilion 88
Saint-Estèphe *70*, 87
St Jean, Ch., California 128, 130
Saint-Joseph 85, 99
Saint-Julien 87
Saint-Nicolas de Bourgueil 102–3
Sancerre 36, 83, 102, *188*; red 102; rosé 96, 148
San Diego 76, 124, 133
Sangiovese (Brunello) grape 116; wine 113, 116
San Luis Obispo County 132–3
Santa Barbara County 133
Santa Clara County 132
Santa Cruz Mountains 132
Santenay 92–3
Sardinia 113, 117
Saumur 162; red 74; rosé 44, 74; Saumur Champigny 74, 103
Sauternes 40, 84, 86, 88, *89*, 147, 163
Sauvignon grape 83, 84, 86, 102, 115; wine 102, 163
Sauvignon Blanc (Fumé Blanc) grape 131, 157; wine 128, 131, 133, 142
Savagnin grape 104
Savennières 103
Savennières Coulée de Serrant 103
Savennières Roche aux Moines 103
Savigny-lès-Beaune 92, 93
Savoie (Savoy) *36*, 76, 79, 84, 85, 104–5
Schram, Joseph 124; Schramsberg 124, 128
Scheurebe *see* under Sylvaner grape
Sémillon grape 70, 83, 84, 86, 131, 136, 138, 139, 163; wine 134, 136, 145
serving wine 196–9; corkscrews *196*, 198; decanting 196, *197*; temperature 196–7; uncorking 196, 198, *198*; wine glasses 198–9, *198*, *199*
Seyssel 105, *191*; Mousseux 105
Sfursat 114, 115
Sherry 53, 55, 118, 190, 202; amontillado 202, *202*; cream 202, *203*; fino 202, *202*; oloroso 202, *203*; solera system 202
Shiraz grape 136, 139
Sicily 112, 113, 117
Siegerrebe grape 110
Soave 115
soil types and conditions 32–3, *32*, *33*, 34, 61, 68, 75, 79, 80, 81, 83, 86, 90, 99, 100, 102–3, 111, 112, 128, 129, 132, 136, 140, 141, 202, 203, 204, 205, 206
Sonoma County 124, *124*, 130, 162
South Africa 77, 78, 80, 81, 139; classification 139
soutirage (racking) 48, 50
Spain 78, 118–20, *118*; classification 118
sparkling wines 21, 50–1, *50*, *51*, 82, 83, 84, 85, 94, 107, 114, 120, 128, 154-5; rosé 50; slightly sparkling 50; *see also* closed vat method, *méthode champenoise*, *méthode rurale*; *also under* Champagne etc.
Spätlese 108, 111
Stag's Leap Wine Cellars 128
storing wine 63, 64
Styria 122
Suduiraut, Ch. 181
Swan Valley 137
Switzerland 36, 46, 122–3
Sylvaner grapes 71, 83, 101, 110, 111, 115; Sylvaner X Riesling (Scheurrebe) 110
Syrah grape *58*, 77, 78, 98, 99, 129, 139, 169

T
table wines (*vins de table*) 14, 108, 113, 118, 120, 121, 123, 139
tannin 26, 42, 46, 48, 66, 74, 78, 208
Tasmania 137
tasting 16–27, 140, 141, 142–85; cards 210–11; conditions 18; fortified and dessert wines 178–9; grape varieties 157–69; hedonistic 16, *16*; horizontal 141, 170–3; professional 16, *16*; red wines 148-53, 170–7; rosé wines 156; robes 180–5; sparkling wines 156–7; technical terms 212–15; vertical 141, 174–7; visual examination 19–21, *19*, *21*; white wine 142–7
Taurasi 116, 117
Tavel *44*, 78, 96, 99
'tears' *see* 'legs'
teinturier grapes 19, 77
Te Kauwhata Vineyards 137
Tempranillo grape 118, 138
Ticino 122, 123

Tokay 53, 139
Tokay grape *see* Pinot Gris
Torrés family 118, 120
Touraine 102, 145, 152, 184; rosé 79
Traminer (-Savagnin) grape 85, 122, 123, 136
transporting wine 62, 63
Trebbiano grape 82, 115, 116, 138
Trefethen Vineyards 128, *128*, 181
Trentino 112, 115, 160; Alto Adige 113, 114, 115
Trento 115
Trockenbeerenauslese 108
Trousseau grape 79, 104
Turin 112, *114*
Tursan 79, 85
Tuscany 82, 112, 113, 116

U
Ugni Blanc grape 82, 105, 139, 204, 206; wine 80
Umbria 113, 116
United States 76, 80, 81, 112, 124–35; *see also under* California etc.
United Vintners 133
Uruguay 138
Utiel-Requeña 120, *121*

V
Valais 123
Val d'Aosta 113, 114
Valdepeñas *118*, 120
Valencia 120, *121*
Valgella 114
Valpolicella 115, 149
Valtellina 114
Vaucrains 90
Vaud 123
vendage see grape harvest
Venegazzu' 115
Veneto 113, 114, 115
Venice 112
Ventana winery 132
Verdicchio 116
Veronese 115
Verduzzo grape 115
Vernaccia di San Gimignano 116
Vienna 122
Vienne 98
Vignes, Jean Louis 133
Vin de Blanquette 84
vin de chauffe 82
vin de goutte 42, 43, 44, 54
vin de marque 94
vin de paille 53, 104
vin de presse 42, *43*, 44, 54
Vin de Savoie 50
Vin de Savoie Chantagne 79
vine diseases 30–1, 34; *see also* phylloxera etc.
vines 28–37; *29*, 32; cultivation 30–1, *30*, *31*, 33; life cycle 28–9, *28*; *see also Vitis labrusca, Vitis vinifera*
vin gris 44; *de Toul* 44, 148; *d'Orléans* 44
Vinho Rosado 121
Vinho Verde 120, 121, 142
vinification 38–55, 68, 73, 97, 118, 140, 141, 144, 203; closed vat 50; red wine 42, *43*, 44, 48; rosé wine 44, *44*, 48; sparkling wine 50–1, *50*, 51; sugar 52–3; white wine 44, 46, *47*, 48, 52; whole-grape 54, *55*
vin jaune 54–5, 104, *192*
Vin Nature de Champagne *see* Coteaux Champenois
Vino Nobile di Montepulciano 113, 116
vins de primeur 54, 78, 99, 106
vins doux naturels (VDN) 53, 78, 83, 190, 200–1
vintage 56–61, *56*, 108, 140, 141, 144; table 216–17; *see also* grape harvest
Viognier grape 85, 98, 99
Vitis labrusca 124, 135
Vitis vinifera 34, 72, 110, 124, 131, 135, 138
Volnay 92, 174–5, 183
Volnay-Santenots 170
Vosne-Romanée 90
Vougeot 90
Vougeot, Clos de 90, *91*
Vouvray 102, 103, 145, 162, 181

W
Wachenheim 111
Washington State 134–5, *134*, 168
Wente Brothers winery 132
Williamette Valley 135
wine, chemical composition 66–7, 113
wine and food 188–95; aperitifs 190; cheese 188, *189*, 194–5; crustaceans 191; desserts 195; eggs 190; farinaceous food 192; fish 191; game 193; hors d'oeuvre and starters 190; meats 190–3; mushrooms 192; poultry 192; shellfish 191; snails 190–1; spicy dishes 193; truffles 192; vegetables 192
wine and health 209
wine bottles *65*, 100, 111, 113, 116
wine glasses 18, 198–9, *198*, *199*; ISO wine glass 18, *18*, *19*, *198*
wine-making *see* vinification
wine presses 40, *40*, 41, *47*, *50*, *55*, 94
Wine Tasting (Michael Broadbent) 140
wood ageing *see* ageing

Y
Yakima River 134; Valley 134
Yalumba winery 136
yeasts 24, 42, 52, 53, 54
Yecla 120
Yquem, Ch. d' *40*, 53, *53*, 86, *88*
Yugoslavia 80
Yvorne 123

Z
Zaca Mesa winery 133
Zinfandel grape 76, 129; wine 128, 129, 133, 184

Bibliography/Acknowledgements

AMERINE, Maynard A. and SINGLETON, Vernon L.:
Wine: An Introduction, revised edition, University of California Press, Berkeley, 1978

ANDERSON, Burton:
Vino: The Wine and Winemakers of Italy, Little, Brown and Co., Boston, 1980; Papermack, London, 1982

BEZZANT, Norman and BURROUGHS, David:
The New Wine Companion, Heinemann, London, 1980

BLANCHET, Suzanne:
Les Vins du Val de Loire, ed. Jema S. A., Saumur, 1982

BROADBENT, Michael:
The Great Vintage Wine Book, Mitchell Beazley in association with Christie's Wine Publications, London, 1980;
Pocket Guide to Wine Tasting, Mitchell Beazley in association with Christie's Wine Publications, London, 1982

BRUNEL, Gaston:
Guide des Vignobles et Caves des Côtes du Rhône, ed. J. C. Lattès, Paris, 1980

DEBUIGNE, Gérard:
Larousse Dictionary of Wines of the World, Hamlyn, London, 1976

DION, Roger:
Histoire de la Vigne et du Vin en France des Origines au XIXe Siècle, ed. Paris, 1959

DOVAZ, Michel:
Les Grands Vins de France, ed. Julliard, Paris, 1979;
Encyclopaedia of the Great Wines of Bordeaux, ed. Julliard, Paris, 1981;
Encyclopédie des Vins de Champagne, ed. Julliard, Paris.

DUIJKER, Hubrecht:
The Great Wines of Burgundy, Mitchell Beazley, London, 1983.
The Good Wines of Bordeaux, Mitchell Beazley, London, 1983.

ENJALBERT, Henri:
Les Grands Vins de Saint-Emilion, Pomerol et Fronsac, ed. Bardi, Paris, 1983

FERET, Claude:
Bordeaux et ses Vins, ed. Féret et Fils, Bordeaux, 1982

FORBES, Patrick:
Champagne: The Wine, the Land and the People, Gollancz, London, 1972; Reynal, New York, 1968

HANSON, Anthony:
Burgundy, Faber, London, 1982 and Boston, 1983

JEFFS, Julian:
Sherry, 3rd edition, Faber, London, 1982 and Boston, 1982

JOHNSON, Hugh:
Pocket Wine Book 1990, Mitchell Beazley, London, 1989
Simon & Schuster, New York, 1989.
Wine, Nelson, Sunbury-on-Thames, 1973; Simon & Schuster, New York, 1975;
The World Atlas of Wine, revised edition, Mitchell Beazley, London, 1983; Simon & Schuster, New York, 1983
The Wine Companion, second edition, Mitchell Beazley, London, 1987; Simon & Schuster, New York, 1987

LEGLISE, Max:
Une Initiation à la degustation des grands vins, ed. Défense et Illustration des Vins d'Origine, Lausanne, 1976

LICHINE, Alexis:
(New) Encyclopaedia of Wines and Spirits, 4th edition, Alfred A. Knopf, New York, 1974; Cassell, London, 1979;
Guide to the Wines and Vineyards of France, Alfred A. Knopf, New York, 1979; Weidenfeld and Nicolson, London, 1979

LIVINGSTONE-LEARMONTH, John and MASTER, Melvyn:
The Wines of the Rhône, Faber, London, 1979 (revised edition 1983) and Boston, 1983

PENNING-ROWSELL, Edmund:
The Wines of Bordeaux, Penguin Books, London, 1985

PEPPERCORN, David:
Bordeaux, Faber, London and Winchester, Mass., 1982

PEYNAUD, Emile:
Le Goût du Vin, ed. Dunod, Paris, 1980

PIJASSOU, René:
Un Grand Vignoble de Qualité: Le Médoc, ed. Tallendier, Paris, 1978

READ, Jan:
The Wines of Spain and Portugal, Faber, London, 1972 (revised editions 1983); Monarch Books, New York, 1978
Pocket Guide to Spanish Wines, revised edition, Mitchell Beazley, London, 1988

ROBERTSON, George:
Port, Faber, London, 1978 and Boston, 1983

ROBINSON, Jancis:
The Great Wine Book, Sidgwick & Jackson, London, 1982
Vines, Grapes and Wines, Mitchell Beazley, London, 1986

SALLE, Jacques:
Dictionnaire Larousse des Alcools, ed. Larousse, Paris, 1982

SCHOONMAKER, Frank:
Encyclopaedia of Wine, Hastings, New York, 1979; A & C Black, London, 1979

SUTCLIFFE, Serena:
The Wine Drinker's Handbook, David & Charles in association with Pan Books, Newton Abbot, 1982

VANDYKE-PRICE, Pamela:
The Taste of Wine, Macdonald, London, 1975; Random House, New York, 1975

VEDEL, A., CHARLES, G., CHARNAY, P., et TOURNEAU, J.:
Essai sur la Dégustation des Vins, ed. Société d'Edition et d'Information viti-vinicoles, Mâcon, 1972

Photographs
Académie du Vin (Steven Spurrier), 15, 17, 19, 20, 23, 25, 41(bottom), 180–5, 187, 197, 198(left and right), 199(left and right)
Agence Photographique TOP, 1, 2, 38, 39, 48(right), 55, 60, 72
Comité national des vins de France (CNVF), 51(top and bottom), 58, 74(left), 75, 76, 80, 83
Food and Wine from France, 206, 207
Michael Freeman, 33, 41(top), 126(top), 133, 135
The High Commissioner for New Zealand, 137
Denis Hughes-Gilbey, 8–9, 11, 12, 16, 30(left and right), 31, 33, 34, 35, 36, 37, 40(top and bottom), 45, 46, 48(left), 49, 50, 52, 53(left and right), 54(top and bottom), 56, 57, 59, 61, 62(top and bottom), 64, 65, 69, 70, 71, 73(top and bottom), 74(right), 77, 81, 82, 88, 91, 92, 93, 94, 96 97, 98, 99, 100. 101, 106, 188, 189, 190, 191(left and right). 192(top and bottom), 193, 194, 195, 204, 205, 208, 209
Chris Jansen Photography, 139
Lightbox Library, 63, 86, 89(top and bottom), 138
Geoffrey Roberts Associates, 29, 124, 126(bottom), 127, 134
Vinos de Espana, 118, 119, 120, 121

Wine Tasting Terms (pp. 212–15)
Laboratoire départementale et régionale d'analyses et de recherche de Tours;
Le centre technique expérimental de l'Institut technique du vin de Tours;
Le comité interprofessionel des vins de Touraine

Equilibrium diagram (p. 27)
E. Peynaud, *Le goût du vin*, Bordas, Paris, 2nd edition, 1983